the complete
holistic dog book

HOME HEALTH CARE FOR
OUR CANINE COMPANIONS

JAN ALLEGRETTI & KATY SOMMERS, D.V.M.

CELESTIAL ARTS
Berkeley • Toronto

Copyright © 2003 by Jan Allegretti and Katy Sommers, D.V.M. All rights reserved. No part of this book may be reproduced or transmitted in any form or by any means, electronic or mechanical, including photocopying, recording, or by any information storage or retrieval system, except for brief review, without the express permission of the publisher. For further information, you may write to:

Celestial Arts
P.O. Box 7123
Berkeley, California 94707
www.tenspeed.com

Celestial Arts titles are distributed in Canada by Ten Speed Canada, in the United Kingdom and Europe by Airlift Books, in South Africa by Real Books, in Australia by Simon & Schuster Australia, and in New Zealand by Southern Publishers Group.

The dogs appearing on pages 76, 254, 255, 282, 294, 295, and 344 all found loving homes with people at Celestial Arts/Ten Speed Press.

Cover and text design by Toni Tajima
Text production by Greene Design
Cover photograph by Birgit Utech/Photonica
Illustrations by Paula Gray

ISBN 01-58761-144-9

Library of Congress Cataloging-in-Publication Data available from the publisher

Printed in the United States of America
2 3 4 5 6 7 — 09 08 07 06 05 04

Contents

Jan's Acknowledgements

This book is the result of a fusion of vision and energy from many people and many different experiences.

Hal Zina Bennett, agent, mentor, treasured friend… Thank you for bringing me this project, and for being a solid rock of integrity, wisdom, and gentleness.

Katy Sommers… Thank you for agreeing to join me in this venture, for your commitment to excellence, and your understanding of who the animals really are.

Veronica Randall, our editor at Celestial Arts/Ten Speed Press… Your enthusiasm for the material, your boundless energy and generosity, and the joy and talent you bring to your work made the process flow through the challenges as well as through the laughter.

The Celestial Arts/Ten Speed Press design team… Thank you for understanding our vision and painting it into the pages of our book.

Carol Maza… When you introduced me to the world of homeopathy so many years ago, you opened up a world of healing as I'd imagined it might be. Thank you for your wise, joyful, and generous teaching.

Lynda McClure… You saw the obvious when I didn't. Thank you for suggesting I formalize the work I'd been doing for so many years.

Bec Kageyama, Dieuwke Pebesma, Lyn Hart, Gale Carcerino, Tish Solomon, Lynn Barclay, Carol LaBranche, and many other wise and beautiful friends… Your loving support and your unfailing belief in my abilities sustain and inspire me.

My mother, Grace Dorolek Allegretti… What a blessing that you always made sure there was a dog in our family, with full access to share sleeping space with any and all of the rest of us. For that good start, and for the times you've cheered me on, thanks, Mom.

The many students and clients and their well-loved dogs…Thank you for sharing the loving, the healing, and the learning.

And most of all, Savannah, Tashina, Ginger, Midge, and Fawn…Thank you for sharing your beauty, your wisdom, your heart, and your spirit.

Dr. Katy's Acknowledgements

My deepest thanks go to the many veterinarians who inspired me to examine a different path within the practice of medicine. Like a sponge, I have soaked up so many ideas and philosophies from countless colleagues at conferences, dinner tables, and walks in the woods. I am especially grateful to Dr. Michael Fox, Dr. Shelly Altman, and Dr. Grace Lui, my earliest inspirations, and Dr. John Limehouse, Dr. Nancy Scanlon, Dr. Ihor Basko and Dr. Kerry Ridgway, all of whom warmly welcomed me into their own practices, offering vision and guidance. I am thankful to the faculty and staff of the International Veterinary Acupuncture Society for opening another door and teaching me a bit of the magic that lies beyond. Dr. Allen Schoen, Dr. Susan Wynn, and many others have done so much to champion the holistic approach to veterinary medicine. Without their important work this book could not have been conceived.

Thank you to our agent, Hal Bennett, for the opportunity for this book and the support during the writing, and to Jan Allegretti, for presenting the vision and allowing the metamorphosis. To Veronica Randall, our canine-loving editor, who had the difficult task of taking the manuscript to completion, to Paula Gray, whose animal artwork never fails to make me smile, and to Toni Tajima and Brad Greene, who provided the design…thank you all.

Friends and family were a huge support during the writing of this book. Heart-felt thanks to Desa Belyea for her steadfast feedback and superb guidance and to Kathy Shearn for her enthusiasm and great dog-walks. I am especially grateful to the wonderful doctors and staff at Mendocino Animal Hospital – my other family at my "home away from home." Their tireless work caring for the animals in our community allowed me precious time to write. Tessa and Silvie – my canine family, provided unwavering support, companionship, and unconditional love during the writing of this book, as you might expect.

My deepest gratitude goes to Lisa Mammina, who put her own projects aside to keep all home fires burning, giving, as always, with an attentive heart. And to my mother, Dottie Harkness, who, in my earliest memories and to this day, shares her great love of animals and nature with me, and who encouraged me throughout life to follow my dreams.

Foreword from Jan Allegretti

Those of us who love dogs share a similar quest—to care for them well, and offer them the best quality of life we can manage. But whether we're looking for the best medicine to give them when they're sick, or adjusting their role as members of the family, at the root of it all is our understanding of who dogs really are—body, mind, and soul. Sometimes it seems there are few clear-cut answers. But then, what's most important is knowing which questions to ask.

Fortunately I never find myself lacking for questions, thanks to the continued offerings of the animals in my life—particularly Savannah. She's a gracious, elegant Great Dane, extremely sensitive and as kind as any creature I've known. Savannah's life hasn't been easy. After two-and-a-half years as a breeder in a puppy mill, she was rescued, only to be left three years later at the local pound. That's where we met. I could see her ribs under her rough, dull coat, and her face had a dark and worried expression. But I loved her gentleness and her serenity. Most of all I loved the way it felt to be in her company.

One afternoon not long after she came home with me, Savannah was sound asleep on the couch when suddenly she began to moan. It was a quiet sound at first, but it had an unmistakable tone of sadness. As she continued to sleep the sound became louder, and more mournful. Soon, without ever opening her eyes, she was up on her elbows, nose pointed to the sky, howling as though her heart would break.

I walked over to where she lay, spoke quietly and put my hands on her. Savannah opened her eyes and looked at me with what seemed like surprise, and maybe a little embarrassment, then let her head fall back onto the armrest. As I continued to talk to her, wondering what kind of dream would make her cry out like that, she responded with expressive sounds that, although there were no words, had the same intonation I'd expect to hear if she was telling me all about her nightmare.

Those first months, Savannah's sad dreams came often. In her waking hours, she was the model of gentleness and good manners, quiet and reserved. She loved our trips to town, but always seemed inordinately uneasy about being left behind. She'd join me on my errands, but if I got ahead of her on our way back to the car, she'd stop in her tracks and look at me with a watchful, stricken face, as though she expected to be left behind; when I called her to the car her eyes would light up, her ears soften, and she'd bound past me and leap through the open car door.

In time Savannah grew more secure—in fact, she blossomed. Her weight improved and her coat came in soft and shiny. She's found her niche as a therapy dog, whose greatest pleasure comes not from roaming the meadows and forests where we live, but from going to town and bringing happiness to the people we meet there. And finally, the disturbing dreams with the mournful cries only rarely trouble her sleep.

Most of us have at one time or another seen our dogs dream. Usually their legs thrash as though they're on a good chase across a field. Sometimes they'll bark a muffled "wfff," as if to warn away an intruder. I've always wondered about the content of those dreams. More recently I wonder what we can learn from simply knowing that dogs dream at all. Doesn't it suggest that they are not only conscious beings, but capable of at least two states of consciousness—that of their dreams and the one they share with us when they're awake? I haven't yet seen a dog wake from a dream and get up to continue the chase that had her legs flailing in her sleep. Is that because they know the difference between the world of dreams and that of wakefulness? What does that suggest about their awareness of consciousness, their "sense of self." And if Savannah's trying past left her to sort through those experiences in her dreams, what does that tell us about the depth and complexity of animal emotions? What does it say about our responsibility to the animals in our care?

I'm luckier than most people, because I'm able to spend most of my days in the quiet company of my animal family. There's just me and Savannah; an aging but very powerful cat named Mazie; and Tess and Tomar, two wise and unfettered horses who come and go over the surrounding hillsides pretty much as they please. We share the land with an extended family of wilder residents who were here long before we were. Ravens, deer, coyote, bear, bobcats, mountain lions, rattlesnakes, lizards, and potato bugs all maintain squatters' rights.

Some people see my lifestyle as a solitary one, but the rich presence of my nonhuman companions gives me the chance to engage them in a way I probably wouldn't if there were people here to talk to. Instead I talk to the animals, and do my best to listen to what they have to tell me. The more I talk, the more they seem to understand what I say. I don't pretend that they understand all the words, but perhaps my words help me focus my thoughts in a way that they, with their innate sensitivity, can perceive. In any case, I'm often caught off guard to notice they've responded to something I've said, when there's no way they could have recognized all the words in the complex sentence I used. Are they reading my mind? How else would Savannah have known what I meant, the first time I suggested she wait in a safe place up on the deck while the horses came through the open gate? If animals don't tune in to our thoughts, how is it that Tess and Tomar know to show up at the barn when I'm ready to feed, whether it's 5 p.m., 8 p.m., or some time in between? And if they can so readily respond to the things we think, what does that say about their capacity to understand other things about their world and ours? What does it suggest about our responsibility to provide them with a lifestyle that honors that understanding?

It's fascinating, and certainly convenient, to find that dogs and other animals understand our thoughts. But there may be more value in exploring what they tell us about themselves. I've come to believe that the amount of information they share through their facial expressions, body language, and behavior (and if we're very perceptive even their thoughts) is limited only by our ability—and our willingness—to receive it. Savannah's face alone conveys happiness, coyness, apprehension, playfulness, disappointment, tenderness, and more, all with the softness or tension around her eyes, the tilt of her ears, or a toss of her head. If I look—*really* look—at that face, I can see her nature, her mood, and sometimes even her desires. But if I'm very honest with myself I realize I don't always watch as closely as I should. It takes courage to see all that's there, because the more I know, the more I must step up to the responsibility of treating her in a way that recognizes her fullness as an intelligent, emotional, conscious being.

So as time goes on I try hard to look more deeply, and perceive more honestly. In the process I find that the animals help me to be more open to the places in myself where emotion is locked away, or where I resist understanding, perhaps because of the responsibility that comes with it. Certainly the animals show me by example what it means to be patient, or honest, or to love and play without reservation. When I notice how all of that helps me find my spiritual center, I can't help but honor the enormous role they play in helping me to live my very best life, the way I was meant to live it. So how, then, do we respond to creatures who offer so much? What do we owe them in return?

Every animal who walks, swims, crawls, or flies is an essential element in the health and beauty of the whole network of life. Each has a consciousness all his own, unique and valuable lessons to teach, and a right to the grace and fullness of life regardless of the direct contribution they may or may not make to humans. For many of us, though, dogs hold a more constant and intimate place in our lives as companions and partners than do other animals. As a result, they play a leading role in our exploration of what there is to learn from a nonhuman teacher. Savannah goes with me everywhere—she's a welcome visitor at the credit union, office supply store, the video rental shop, and of course the feed store. Our dinners come from the same pot, and we sleep side by side, breathing the same air. Day after day I'm in the company of her quiet gentleness, her patience, her simple beauty. There's no question I'm changed by her presence. And day after day I wonder what I've yet to learn about who she is, the depth of her understanding and the range of her emotions. I've seen the joy in her eyes when a child meets her in town, delighted by her huge, sweet presence, and Savannah turns to look at me as if to share her pleasure. I've also seen the disappointment in her expression when she has to spend another boring day on her own while I work away at the computer or on the phone, or when her dog friend runs off to follow a fresh scent rather than stay with her and play. How difficult is it for her to spend so many days idle on the couch, or watching who-knows-what across the distant valley?

It's an ongoing quest, to find the ways to understand who Savannah is—and who all manner of creatures are—and to find the best ways to care for her and honor her in all her dimensions. It seems I'm somewhere midway in a long process of learning. Twenty years ago when the dog in my life was a very ladylike rescued Doberman named Ginger, I was proud to feed a "premium" brand dog food, and give her a fluffy cushion to sleep on near the foot of my bed; she got every vaccination that was available and antibiotics at the first sign of illness. Now, Savannah's meals are home-cooked organic fare, and her "cushion" consists of the left side of my bed. Thanks to the healing benefits of homeopathy, herbs, good nutrition, and bodywork, I'm able to provide health care that works *with* her body's wisdom to support her physically as well as emotionally.

But I struggle with the ways I'm not always able to make her happy, or fall short in helping her realize her potential in "bringing happiness" to people besides myself. Yet, as is true for all of us, life is less about perfect happiness than about the wholeness with which we engage it. So I take pleasure in the smile I see on Savannah's face when we play or cuddle, or when we're in town and she's putting smiles on the faces of children we meet there. And now, when she has a bad dream, I sit by her side and we howl together, two noses pointed to the sky, pouring all the sadness from our hearts until the howl becomes a triumphant song—two voices sharing life's sorrows and joys, loving and learning from one another.

Wherever you are on your own quest, I hope this book will become a helpful companion as new questions arise day by day. And as your dog's true nature continues to unfold before your eyes, I know you'll discover new ways to provide excellent care, and deeper and more rewarding ways to share life's lessons with one another.

Foreword from Dr. Katy Sommers

One crisp September morning in 1980, I was called upon to treat a dying foal. I administered the conventional therapy for foal diarrhea—fluids and antibiotics—as taught to me while training at one of the country's finest veterinary schools. That same day, the local medicine man was called to do his healing. I watched as he chanted and danced and blew gray-green smoke into the nostrils of the wobbly foal. The next day, the foal made a rather unexpected recovery, and I asked a Navajo woman which healing method we should credit. Her reply, through a translator, was simply, "Does it matter?"

What I have learned, in more than twenty years of practicing veterinary medicine, is that some things matter, and some things don't. What matters in my daily practice is that the animals move toward a greater level of health and vibrancy whenever possible. In my mind, and in the wisdom of my Navajo friend, it matters little which avenue is taken to reach that healing, as long as the support for better health comes with compassion and empathy for the animal. How a person raises a puppy, and how the puppy is nourished, guided, supported emotionally and physically, all matter in the life of that very special canine being. The relationship that an individual or family has with their companion animals matters when it comes to the health and longevity of those animals. And the deep connection that is possible between individuals, even of different species, can open a new reality and inspire healing on both sides: As we are healing them, they are healing us!

Like many veterinarians today, exploring the options of alternative and complementary healing methods has given me a wider range of therapies to benefit my patients. Sometimes, conventional treatments just don't exist for a particular problem or, while the latest medical advance may hold dramatic promise for an illness, it may be unaffordable for a struggling young family. At other times, the greatest healing comes from a combination of therapies, both conventional and alternative. A cancer patient may need radiation and surgery for survival, but it may be the alternative therapy I prescribe, and the family administers, that enhances the quality of life of that patient.

When a patient's longstanding skin problem resolves after a combination of dietary changes, nutritional supplements, and a short series of acupuncture treatments, my clients have taught me that it doesn't matter which therapy had the greatest impact. We are thankful for the greater level of long-term health and comfort for their animal friend! And when a patient stops vomiting after a homeopathic remedy is administered, or is less stiff and painful after an acupressure treatment is performed by a caregiver, it doesn't matter that a comprehensive scientific explanation may not yet exist.

In these pages, you will find many of the ideas and health concepts I try to share with my human clients when they bring their animal companions to my veterinary hospital. This book most assuredly is not meant to replace the important veterinary care your dog will receive throughout life, but instead embraces the idea that support for vibrant health begins at home. The concept of holistic health care means addressing the harmony of mind, body, and spirit of an individual that together *promote* health. This includes lifestyle considerations, such as nutrition, exercise, play, stress prevention, and rest—all of which you will be able to provide for your canine friend. While your veterinarian is a vital member of your dog's healthcare team, you have, as the primary caregiver in your dog's life, the most important role to play when it comes to disease prevention and support for his emotional, social, and physical needs. By creating a strong foundation for good health, you are in fact supporting your dog's natural healing ability.

Included also, is the wisdom of many holistic veterinary practitioners who've shared their knowledge and offered support during my own quest to offer a greater level of healing to my patients, as well as thoughts, therapies, and a very different perspective that comes from Jan's personal experiences with animal healing. My greatest teachers, the animals themselves, have contributed throughout and inspired the whole of this book. I feel blessed to have found a calling that gives me the opportunity to learn from and connect with so many extraordinary animal beings each day. I hope this book will serve as a useful guide, not only to benefit your dog's health, but to strengthen the precious bond that connects you to the wonderful canine companions in your life.

1 part one

Tessa, Labrador Retriever/Springer Spaniel cross.
1985–2002. Adopted by Dr. Katy Sommers at
6 weeks old from the Domestic Animal Protection
Society of Ukiah, California.

Silvie, Terrier cross. Found in 1989 at 8 weeks
old shivering under a truck in a rainstorm,
downtown Ukiah, California. Silvie supervises
the Mendocino Animal Hospital with Dr. Katy.

part one

a holistic lifestyle
THE FOUNDATION OF GOOD HEALTH

FOR MANY OF US our first experience with holistic health care starts with a packet of herbs, or a bottle of nutritional supplements recommended by a friend, or an article in a magazine. For others it begins when a family member—human or nonhuman—becomes ill, and conventional treatments just seem too invasive, or carry the risk of too many side effects. In an effort to find a gentler alternative we may seek out a health food store and explore the aisles filled with "all natural" remedies.

But holistic health care for your dog, as for any other member of the family, begins with a lifestyle, one that takes into account his physical as well as emotional well-being. It's a lifestyle that supports the animal's innate wellness with wholesome nutrition, a nurturing environment, and the opportunity to be a happy, well-adjusted member of his human and canine community. A holistic lifestyle lays the foundation for good health so that your dog's "life energy" will be vibrant, strong, and unencumbered. When this foundation is in place, your dog will thrive, and his own healing capacities will ward off most of the health problems that might otherwise

come his way. If he does succumb to an illness or injury, he will be better able to respond to the support of natural remedies like nutritional supplements, herbs, and homeopathic remedies to bring his system back into balance.

There are three fundamental elements to consider as you create a holistic lifestyle for your dog: 1) wholesome, life-giving nutrition; 2) a home environment where he feels secure, where his emotional needs are met, and where he is physically safe; 3) the opportunity to participate in a human-canine social community. Giving your dog the best in these areas will work wonders in preventing illness and other problems down the road.

Nutrition

Your dog's diet is a key factor in maintaining his health. Many problems can be traced directly to shortcomings with the diet, while wholesome, life-supporting food allows your dog's system to function at its best. Good nutrition supports your dog's natural healing energies so that, if he does become ill, he can respond quickly to the gentle healing effects of natural medicines. If, on the other hand, your dog's diet is less wholesome, or includes substances that make a poor—or even negative—contribution to his well-being, his vital energy will be compromised. He'll be more susceptible to invasive or degenerative disease, and may need more invasive treatments to slow the progression of illness.

Most of us have been taught that the best way to feed our dogs is to buy a commercial dog food that is "nutritionally balanced" to provide everything they need. We find a brand that we feel we can trust, one that our dogs like, and feed it religiously—day after day, month after month, year after year. Often we resist our friend's pleas for table scraps because we've been taught that they are unhealthy for him. With the best of intentions we adhere to this feeding regimen throughout the life of our beloved companion.

For many years, this plan was consistent with the advice of most experts, including veterinarians and certainly the manufacturers of dog food. But this is changing, for reasons you'll easily understand. Step back for a moment and consider how it compares with everything else you know about nutrition as it applies to your own diet. Do you rely on prepackaged food for your own meals? Are you concerned about chemical additives like artificial colors, flavors, and preservatives? Do you try to eat some fresh vegetables and fruits each day? What about variety? Do you eat the same foods every day of the week, every meal of the day? If you're reasonably health-conscious, chances are you strive to eat a wide variety of fresh, wholesome foods with a minimum of chemical additives. You may even have experienced the benefits of eating organic foods.

Now consider this: When you feed your dog a commercially prepared dog food day after day, it's the equivalent of feeding yourself and the rest of your family the same brand of "100% nutritionally complete" breakfast cereal three meals a day, seven days a

week, year after year, throughout your entire lives. There's actually very little difference. Chances are you wouldn't dream of adopting such a diet for the humans in your family. Why should the guidelines for your dog's diet be any different?

To stay in the peak of health, your dog needs a broad range of foods to provide a variety of nutrients, just as you do. A steady diet of the same prepackaged food simply cannot do this, for a number of reasons. First, when commercial dog food is prepared for packaging, the processing that is required destroys many of the vitamins and other nutrients. What's more, it's very difficult to know exactly what is in most dog foods. The quality of meats and grains used varies dramatically. Terms like "by-product" and "meat meal" may indicate a perfectly acceptable food source—or mask a waste product that you would never consider feeding your dog if a more descriptive name was used on the label.

Many commercial dog foods contain chemical additives used to improve their appearance (so they will look tasty to you), their flavor (because much of the natural flavor has been processed away), and to preserve them (so that they can sit on your grocer's shelf and in your cupboard for months—or even longer). Not only is much of the nutritional value lost during processing, these additives may actually undermine your dog's health.

What may be most troublesome is that, in reality, there is no such thing as a commercial food—or, for that matter, any other single diet—that is "100% nutritionally complete" for every dog. Contrary to manufacturers' claims, when you feed the same food every day you run a risk that your dog will *not* get all the nutrients he needs. Nutrition is an evolving science, and absolute evidence that all dogs need a given amount of a particular vitamin or mineral simply does not exist. What's more, dietary requirements vary from one animal to the next, and it would be impossible to guarantee that your dog's needs are met by any one brand of food. The best way to assure that he gets all the nutrients he requires is to feed a variety of foods, so that his body can draw different substances from different sources. That's not possible when he is served the same food at every meal.

What You Can Do: Consider adopting one of these mealtime alternatives

- Prepare fresh, home-cooked meals.
- Reevaluate your choice of prepackaged food, and rotate between several brands that meet your rigorous new standards of quality.
- Develop a routine that combines fresh food with an exceptionally high quality prepackaged brand.

You'll find a more complete discussion of these options in Chapter 3, A Wholesome Diet. We encourage you to give careful thought to this vital element of your dog's health care. This is the first step in creating a lifestyle that maintains good health and prepares him to recover from any problems that do arise.

A Healthy Home Environment

When we recognize the importance of caring for our dogs as physical *and* emotional beings, the need to create a safe and happy home environment becomes clear. Your home, after all, is where your dog's primary physical and emotional needs will be met. Your home should be a safe place for him, which means that he is sheltered not only from the elements, but also from stress and from unseen hazards that might jeopardize his health. Your home should be a place where he can feel secure, a place where he is loved.

PART OF THE PACK, PART OF THE FAMILY

Like their wild ancestors, dogs are pack animals. They rely on the companionship of others to meet their considerable needs for social interaction and physical safety. In the wild, those "others" are the extended canine family. When we bring a domesticated dog into our household we become his pack, and assume the responsibility of meeting his needs for social interaction and protection. In return, our dogs contribute a wealth of emotional energy to the rest of the family. They make us laugh, they lick our tears away, and they offer the unconditional love that we all know we can count on. When given the opportunity, they often welcome the chance to share responsibility for protecting our homes and family members, and perform other extraordinary tasks such as search and rescue for the lost, guidance for the blind, assistance for the deaf, and animal-assisted therapy for the ill and elderly. What's most important from your dog's perspective is that he be included as an integral part of your family.

Unfortunately, in many cultures it is assumed that dogs can live adequately, both emotionally and physically, in isolated circumstances, either in outdoor kennels or, worse, chained to a stake. Some families want the companionship of a dog, but are reluctant to bring them into their homes. Others may allow a dog to share their home during the day, but then send him outside to spend the night alone in a doghouse. As difficult as it may be, it's important to give careful consideration to the emotional needs of the dog, as well as the desires of the human family. Adopting an animal into a family that is unable, for whatever reason, to provide for his physical health and his emotional wellbeing is an unfair choice for everyone. Not only will your dog deal with loneliness, anxiety, and frustration, but you will miss out on the rewards of understanding his emotional world, and of all he has to give in return.

isolation and confinement

Keeping a dog tied to a stake or locked in a kennel may actually be tantamount to a death sentence. Dogs who are forced to endure regular, extended periods of isolation or confinement are likely to develop behaviors that make them even less welcome members of the family. Hours spent at the end of a chain or alone in an enclosure force these animals to deny their needs for social interaction, physical exercise, and a sense of safety. Out of frustration they may bark incessantly, dig or chew up their environment, or even become aggressive. In sharp contrast to their natural preferences, they are forced to urinate and defecate in the same area where they eat and sleep, and as a result may become poor candidates for successful house training.

These dogs often end up at animal shelters, disposed of by their humans who fail to understand that the animal's disruptive or destructive behavior is his only way of expressing his unhappiness. Once deposited at the shelter, their prospects are grim: With the vast numbers of animals that pass through shelters and pounds every month, those with behavior problems, regardless of the cause, are often among the first to be euthanized.

MINIMIZE STRESS—IF AND WHEN YOU CAN

We all know the hazards of living with stress. We've read numerous articles about its effect on our health, and have explored a range of ideas to minimize the causes of stress in our lives. It's equally important to recognize and minimize the stress in your dog's life. Maintaining his peace of mind is an important aspect of maintaining his health, just as it is for you.

The following are some common causes of stress in a dog's life. While the list is by no means complete, it will help you fine-tune your ability to think about events from your dog's point of view.

What You Can Do: Simple coping strategies for complex problems

🐕 **You're away from home most of the day and your dog is left alone.** Knowing what to expect—which includes knowing that you'll return in the evening—will help make the separation easier for your friend. Try to maintain a regular routine for him before you leave in the morning and when you come home. A brief walk at the beginning and the end of the day will allow him to investigate the world beyond his backyard and offset the boredom of the long hours he'll spend home alone. Just a few minutes of playtime in the morning may burn off a little excess energy and help him relax while you're gone. When you return, greet him cheerfully but

the stress response

There's a predictable set of physical responses that occur in the body when your dog is stressed, whether it's emotional stress from being isolated in the back yard, or physical stress such as major surgery. In the wild, the stress response prepares your dog's body for "flight or fight" when he perceives impending danger. The amygdala, the brain's alarm center, sends a signal to the pituitary gland, which then sends hormonal messages to the adrenals to secrete adrenaline and other hormones. The result: A massive mobilization of energy to prepare your dog to flee danger or, if necessary, combat it.

There's a second phase of the stress response that kicks in when the stress doesn't go away. The body prepares to defend itself for a long-term battle, with the master gland, the pituitary, again directing the release of hormones. This time the pituitary calls on the thyroid to increase its hormonal production, which accelerates the metabolism, and directs the adrenal to rev up its production of cortisol. The effect this time? Blood sugar levels rise, the blood-clotting mechanism goes into high gear (just in case it's needed) and, most importantly, the immune system readies itself to be better able to react to invaders.

Here's where the body's defense mechanism becomes a double-edged sword. **Repeated or chronic negative stress from emotional unhappiness, fear, or fatigue can lead to exhaustion of these vital bodily resources, paving the way to immune system depletion. This leads to the increased susceptibility to disease, including cancer.**

Your dog doesn't need to be protected from every little stress in life. What he does need is an environment in which he's not repeatedly exposed to stress, and where he feels safe so that he can enjoy a relaxed and a happy emotional state.

calmly—too much excitement may add to his anticipation and make the wait more difficult. Before you begin tackling your "to-do" list for the evening, take a few moments to focus just on your dog, whether in play or by quietly stroking or brushing him. A small amount of your undivided attention will go a long way to reassure him of how important he is to you. Also, try to include him as much as possible in your other activities—let him ride in the car with you when you run errands on Saturday, or let him follow you around the house while you clean.

- **His relationship with another dog is volatile.** Your dog needs to be able to relax in his home and in his outside play area. If you have more than one dog and they frequently get into spats, consulting an animal behaviorist may help you understand and sort out unsettled dominance issues that may be triggering the problems. If your dog feels threatened by a neighborhood bully, even from the other side of the fence, the anxiety may be causing him to feel stress whenever he's outdoors. Though it may be difficult to approach the neighbor dog's guardian, asking him or her to work with you to bring peace to your backyard could be crucial to maintaining your dog's peace of mind—and your own.

- **There is emotional turmoil among human members of your family.** It's important to remember how sensitive our nonhuman family members are. Your dog is affected by your emotional state, so try to avoid exposing him to the stress you or others are feeling. Above all, be sure to protect him from becoming the focus of others' frustrations, and reassure him that he is not the source of anyone's anger. When tempers do erupt, everyone concerned may benefit from an extra game of fetch or a peaceful walk in the woods.

The list of possible stress factors is different for every home and for every dog. The more you are able to tune in to your companion's emotional nature, the more quickly you will recognize the signs that he is feeling ill at ease, and take steps to reassure him. When you do, not only will you help to ensure his health and well-being, but you will deepen your relationship with him as well.

Socialization and Training

As we know, dogs are highly social beings. Like their wild cousins, they have a complex array of behaviors through which they interact with other canines. When we bring dogs into our homes, we also bring them into our culture—our human pack, if you will. Unfortunately, some instinctive canine behaviors do not work as well in the context of human society. Part of our responsibility to our dogs is to ensure that they will thrive in the society in which they live, as well-adjusted, respectable members of the community. Socializing your dog at an early age allows him to learn what to expect from other creatures in his world, and how to interact with them. Teaching him how to behave will help him to be a welcome participant in your household and your activities, as well as help prevent behavior that might endanger him or others. Together, socialization and training complete the picture of a well-adjusted, healthy dog.

FRIENDLY DOGS IN THE MAKING

You can begin to provide the right foundation for your dog to blossom mentally when he is still a puppy. There is a critical period of socialization that occurs between 6 and 12 weeks of age. Puppies are very sensitive during this time, and what happens (or doesn't happen) in this period can have a lifelong effect on your dog's behavior and personality. In other words, if good things happen, such as positive and gentle interactions with children, adults and other animals, your puppy will carry this memory with him for life. On the other hand, if he is poorly socialized during this period he may tend to startle easily later on, or become fearful in situations that are actually harmless. He may behave unpredictably, or simply have a difficult time adapting to change.

Let's look at some examples. Cinder, an 8-week-old black lab puppy, came home to her new family on the Fourth of July. Everyone played and cuddled with her all day. That evening they headed into town to see the fireworks. Before they left they set Cinder up in the garage with a bed and plenty of toys and food. However, as the evening wore on, she could hear the sound of firecrackers exploding outside the garage where she waited all alone. The tremendous terror she felt from being forced to deal with the experience on her own in a strange place left Cinder with a lifelong fear of thunderstorms, backfiring cars, and other loud noises. On another Fourth of July a few years later, her panic was so intense that she ran through a plate glass door.

Danny, an exuberant pointer pup, led a mostly solitary life for his first 9 months. He spent much of his day alone in the backyard—his family only interacted with him before and after work. Soon, he had a difficult time dealing with anything new. While he loved his family, he was aggressive with people he didn't know. Fearing that Danny might eventually injure someone, his family left him at a shelter a few days after his first birthday.

Cinder and Danny's families didn't realize they were laying the groundwork for a lifetime of chronic fears. By having a healthy respect for the importance of socialization, and dedicating time and positive energy to your puppy during those important early weeks of his life, you will strengthen your bond and prepare him for a well-adjusted future.

What You Can Do: Provide good socialization experiences

Follow these suggestions during your puppy's first few months to help him become a friendly and confident adult dog.

- **Introduce your puppy to a variety of people,** creating an enjoyable experience with each of them. Make a point of including people with different physical characteristics: tall people, young children, men with facial hair, people wearing hats, people of different races and ethnic groups, vivacious people, and quiet people.

- **Use food, toys, and lots of affection** to create pleasant experiences in a variety of situations— riding in the car; trips to friends' homes, and visits to the grooming parlor or veterinary clinic. (When your puppy is out and about, remember to protect against distemper and parvovirus exposure—see page 33.)

- **Introduce your puppy to other species of animals** that he will be likely to meet later on, such as horses, cats, birds, or reptiles. Make sure the experience is a positive one by choosing friendly individuals and providing lots of supervision and positive reinforcement. Let him take his time approaching the new animal; if he is reluctant, allow small advances and use treats and encouragement to reassure him.

- **Never force a fearful puppy into a new situation.** Be patient. Demanding that he accept being touched by someone he is afraid of is *not* good socialization, nor is overwhelming him with new experiences before he's ready. Remember, each dog has a unique personality, with his own way of relating to the world. Watching him respond to each situation will give you valuable information about his individual nature. Respecting who he is will go a long way toward building a foundation of trust between the two of you.

THE VALUE OF PUPPY CLASS

Many people have reared their dogs and trained them at home to be wonderful canine citizens, without ever taking them to a class. However, puppy classes offer many wonderful benefits that are well worth considering. It will take some extra time and effort, but if you do make this investment in your new young friend, you'll find that he:

- learns valuable canine social skills by meeting and playing with other puppies

- learns appropriate use of his mouth, avoiding biting problems later

- benefits from having his guardian learn about normal puppy behavior

- becomes relaxed and secure with different elements in his environment

- learns to socialize with people other than immediate family members

- learns basic "good manners" that will make him welcome wherever he accompanies you

- has less chance of developing behavioral problems in the future

An unsocialized puppy, on the other hand, may:

- never learn basic skills for interacting with others

- become fearful and aggressive

- feel isolated and become desperate for interaction

- become anxious in unfamiliar surroundings and around strangers

- develop inappropriate social behaviors that frighten or frustrate his guardian

- be relinquished to a pound or euthanized when his guardian becomes frustrated or fearful

(Sophia Grossi, personal communication, 2001)

AGGRESSION:
A guide to prevention

Aggression is the most serious behavior problem your dog can develop. Reports of dog bites, especially to children, have reached epidemic proportions in the United States. Even if your dog doesn't bite but shows aggressive tendencies, you may be concerned not only for your personal safety, but also for liability issues, such as loss of homeowner's insurance or lawsuits from a victim. If your dog bares his teeth at the mail carrier or a delivery person, for example, a concerned landlord might consider your dog a potential risk to the apartment complex, and perhaps attempt to deny housing for you and your family. If your dog is on a leash and lunges aggressively at another leashed dog, causing a fall or injury in the process, the aggressive behavior might be grounds for legal action.

In the wild, aggression is a normal canine behavior. Dogs are aggressive when they protect themselves, hunt for food, or defend their territory and family. Domestication has toned down these behaviors, but a variety of factors can influence and aggravate the development of serious aggression problems. Aggressive behavior may be based on fear, dominance, protection of territory, or even of a guardian. While genetics, past abuse, or traumatic experiences might also contribute, inadequate socialization and improper handling and training are commonly at fault.

An unsocialized dog is often filled with anxiety. When he encounters things that frighten him, he may try to flee or protect himself the only way he knows how. Without socialization skills, he doesn't have many options in a new and uncomfortable situation. If he lacks experience meeting different kinds of people, he may bite a stranger, even when the stranger is not behaving in a threatening way. If he hasn't learned how to inhibit his bite and use a "soft mouth" through proper handling and play-biting with other puppies, he may cross the threshold and inflict damage in a sudden, seemingly unprovoked attack.

selecting a trainer

1. Choose a trainer who believes in *positive* reinforcement to prevent or minimize inappropriate behavior, and who avoids aversive control or negative reinforcement techniques that are not only less humane but also less effective. For instance, good trainers don't object to using food as a positive training tool, in fact they encourage it. Avoid trainers who insist on using choke chains or pronged collars. Head collars such as Gentle Leader or Halty are humane alternatives if used gently, without jerking or twisting your dog's neck. (To reduce the risk of neck injury, head collars should *always* be used *along with* a flat collar or, in some cases, a harness.)

2. Observe one or two classes before participating with your dog. Are the dogs and the people happy? Interview participants. Choose a trainer who treats everyone, dogs and people alike, with respect.

3. Avoid trainers who don't share with you *first* exactly what they plan to do. Don't ever be afraid to trust your own intuition and stop a trainer if she is doing something with your dog that you don't like.

4. Choose a trainer who offers you an understanding of dog behavior, and tells you the "whys" and the "what fors" when you and your dog are learning something new.

5. Watch your dog's response to the trainer and to training activities. Observe his facial expressions, his body language, his willingness—or lack thereof—to be in close proximity to the trainer. Trust the messages he gives you. If he appears frightened or confused, he is not having a positive experience. Be sure your trainer is willing to address those issues with compassion, and to provide your dog with the understanding and encouragement he needs.

Unfortunately, when improper socialization and training are at the root of the aggression, well-meaning guardians are often left dumbfounded, particularly if they lack a clear understanding of normal dog behavior. They may rush to a behavior specialist or veterinarian for advice, or broken-heartedly leave their beloved friend at a pound for euthanasia. Prevention is so much easier than treatment after the fact. Avoid a potentially dangerous or even tragic scenario by using the following guidelines.

What You Can Do: Make each new situation a learning experience

- 🐕 **Make socialization of your dog or puppy your TOP priority.**

- 🐕 **Learn about normal canine behavior** through dog classes, books, your veterinarian, and other resources.

- 🐕 **Teach your dog to accept being physically handled all over his body,** including his face and paws, using praise and small treats in the process.

- 🐕 **In new situations, learn to recognize the body language and postures of your dog**—when he is feeling threatened, protective, anxious, or fearful—and keep him and others out of harm's way until the situation can be changed.

- 🐕 **Seek behavioral counseling** for your dog at the first sign of trouble with aggression.

- 🐕 **Never, *ever* use physical punishment or abusive training techniques.**

PLAYTIME: NOT JUST FOR PUPPIES

Just like their wild cousins, domestic dogs engage in play behavior from early puppyhood on through adulthood. Young wolves and coyotes learn essential hunting skills through play, as well as the proper etiquette of social interaction within their canine families. While our companion dogs don't need to know how to hunt and kill other animals, their playful antics help them learn the social skills necessary to behave appropriately in the company of humans as well as other dogs. For all dogs, whether wild or domestic, young or old, play provides physical activity and mental stimulation, and helps fill the need for social interaction. When you provide plenty of opportunities for your dog to play, you are making a valuable contribution to his physical, mental, and emotional well-being.

Here are a few ideas to help you help your dog get the most from his playtime:

- **Rotate toys**, offering different ones every few days. Choose some toys for chewing and some for fetching. Offer plenty of interactive toys that your dog can use to entertain himself. Knotted rope toys, sturdy balls or other oddly shaped items to toss, or toys that distribute treats when he pushes them around the yard can help keep him stimulated. Nontoxic chew toys provide a valuable way for him to satisfy his need to chew, and can also help him relax after a period of activity.

- **Offer a variety of playmates.** Some dogs would choose playing fetch with you any day over a trip to the dog park. Be sensitive to who your dog enjoys playing with. Always introduce new playmates slowly, and monitor activity closely in the beginning to be sure aggressiveness will not be a factor.

- **Offer sufficient play opportunities.** Young dogs and very active dogs, of course, need play periods scheduled more frequently. See what a wonderful difference play opportunity makes when you are looking for quiet time with your dog later in the day.

DOGS WHO LIKE STRUCTURE

Some dogs, especially working breeds, are looking for a "job" to do. Their guardians are often perplexed about why they tear up the rose bed or chew up the couch. The answer is often simple: These dogs were bred to do more than protect the yard and watch television with the family.

There are many exciting games and jobs you can offer your dog. Some dogs truly enjoy the extra training in obedience work, agility, search and rescue, and frisbee or flyball. Be sure your dog resonates with the activity you choose for him, and be very cautious when selecting a trainer. Keep an eye on your dog's energy level, and allow time for rest at reasonable intervals during vigorous activity.

the tao of the dog

The ancient philosophy of Taoism has a very important precept called *wu-wei*, which translates to "not doing." By practicing wu-wei, you are relating to your dog without force or interference. This "art of doing nothing" will give you a better understanding of who he really is.

Take your dog to a dog park, or a protected nature area where he can safely be off leash. Try just sitting for an hour or two, and quietly observe your friend. As you watch him move through this new environment, try to imagine what it is like to hear sixteen times better than you do, and have a sense of smell a hundred times better than your own. Which activities give him joy? How does he sense danger, and how does he respond to it? What is his connection to you? Is it comfortable and easy, or does he experience anxiety whenever he drifts away from you?

If past problems suggest your dog is not ready to be off leash with strange dogs and people, have a friend take your dog for a walk on a long leash. Go along, but only as a passive observer, not as a participant. Walk in silence, putting all your attention on observing your dog. Can you see him "talk" through his body language? Do you recognize the difference between a big, slow, tail wag that means, "I'm happy," and the fast, sharp wag that indicates stress or uncertainty?

Which parts of the walk does he enjoy most? When is he stressed or unsure of himself? How does his expression toward each passerby change? Is he submissive, or does his body language suggest, "Stay away from me"? Most importantly, how does your dog respond to the direction of your friend when there is tension in the situation?

You can practice wu-wei with your dog at home, too. If your dog is relegated to the back yard or a kennel every day, try sitting a few hours there with him. Perhaps you'll come to understand why he tears up the rose bed! Or you may decide that a softer bed on that concrete floor might not be such a bad idea after all. Just observing your dog in a passive and open way, you will be better able to interpret his unique communication style and know more intimately what makes him tick. No doubt, you will likely see your relationship with your canine companion deepen in many wonderful ways as you come to know the "Way of the Dog."

EXERCISE:
For physical *and* mental health

"Flowing water never stagnates, active hinges never rust." A great Chinese physician, Sun Ssu-mo, wrote these words over a thousand years ago. The Taoist tradition in China is one of the most complete preventive health care systems, in which exercise is recognized as vital in maintaining optimal balance in both the physical and mental energy systems that make up the life force of an individual. While we are more aware today of the role of exercise in maintaining our own health, we may forget that these same benefits pertain to our dogs. You can provide the exercise your dog needs in a variety of ways. Whatever form you choose, there are a few important guidelines you will want to follow:

- Too much exercise for young, growing dogs can lead to developmental bone disease that could be permanent. For dogs less than a year old, limit strenuous exercise. While jogging with your puppy might seem pleasant for both of you, the steady pace, especially on flat paved surfaces, is the worst thing for his underdeveloped bones. A better alternative is short sprints, no more than 20 minutes at a time, that include some varied terrain, with plenty of changes of direction. This will help avoid stressing your dog's musculoskeletal system.

- If your dog shows pain, stiffness, shortness of breath, or a reluctance to move after exercise, consult your veterinarian. There may be underlying problems.

- Use the same commonsense rules you would apply to yourself. Start gradually on any new program, have warm-up and cool-down periods, and offer access to plenty of fresh water.

Recommended Reading

The Culture Clash. Jean Donaldson. Berkeley: James and Kenneth, 1996.

Dogs Never Lie About Love: Reflections on the Emotional World of Dogs. Jeffrey Moussaieff Masson. New York: Crown, 1997.

The Hidden Life of Dogs. Elizabeth Marshall Thomas. Boston: Houghton Mifflin, 1993.

Minding Animals: Awareness, Emotions, and Heart. Marc Bekoff. New York: Oxford University Press, 2002.

Pack of Two: The Intricate Bond Between People and Dogs. Caroline Knapp. New York: Dell, 1998.

an ounce
of prevention

SUPPORT FOR GOOD HEALTH comes in many forms. It includes the measures you take to prevent accident and injury, your routine medical care and parasite control, and even your positive energy and intentionality. And as obvious as it may seem, we sometimes forget that the most important thing you can do is simply to pay close attention to your dog.

What Is Your Dog Telling You?

Every hour of every day, your dog provides you with a wealth of information about her physical and emotional health. How does she move, sit, or chew? What do you notice when she interacts with others? Has she changed her sleeping posture, or does she seem reluctant to tackle the stairs? Does she lick one part of her body more than usual, or seem weak on one leg when she gets up? Is she more irritable, or more clingy? There's an enormous amount of information just in the expression on your dog's face. Look deeply into her eyes. Do you see a peaceful, happy look? Do you see tension, discomfort, or fatigue?

Your touch is another wonderfully sensitive tool for evaluating your friend, and learning the topography of your dog's body can deepen the connection between the two of you. Use your sense of smell to detect subtle changes in odor from the ears, skin, and breath. Listening is important, too. Learn the normal sounds your dog makes when she's sleeping, and the rhythm of her breathing after a vigorous game of catch. A change in your dog's breathing pattern or her bark, or retching, coughing, and gagging are all unusual sounds that need further investigation. Careful attention can enable you to use homeopathy, herbs, acupressure, or other home treatments to rebalance his health before a major problem arises. Sharing your observations with your veterinarian will make it easier for him to assist you.

THE DOG SCAN:
How to do a home physical exam

While a home physical doesn't replace a comprehensive veterinary exam, it is valuable as an early warning system and allows you to be involved more personally in preventing or detecting illness or injury in your dog. Think of the Dog Scan as more of a "touch session" than a medical evaluation, and your dog will think of it that way too. Choose a quiet room, free of distractions, and be sure you are in an attentive mode, letting the other issues of the day fall away before you begin. Your objective is to detect irregularities in your dog's physical body, and to look for areas of soreness or discomfort. You can include a massage if you like, or even a little acupressure. There are many ways to do the scan, but if you follow the same routine each time, you're less likely to forget an area. Performing your Dog Scan weekly is a good idea. That way you'll quickly detect changes that can escalate rapidly in older animals, and your younger dog will enjoy the frequent attention, too.

1. **Start at your dog's head.** Look into her eyes. Are they clear, bright, and moist, with no discharge or redness? Peer into the ear canals. There should be little odor, and no redness or discharge. Lift the lips and look at the gums. Are they pink and moist? Look at a few different dogs to get a sense of what normal gums look like. A pale color might mean anemia or circulatory problems, while bluish gums mean a lack of oxygen; both abnormalities suggest a need for veterinary evaluation. Spend a little time feeling and examining the mouth further, checking for dental tartar and periodontal disease, growths on the gums or tongue, and any unusual odors. Believe it or not, some dogs really do enjoy a gum massage! Dogs who become accustomed to having their mouths handled will be more relaxed during a veterinary dental exam. They'll also be more likely to permit you to extract a stick or bone lodged in the roof of their mouth, should the need arise.

2. **Run your hands along your dog's back, paying attention to the skin and coat.** Is her fur dry and lackluster, or is it shiny with healthy skin? Part the hair to check for dandruff (looks like salt), flea debris (looks like pepper), and excessive oiliness, redness, or odor. Dogs with excessive "doggy odor" are frequently suffering from skin disorders, which can be related to allergies, poor diet, or skin infections such as yeast. If the coat or skin is not in top condition, see Chapters 3, A Wholesome Diet, and Chapter 9, Treating Illness and Injury: The Skin, for supplements that may help.

3. **Now move your hands over the body with deeper pressure,** palpating the contour of the muscles for symmetry, and at the same time feeling for abnormal lumps and bumps. By this time, your dog is probably lying on her side, and you will need to roll him over to complete the scan. Before you do, be sure to look under the tail at the anal area, checking for tumors or discharges. Check the genitals, and if your dog is a female palpate each nipple and mammary gland thoroughly for hidden tumors: small ones (pea-sized) might not be visible, but if you find them with your hands and alert your veterinarian you may pick up a cancer before it's had a chance to spread.

4. **Next, gently move each joint, and compare the flexibility in the left and right legs.** There should be no pain, crackling noise, or discomfort when a limb is moved through its normal range of motion. Once again, move your hands down the back starting at the shoulders, and feel for areas of tightness, board-like stiffness, heat, or tenderness. These are areas that may need bodywork with massage, acupressure, acupuncture, or a chiropractic adjustment.

5. **End your session with quiet petting and stroking,** making mental notes of any suspicious changes or areas you feel need further evaluation.

ROUTINE VETERINARY CARE:
The annual check-up

Some holistic veterinarians and many animal caretakers feel an annual exam by your vet is not necessary for young, vital dogs, and recommend this service only for

Body condition score

1. Very thin ▶

The ribs are easily palpable with no fat cover. The tailbase has a prominent raised bony structure with no tissue between the skin and bone. The bony prominences are easily felt with no overlying fat. Dogs over six months of age have a severe abdominal tuck when viewed from the side and an accentuated hourglass shape when viewed from above.

◀ 2. Underweight

The ribs are easily palpable with minimal fat cover. The tailbase has a raised bony structure with little tissue between the skin and bone. The bony prominences are easily felt with minimal overlying fat. Dogs over six months of age have an abdominal tuck when viewed from the side and a marked hourglass shape when viewed from above.

3. Ideal ▶

The ribs are palpable with a slight fat cover. The tailbase has a smooth contour or some thickening. The bony structures are palpable under a thin layer of fat between the skin and bone. The bony prominences are easily felt under minimal amounts of overlying fat. Dogs over six months of age have a slight abdominal tuck when viewed from the side and a well-proportioned lumbar waist when viewed from above.

◀ 4. Overweight

The ribs are difficult to feel with moderate fat cover. The tailbase has some thickening with moderate amounts of tissue between the skin and bone. The bony structures can still be palpated. The bony prominences are covered by a moderate layer of fat. Dogs over six months of age have little or no abdominal tuck or waist when viewed from the side. The back is slightly broadened when viewed from above.

5. Obese ▶

The ribs are very difficult to feel under a thick fat cover. The tailbase appears thickened and is difficult to feel under a prominent layer of fat. The bony prominences are covered by a moderate to thick layer of fat. Dogs over six months of age have a pendulous ventral bulge and no waist when viewed from the side due to extensive fat deposits. The back is markedly broadened when viewed from above. A trough may form when epaxial areas bulge dorsally.

Reprinted with permission from Hand, M. S., Thatcher, C. D., Remillard, R. L., Rondebush, P., *Small Animal Clinical Nutrition, 4th Edition.* Topeka, KS: Mark Morris Associates, 2000.

puppies and senior dogs. Only you can determine what's right for you and your dog. However, you may want to consider how a yearly visit to your veterinarian can serve both you and your companion.

First, the annual meeting is a way to establish a strong bond between the three of you. Your vet can get to know you and your objectives for the health of your animal friend. Obviously, meeting on an annual basis also gives him better knowledge of your dog, her personality, her physical development, and the special relationship the two of you have. It also gives you the opportunity to get to know and develop confidence in him. Ideally, you and your vet will be the key players in a "healing team" should your dog experience a health crisis later in life.

Second, this visit is a time for you and your veterinarian to exchange new information and share ideas regarding diet and home health care. As the holistic approach to animal health care broadens, there is a marked shift in favor of prevention of disease rather than simply treating disease after it occurs. As the trend continues veterinarians will be more informed about ways to *keep* your dog healthy than ever before.

Another benefit of the annual visit is that your dog will get a thorough medical examination. Small problems or subtle changes may be detected before they develop into larger ones. Even though you may be very much in tune with your dog, she is by nature inclined to live stoically with health imbalances, so that you may not realize they exist. Your vet will use the ophthalmascope, otoscope, and stethoscope to evaluate the deeper structures of the eye, ear, and chest cavity. His skilled hands will perform deep palpation to detect any abnormalities in the abdominal organs, back muscles, tendons, joints, or prostate.

Finally, the veterinarian's office can be a scary place for your dog, especially if she only goes there when she is sick and hurting. Regular visits, particularly when she is well and would not be subjected to painful or frightening procedures, will help minimize her stress if a stay in the hospital becomes necessary.

Dental Care

Brushing and flossing are basic components of human hygiene, yet maintaining the health of gums and teeth is one of the most overlooked parts of basic dog care. Problems creep up slowly, and an estimated 80% of dogs have gum disease or some other preventable dental problem by the time they reach 5 years of age.

Tartar build-up not only causes bad breath, it allows bacteria to become trapped at the edges of the gums, where the invading organisms release toxins that injure oral tissue. The inflammation that follows allows bacteria to move deeper into the tissues and loosen teeth. Bacterial toxins can enter the blood stream, possibly infecting kidneys, lungs, liver, and heart. Over time, the chronic accummulation taxes the immune system, too. Obviously, minimizing tartar build-up can maximize health. By practicing some basic home dental care for your dog, you decrease the need for professional cleaning and extractions.

Will eating ordinary dry kibble prevent tooth and gum disease? There's just no evidence that it will. That's why the market is being flooded with new dog foods that are specially formulated as "dental diets." While these may work for some, it is likely that meals you create at home will be healthier overall than a commercial food offered for dental cleaning purposes. What's more, holistic veterinarians often note that many dogs on home-prepared diets don't seem to have a significant amount of tartar accumulation or gum disease. It makes sense, then, to choose a diet based on optimum health and nutrition and, if necessary, control tartar build-up with brushing.

Even if tartar is already beginning to build up on your dog's teeth, brushing them for just 20 to 30 seconds a few times a week, or even daily, can work wonders—and many dogs enjoy the attention and interaction. Use a soft toothbrush or, for larger dogs, a finger-toothbrush (it's like a rubber thimble that fits snugly over your index finger). To start with, dip the toothbrush in beef or chicken broth, or a mild garlic solution. Just allow your friend to lick the brush several times a day until she learns to associate it with a tasty treat. Once she's familiar with it, you can begin to actually brush the teeth. Use circular motions, stroking away from the gum line, and move along the outer surfaces of the teeth. Luckily, because of the way your dog's teeth fit together, tartar formation on the inside surfaces next to the tongue is not usually a problem. For the most part, her teeth can be brushed with her mouth closed.

Once you've established a routine, you'll be ready to add a tooth cleaner to the brush. Enzyme toothpastes for dogs contain lactoperoxidase that combines with naturally occurring ions in saliva to produce an antibacterial effect. Look for other products that contain walnut shells for abrasive action, zinc and vitamin C for healthy gums, or acetic acid, which binds minerals that lead to plaque formation.

People who feed raw food diets often find very little need to brush their dogs' teeth. This is not surprising, since tough chunks of raw meat contain stringy connective tissue fibers that act like floss. Braised or seared meats can be just as effective. Chewing on bones, however, carries a risk of tooth fracture. (See page 58 for the pros and cons of raw foods diets before making the decision about what's right for you and your dog.)

Rawhide chews have been shown to decrease tartar. However, some of these products, especially those produced outside the United States, are contaminated with bacteria that can lead to diarrhea and illness. Dried cow hooves and other hard-pressed rawhides can occasionally break teeth or become lodged in the intestinal tract. These products can also pose problems in multiple-dog households, where one dog may bolt down a large portion in an attempt to prevent another dog from access to the chew. Safer alternatives include chews made from carrot and other vegetable sources, or even nylon or other synthetic varieties of chew toys that are meant to be gnawed on, rather than ingested.

Routine Grooming

Different dogs require different amounts of grooming to keep them comfortable year-round, with shiny coats and healthy skin. Genetics, breed, and lifestyle are all factors that affect individual needs. A Sharpei, susceptible to a host of skin diseases and allergies, may require frequent bathing. An Afghan might need daily brushing to maintain that long, silky coat, while any lap dog needs regular nail trimming to prevent nail injury and excess tension on the ankles. And let's face it, if your dog enjoys rolling in the most "fragrant" deposits she can find, your bathing and grooming schedule might reflect the sensitivity of your own sense of smell!

Here are some general guidelines:

1. Brushing and combing prevents mats and tangles, and allows you to inspect for fleas and ticks. Use a soft brush, keep sessions brief if your dog is sensitive, and reward her for being cooperative. If you don't have the time, enlist the help of a professional groomer.

2. Frequent shampooing can remove natural oils that keep skin healthy, and should include the use of a conditioner to help restore moisture. However, unless your dog has a skin condition that requires frequent baths (see Shampoo Therapy, page 167), you rarely need to shampoo more than every 2 to 3 months, if at all.

3. Learn how to do your own nail trim—a vet assistant or groomer can teach you. Begin handling your dog's feet at an early age to make this procedure easy for the rest of her life. Most active dogs won't need a pedicure, as nails will wear down nat-

urally, but routine inspection of the nails is a good idea. Pay close attention to the dewclaws, as they are more prone to overgrowth and can even become imbedded in the sensitive pads if left unchecked.

4. If your dog's coat is heavy and you live in a hot climate, consider giving her a total body shave in the summer. Clipping the body, with special attention to the feet, can also help prevent plant seeds, or **foxtails**, from becoming entrapped in the coat where they could migrate and penetrate the skin.

5. The anal glands, beneath the skin on each side of the anus, normally secrete a thin fluid. They can become impacted with thicker secretions, causing your dog to scoot across the floor, lick, or chew at the anal area, or even chase her tail. Groomers often empty, or *express*, these sacs as a matter of routine. However, unless your dog shows any of the signs of discomfort listed here, it's best not to include this in your regular grooming practice.

Spaying and Neutering

Oscar, a miniature Dachshund, was killed by a car on his first birthday. Big, shaggy, lovable Jezebel should have outlived her mother, but she died at 10 years of age due to mammary (breast) cancer. Parker, a regal Doberman, developed a life-threatening prostate infection. His family could not afford the cost of surgery to save him, and he was sadly euthanized when he was 8 years old. What did Oscar, Jezebel, and Parker have in common? Spaying or neutering early in life could have prevented their untimely deaths.

Spaying is the term used for the surgical removal of the ovaries and uterus in the female dog. Neutering is another term for spaying, but more commonly refers to the surgery done to remove the testicles of male dogs. Both surgeries are done for the following reasons:

- to curb roaming and wandering, which may lead to injury, unwanted pregnancy, and unhappy neighbors

- to decrease risk of disease and increase life span

- to protect against reproductive (especially mammary) cancers

- to decrease unwanted behaviors, especially aggression toward other dogs

The majority of people today spay and neuter their companion animals. Most of us are sadly aware of the extreme overpopulation of cats and dogs in this country, and do not wish to add to the millions of animals killed each year in shelters and pounds. For every home found for a puppy that you breed, even a purebred, there is one less home for a puppy or adult dog waiting in a shelter. And yet, myths and concerns about the wisdom of spay and neuter procedures still exist.

A common claim about neutered animals is that they don't perform successfully in their work. Dogs themselves can best debunk this myth. Spayed or neutered canines are heroes in search and rescue operations, and lovingly serve as assistance dogs. Neutered dogs routinely score top honors in sheepdog and hunting trials, win the Iditarod, and compete successfully in the obedience and agility arena.

Some people feel that spaying or neutering is "unnatural," and that dogs should therefore be left unaltered. It might be best to examine the differences between wild canids and domestic dogs before we make any assumptions here. After all, the natural environment of canines *has* been altered. By living with us, they no longer engage in many natural wild behaviors such as roaming in packs, hunting and killing their food, and sleeping in the snow.

An important difference exists between the reproductive capacity of wild dogs and our domestic canine companions. Environmental conditions affect their natural heat cycles, and litters are smaller and less frequent in the wild. Domestic dogs usually have two heat cycles a year. This continuous cycling causes wide fluctuations in hormones, creating a very real risk of two life-threatening conditions: mammary cancer and **pyometra** (which means "pus filled uterus"). Because estrogen plays a role in mammary tumor development, dogs who have had more than two heat cycles have a one-in-four chance of developing this type of cancer. Fortunately, the chances are almost nil for dogs spayed before or after their first heat. Pyometra is more common in middle-aged (unspayed) females, and usually occurs about four to six weeks after a heat cycle. Symptoms (loss of appetite, thirst, and lethargy) are often subtle until the uterine infection is advanced. Spaying at this point may be necessary to save the dog's life, but the illness makes it more complicated, expensive, and risky.

It is probably not "natural" for domestic male dogs to remain sexually intact, and yet have no natural breeding opportunities. This creates emotional stress that often results in behavioral problems. The continuous production of testosterone may create aggression toward other dogs, as well as prostate disease, testicular cancer, and tumors of the anal region. Like females, neutered males have longer life spans, and usually appear emotionally happier in their domestic environment.

THE HOLISTIC APPROACH TO SPAY AND NEUTER

If you have concerns about spay or neuter surgery, ask your vet to explain the operation, and be sure you are comfortable with the surgeon who will perform the procedure and with his clinic. Holistic veterinarians often use special protocols, remembering that the mind—as well as the body—of the animal needs support throughout the surgery and healing process. (See Chapter 10, When Your Dog Is Seriously Ill.) If possible, let your dog visit the clinic beforehand so she can get to know the sights, smells, and sounds of the place before the "big day," and maybe even receive treats from the staff.

PREVENTING SIDE EFFECTS OF SPAYING AND NEUTERING

No medical procedure is without side effects. Fortunately, the most common side effect of spaying and neutering is **obesity**, and it is entirely preventable. There is no question that removal of reproductive organs can slow the metabolism. In addition, the surgery is often performed around the time a young dog's growth rate is slowing down. As a result, she needs to consume fewer calories, yet many guardians continue to feed a puppy diet that is high in fat, or they simply feed too much food for their dog's new level of activity and maturity.

How can you prevent your dog from gaining weight? Feed according to her activity level, maintain a good exercise program, and monitor her weight and Body Conditioning Score (see page 15) monthly for the first year after surgery. With careful observation, you can modify the diet before obesity sets in. As with humans, once the pounds are there, they're not easy to get off.

Preventing obesity and maintaining daily exercise may also help prevent urinary incontinence, another side effect of spaying and, less often, of neutering. Fortunately, this disorder affects only a small percentage of dogs. Large breeds, primarily females, are most at risk. Uncontrolled urine leakage can be intermittent, and often begins years after the procedure. It is believed that the absence of sex hormones is linked to the loss of urinary sphincter control in some dogs. Anything you can do to help maintain optimum health and muscle tone will help prevent incontinence. Ensuring your dog has plenty of opportunities to empty her bladder is also important, as chronic overdistension of the bladder will strain the sphincter.

BREEDING ANIMALS

The intentional breeding of any dog is a controversial issue when *every hour*, thousands of healthy dogs are killed for lack of loving homes. In addition, producing healthy dogs who will not inherit genetic diseases or dysfunctional personality traits is complicated and almost impossible, so the genetically diverse mixed breeds are generally considered healthier than purebreds. Breeding an animal should never be done without careful thought about who is benefiting from such a proposition, as well as a thorough understanding of the risks to the dog, her future generations, and other members of her species.

Cosmetic Surgery

Cosmetic surgeries probably have no place at all in today's enlightened age. **Tail docking** was started by the Romans, who thought the practice would prevent rabies. The perpetuation of this practice in certain breeds appears to be nothing more than a fashion statement. Amputating the tail of a dog is, in fact, removing an important body part used for balance, maneuvering, and communication. If dogs could tell us their opinions, it's likely they'd have much to share about how it feels to have a segment of their vertebral column and sensitive nerves amputated. Even when performed at the recommended age of just 2 to 5 days old, every pup shrieks with pain during the procedure, and the occasional dog seems bothered for life, perhaps due to a sort of phantom pain.

Ear cropping—or more accurately "partial ear amputation"—was initiated for equally misguided reasons, and the procedure results in even more emotional and physical pain and suffering. During the critical period of social and psychological development, the pup must enter the hospital alone for surgery. The trauma continues as the sore ears are taped, racks are applied, and the painful tissue is handled repeatedly during the weeks following surgery.

According to the *Nei Jing*, one of the most ancient texts on acupuncture, "The ear is the meeting place of all the [energy] channels of the body," leading practitioners of Traditional Chinese Medicine to further question the impact of ear cropping on health. In fact, the ear has so many useful acupuncture points that a system of acupuncture, called **auriculotherapy**, was developed in the 1950s in France. This healing system is widely practiced throughout the world today, using powerful energetic points in the ear to heal distant regions of the body. What's more, cropping the ears interferes with an important mode of expression for your dog, in a sense depleting part of her vocabulary. Training the newly designed ears into a continuously erect posture deprives him of some of the normal ear postures used in communication with other dogs.

Even **dewclaw removal**, sometimes done with the intention of preventing injury, should not be considered a minor, elective surgical procedure. It is, in fact, the same as amputating your thumb!

Understanding Parasites: Living with and without Them

A parasite is an organism that lives in or on the body of another and derives nutrients from its host. All dogs have parasites, but not all of them are harmful. Take the Demodex mite, for instance. This microscopic critter lives deep in the skin follicles of all dogs, kept in check by the natural defenses of the dog's immune system. In a faulty immune system, these tiny parasites can wreak havoc, multiplying out of control and causing hair loss and nasty skin eruptions. Fortunately, you don't need to worry about attacking the Demodex mites unless they are attacking your dog.

This applies to other parasites as well. Two common annoyances are the **flea** and the **tick**. For some dogs, that's all these parasites are: little annoyances. Dogs get the occasional tick or flea and deal with it. They've evolved to do just that. It seems that healthy animals simply aren't likely to be plagued with large parasite burdens, and the occasional flea just isn't a big deal.

But when health is out of balance, such as when a dog is allergic to flea saliva, life can be miserable. A single bite can cause intense itching for as much as two weeks. Excessive scratching can create secondary skin infections, which compound the discomfort. If the environment is loaded with fleas, small dogs can develop serious anemia from too many bites. And ingesting a flea can also transmit the common and unsightly tapeworm.

As another example, the occasional tick might be tolerable; a serious infestation can lead to serious illness. Lyme disease, which can be transmitted by ticks, has been known to cause fatalities due to kidney failure, in addition to the arthritis more commonly associated with Lyme. Other infections, Rocky Mountain Spotted Fever, Erlichiosis, tick paralysis, and Bartenellosis are just some of the diseases caused by tick bites.

Similarly, internal parasites can cause little or no health problems for your dog, or they can pose a major health crisis. Intestinal parasites, such as **tapeworms**, are often more a cosmetic problem than a health risk. No one enjoys seeing those crawly segments on their dog's hind end, but most dogs can harbor a tapeworm or two without a problem. This isn't to say you shouldn't try effective, natural flea-control measures, but tapeworms just don't seem to rob your dog's body of important nutrients the way other intestinal parasites like hookworms and whipworms can.

While a colony of **heartworms** living in your dog's heart can be life-threatening, harboring just a few of these parasites rarely does much damage. The mosquito-transmitted larvae may enter your dog's system, but many dogs mount their own immune response that keeps the parasite in check. Heartworms have a natural life cycle and, if only a few are present, they may die out on their own after a number of years without causing major health issues. But for a dog with a hypersensitivity to the worms, or one with a large number of worms, the problem can be catastrophic. Heart failure, kidney and liver damage, and sudden death may result.

So how do you know when to mount an all-out attack on parasites and when to adopt a "live and let live" approach? This is a complex question, but these simple guidelines will help.

What You Can Do: Prevention versus control

🐕 **Keep your dog healthy by feeding a high quality diet.** Healthy animals have fewer parasite problems.

🐕 **It's easier to prevent a parasite infestation than to control an existing one.** Follow a routine grooming program. This helps you monitor your dog for external parasites. Removal of dog and cat (and raccoon) feces at least weekly from your yard will eliminate the majority of eggs from intestinal worms before they become infectious.

🐕 **When treating parasites, start with safe, natural products with a proven track record.** Before resorting to chemicals, seek veterinary advice. Avoid over-the-counter chemical products. They are less effective and more toxic to you, your dog, and the environment. For more information, see Chapter 9, Treating Illness and Injury: The Skin.

🐕 **If your dog does not live in or frequent a heartworm-infected area,** you can safely skip the preventive medication. If heartworms exist in your area, use a monthly, allopathic heartworm prescription recommended by your veterinarian. If you have trouble remembering to give the medication, ask your vet about administering the semiannual heartworm prevention injection. (NOTE: The majority of holistic veterinarians concur that there is no fail-safe natural control for this serious disease, and there is no way to know whether your dog will pick up a serious infection or not.) If your dog does test positive for heartworms through standard blood tests, consult your holistic veterinarian before treatment. If your dog shows no symptoms, you may want to try holistic support and immediate use of the monthly heartworm preventive medication. Studies show that early cases of heartworm infection may actually be eliminated by a number of monthly doses. Retest in 4 to 18 months to be sure this approach has been effective for your dog.

If you suspect an intestinal parasite problem, submit a sample of stool to your vet for microscopic examination. If you have small children in the home, talk to him about worming program to avoid transmission of parasites to humans. Be cautious about treating a suspected worm infection on your own. Some over-the-counter herbal parasite cleanses are excessively harsh, and if your dog is not actually infected, the treatment may not be needed at all.

FLEAS AND TICKS: The commitment to a chemical-free approach

Fleas and ticks have been with us for millions of years, and chances are they'll be around for some time to come. A multibillion-dollar industry exists to produce chemicals to control them. The newer products are unquestionably safer and more effective than anything available in the past, but as with all chemicals, resistances develop, more products have to be developed, and the cycle continues. Many of us are concerned about the environmental impact, as well as the impact on the health of our dogs, and rightly so.

If you've decided on a chemical-free approach, don't expect a quick fix. In some areas of the country it takes a real commitment, especially if your dog suffers from flea allergies or is at risk for tick borne disease. There is also a good deal of misinformation disseminated about some "natural" flea and tick products. They can be toxic, ineffective, or both. Beware of false claims, and *never* assume that what is safe for a dog is safe for a cat. With those thoughts in mind, however, there is much you can do to control fleas and ticks without the use of harmful chemicals. Consider the following suggestions, and remain diligent and patient. The results can be well worth the effort.

CONTROLLING FLEAS— NATURALLY

The most natural product available to you is the **flea comb**. Fleas become trapped in the comb's tiny, close-set tines as it glides through your dog's coat. Dipping the comb in a bowl of soapy water will drown the fleas and prevent reinfestation. *Bathing alone is ineffective for flea control.* No matter what product you use, fleas will jump back on after the bath. However, **flea repellents** work for some, and seem to be useful when infestations aren't severe. Oral remedies include garlic, brewer's yeast, or thiamin supplements. Topical remedies such as pennyroyal, citronella, and eucalyptus oils also repel fleas, but can be toxic to puppies and cats. Some guardians have had success with a light, daily application of a natural flea repellant formula for adult dogs recommended by Dr. Ihor Basko, a holistic veterinarian in Hawaii: Combine 1/2 ounce citronella oil, 1 ounce eucalyptus oil, 4 ounces aloe vera juice, and 4 ounces witch hazel extract. **Cedar beds** make effective repellents, as long as covers are washed routinely.

If flea combs and repellents don't solve the problem, look to the environment. One female flea lays about 30 eggs a day. No matter how well you "deflea" your dog, the presence of eggs, larvae, and pupae in the house or yard ensures reinfestation.

Indoors: Homes with central heating and wall-to-wall carpeting are perfect environments for flea development. Thoroughly **vacuum** cracks, crevices, upholstery, and carpets weekly. Pay attention to areas under furniture and appliances where larvae will crawl to avoid light and vibration. Seal and empty the vacuum bag so fleas can't crawl out. If you have a thick, plush carpet, consider a **professional carpet treatment** or home treatment with a borate-based product (Flea Busters, Rx for Fleas) unless there are animals or people in the house with respiratory disease. **Wash small area rugs and bedding** in hot water weekly; dry in a hot dryer.

Outdoors: Raccoons, possums, and other wildlife who frequent the yard can bring in thousands of fleas. Moist, shady areas and the places your animals spend most of their time are the problem spots. Apply a **natural nematode lawn product** to devour flea larvae. **Diatomaceous earth** is also suitable for outdoor use.

Even with the most comprehensive approach to natural flea control, it's essential to remember that **the best protection against fleas is your dog's vibrant good health**. That starts with a safe and happy environment, as free from stress as possible, and relies heavily on a wholesome diet that's free from artificial additives. When a dog's system is not laden with the by-products of poor quality ingredients and chemicals, health is more likely to flourish and the skin and coat will bloom. Fleas and other parasites are less likely to thrive when your dog's immune system and his skin's natural oils are able to do their job.

During those seasons when fleas are most abundant, some feel it may help to give your dog a little extra insurance with a bit of **fresh garlic** and **nutritional yeast** added to each meal. Garlic stimulates the

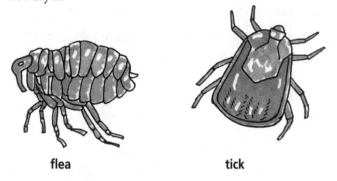

flea   tick

when natural remedies just aren't enough

On rare occasions a more aggressive approach to flea control is warranted, such as when:

🐕 natural remedies have been unsuccessful in alleviating the problem

🐕 your dog is suffering from severe flea allergic dermatitis

🐕 there is such a large flea infestation that your dog is miserable

🐕 due to young age or small size, your dog is at risk of life-threatening flea bite anemia

Products containing insect growth regulators, or **IGRs**, are available as environmental, topical, or oral treatments (Program). They are not true pesticides, but are used to control flea fertility.

I find sprays, dips, and over-the-counter spot-ons to be more toxic and less effective than prescription monthly spot-ons such as imidacloprid (Advantage) and fipronil (Frontline). I have seen serious problems and death in cats from over-the-counter spot-ons, and if your dog enjoys the company of cats he can bring serious risk to his feline friends if he's been treated with one of these chemicals. While side effects of veterinary-prescribed products tend to be mild and treatable by discontinuing their use, keep in mind that complete information about side effects may not be available. Products presumed to be safe have at times been found to be detrimental to health only after many years on the market.

If you feel you must resort to the use of chemicals, I suggest limiting their use to a short time frame. Two to three months may be long enough to break the life cycle of the fleas and reduce the infestation. During this time, work on improving the general health of your dog through nutrition and other means, and reduce environmental infestation, so that further reliance on chemicals can be minimized. This is especially important because, if you continually resort to intermittent chemical use, you may create a colony of fleas that are resistant to those products.

When tick season is in full swing and a client requests more complete control than they are getting from natural methods, I let them know the following:

- Collars that contain amitraz have been shown to be very effective, but also toxic. Ingestion of a piece of collar (as by an inquisitive puppy) is a true emergency, requiring the administration of an antidote and careful monitoring by a veterinarian.

- Many find fipronil (Frontline drops or spray) to be effective enough for tick control without the worry of collar ingestion, and much less toxic than over-the-counter spot-ons. Use should be suspended when ticks are not in season.

Of course, if you can get by without using any chemical forms of flea and tick control, your dog will be the healthier for it. —*Katy*

immune system, and some holistic practitioners believe both supplements act as deterrents to the tiny predators.

CONTROLLING TICKS— NATURALLY

Like using a simple flea comb, **removing ticks by hand or with a tweezers** is the only real chemical-free approach that is completely effective. Fortunately, transmission of Lyme disease usually does not occur unless the tick is attached for 24 to 48 hours, so diligent tick patrol can prevent serious infections. Don't forget to check the groin and armpit region, and look closely around the eyes and ears and between the toes.

As with fleas, keeping your dog in the best of health will make her less susceptible to the onslaught of large numbers of ticks. Some holistic practitioners believe that adding garlic and nutritional yeast to the diet may make the skin less attractive to ticks, so that they are less likely to attach.

For **environmental control** of ticks in areas where dogs are confined, keep grass mowed and shrubs trimmed, and remove excess debris such as wood- and burn-piles. Amazingly, some ticks can lie in wait for years, and become active when pheromones (natural chemicals produced by passing animals) stimulate them to jump and attach. When you walk your dog in rural areas, staying on open roads and out from under low-lying branches can reduce exposure to ticks. Natural repellent sprays are usually not strong, but when applied just before a walk they can deter ticks by masking the natural pheromones of the dog.

If, like most dogs, your friend loves to run through the underbrush, chasing down scents on your walks through the countryside, don't feel you need to deprive her of this delicious part of her life. Just make it a practice to go over her inch-by-inch later in the evening and, if you wish, combine the manual "de-ticking" with a much appreciated massage.

Environmental Hazards: Keep Your Dog Safe

A shrinking ozone layer and increasingly toxic and pervasive pollution means all creatures—including our dogs—face health issues as a result of the environment, and sometimes dogs have an even more serious exposure than we do. Dogs who live in households with smokers have ten times the risk of lung disease compared to people, because smoke tends to hang low in a room and their exposure to the toxins in second-hand smoke is greater. They also tend to sleep and play in closer proximity to lawn and garden chemicals than their human family members. One study showed a significantly increased risk of lymph node cancer in dogs living where lawn herbicides that contain 2,4,D were heavily used. Even solar-induced skin cancers are on the rise in dogs and cats.

Fortunately, much that we do to protect ourselves can be done for our dogs as well. Whether you eat organically, commit to a chemical- and pesticide-free home and yard, or use as few products as possible that contain environmental pollutants, your dog will benefit from decreased toxin exposure just like the rest of your family.

Specific household toxins and hazards you should be aware of are identified on pages 26, 27, and 28. Fortunately, there are now safer alternatives to many of the commonly used household cleaners, pesticides, and other chemicals. Consider making the switch to nontoxic products and discarding those you no longer use. Other items that aren't normally considered hazardous to you or other members of your family may be deadly for an inquisitive young pup. Simple measures, like covering exposed electric cords or making sure your prescription medication doesn't get left out on a table top, may be all it takes to prevent a fatal accident.

COMMON HOUSEHOLD HAZARDS

Potentially Harmful Substances	What You Should Know
Pesticides, insecticides, and herbicides: many harmful varieties, especially those that contain organophosphates, carbamates, DEET, diazanon, or 2,4,D.	Antidote may be required. See your veterinarian if ingestion occurs. If you must use a deterrent, consult your holistic veterinarian for the safest alternatives.
Snail bait products that contain metaldehyde.	A common cause of dog poisoning; causes drooling, diarrhea, shaking, coma, and death. As a safer alternative, use SLUGGO (made with iron phosphate) from Monterey Lawn and Garden Products; Phone: (559) 499-2100; Website: www.montereylawngarden.com
Rodent bait products that contain anticoagulant (warfarin) Newer, more potent and toxic products are continually being produced.	Ingestion of warfarin product may require antidote with prescription variety vitamin K1; YOUR DOG MAY NOT SHOW SYMPTOMS UNTIL IT'S TOO LATE. Seek veterinary help if ingestion is even a possibility. Instead of poisons, use mousetraps that do not kill mice but allow their release in an alternate location.
Plants: ornamental/indoor/outdoor, especially castor bean plant, poinsettia, dieffenbachia, philodendrons, foxglove, oleander, milkweed, sago palms, rhododendron family.	Seek immediate veterinary support if your dog shows signs of vomiting, diarrhea, or other illness after plant ingestion. Some (such as sago palm) can be fatal within hours. Keep ornamental plants out of reach of inquisitive puppies.
Garbage and spoiled food	May contain potent toxins; can cause milder gastro-intestinal symptoms or more severe neurologic symptoms.
Foods that can poison: chocolate, macadamia nuts, possibly grapes/raisins, many mushroom varieties, unwashed food with heavy pesticide residue, unhulled black walnuts (due to fungus in some hulls).	Keep Out of Reach; do not feed (currently, reports of toxicities from small amounts of grapes or raisins in dogs are under investigation); the inquisitive nature of young puppies makes them particularly at risk for mushroom poisoning.

COMMON HOUSEHOLD HAZARDS

Potentially Harmful Substances	What You Should Know
Prescription drugs	Keep Out of Reach. Call hotline or your vet should your dog ingest any prescription medications.
Over-the-counter medications including ibuprofen, pseudoephedrine	Keep Out of Reach, as for prescription drugs. Consult your vet before giving any over-the-counter drugs to your dog.
Recreational drugs, including marijuana	Keep Out of Reach; do not feed.
Household cleaning products	Choose products made from natural ingredients that are nontoxic to humans, animals, and the environment.
Electrical cords	Young and inquisitive dogs are at particular risk of electrical shock from chewing on electrical cords. Cover exposed cords with PVC pipe, or tape them to the floor to make them less inviting.
Fumes from household appliances or products	1. Be sure gas appliances are functioning properly and vented to the outside, and use exhaust fans when cooking. Avoid kerosene heaters if possible. 2. Maintain air conditioners, air ducts, and filters, especially in newer airtight homes. 3. Use aerosol household products only in well-ventilated areas. If you need to wear mask to paint or varnish, then your dog should be removed from the area!
Heavy metals: lead-painted wood, other lead or zinc objects.	Keep Out of Reach. Toxic if ingested or chewed.
Petroleum products and industrial solvents, including gasoline, kerosene, motor oil.	Toxic if ingested or absorbed through the skin. Call poison hotline in the event of ingestion or topical exposure.

COMMON HOUSEHOLD HAZARDS

Potentially Harmful Substances	What You Should Know
Ethylene glycol-based antifreeze products	Animals are attracted to the sweet smell and taste and 2 ounces can kill a medium-sized dog. Symtoms can be delayed for days, and survival is rare. An estimated 90,000 pets died in 1 year due to antifreeze ingestion. 1. Repair radiator leaks and control spills. 2. Use Sierra Antifreeze, made with safer propylene glycol. Phone: (800) 323-5440 Website: sierraantifreeze.com 3. If your animal ingests even a small amount, contact an emergency veterinary clinic or hotline immediately. DO NOT WAIT FOR SYMPTOMS TO DEVELOP.

Prepare for the Unexpected

Part of your role as canine caregiver is to be ready to respond to the unforeseen events that may impact your dog's health, or even threaten her life. *You* may keep the back gate locked, but someone else may be careless. Being prepared for the unexpected will make a huge difference.

What You Can Do: Be prepared

- **Provide Proper ID.** A microchip can be placed under your dog's skin at the time she is neutered, or as part of a routine office visit with your veterinarian. The chip contains a code that can be read with a scanner that vets, humane societies, and shelters keep on hand. By calling an 800 phone number, these caregivers can then use the code to access information left on record by you. The information can be used to reunite you and your friend, or even describe medication she may need. If microchipping isn't appropriate for you, an ID tag attached to a break-away collar will be suitable in most situations.

- **Be ready to respond quickly if your dog is poisoned.** If your dog ingests a poisonous substance, a swift response can mean the difference between life and death. Have emergency phone numbers available and an action plan in mind *before* you need them.

- **A Poison Control Hotline 888-4ANI-HELP (888-426-4435)** is maintained by American Society for the Prevention of Cruelty to Animals (ASPCA) 24 hours a day. For a fee ($45 as of this printing) they will answer questions about toxic substances that may be around your home, or assist you or your veterinarian in providing the proper treatment for your dog in an emergency. They will even help you assess whether or not a trip to the vet is necessary.

- 🐕 **Keep your veterinarian's phone number next to your phone along with other emergency numbers.** Having this information at your fingertips in an anxious moment will help you as well as your dog.

- 🐕 **Locate the 24-hour emergency veterinary care facility nearest you** and keep that number and address handy as well.

DISASTER PREPAREDNESS FOR DOGS

Here in Northern California, earthquakes, fires, and mudslides are not uncommon. Other areas of the country routinely cope with hurricanes, tornadoes, and floods. Wherever you live, it is essential to have an emergency evacuation plan for all members of your family—including your animals. Even if you aren't at home when disaster strikes, the following suggestions will help a neighbor, a rescue worker, or a good samaritan escort your dog to safety.

What You Can Do: Before a disaster occurs

- 🐕 **Make sure your dog has some form of identification** (microchip, tags).

- 🐕 **Keep a leash near the door for each dog.** She may not need it when walking with you, but frightening circumstances may call for the extra control provided by a leash.

- 🐕 If you have a small dog (or cat), **keep a crate or traveling carrier available** in a hall closet close to the front door (not buried in the basement, attic, or other inaccessible place).

- 🐕 **Keep a kit with evacuation supplies in a waterproof box** in the same closet near the door. Include microchip information, current photos, a fresh supply of any medications your dog must take, and contact information for your place of work and for a friend who can care for your dog in your absence. Contact the American Veterinary Medical Association (AVMA, www.avma.org) for an evacuation kit checklist.

- 🐕 **Place stickers on all doors to notify rescue personnel that animals are in your home,** and where to find your evacuation supplies.

- 🐕 **Talk to your neighbors about implementing a joint disaster response plan.** Most states have a plan organized by local veterinarians. To find out more, contact the AVMA.

Vaccination:
The New Thinking

Imagine for a moment that your child has just completed her regimen of childhood vaccines. As you leave, you are told to return for booster shots for diphtheria, tetanus, whooping cough, mumps, and measles *every year* for the rest of her life. Most parents would rebel, demanding to know why such a protocol was needed. Yet many dogs are vaccinated yearly for as many as 5 or even 9 diseases. This practice continues despite the fact that the AVMA's *Position Statement on Biologics* states, "Questions over duration of immunity and the search for the optimal revaccination interval have reminded veterinarians that vaccination is a complex medical procedure." Simply put, even among experts little is known about how long a dog is actually protected.

None of us wishes to see our dog succumb to a serious or life-threatening disease because we failed to vaccinate him, but there are serious, even life-threatening side effects from vaccination as well (see page 34). Fortunately, vaccine problems are uncommon, but certain breeds or families within a breed appear to be more predisposed to adverse reactions (see page 35). And of course, even if the risk of a serious side effect from a vaccine is low, if it happens to *your* dog, the statistics don't seem very important.

The goal of a vaccination program should be to provide **benefit** in the form of protection against serious diseases that truly threaten your dog, while minimizing the **risk** of adverse side effects. Your veterinarian can help you evaluate the **risk-benefit ratio** of each vaccine and the prevalence of regional diseases in your area.

ARE WE OVER-VACCINATING?

The current practice of revaccinating dogs every year has no scientific basis, and never did. There is no published data that proves this practice is necessary. In fact, only recently have studies been conducted to determine how long a dog is likely to be protected by a particular vaccine. Many human vaccinations need boosters only about every ten years, and there is reason to believe that some vaccines for dogs might last as long. Studies now underway indicate that immunity to *most* common diseases in dogs is, in fact, very long lasting. While more data are needed, it is likely that some vaccines will provide a lifetime of protection after just one initial series of injections.

Another factor to consider is that no two dogs react alike to a vaccine, due to differences in genetic make-up and individual variations in the functioning of the immune system. Revaccinating a dog that is already protected by a previous inoculation stimulates the immune system unnecessarily, does nothing to improve resistance to the disease, and may increase the risk of adverse reactions. In addition, the common practice of administering several different vaccines at the same time—often in the form of a single injection known as a **polyvalent** vaccine—causes undo risk to dogs as well. If a vaccine reaction follows, it is impossible to determine which vaccine caused the problem. What's more, the over-burdening of the immune system caused by frequent vaccination is compounded when five or six disease factors are given at the same time. Fortunately, most veterinarians are giving individual vaccines separately, and changing to longer intervals between boosters. If yours is not, ask why.

IS ANTIBODY TESTING THE ANSWER?

If the available data can't pinpoint the length of time a vaccine will prevent disease, what other means can we use to guide us? There are blood tests, called **titers**, that measure whether the immune system has produced the needed antibodies for protection against diseases such as parvovirus and distemper. Unfortunately, these tests can't always reliably predict a patient's immune status for every disease, and interpretation can be tricky; some dogs with low levels of antibodies still seem to be resistant to disease. This is probably due to another part of the immune system, termed **cell mediated immunity**, which can't be measured in blood tests but does provide protection.

VACCINOSIS: What does it mean?

Vaccinosis is a term coined by Compton Burnett, a turn-of-the-century physician, to describe a chronic disease state whose origin may be linked to the administration of vaccines. Associated problems may include skin eruptions, ear disease, respiratory ailments, thyroid disease, chronic diarrhea associated with inflammatory bowel disease, cystitis, emotional and behavioral disorders, seizures, and a host of autoimmune diseases. Some holistic practitioners suspect that rabies vaccination may be a factor, particularly when symptoms bear some resemblance to the rabies disease itself. Those symptoms include seizures, paralysis, encephalitis and other neurological disorders, as well as aggression, hypersensitivity, and fearfulness.

While the term vaccinosis is generally used only by holistic practitioners, most vets seem to agree that some chronic illness, such as autoimmune disease, can be induced by vaccination. Unfortunately, an accurate assessment of vaccine-related problems is difficult, in part because most veterinarians don't report adverse reactions to regulatory agencies like the United States Department of Agriculture (USDA) or to vaccine manufacturers. In addition, it is virtually impossible to confirm a cause-and-effect relationship between vaccines and chronic problems that may develop over the lifetime of the animal.

VACCINOSIS: Homeopathic prevention and treatment

Some holistic practitioners recommend giving a homeopathic remedy immediately following vaccination to prevent an adverse reaction. Others prefer to treat acute reactions only when and if they occur, or chronic disease states in cases where the origin may be related to a vaccine. Still others avoid using vaccines altogether, and choose instead to administer homeopathic nosodes (see page 32). If you do choose to vaccinate, the following suggestions may be helpful.

- **When using homeopathy as a preventive measure,** common remedy choices are Thuja, Sulphur or Silicea; for protection after a rabies vaccine, Lyssin, which is made from the saliva of a rabid dog.

- **If your dog has a localized reaction or becomes ill** 24 hours to 21 days after a vaccine, choose a remedy that matches the symptoms you see. Some common choices are:

  Apis for a hot, swollen area at the site of the injection

  Ledum for a cool, swollen area at the site of the injection

  Silicea for infections at the site of the injection; chilliness; weakness in the hind limbs

Sulphur for seizures; skin eruptions; digestive disturbances

Thuja for exhaustion, depression; neurologic, digestive, or respiratory disturbances; skin eruptions

NOTE: *Any vaccine reaction should be reported to your veterinarian.*

- **For chronic illness that you suspect may be related to a vaccine**, begin with a dose of **Thuja**; if symptoms resemble those of rabies, particularly neurologic symptoms or aggression, and your dog has received a rabies vaccine, choose **Lyssin**. In all cases, as for any chronic illness, base your evaluation on the full range of symptoms and traits. (See Chapter 5, Homeopathy: Like Cures Like.) NOTE: Treating vaccinosis is complicated due to the many layers of disease. An experienced homeopath can help your dog achieve a complete recovery.

ALLOPATHIC RECOMMENDATIONS FOR VACCINE REACTIONS

If a vaccine-related problem occurs, the most important response is this: **Do not revaccinate!** The chance of another reaction is high. There are many different types of vaccine reactions, and your dog may experience an even more severe one next time. Many veterinarians recommend pretreating a reactive dog with antihistamines or cortisone prior to the next vaccination to ward off a future problem. However, in this scenario your dog gets not only a yearly vaccine, but an annual cortisone shot as well! Consider this protocol only if antibody titers, regional issues, and other indicators suggest a legitimate need for the vaccination, and beware that these procedures are not foolproof in preventing reactions. In any event, heed the message your dog's reaction might be telling you—that a more holistic approach to supporting his overall health and constitution is probably wise.

A HOLISTIC APPROACH TO VACCINATION

There is another approach to vaccination that, while controversial, makes sense to many people: Keep your dog in optimum health with a robust immune system and she will not need a vaccine to protect her from a disease, even if she is exposed to it. One way to achieve this is to feed a healthy diet, minimize exposure of young animals (less than a year old) to diseases, and avoid genetic lines of breeding that are known to have weak immune systems. Unfortunately, there will always be some individuals who, due to genetic susceptibility and their level of exposure, will still sicken and die if not vaccinated, no matter how well you care for them. This perspective holds that it's simply a matter of "survival of the fittest" and can be viewed as nature's way of weeding out the weaker animals of the species.

Unfortunately, what might be good for the species as a whole is not always good for an individual. Many guardians are searching for a middle ground, one that avoids overuse of vaccines, yet protects their valued friend from serious or life-threatening illness. Here are some guidelines to consider.

- Since young animals are most likely to succumb to infectious diseases, vaccinate puppies for the most life-threatening diseases like parvovirus and distemper.

- Instead of the customary regimen of 4 or more doses before maturity, give parvo and distemper vaccines at 9 weeks of age, followed by a booster at 12 weeks. Your veterinarian may be able to provide separate, rather than polyvalent, doses, and can guide you to vaccine brands that provide good protection and minimal side effects if you choose to administer the vaccine yourself.

- Avoid unnecessarily exposing your puppy to diseases before her immune system is fully developed. Be sure her abbreviated vaccine series is complete before you take her into public places or allow her to mingle with dogs with unknown vaccine histories.

- Rabies vaccine protocols are subject to state and county regulations regarding the animal's age and the frequency of inoculation. However, if your dog is in poor health or suffering from a serious illness, your veterinarian can contact local Animal Control officials who may allow you to postpone vaccination until your dog is well. Similarly, if your dog has had a life-threatening reaction to a rabies vaccine, inquire about exemption policies in your area.

- If your dog is an adult, reevaluate your options before you continue with your next round of booster vaccines. Ask your veterinarian to keep you informed of the most recent vaccine schedule changes based on the latest research. *Never* vaccinate an individual who suffers from an immune system disease, who is not in good health, or who is unlikely to be exposed to the disease in question.

NOSODES:
A homeopathic alternative?

Nosodes are homeopathic preparations made from the tissues or discharges of diseased animals. They are used by some homeopathic veterinarians to prevent disease in lieu of vaccinations. Although some practitioners report good results, we do not have clear evidence that nosodes provide reliable long-term protection. They are prescription medicines and therefore should only be given under direct supervision of a homeopathic veterinarian.

CURRENT VACCINES:
Expand your awareness

■ **Bordatella or "Kennel Cough":** An upper respiratory infection that causes a persistent, dry, hacking cough. It is highly contagious and may last for several weeks.

Who's at risk: Dogs who congregate in closed-air environments such as boarding kennels, dog shows, and veterinary hospitals, as well as dogs who have contact with saliva or air-borne particles coughed up by infected dogs.

The vaccine: Available either in drops administered into the nostrils, or as a standard injectable vaccine. Duration of immunity is unknown, although it is believed to be short-lived, leading some people to vaccinate dogs who are frequently exposed, for example at dog shows, every 6 months.

This is a bacterial disease, curable with antibiotics, or with alternative therapies in most cases. It is not life threatening, and so the need to vaccinate is highly questionable. However, to help prevent outbreaks, vaccines are frequently required by boarding facilities.

■ **Canine Distemper:** One of the most serious canine diseases, with an alarmingly high death rate. Infection attacks the respiratory, gastrointestinal, and neurologic systems. Treatment, especially if complemented with alternative therapies, can save some dogs, although permanent brain damage can result.

Who's at risk: Unvaccinated puppies are at risk of ingesting environmental viral particles deposited by infected domestic or wild dogs. Fortunately, years of vaccination have reduced the prevalence of the disease in some areas, however contamination is widespread in others. Adult dogs are usually immune due to natural or vaccine-induced immunity.

The vaccine: Distemper virus is commonly added to a polyvalent vaccine. Fortunately newer vaccines for distemper alone may soon be available. Because the disease is so devastating and difficult to treat, **consider vaccinating all puppies**. (See general vaccine information.)

■ **Canine Parvovirus:** Causes severe intestinal infection leading to vomiting, bloody diarrhea, dehydration, and sometimes death. Even with aggressive treatment, mortality is at least 15%.

Who's at risk: The incidence in a given area varies according to a number of factors, including weather, contamination of the area from previous outbreaks, and the percentage of dogs that have been vaccinated in the vicinity. The virus can persist in the environment for as long as several years, so any dog can be at risk. Most fatalities occur in the young; adult dogs usually get only mild infections. Breeds at high risk are American Pit Bull Terriers, Rottweilers, Doberman Pinschers, and Labrador Retrievers, but any breed may be effected. Unvaccinated dogs are reportedly 10 to 12 times more likely to become ill than those who have been properly vaccinated.

The vaccine: Parvovirus protection is included in polyvalent vaccines, but is also available separately. Problems with the vaccine have been related to high levels of maternal antibodies in the puppy's system, which can interfere with its effectiveness. The antibodies decrease as the pup grows older, creating a window of vulnerability in which the puppy is most at risk of infection, even if a vaccine has been given earlier. This is why it is typically administered at intervals. Newer vaccines are reported to break through maternal antibody interference, and are effective at a much earlier age (12 weeks), thereby reducing the number of inoculations needed.

Not only is parvovirus potentially deadly, most cases cause a lot of pain and suffering. Hospitalization is likely, often during the pup's critical period of socialization. It's a miserable and frightening experience, and not all puppies survive. **All puppies should be vaccinated unless the disease does not exist in their community.**

■ **Coronavirus:** Transmitted in much the same way as parvo, but a much milder intestinal virus that causes only mild diarrhea and illness, unless it is contracted at the same time as parvovirus.

Who's at risk: Similar to parvovirus, young animals are primarily at risk. Infection may go unnoticed in an adult dog.

The vaccine: Often included in a "7-way" polyvalent form, but it is also available separately. Because the infection is so mild in adult dogs, most veterinarians agree this vaccine can be skipped. Puppies vaccinated against parvovirus will also show only mild symptoms from a coronavirus infection.

■ **Leptospirosis:** Can lead to kidney or liver failure, and death in about 10% to 20% of the cases treated. Chronic kidney failure often persists in dogs who survive.

Who's at risk: Dogs who have contact with wildlife (particularly skunks, raccoons, and opossums), herding dogs, or those in contact with livestock or livestock waste; also dogs who roam the countryside or drink from contaminated ponds or flooded areas. Transmission is often through contact with the urine of infected animals.

The vaccine: Probably has the highest rate of adverse reactions, particularly in miniature breeds. It has been reported to suppress the immune system in dogs less than 16 weeks of age. A number of vaccinated dogs have contracted leptospirosis because the vaccine did not protect against the strain of the disease, or **serovar**, prevalent in their particular environment.

Consider this vaccine *only* if this disease is present in your area, if the vaccine is effective against the serovar that causes disease in your area, and only if your dog is at risk due to contact with wildlife, or with waste water or ponds in areas frequented by wildlife. Wait until your dog is at least 16 weeks of age, and administer it separately from other vaccines.

■ **Lyme Disease:** Caused by a spirochete (*Borrelia burgdorferi*) and transmitted by certain tick species, Lyme causes arthritis, fever, and lethargy. In rare cases, kidney failure, heart problems, and neurological dam-

---

PROVEN POTENTIAL PROBLEMS ASSOCIATED WITH VACCINES

Anaphylactic shock due to allergic reaction to the vaccine

Transient (temporary) suppression of the immune system after vaccination

Autoimmune disorders (diseases in which the body's immune system attacks its own tissues after being "confused" by a stimulus such as a vaccine, drug, or other foreign substance); may affect muscles, joints, bowel, liver, thyroid, kidney, blood, skin, mucous membranes, eyes, or other tissues.

Neurological disorders (problems with nervous system or nerve function)

Vaccine-induced tumor formation (confirmed in cats)

Transient infections (short-term incidence of the disease for which the dog was vaccinated)

Long-term infected carrier states (the animal tests positive for the disease but shows no symptoms)

Permanent hair loss at vaccination site

---

age may occur. Diagnosis can be difficult, and chronic disease states similar to those seen in people may exist in dogs, but the evidence is unclear.

Who's at risk: Dogs in certain geographic areas (northeastern states, mid-Atlantic, and the upper north central regions of the U.S., as well as several California counties) where ticks that carry the Lyme spirochete exist. Susceptibility seems to vary dramatically from one dog to the next—some can be loaded with infect-

SUSPECTED POTENTIAL PROBLEMS ASSOCIATED WITH VACCINES
Kidney failure
Thyroid dysfunction
Fertility problems (especially if a vaccine is given while the dog is in heat)
Allergic skin disease
Seizures
Chronic pain
Aggression and other behavioral problems

BREEDS WITH HIGHER RISK OF PROBLEMS ASSOCIATED WITH VACCINES.
Akita
American Eskimo
Chihuahua
Cocker Spaniel
Fox Terrier
Harlequin Great Dane
Jack Russell Terrier
Springer Spaniel
Weimaraner

(Adapted from *Current Veterinary Therapy XI*, by T. Phillips and R. Schultz, and personal communication with W. Jean Dodds, D.V.M.)

ed ticks and show no symptoms while others become ill after much less exposure. The reason is still a mystery, but the immune system reactivity of the individual dog is certainly a factor.

The vaccine: Reactions at the site of vaccination have been reported; a more purified vaccine has recently been released with fewer injection site problems, but controversy exists over the effectiveness of the vaccines. Some vets suspect problems with vaccine-induced arthritis or kidney disease, but studies have not yet confirmed this. That makes the usual concern about over-stimulating the immune system with repeated vaccination even more of an issue.

Lyme's symptoms arise as a result of the immune system's *response* to the organism rather than the organism itself, so some worry that "priming" the immune system repeatedly with vaccines might be counterproductive. This, combined with the variation in susceptibility from one dog to the next, has led some vets to wonder if perhaps letting dogs develop their own immunity might be best.

Too many dogs receive this vaccination even though they will never see an infected tick in their lifetime. **Confirm that the disease is truly a problem in your area before you even consider vaccinating your dog**. An effective tick control program may be a more sensible approach that will also protect your dog against other tick-transmitted diseases for which there is no vaccine.

■ **Rabies:** An acute viral disease of the central nervous system that can affect all mammals—including humans. It is transmitted through a bite wound from an infected animal. The disease is untreatable, death is certain, and many individuals and animals are likely to be exposed when a dog contracts rabies.

Who's at risk: Dogs in contact with wildlife.

The vaccine: Many holistic veterinarians, and particularly homeopaths, share concerns that chronic illness or behavior disorders may occur in dogs as a reaction to rabies vaccines. The vaccine has been associated with the formation of malignant tissue tumors in cats, but to date similar cases have not been confirmed in dogs.

Many dogs will never be exposed to rabies because they spend the majority of their time indoors, or don't frequent areas where the disease is a problem. However, most local ordinances require that every dog be vaccinated either annually or every 3 years, depending on where she lives. If your dog is ill or has been diagnosed with vaccinosis by your holistic veterinarian, ask for a note excusing your friend from rabies vaccinations, and inquire about exemption policies in your area. A rabies antibody titer, to evaluate immunity from previous vaccination, can be performed at Kansas State University from a serum sample submitted by your veterinarian. However, even if the test indicates your dog is still protected, chances are it will not satisfy statutory vaccination requirements.

a wholesome diet

a WHOLESOME DIET may be the single most important factor in maintaining our dogs' good health. But what exactly is a "wholesome" diet? Nutrition for our domesticated animal friends is a hot topic of controversy today. There is the multibillion-dollar pet food industry vying for our dollars with impressive claims about their products in full-page magazine ads and prime-time television commercials. There is also a vast network of individuals on the internet and elsewhere promoting a variety of dog diets, many of which prove frighteningly unhealthy.

Maybe you have been rethinking your dog's diet for some time. You'd like to sneak tonight's leftovers into his bowl, but don't know if your veterinarian would approve. A friend is feeding her dog a "raw foods diet" and swears by it, but you aren't sure if bones are safe. Perhaps you've made a commitment to provide your dog with a healthier commercial food, without a lot of additives and by-products. But there were so many choices at the pet store, you came away more confused than ever.

Well, take heart. With some solid information and a little bit of common sense, the right choices are easier than you think.

The ideal diet for your dog would be:

- fresh and unprocessed, organic when possible
- balanced and full of variety
- made with high quality ingredients
- made without additives or preservatives
- tasty, enjoyable, and satisfying
- inexpensive, quick, and easy to prepare

This looks a lot like an optimum diet for humans, right? The truth is, domesticated dogs have adapted very well to eating what we eat. But perhaps you're a bit perplexed, because you've been told not to feed your dog "people food." The myth that the food we eat is bad for dogs is quietly being debunked, with more and more dogs enjoying improved health and other benefits from entirely home-prepared meals, or from having their commercial dog food supplemented with fresh foods.

CLUES FROM YOUR DOG'S ANCESTORS

Before dogs began living so intimately with us, their diet in the wild was quite a bit different from what it is today. They caught or found their food and ate it raw. That's been the impetus for the recent popularity of raw diets and, while many, many dogs thrive on a balanced raw foods regimen, it doesn't really duplicate nature's feeding plan either. Why? For one thing, today's packaged and butchered meats hold a higher risk of disease transmission than the fresh-killed animals eaten by wild canids. For another, factory-farmed meats are laden with hormones and antibiotics that may compromise your dog's health. Most significantly, wild dogs foraged and varied their menu instinctively to meet nutritional needs. Their instincts also guided them to use a natural healing system of "food therapy" by seeking out certain plants to eat when they were ill, or when they suffered from a mineral or other nutrient deficiency.

If it's not possible—or even advisable—to duplicate the diet of a wolf or a coyote, does that mean our dogs should just eat what we eat? What about differences in nutrient requirements? Is our diet really balanced for them?

The answer is, our dietary needs are similar—but not exactly the same. While it's possible—even easy and beneficial—to adapt our own diet to meet the nutritional needs of our dogs, not *all* the rules of human nutrition apply to the canine part of the family. For instance, dogs require different amounts of protein and calcium. Also, some foods we tolerate easily just don't sit as well with your dog. The occasional chocolate bar probably won't do you any harm, but the theobromine compound in it could be toxic to your dog.

Years of research have provided guidelines for the nutrient requirements for dogs in different life stages. Of course, since no two dogs are alike, individual needs vary within those guidelines according to, among other things, genetic make-up, activity level, and health.

Genetic variation explains why one dog will look healthy and appear to thrive on one dog food or diet, while another will eat the same thing and look dull, act sluggish or hyperactive, or even become ill. It's easy to see how a 14-year-old Chihuahua might have different needs than a 4-month-old St. Bernard, but sometimes the differences are subtle. It's not uncommon for two dogs of the same age and breed to have different needs due to differences in metabolism, allergies, or other health issues. A diet your neighbor swears by may give your dog loose stools or chronic ear infections; the food you fed your last dog for years and years may leave your newly adopted friend with flaky skin and bad breath.

Commercial manufacturers follow minimum and maximum nutrient requirements established for the "average" dog. However, sometimes a nutrient can be unknowingly present at a marginal level in a brand's formula, leading to serious health consequences in some individuals who eat this diet day after day. As you'll see later, feeding a *variety* of foods is the "golden rule" for a healthy diet for your dog.

Nutrition 101

Welcome to Nutrition 101. You may be surprised by how much you already know. For starters, as mammals our dogs have many nutrient needs that are *similar* to our own. Everything they need can be divided into six basic categories: water, protein, carbohydrates, fat, vitamins, and minerals.

WATER

Not only does your dog need access to fresh water, but the quality of the water is important, too. If you avoid a source of water for yourself due to questionable quality, consider the same for your dog. In other words, if you don't drink from the tap, should your dog? Chemical additives, such as chlorine and fluoride, can be just as harmful to him as they are to you. And while dogs drink from ponds, puddles, and other places we see as disgusting, bacterial contamination and exposure to parasites such as Giardia are known risks. Carrying a bottle of fresh water along on hikes can reduce the need for your dog to drink from risky sources.

Remember to change your dog's water regularly, use bowls made of stainless steel, ceramic or glass, and keep the bowl clean.

PROTEINS AND AMINO ACIDS

Proteins are complex molecules made up of amino acids. Protein is part of the basic structure of many body tissues including tendons and ligaments, blood, muscles, nails, hair, and even hormones and disease-fighting antibodies. Dietary protein comes from muscle and organ meats, fish, eggs and dairy products, corn, soy products, legumes, and grains.

Your dog utilizes the amino acids from dietary protein to create proteins for his own tissues. Although some amino acids can be synthesized within the body, others must be provided in the diet. **Essential amino acids** are those that your dog can't manufacture on his own. They are arginine, histidine, isoleucine, leucine, lysine, methionine, phenylalanine, threonine, tryptophan, and valine. When your dog is ill or under stress, some amino acids not truly considered "essential" must also come from food. The interesting thing is, your dog must have the *full* complement of amino acids needed for each tissue when it's time to manufacture new proteins. If just one of these building blocks is missing, the desired protein can't be created.

Two important characteristics of dietary protein are **digestibility** and **quality**. Quality refers to the complement of amino acids that make up the protein source. Eggs, for example, are considered one of the best sources because they have all the essential amino acids in good quantity *and* they are easy to digest. The more digestible a protein is and the higher the quality, the less your dog needs in his diet.

Varying meals to include two or more protein sources over the course of a week or two may provide a better overall complement of amino acids. Soybeans, for instance, are high in tryptophan. Barley is low in tryptophan, but provides a variety of other amino acids. The two together offer a good balance. Animal meat sources such as beef, fish, and liver are considered good quality proteins, so balancing different amino acid sources is not usually an issue unless you are feeding a vegetarian diet. A vegan diet, without eggs or dairy, needs a variety of protein sources over a period of several days to provide the full complement of amino acids.

HOW MUCH PROTEIN? This is a tricky question. Remember that the **quality** and the **digestibility**, in part, determine how much your dog needs. A diet based on eggs would need a smaller percentage of protein than one based on grain or soy. Guidelines have been established based on the protein sources commonly used in dog foods today, suggesting at least 22% protein for growing puppies and nursing moms, and at least 18% for adult daily allowances, with adult maintenance diets usually not exceeding 30%. This is based on **dry matter** proportions, or what you will read on a bag of dog food. Homemade diets often figure protein amounts by volume or percentages. In this context, they may make up 30% to 60% of the total volume of food, because fresh foods contain more moisture. In addition, feeding a **variety** of ingredients as part of a home-cooked regimen means the percentage need not be as strict as when feeding the same commercial food day after day.

Manufacturers must follow certain guidelines to claim their foods are "complete and balanced." They can use lesser quality proteins, as long as they are providing all the essential amino acids your dog needs. You will commonly see corn as the first ingredient on the label of dry dog foods. While you may think of corn as a carbohydrate, it's actually being used as a cheap source of protein. Combining it with lower percentages of other protein sources rounds out the amino acid content required.

But remember, the minimum and maximum levels of protein that manufacturers must provide are not necessarily what is ideal for every dog. For instance, levels should increase when dogs are working hard, exercising frequently, or dealing with cancer, while dogs with kidney disease should receive less. It was once thought that older dogs in general should have less dietary protein, but more recent studies have found this to be false. Protein is needed to support the aging immune system and body tissues. Even so, some companies still market low-protein diets for senior dogs.

The best way to evaluate the protein content of your dog's diet is to critically assess how he looks and feels. Dry, brittle fur and poor muscle development may be signs that your dog is getting **too little protein**. If he is eating a commercial food with adequate levels stated on the label, the quality or digestibility may not be good enough. Less visible problems can include anemia, infertility, growth problems, or a less-than-robust immune system.

Too much protein is rarely a problem, unless your dog has impaired liver or kidney function, or a dietary allergy to a particular protein source. Early kidney or liver troubles may go unnoticed, but periodic blood tests by your veterinarian can help you monitor internal functions. If you suspect an allergy to a particular protein, try eliminating it from the diet for 8 to 10 weeks.

A rare side effect of too much protein is the development of fear-related aggression. If you've seen signs of this in your dog, try reducing the protein content, then look for behavioral changes.

CARBOHYDRATES

It's interesting to note that most dogs don't have an absolute need for carbohydrates; they can get their energy from proteins and fats. Yet carbohydrates, usually from rice, corn, or other grains, are common in commercial foods, and sometimes make up as much as 30% to 60% of the diet. This is because they are less expensive sources of energy (or calories) than proteins and fats. Although dogs in the wild would consume no grains and very little vegetable matter (usually from "grazing," and as part of the stomach and intestinal contents of the prey they consume), the excess starch is usually well tolerated by most domestic dogs. While some people prefer to provide a diet closer to the ancestral diet of wild dogs, keep in mind that thousands of years of domestication has allowed most dogs to adapt to a diet similar to ours. Whole grains can provide iron, minerals, fiber, and other beneficial nutrients. Vegetables and even fruit offer important phytonutrients, fiber, and trace minerals.

Some dogs have specific enzyme deficiencies that can lead to carbohydrate intolerances. Symptoms include skin and ear problems, flatulence, and diarrhea. These dogs do better on low-starch or enzyme-supplemented diets.

Carbohydrates *are* essential for pregnant and nursing dogs, puppies, and dogs with very high energy needs, all of whom benefit from the quick energy source in addition to the protein and fat in the diet.

FATS

Fats, along with proteins and carbohydrates, are the main sources of dietary energy, in the form of calories. Age, breed, activity level, and neutering are important factors in determining your dog's caloric requirements. Geographical climate and the insulating capabilities of your dog's coat also effect energy and fat requirements. A dog recovering from disease, infection, injury, or cancer often needs extra sources of energy, usually as both protein and fat, as these conditions draw a lot of energy and calories from the body.

In addition, without fats your dog cannot absorb the fat-soluble vitamins A, E, D, and K. Fats also contain **essential fatty acids**, or EFAs, required for healthy skin and coat, eyes, brain, and other tissues.

Too little fat in the diet will result in fatty acid deficiencies. Symptoms include poor coat, skin infections, chronic ear problems, poor wound healing, and reproductive troubles.

In stark contrast, **trans-fatty acids**, found in margarines and packaged foods that contain partially-hydrogenated oils, are fats that have been chemically altered, and are suspected of compromising the immune system. Until more solid information is available regarding their effects on dogs, fat sources that contain partially-hydrogenated oils should be avoided.

HOW MUCH FAT?
Young dogs, pregnant dogs, nursing mothers, and hard-working dogs need a greater amount of energy from fat. Fat requirements are also higher in those recovering from severe injury or illness, or dealing with cancer. Other conditions, such as pancreatitis or obesity, indicate a need for a low-fat diet. Your dog's Body Condition Score (see page 15) is your best guide to determine the amount of fat he should receive.

VITAMINS

The best source of vitamins for your dog is fresh, wholesome food, just as it is for you. An insufficient amount of a vitamin will eventually lead to deficiency symptoms, even though mild inadequacies may not be noticed for some time. Nutritionists recognize that many vitamins and other nutrients can be beneficial at levels *beyond* what are considered the minimum daily requirements, both for humans and for dogs. In addition, vitamin-like substances, such as biflavonoids and carotenoids, are now considered as essential as vitamins for some animals under certain conditions.

One interesting difference between dogs and humans is that dogs can create their own vitamin C. That doesn't mean this isn't an important supplement under certain conditions, because during stress or disease your dog's C production might be decreased.

Your dog always needs extra vitamins:

- while growing, pregnant, or nursing
- when the appetite is down, and an inadequate amount of food is taken in
- while taking diuretics or suffering from diabetes or kidney failure, when a large amount of urine is produced
- during periods of emotional or physical stress
- while taking certain antibiotics, especially trimethiprim-sulfa combinations

Dog food manufactures must add vitamins in addition to what is present in their food sources, because processing and storage destroys many of the vitamins nature provides. Unfortunately, determining the correct amount is largely guesswork. In any case, the quality of the synthetic vitamins in no way matches the quality of those in fresh foods.

Some holistic veterinarians recommend a daily vitamin supplement for most dogs. Vitamin supplements should be given with meals for best absorption, however it's best not to add the vitamins before cooking or heating. Crush the tablet into the food just prior to feeding. If you are giving a human vitamin-mineral supplement use a half tablet daily for small dogs, a whole for large. Some veterinary supplements use human-grade vitamin sources, and offer megadoses for specific conditions. Vitamins derived from whole food sources are the most easily absorbed by the body and should be given every other day. Check the label for source information.

MINERALS

Minerals make up less than 1% of your dog's body weight, but are essential components of bones, teeth, and body fluids. They also support the function of enzymes and hormones, and are necessary for proper growth. There are 18 minerals that are essential to your dog. Some are considered macrominerals because they are needed in larger amounts.

IMPORTANT VITAMINS FOR YOUR DOG

Vitamin	Common Sources	Signs of Deficiency	Comments
Vitamin A	Liver, fish oils (cod liver, salmon, herring), eggs, dairy products	Night blindness, dry eyes, skin diseases, poor reproduction Note: Because vitamin A is stored in the liver, toxicity associated with over-supplementation occurs in rare cases.	One of the most variable nutrients in the diet due to variable levels of the vitamin in meats, and of carotenes (the precursor of vitamin A) in plants. Sometimes used in megadoses for skin problems, particularly in Cocker Spaniels.
Vitamin D	Marine fish oils, fresh water fish, egg yolks; smaller amounts in dairy products, beef, and liver	Problems with bones and growth, including osteoporosis.	Excess vitamin D can cause bone problems, too, and may also adversely effect calcium levels.
Vitamin E	Vegetable oils, seeds, grains, bran, wheat germ	Problems with immune system, skin, and muscle.	An excellent antioxidant.
Vitamin K	Leafy greens, alfalfa, seeds, liver, fish	Poor blood clotting.	Vitamin K_1 is the antidote to poisoning by warfarin and related mouse baits.
Vitamin B (thiamin, riboflavin, niacin, B_6, pantothenic acid, folic acid biotin, choline, and B_{12})	Whole grains, nutritional or brewers yeast, liver, beans, dairy products, nuts, green vegetables, spirulina	Problems with growth, skin, and muscles; appetite loss, diarrhea, weight loss, diseases of the mouth; many other systems also affected.	Vitamin B_{12}, in particular, is present only in very low levels in plants, so vegan diets must be supplemented with B_{12}.
Vitamin C	Fruits, vegetables, organ meats	No signs of deficiency reported, as dogs synthesize their own vitamin C.	An important antioxidant, used in prevention and treatment of diseases; dog's own vitamin C production may be low during some illnesses.

Calcium and phosphorus are essential macrominerals that must be balanced and given in correct proportions. **Too much calcium** in growing, large breed puppies can cause problems with bone development. **Too much phosphorus** can damage kidneys. Homemade diets require additional calcium supplementation, unless they are based on raw, meaty bones.

Trace minerals such as iron, zinc, and manganese need only be present in tiny amounts, but still serve very important functions. Minerals interact with each other; too much of one can interfere with the absorption or availability of another. For example, too much calcium may interfere with zinc absorption. Breeds susceptible to zinc deficiencies include Bull Terriers, Malamutes, and Huskies.

Dog food manufacturers attempt to provide a balanced source of all the minerals your dog needs based on estimated requirements derived from mineral balance studies. Nevertheless, some commercial foods contain excessive amounts of minerals. Dogs on home-prepared diets do well on either human-grade vitamin-mineral supplements or those supplied by a veterinarian, when they're given in sufficient quantity. Look for chelated minerals, a form that appears to provide better bioavailability.

Nutrition and Disease: Food as Therapy

When your dog is sick, feeding him foods that are high in a particular nutrient that he needs will provide added resources for his body to draw on as it heals. Certain foods have specific effects on the body, such as aiding digestion or supporting the nervous system. Herbal medicine is actually a form of food therapy, as it involves ingestion of a plant to encourage healing.

Specific diet modification for certain diseases can greatly improve health, even in the most serious and critical situations. If your veterinarian diagnoses a disease process in your dog, one of your first questions should be, "How can I alter my dog's diet to help fight this disease?" While not all vets are versed in home diet preparation, they are knowledgeable about nutritional adjustments that may be helpful, such as protein modifications for liver and kidney disease, dietary changes to prevent bladder stone formation, fiber supplementation for gastrointestinal disease and diabetes, or carbohydrate restriction for some cancers.

TCM FOOD THERAPY

In Traditional Chinese Medicine (TCM), foods are commonly used to rebalance energy and promote healing. Some foods are considered "warming,"—not because you serve them hot, but because they give a feeling of internal warmth, or balance your dog's **yin** and **yang**. Warming foods such as oats, chicken, or lamb are good for older dogs with poor circulation and arthritis, as they help aid digestion and invigorate circulation. Some foods can affect particular organs; some are considered relaxing or calming, others more stimulating for sluggish or tired animals.

Cooling (Yin) Foods

- raw fruits
- turkey
- bulgur
- millet
- broccoli
- cod
- tofu
- yogurt
- spinach

Warming (Yang) Foods

- cooked root vegetables
- lentils
- garlic
- oats
- lamb
- winter squashes
- beans
- chicken
- ginger
- venison

Neutral foods

- beef
- rice
- carrots
- eggs
- pork
- liver
- potatoes
- corn
- duck

In addition to selecting certain foods to help your dog heal, you can augment his diet with supplements that deliver substances (already found naturally in food) to relieve symptoms and help cure the underlying disease. They can also be used to help prevent disease. Fatty acids, fiber, antioxidants, pre- and probiotics, and neutraceuticals are among the natural food supplements that can support your dog's health and healing process with a minimum of side effects.

ESSENTIAL FATTY ACIDS:
A "must" in your dog's diet

There are two kinds of fatty acids that are essential to good health—omega-3 and omega-6. Supplementing with these, beyond the minimum requirements, can benefit your dog when he's healthy as well as when he's fighting disease. For example, the inflammation associated with many skin problems, allergies, or arthritis can be improved by adding omega-3, over and above what your dog is getting in his food. Dogs suffering from kidney disease, heart disease, or cancer can benefit as well, and may even live longer. Omega-6 supplements often help improve dry skin and a poor coat.

Soybeans and corn provide omega-6 fatty acids, as do vegetable oils such as corn, soy, safflower, and sunflower. Borage oil, black current oil, and evening primrose oil are also excellent sources. Marine fish oils from salmon or other cold water fish are considered the gold standard in supplying omega-3s. Salmon oil may be the best choice, since it does not appear to carry the high levels of mercury sometimes found in other deep-sea fish. Flaxmeal (made by grinding flax seed in a food processor or a coffee grinder) and

flaxseed oil contain both omega-3 and omega-6 oils. Hempseed oil is another alternative.

Eicosapentaenoic acid, or EPA, is an omega-3 fatty acid that is found only in animal sources, particularly the fish oils. Extensive research has found that it is particularly effective in combating inflammation and protecting against cancer. Flax oil contains another omega-3 fatty acid, ALA, that must be converted by your dog's body into EPA. Studies indicate dogs may not convert this well, so most veterinarians agree fish oils are superior when omega-3 fatty acid supplements are needed.

No one knows the exact ratio of omega-3 to omega-6 that is most beneficial to our dog friends. The amount provided in commercial foods and supplement preparations varies. Some manufacturers mix fish oils, flax, borage, and vegetable oils to provide a variety. You can do this, too. Simply puncture a capsule of borage, hemp, or evening primrose oil and a vitamin E oil capsule, mix with a few teaspoons of marine fish oil, and add to a tablespoon of extra virgin olive oil or other vegetable oil. Be sure to refrigerate. Alternate with flax meal or flaxseed oil, and you've covered all the bases. Keep the following points in mind when using these preparations:

- Oils are prone to oxidation and breakdown. This completely counteracts their health effects. Store oils in the refrigerator, purchase them in small quantities, and use before the expiration date. If you are using flax oil, consider switching to freshly ground flax seed as a fresh and healthy alternative; be sure to clean the grinder after each use.

- It takes 8 to 12 weeks to see the benefits of fatty acid supplementation. Be patient!

- It is important to supplement with vitamin E when adding fatty acids to avoid deficiency and increase the benefits.

- Introduce fatty acids gradually to avoid intestinal upset.

- High doses of fatty acids in some individuals can alter blood clotting, especially if used with other compounds that thin the blood or affect clot formation, such as aspirin or gingko. Consult your veterinarian if your dog has a known clotting problem.

WHAT ABOUT FIBER?

Fiber is a type of carbohydrate that differs from starch in that it is not digested in the intestines by enzymes, but is instead fermented by bacteria in the colon. Fiber promotes normal bowel function and maintains colon health. Because our dogs have a shorter intestinal tract than we do, their digestive system is designed to receive a lower bulk diet than ours. Nevertheless, a small amount is healthy for all dogs, and adding extra fiber can help manage certain chronic conditions, such as constipation and difficult defecation. Extra fiber corrects some diarrhea problems, and may improve blood sugar control in diabetic dogs.

Psyllium is one of the best natural sources of fiber, particularly the hulls or husks. The seeds tend to swell when ingested, and are therefore not as gentle. A good starting dose, depending on your dog's size, is ½ to 2 teaspoons. Whole grains, sweet potatoes, and pumpkin are excellent fiber sources that also contain vitamins and other nutrients.

If you would like your dog to lose some weight, substitute part of her diet with a high fiber, natural breakfast cereal or some cooked oat bran. These are excellent choices for diabetic dogs as well.

ANTIOXIDANTS:
What's all the fuss?

To grasp the importance of antioxidants, let's look at the concept of **free radicals** for a moment. These are highly reactive molecules in the body that attack and destroy cell membranes, DNA, and proteins, in a process known as **oxidation**. Normal metabolism produces free radicals; stress and exposure to toxins in

EXAMPLES OF SUPPLEMENTAL ANTIOXIDANTS

Vitamin A
Vitamin C
Vitamin E
Alpha-lipoic acid
Beta carotene
Bioflavonoids
Coenzyme Q10
Grape seed extract
Green tea extract
Milk thistle
SAM-e
Selenium
Superoxide dismutase (SOD)

SOME CONDITIONS THAT BENEFIT FROM ANTIOXIDANT SUPPLEMENTATION

Allergies
Arthritis
Autoimmune diseases
Cancer
Cataracts
Dermatitis
Diabetes
Food allergies
Heartworm disease
Immune suppression (ie: viruses, chemotherapy)
Inflammatory bowel disease
Liver disease
Radiation burn (dermatitis caused by sun exposure, or radiation therapy for cancer)

food and the environment increase the formation of these dangerous molecules. Oxidative damage by free radicals is on the increase and is now associated with many chronic diseases, as well as the degenerative changes associated with aging.

Enter **antioxidants**—the body's natural defense against free radicals. They scavenge these toxic molecules, reducing cell damage and fortifying the immune system in the process. By attacking free radicals, antioxidants not only protect health, but also provide a natural way to fight the inflammation and damage associated with disease.

Fresh foods provide a wealth of antioxidants, but with the immune challenges our dogs are exposed to everyday, adding a blend of antioxidants to the diet is a good idea.

THE POWER OF PROBIOTICS

When your dog is healthy, his intestines contain millions of beneficial bacteria that help process food, ward off harmful organisms, and support his immune system. **Probiotics** are natural products that contain one or more strains of live, friendly bacteria. They can be given orally to improve the balance of intestinal microorganisms and aid digestion. You are probably familiar with live yogurt cultures containing acidophilus organisms. Acidophilus is one of the beneficial strains often identified in probiotic supplements. Lactobacillus, bifidobacterium, and other names are often listed as well.

Maintaining the normal **intestinal flora**, or organisms, creates an optimum environment for the intestines to function properly. Probiotics can be given in times of stress or in old age, or when the normal gut bacteria have been damaged due to antibiotic or steroid usage, heavy parasite burdens, intestinal infection, or after a major illness or surgery. Probiotics can also help with diarrhea associated with inflammatory bowel syndrome or to support the body as it fights infection.

Most supplement labels include recommended dosages, but giving a human-sized dose is safe for dogs. Be aware that shelf life is an issue. To be of any benefit, it must contain live organisms at the time you purchase it, and of course when you feed it to your dog. Many preparations require refrigeration to remain viable. Check the label for the manufacturer's storage recommendations and for expiration date.

WHAT ABOUT PREBIOTICS? Prebiotics are nondigestible, complex carbohydrate food supplements that stimulate the growth of beneficial gut organisms. Fermentable fibers, particularly fructo-oligosaccharides, or FOS, seem to be the most effective prebiotics, stimulating the growth and proliferation of bacteria such as bifodobacterium and lactobacillus. Because they lay the foundation for the growth of healthy bacteria, prebiotics are often given in conjunction with probiotics for a more lasting effect.

NUTRACEUTICALS:
Are they really foods?

Nutraceuticals are products made from natural substances, often refined and concentrated, then administered in dosages larger than the body is accustomed to in order to achieve a specific healing affect.

Let's take **glucosamines** as an example. Glucosamines are produced naturally in the body and are necessary for the repair of connective tissues and mucous membrane linings, as well as for lubrication of the joints. They can be refined from sources in nature (from cattle and poultry, as well as sea animals), and used to augment the body's own production.

Sometimes animals are deficient in glucosamine production, or the body may use up more than it produces. In arthritis, for example, the ongoing joint degeneration creates a higher demand for the body's glucosamine. Supplementation can profoundly reduce the symptoms of arthritis, as well as other diseases such as colitis and other bowel problems, disc pain, and some bladder conditions.

Because they are natural compounds, and chemically identical to substances that occur naturally in the body, they carry very little chance of side effects compared to more potent drugs used to treat the same conditions. Occasionally, glucosamines in high doses can cause an upset stomach or diarrhea, but more serious side effects just aren't a problem. Unfortunately, as with most nutraceuticals, treatment with glucosamines may also take longer to show results. Rarely are benefits realized in less than 2 to 4 weeks. In addition, if you are committed to refraining from the use of animal products, you may want to consider vegetarian sources for alternative healing aids. (See page 186 on Arthritis)

A vast array of products and supplements on the market today contain nutraceuticals, and manufacturers often make wildly unsubstantiated claims. Watch consumer reports for product reliability and choose from sources you feel comfortable with, or consult your holistic veterinarian.

Preventing and Managing Obesity

Let's talk about how *too much* of a good thing can lead to trouble. An estimated 45% of dogs in the United States are at least 15% overweight. Why?

- Feeding recommendations for commercial pet food are generally excessive for most companion animals. Following label instructions results in feeding 5% to 15% more calories than most dogs need.

- Commercial foods are sprayed with fats to make them tasty. Dogs often continue to eat for the good taste, even after they feel full and have taken in plenty of calories.

- Neutering surgeries typically reduce physical activity and slow metabolism slightly. Neutered animals usually need 25% fewer calories than unneutered ones.

- After puppyhood is over and full growth is achieved, caloric needs decline. Failure to cut back on feeding portions means the extra calories turn to fat.

- Although it is more convenient to feed two or more dogs in the same household the same food in the same amounts, individual needs and breed variation should be considered. For instance, Beagles, Golden Retrievers, and Labradors need less energy in their food and are therefore prone to obesity if fed the same amount per body weight as, say, Dalmations or Dobermans.

- We may like to reward our dogs with extra treats, which often add more calories than we realize—which, again, turn to fat!

So what's so bad about being overweight? Just as with people, extra weight can aggravate arthritis and heart disease, as well as increase the risk of herniated discs in the back or torn ligaments in the knees. Overweight dogs have more difficulty tolerating heat and are more prone to skin problems. Obesity increases the risks associated with anesthesia and surgery, should they be necessary. And because overweight dogs feel lethargic and less interested in exercise, the cycle continues with more weight gain and sluggishness.

What You Can Do: Prevention

🐕 Calories in...calories out! No two dogs, even the same size and breed, have the same requirements for calories, so avoid rigid adherence to recommended amounts, whether you are feeding a home-prepared diet or a commercial food. Use your dog's Body Conditioning Score (see page 15) to guide you.

🐕 **Keep your dog well muscled through regular activity.** Muscle tissue actually burns calories faster than fatty tissue but, more importantly, it also gives your dog a sense of well-being.

🐕 **Feed high quality food,** with the right balance of vitamins and minerals to keep his metabolism running smoothly.

🐕 **Make sure your entire family (and perhaps your neighbors and friends) realize that you are dedicated to keeping your dog fit.** Just a few extra treats can really add up, especially in small dogs. Consider rewarding him with extra play time or special one-on-one love time with you instead. If possible, weigh your dog periodically to help monitor his progress.

What You Can Do: When your dog Is overweight

🐕 **Evaluate your feeding practices** to ensure you are not providing too many calories for his size and activity level. Are you feeding high calorie treats? Consider a change to rice cakes or carrot sticks. Vegetables can be satisfying and add fiber, but contain minimal calories. Consider lowering the amount of fat in your dog's diet. Try a low-fat cottage cheese and rice recipe for a while. Most dogs love it.

🐕 **Your dog's metabolism may function more slowly as he ages,** so he may require less food. Thyroid hormone levels may drop in senior dogs, also slowing their metabolism. A blood test can evaluate thyroid function if your dog is overweight despite a calorie-restricted diet.

🐕 **Try feeding three smaller meals a day,** instead of two. Eating small meals minimizes the amount of carbohydrates and proteins that are converted to fat. Provide small amounts of omega-3 fatty acids from fish oils to help the body burn fat. Other metabolism enhancing supplements include the amino acid L-carnitine, the trace

---

low-fat recipe for weight reduction

(Feeds a 35-pound dog for one day)

1/2 cup 1%-fat cottage cheese

2 cups long-grain brown rice, cooked

1/2 teaspoon olive or other vegetable oil

1/4 teaspoon potassium chloride (salt substitute)

1 Tablespoon bonemeal, or 2 calcium carbonate tablets, or 1 to 1 1/4 teaspoons calcium carbonate

1 (human) daily vitamin-mineral supplement

1 to 2 tablespoons raw or lightly steamed vegetables (optional)

1 to 2 teaspoons bran cereal or oat bran (optional)

- The amounts listed are meant to achieve a normal body weight of about 35 pounds. Adjust recipe proportionally for larger or smaller dogs.

- The optional vegetables provide few available calories if served raw; if lightly steamed they will provide more.

- The optional vegetables and fiber may help some dogs feel more full, but they may also increase your dog's stool volume.

- Potassium chloride salt substitute is available at most grocery stores.

(Adapted from *Home Prepared Dog and Cat Diets: The Healthy Alternative*, D.R. Strombeck)

---

mineral chromium, as well as alpha lipoic acid, inositol, and ginger.

🐕 **Start each day with a good walk to get the metabolism going.** Maintaining fitness through exercise is essential for dogs with weight problems.

PUTTING IT ALL TOGETHER

With a few minor differences, your dog's nutritional needs for optimal health are very similar to your own. He needs the basic food groups—water, carbohydrates, protein, fats, vitamins, and minerals—provided in such a way that the diet is balanced and as fresh as possible. The energy your dog needs comes from foods that contain carbohydrates, proteins, and fats. Too much food energy (calories) leads to obesity; portions should be tailored to meet individual needs.

Whether you feed a top quality commercial diet or the more optimum home-prepared fresh food, adding a fatty acid supplement and antioxidants can help prevent and manage disease. Fiber sources and probiotics can be added for digestive health, and nutraceuticals can be used to correct specific imbalances as needed.

Commercial foods attempt to balance nutrients based on guidelines for the average dog. However, since each dog is unique, not every dog will thrive on these formulas. (See discussion beginning on page 63, Feeding Commercial Food). Home-prepared meals may be the solution. What follows is an easy guide to help you feed fresh foods. Remember, food is the foundation for health, and healthy food is good medicine!

A Fresh Food Diet

Without question, one of the most fundamental ways to maintain your dog's good health is to provide him with a diet that offers balanced nutrition from the best quality ingredients available, free of artificial additives. The best way to ensure that he gets this is to prepare fresh food for him. Why is a homemade diet so good for your dog?

- **Wholesome ingredients:** When you cook for your dog you know exactly what he's eating: fresh ingredients, organically produced if possible, and

good diet, good health

As a teacher of holistic health care for animals, I've become absolutely convinced that, next to a safe and loving home, nutrition is the single most important factor in the health of our dogs. Time and again, before a homeopathic or herbal protocol is even implemented, dogs begin to get well just from a change in their diet. Whether they suffer from lameness, skin trouble, behavioral problems, or digestive ills, feeding fresh foods almost invariably makes them better. I'll even go so far as to say that many difficulties are resolved *just* from cleaning up the diet, without ever going on to a remedy or treatment. I've come to believe that the toxic substances, even in "premium" brand dog foods, are major contributors to health problems in our dogs. When we spend the extra time and energy to prepare fresh, home-cooked meals—or, if that's not possible, to research and choose a top quality, natural commercial food—we make an investment in our dogs that returns enormous dividends in saved vet bills and in years of vibrant good health for our beloved companions. —*Jan*

of human grade (not the lesser quality by-products that often go into commercial dog foods) free of chemical preservatives, colorings, and flavor-enhancers.

- **Variety:** Eating a broad range of foods over the course of a week or a month minimizes the chance of nutritional deficiency or excess.

- **Flexibility:** A home-cooked diet can be modified to suit your dog's dietary needs, address health issues, and satisfy his preferences in ways that no commercial food can.

IT'S EASIER THAN YOU THINK

Before you turn the page in frustration at the prospect of yet another meal to prepare every day—wait. It really doesn't have to be a drag. Meeting your dog's needs can fit smoothly into your existing lifestyle—including your shopping, cooking, and eating habits. Cooking for your dog requires only a minimal adjustment to your daily routine.

- **Use the food you already cook for yourself to create a diet that meets your dog's needs.** As long as you're already eating a reasonably healthy diet, simply modify the proportions and add a few supplements to create nutritious meals for your dog right from your existing shopping list—even out of the same pot of food you're simmering for your own dinner. If your own diet is more quick 'n easy than fresh 'n wholesome, this is an excellent opportunity to let your dog inspire you to make changes that will benefit you both.

- **Cook in large batches.** Prepare one-pot meals, in batches large enough to last several days. It doesn't take long to toss some lentils or chicken, rice or potatoes, and a few vegetables into a pot. In less than an hour you'll have a tasty meal for your dog—and for you, too, if he's willing to share. Freeze or refrigerate leftovers in single-serving containers for subsequent meals that will be almost as easy to prepare as opening a can of that "other" dog food.

- **In a pinch, whip up some "doggie fast food."** Develop a repertoire of super-quick meals for days when you're particularly short on time, from staples you always have on hand. While they not may meet all of his dietary needs in one meal, the wholesome ingredients will keep him healthy, satisfied, and energized. In the context of a sound dietary program, he'll thrive by drawing nutrients from a variety of foods, over the course of several days or weeks. (See page 56 for suggestions.)

- **If you need to, use a high quality prepackaged food as a back-up.** You may find it helpful to have a high quality commercial dog food on hand for convenience, or to supplement your home-made meals until you gain confidence. Be sure to choose a food that is "all natural"—that is, made with no artificial additives—and, if possible, made with human-grade ingredients. Refer to the guidelines in Selecting a Commercial Food, beginning on page 66.

PREPARING A HEALTHY MEAL

By preparing your dog's meals you can modify proportions of ingredients to suit his body type, his age, his activity level, even his breed. Given those modifications, most dogs do well on a diet that falls within these guidelines:

Protein: **Your dog's diet should include about 30-60% protein foods by volume.** In other words, if your dog eats about 1 cup of food at each meal, $1/3$ to $2/3$ of a cup will be a protein-rich food. Because proteins are usually more costly, you may start with a diet that is closer to 30% protein. If your dog is very active, isn't thriving, or is just a little picky with her food, you can easily increase the proportion. If you are feeding a diet based on raw meat and bones, pro-

A HOME-COOKED MEAL: THE BASIC INGREDIENTS

So what exactly should you put in your dog's dinner bowl? Here are some easy guidelines with some sample foods to get you started. Remember to vary the ingredients for optimum nutrition.

WHAT KIND OF FOOD?	HOW MUCH?	WHICH FOODS ARE THEY?
Protein	30% to 60% of the meal	Meat, eggs, beans, lentils, tofu, peanut butter
Carbohydrate	30% to 60% of the meal	Rice, potatoes, winter squash, millet, quinoa, rolled oats, barley, whole grain bread
Vegetables	10% to 30% of the meal	Broccoli, green beans, carrots, spinach, chard, Brussels sprouts, cauliflower, tomatoes, turnips
Calcium supplement (particularly important for dogs on a meat-based diet)	For adult dogs, 500 to 600 mg per 10 to 15 lbs body weight per day, double for nursing moms and puppies.	Eggshells, bonemeal, dicalcium phosphate, calcium carbonate
Fats	1 tsp to 1 Tbsp per day	Fish oil, flax oil, canola oil, olive oil, hemp oil, ground flaxseeds
Vitamin-mineral supplement	For dogs over 20 lbs, 1 tablet per day; for dogs under 20 lbs, 1/2 tablet per day. If supplement is made from whole foods, feed every other day.	Human grade multivitamin-mineral supplement that provides 200% or less of human RDA
Nutrition boosters	Amount varies depending on the booster. See chapter for guidelines.	Probiotics, spirulina or blue-green algae, wheat germ, garlic, nutritional or brewers yeast, alfalfa, lecithin

tein levels will automatically be near the higher end of the range. High quality protein sources include:

- **Fresh, lean meats**—Chicken, turkey, lamb, venison, pork, or beef. Meat should be cooked, or at least seared on the outside to destroy salmonella, E. coli, or other bacteria. (See page 58 for information about raw foods diets.) NOTE: Since meats are relatively high in phosphorus, when they are your primary source of protein it's especially important to add a calcium supplement to ensure the proper calcium-phosphorus balance.

- **Eggs**—Raw eggs offer the most nutrition, but may pose a slight risk of salmonella or other bacteria that may be harmful to very young, old, or weak dogs. For those dogs, cook eggs thoroughly.

protein—really?

High carbohydrate foods such as wheat, oats, barley, and potatoes, actually provide a significant amount of protein. While a diet of these foods alone would be unlikely to provide adequate protein to meet your dog's needs, they do make a notable contribution.

- **Beans and other legumes**—Lentils, split peas, adzuki beans, mung beans, and other small beans cook quickly, and can usually be fed whole. Larger, firmer beans such as pinto, soy, red, white, or garbanzos should be puréed in a food processor after cooking. Cook beans thoroughly, until very soft, for easier digestibility. Canned beans are a convenient option. Tofu, made from soybeans, is highly nutritious and easy to digest. Peanut butter is an inexpensive and convenient choice, however due to its high fat content it may be best saved for an occasional fast-food treat. Avoid brands that contain added sugar or salt.

Carbohydrates: About 30% to 60% of your dog's diet will be made up of foods high in carbohydrates.

- **Grains**—Rice, millet, barley, and quinoa are just a few examples. As with beans, cook your dog's grains a little longer than you might cook your own, to enhance digestibility. Rolled oats and barley can be fed raw.

- **Starchy vegetables**—Potatoes, sweet potatoes, and winter squash are alternatives that most dogs love. Corn should be puréed to make it more digestible. However, cornmeal or polenta is a tasty alternative that, when cooked thoroughly, is easily digested.

Vegetables: About 10% to 30% of your dog's diet should consist of fresh vegetables. Serve raw or lightly steamed. Light cooking makes them easier to digest, but too much cooking destroys nutrients. Add the cooking water to your dog's meal for a little extra nutrition. Different colored vegetables contain different antioxidants and phytonutrients, so try a different color every few days.

- **Green, leafy vegetables**—Spinach and leafy chard can be fed raw, finely chopped or puréed. However, they tend to spoil quickly, and should be added to your dog's meal just before serving. Dense greens, such as kale and collards, should be lightly steamed. Any dark green, red, and purple vegetables will add an abundance of vitamins, antioxidants and other phytonutrients.

a note about organics

Even the freshest foods may contain residue of chemical pesticides, herbicides, and fertilizers, as well as hormones and antibiotics in the case of meat, that are used in the growing process. Organic foods have been raised without these potentially harmful substances, and without genetic engineering. While the cost of organically grown produce and meats is often higher than their commercially produced counterparts, their nutritional value is greater. If you share your dog's organic meals, you'll probably find they taste better, too!

- **Cruciferous vegetables**—Broccoli, cabbage, Brussels sprouts, cauliflower, chard, kale, and mustard greens. Most can be fed raw, if finely chopped, but broccoli and Brussels sprouts actually provide more nutrition if lightly steamed. Their antioxidant properties have been linked to a lower incidence of cancer in humans, however studies show that cooking reduces the cancer-fighting properties.

- **Green beans**—Many dogs consider these a favorite, tasty addition to their meals. They can be fed raw or cooked.

- **Tomatoes**—Cooked tomatoes and tomato sauce are especially high in cancer-fighting lycopene, an antioxidant with twice the power of beta-carotene.

- **Summer squashes**—Zucchini, crookneck, and starburst. Should be lightly steamed or shredded to enhance digestibility.

- **Root vegetables**—White parsnips, purple turnips, red beets, and orange carrots are rich in antioxidants and other phytonutrients and provide plenty of fiber. Although best if lightly cooked, they can also be fed raw, but should be finely diced or shredded to enhance digestibility.

Some caution should be used with onions, which have been linked to heinz-body hemolytic anemia in dogs due to a compound in the onion that contains sulfur. Although the anemia can be severe, evidence suggests that a fairly large amount of onion must be consumed before any symptoms appear.

Fruits: If your dog is unaccustomed to eating fresh fruit, she may be reluctant at first and need a little coaxing. She will benefit from the many vitamins and antioxidants in a sweet orange, a banana, or a fig while crunchy apples and pears exercise the teeth and gums. Fruits can be fed as a treat or added to a meal. Here are a few notes of caution:

- Recent reports from a national poison control center indicate that grapes and raisins have been associated with acute kidney failure in a number of dogs. Until further study is done, it's best to avoid sharing these with your dog.

- Be sure to remove the pits from stone fruits, such as peaches, plums or nectarines, as the jagged edges may be harmful to teeth and gums.

- If your dog is diabetic, the amount of fruit should be limited.

Calcium: Calcium is perhaps the single most important supplement for a successful home-cooked diet. Even if you are feeding a variety of foods, you'll need to provide an extra source of calcium to adequately meet your dog's nutritional needs. **Calcium carbonate** is routinely recommended by veterinary nutritionists, and it's readily available in most grocery stores and pharmacies. A **600 mg calcium carbonate tablet (or 1/2 teaspoon of the powder form) for each 10 to 15 pounds of body weight daily for most adult dogs; growing puppies need twice as much.**

Bonemeal or **dicalcium phosphate** can be substituted in similar amounts, but should not be used if your dog has kidney disease. The more bioavailable forms of calcium marketed for human use (gluconate, citrate, or coral calcium) should require lesser amounts to meet your dog's calcium needs.

Eggshells are a form of calcium carbonate, and may be crushed and added to the meal as a convenient supplement. Cook the shells in a 350° oven for 10 minutes (or 1 to 2 minutes in a microwave) to kill salmonella or other bacteria; store in the refrigerator. One large cooked eggshell provides roughly 2000 mg calcium. **Feed 1 eggshell per 40 to 60 pounds body weight.**

NOTE: Commercial dog food contains adequate or even excessive amounts of calcium and phosphorus, so if you feed *some* prepackaged meals, you don't need

THE IMPORTANCE OF CALCIUM

According to the veterinary text, *Small Animal Clinical Nutrition*, failure to meet calcium and mineral requirements is one of the most common problems with feeding homemade diets. In fact, *a calcium deficiency is possible on any home-prepared diet that isn't supplemented*. In addition, the ratio of calcium to phosphorus is important for your dog's health. This ratio should fall somewhere between 1:1 and 1:2. Meat-based diets are particularly low in calcium and high in phosphorus, and a dog on this type of diet without adequate calcium supplementation would get a ratio closer to 1:10.

Getting the right amount of calcium is most critical for:

Young, growing, large breed puppies: Excess calcium can lead to bone malformation that can cripple a dog for life. Deficient calcium, or improper ratios of calcium and phosphorus, can also affect bone development.

Pregnant and nursing mothers: Excess calcium leads to fetal problems, while inadequate amounts can weaken the bones of the mother or lead to seizures due to low blood calcium.

Dogs in kidney failure: Kidney function declines with age. Excess calcium can cause damage to weak kidneys. Excess phosphorus (as supplied by bonemeal or dicalcium phosphate) can accelerate the progression of kidney disease; proper phosphorus restriction, based on lab tests, can slow the decline of the kidneys.

Dogs suffering from cancer, parathyroid disease, or a history of calcium oxalate urinary stones: These conditions require strict calcium regulation of the diet, and veterinary advice is essential.

Dogs taking long-term medications: Calcium interferes with absorption of some antibiotics (tetracyclines, enrofloxin). Heart medications (calcium channel blockers, atenolol) may be affected by excess calcium, and some antacids may effect calcium absorption.

to supplement as heavily. Many holistic vets recommend **1 heaping teaspoon of calcium carbonate, or 1 level tablespoon of bonemeal, per each pound of meat you add to the diet.**

Fish oil or vegetable oil: 1 teaspoon to 1 tablespoon per day, depending on your dog's size, weight, or any health concerns. Meat-based diets usually contain adequate fat, but supplementing with oils, especially fish oils, promotes optimal health. Best choices are salmon oil, or canola, olive, flax, borage, or hemp oil. Ground flax seeds are a fresh and healthful alternative.

Vitamin-mineral supplement: For dogs over 20 pounds, 1 human multiple vitamin-mineral tablet (that doesn't exceed 200% of human needs) per day. For dogs under 20 pounds, feed ½ tablet per day. If the supplement is made from whole foods, feed the above dose every other day.

There are several vitamin supplements formulated just for dogs, or even for dogs at a particular stage of life. However, because of higher nutrient levels, a good multivitamin intended for human use is an even better choice.

- As with any packaged food, read labels and avoid products that are made with artificial colorings, flavorings, or chemical stabilizers.

- Tablets made from concentrated whole foods are more likely to contain synergistically active ingredients, and are preferable to those that contain only isolated active ingredients.

- See page 42 for a table of vitamin supplementation that is particularly important for your dog.

Nutrition boosters: Augment your dog's diet with the vitamins, minerals, antioxidants, enzymes, and other nutrients provided by these high-powered whole foods. They contain an array of substances that work synergistically, so that nutrients are more easily assimilated into your dog's body. **Try feeding 1 or 2 nutrition boosters at a time, rotating through the list on a weekly basis.** If your dog has a particular dietary need, you can provide at least a portion of his requirement by using one of these whole foods in addition to, for example, a vitamin tablet. (NOTE: Recommended amounts listed below may be fed "per meal.")

- **Probiotics**—Acidophilus, bifidus and other bacteria that are essential to a healthy digestive system; may help support the immune system; important for dogs fighting an infection or those have taken antibiotics; available in capsules, powder, or liquid. **Follow feeding guidelines on the package, making proportional adjustments for your dog's body weight.**

- **Spirulina (blue-green algae)**—A true "super food," spirulina is an abundant source of minerals, including iron, as well as B-vitamins, chlorophyll, superoxide dismutase (SOD), and other antioxidants; available in tablets or powdered form. **Feed about 1/4 teaspoon per 30 pounds body weight.** (NOTE: Some strains have been harvested from sources that are contaminated with heavy metals.

lead contamination in calcium supplements

There is a great deal of controversy over the best source of calcium. Lead content in calcium supplements is a real concern, and recent reports suggest that unhealthy levels can be present in natural sources such as bonemeal and oystershell, as well as pharmaceutical forms. Some states, such as California, have adopted regulations that are more stringent than those provided by federal law for the allowable levels of lead contamination.

If the label on your calcium supplement doesn't say, "essentially lead-free," contact the manufacturer for more information about the lead content in the product.

Ask the manufacturer whether their source has been checked for contamination.)

- **Wheat germ**—High in vitamin E and many B vitamins; available raw or toasted. (Refrigerate, as it spoils easily.) **Feed about 1 teaspoon to 1 tablespoon per 30 pounds body weight. Because it's high in fat use with caution in overweight dogs.**

- **Garlic**—Stimulates the immune system and may help fight viral, bacterial, and fungal infections;

DOGGIE FAST FOOD

Too busy to cook? Worked late last night and didn't have time to shop? You thought you had one more single-serving of your dog's food in the freezer, but now it looks like Uncle Jim must have eaten it?

You've got your home-cooked meal routine down to a science, but every now and then you need to whip up a quick meal from scratch in a flash. Here are a few ideas that will let you light up those big, hungry brown eyes, even if your cupboard is down to the bare basics.

(Please keep in mind that the recipes that follow are not nutritionally complete on their own, nor are they intended for use on a daily basis. We offer them as occasional choices within the context of a well-balanced, varied nutritional plan. All recipes have been taste-tested by our eager canine food editors.)

Lunchbox Peanut Butter Sandwich
This one is really simple. Layer slices of whole-grain bread with peanut butter. Break the sandwich up and toss with plain yogurt and a fresh, diced apple. That's it. You're ready to go.

Eggs 'n Toast
Break a few slices of whole-grain bread into a bowl and moisten with soy or dairy milk. (Toasting the bread is optional.) Add a bit of spirulina or fresh alfalfa (also optional). Top with 1 fresh egg or 2 or 3. (Let's see, how many eggs per pound of body weight?) Yum.

California Cuisine
Your dog will be the coolest canine in the county. Toss tofu with raw rolled oats or barley. Add the juice from the tofu to moisten. Add spinach leaves, alfalfa sprouts, or a sprinkle of spirulina.

My Dish Is Your Dish
This one may be the easiest of all, but it assumes a certain level of healthful dining on your part. Simply share whatever you're eating with your buddy. If you've been following our guidelines so far, you can be sure that if it's good enough for him, it's good enough for you!

---

believed to aid in discouraging parasites. **Feed about 1/4 clove per 30 pounds body weight.**

- Nutritional yeast—High in B-vitamins, as well as lysine and other essential amino acids; also believed to aid in discouraging parasites. **Feed about 1 teaspoon per 30 pounds body weight.**

- Alfalfa—High in minerals, particularly those that maintain the health of bones and joints; available in powdered form or as sprouts. **Feed about 1/8 teaspoon of powder per 30 pounds body weight.**

- Lecithin—Aids in absorption of fat-soluble vitamins such as A, D, E, and K; may support mental alertness and help correct some neurological problems. **Feed about 1/4 teaspoon per 30 pounds body weight.**

Specialty Diets

CAN DOGS BE VEGETARIAN?

As more and more people adopt a vegetarian diet for themselves, they also consider eliminating animal products from their dogs' diets. But is this really a healthy choice for our canine companions? Didn't they evolve as predatory carnivores, existing on the raw flesh of their prey? Yes—and no. It's true that your dog's ancestors were wild dogs whose diet consisted primarily of the animals they killed. But the canines we live with today are genetically far removed from their wild counterparts. Think about it—does a Dachshund appear to have the identical genetic profile of a wolf? Of course not. Due to centuries of selective breeding and adaptation, the dog who sleeps at your side is substantially different from her ancestors. What's more, the meat we feed him is substantially different from the wild game consumed by her predecessors. The cows and chickens of today are also the result of extensive selective breeding, and their flesh carries the residue of hormones, antibiotics, and the pesticides applied to the grain they eat—hardly the same as a freshly killed jackrabbit.

The fact is, even a wolf or a coyote is not a true carnivore. A wild canine nibbles on grasses and other vegetation, as well as the stomach contents of his vegetarian prey. He's actually more of an omnivore, or an animal that consumes both animal and vegetable foods. All things considered, it's reasonable to assume that our dogs *can* rely on non-animal sources for a healthy diet.

In fact, **many dogs actually blossom when switched to a meatless regimen**, with glossier coats, fresher breath and cleaner teeth, more energy at play, and a more peaceful disposition overall. Removing animal products from the diet may even help overcome some health problems, including allergies, behavioral disorders such as aggression, hypersensitivity, or anxiety, and even seizures. It also eliminates the possibility of exposure to toxic residues in the flesh of farm animals that are not organically raised. In some cases, dispensing with most or all meat from the diet helps overweight dogs trim down while still enjoying ample, satisfying meals. And if you're a vegetarian, the option may come as a relief if serving meat in your house is uncomfortable for you.

MAKING THE SWITCH To make the switch to meatless fare for your friend, simply choose vegetable sources for the protein component of his meals. Vegetable proteins are not digested as completely as those derived from meat or dairy, so the proportions may need to be a little higher. Variety is particularly important, to be sure your dog gets the balance of amino acids he needs (see page 39). The suggestions on page 62 will give you lots of ideas to try. Here are a few additional guidelines that you may find helpful:

- When using beans as your protein source, remember to cook them until soft, and purée the bigger, firmer varieties.

- Even if you avoid eggs in your own diet, consider including them in your dog's menu. Dogs are not at risk for elevated cholesterol levels, so it's difficult to find a downside to the excellent nutritional value eggs offer canines. If the inhumane treatment of chickens is a concern, buy those produced by cage-free hens.

- Vegetarian dogs need either a vitamin B_{12} tablet weekly, a daily multivitamin, or B_{12}-rich spirulina on a regular basis.

- Remember to follow the golden rule of nutrition: Variety, variety, variety. Give him lentils on Tuesday, black beans on the weekend, eggs on Sunday morning. If providing a varied diet is difficult for you, follow a balanced, veterinary formulated recipe.

- If you need to rely on a commercial dog food, there are vegetarian varieties available, however the same concerns about processing, preservatives, chemical additives, poor quality ingredients, and lack of variety apply. Follow the guidelines beginning on page 66 to help you make the best selection.

Once your dog starts his new diet, watch for changes—for better or worse—in his health or behavior. A brittle coat, low energy, or weak muscles may be a sign that he's not getting enough protein. If so, be sure the protein source is easily digestible and of good quality. Cook beans a little longer or purée them; increase the amount of protein, or try different sources such as eggs or tofu.

On the other hand you may find your dog's coat becomes softer and shinier, his energy increases, he's less afraid of those thunderstorms, his breath is fresh, and that nasty build-up on his teeth seems to be going away. If that's the case—celebrate and carry on!

RAW FOODS DIET

Let's face it. Dogs don't cook. Raw food provided all the nutrients dogs needed for thousands of years, and today many people believe that a raw foods diet is the healthiest choice.

Cooking can make food less nutritious in a variety of ways:

- It destroys vital enzymes and antioxidants.

- It can denature proteins and destroy amino acids.

- High-temperature cooking changes molecular structure, and studies show that cancer-forming compounds can be produced under these conditions.

Most raw foods plans are based on raw meats and bones, with smaller amounts of raw vegetables and supplements. Raw bones, with their high calcium content, are usually supplied as chicken necks and backs, so there's no need to supplement with calcium or joint supplements. Many people who have switched their dogs to a raw foods diet report healthy skin and a shiny coat, clean teeth and fresh breath, and apparent resistance to diseases, parasites, and allergies.

Is there a down side to a raw foods diet? That depends on who you ask. Most holistic veterinarians acknowledge that there are certain risks involved with feeding raw meat and bones. Present day sources of slaughterhouse meat and factory-farmed eggs are often contaminated with salmonella, E. coli, and other bacteria. Although dogs, with their shorter digestive tracts, seem more resistant to this type of food poisoning, bouts of diarrhea—probably due to bacterial contamination—are not uncommon in dogs fed raw meat. Puppies, senior dogs, and dogs in poor health are most likely to be affected. A serious problem can cause dehydration or even toxic shock, requiring veterinary intervention. An additional concern when feeding raw meat is the possible bacterial contamination of food preparation surfaces or containers, which could expose human family members. This can be prevented by careful attention to standard food safety practices.

Raw bones can also present a risk. Usually *cooked* bones are blamed for intestinal obstruction or constipation, but as feeding raw bones has become more popular, surgeries to retrieve those are on the rise as well. Damage, although rare, can be serious and even life threatening. In addition to intestinal damage, bone shards, even when raw, can occasionally lodge in the roof of the mouth or fracture teeth. Since most raw foods diets rely on bones as the primary source of calcium, if you decide *not* to give your dog whole raw bones, you need to be committed to grinding them or adding a calcium supplement to avoid a deficiency.

Finally, if your dog has chronic health problems, consult your vet before switching to a raw foods diet. While it may eventually benefit your dog's health, if his system is weak or compromised he might need added nutritional support or other special adjustments during the transition.

Feeding Commercial Food

There's no doubt that a home-cooked diet, carefully balanced nutritionally with the most wholesome and fresh foods possible, is the very best diet your dog could receive. But for many of us, there are a variety of reasons why home-prepared meals just aren't always possible. Commercial dog foods are a huge convenience for busy guardians, so it's no surprise that the pet food industry has become a multi*billion*-dollar business worldwide.

Manufacturers are beginning to realize the importance of appealing to consumers who want more wholesome ingredients and less harmful additives in their dog food. A plethora of "natural" and "super-premium" foods has hit the market in recent years from companies large and small. The result? A bewildering array of commercial dog foods, each with its own claims and come-ons, that can leave you standing in the aisle scratching your head.

WHAT TO LOOK FOR

Obviously, you want a diet that is nutritionally balanced, and most manufacturers claim their dog food qualifies. You also want a diet that has ingredients of predictable quality. Reading labels can help, once you know what to look for and what to avoid. But information about quality isn't on the label, and few manufacturers are willing to share much detail with you. Besides, wording can be tricky, and guidelines aren't as stringent as they are for human food labeling. Also, keep in mind that marketing is one thing, and performance is another.

When evaluating *any* food, pay close attention to how your dog looks and feels on the diet. Is his coat soft and glossy? Is his skin in good condition? Does he have good muscle tone? Are his stools consistent and neither scanty nor voluminous? How is his energy level? Are his eyes bright? These qualities will give you a good sense of how well the food is meeting his needs, although they do not *guarantee* that his dog food is as good as you hope. Some health problems that may result from poor quality ingredients may take years to show up.

COMPLETE AND BALANCED— OR IS IT?

The American Association of Feed Control Officials, or AAFCO, sets standards for measuring the nutritional adequacy of animal foods, and evaluates how well commercial products measure up. There are three ways commercial manufacturers can substantiate the quality of their dog food relative to AAFCO standards. The first is to pass a feeding trial approved by the association. The trial is performed in a laboratory, and assesses how acceptable the food is to dogs and whether it provides the proper level of nutrients to prevent deficiencies. Sounds good? Perhaps. But who runs the trial? The dog food company or an outside contractor that reports to the company? A conflict of interest could affect the data, especially since some of the criteria are very subjective when it comes to symptoms of deficiencies. Another flaw is the length of the trials. Certain deficiencies, vitamin A for instance, may not show up for months, well after the trial is over. And what may be fine for one dog, day after day, year after year, could lead to serious deficiencies in a dog with a different metabolism or genetic make up. There have been tragic cases of heart problems as a result of some cats consuming the same brand of food for a number of years. Even though the product passed the criteria for "complete and balanced," these animals suffered, and some died as a result.

how jan cooks for savannah

I'm a vegetarian. So is Savannah. Since Savannah is a Great Dane, I cook in big batches. I'll soak black beans or garbanzos overnight and let them simmer a few hours the next morning. I toss lentils, mung, or other small beans right in with my rice and cook both in the same pot. Split peas (her favorite!) mean soup for both of us in about an hour's cooking time. As an alternative to rice, I use potatoes or corn polenta, and often add raw rolled barley after cooking.

For her vegetables I rotate through steamed broccoli, which we share, green beans, which we don't—she loves 'em, I never did and never will—or raw cabbage, chard, spinach, or other greens.

I've never seen a flea on Savannah, but we do live in an area where ticks and heartworm are a concern. To keep both at bay I add fresh chopped garlic and nutritional yeast to her meals.

I like to combine her beans, grains, vegetables, garlic, and nutritional yeast and store the mixture in single-serving containers in the refrigerator or freezer. That way I have meals for three or four days ready to go. At serving time I add supplements. Currently she gets alfalfa for joint health, vitamin C for joints and overall immune system support, probiotics to combat ear infections, and coenzyme Q10 for her gums. A top-dressing of canola (GE-free, of course), olive, or safflower oil adds essential fatty acids and makes the meal particularly inviting.

In addition to our standard fare, we have a few favorite meals that we share every now and then. In the wintertime we enjoy a hearty stew of black beans, sweet potatoes, cabbage, and corn. As a special treat we love whole wheat pasta topped with tomato marinara sauce and broccoli or spinach. I like it just as is, but sometimes I add a little tofu or beans to Savannah's. Other times she eats it just as I do, and I know she'll get her optimum protein ration in tomorrow's meal. (Remember the golden rule: Variety, variety, variety!)

A couple of times a week Savannah gets raw eggs, the cage-free variety, served over organic spouted whole-grain bread moistened with soymilk, and often with a bit of spirulina mixed in. It's a special treat for my sweet girl—when she hears those eggs crack she comes running. And the whole meal takes about three minutes to prepare, start to finish.

For snacks, Savannah knows where the carrots and apples live in the refrigerator. As a special delicacy, I make large-dog-sized treats by letting organic whole grain bread or buns dry till they're hard and crunchy. For take-along treats that fit in my purse or pocket, I buy wholesome, all natural, vegetarian dog biscuits.

how dr. katy cooks for silvie

Although I'm a vegetarian, my little 14-year-old terrier Silvie is decidedly not. I can get her to eat lightly steamed veggies (squashes, spinach, and cauliflower are her favorites) by puréeing or mashing them. But like some kids, she'll try to eat around them if they aren't well mixed into her food!

Silvie's a diabetic, which means in addition to twice-daily insulin injections, she needs to eat controlled portions at the proper time of day to best manage her blood sugar. Initially, I contacted the veterinary nutritional consultants at petdiets.com for recommendations on a balanced diet that would be A) low fat, as she tends to put on weight, B) high in fiber for better blood sugar control, and C) meat based, as she cleans her plate best that way! Their guidelines helped me fine-tune the portions of carbs, protein, fat, and calcium for her condition.

My partner is an excellent shopper, so the variety in Silvie's meat portion (beef, turkey, and chicken) sometimes depends on what's on sale. We try to use organic meats when possible, and because little Silvie eats only about 2 to 3 ounces a day, it's quite affordable. Her less favorite scrambled eggs and tofu sometimes replace the meat. We often cook 2 or 3 day's worth at a time, storing separate portions in Ziplocs in the refrigerator.

Silvie's carbohydrates come from the same grains we eat. Her favorites are couscous, brown rice, barley, and small chunks of whole-wheat bagels soaked in a little milk. We mix in a heaping $1/2$ teaspoon of calcium carbonate powder daily, and either a little leftover oatmeal or organic, high-fiber cereal and some veggies. Every other day, she gets one of my own food-based multivitamin-mineral tablets with antioxidants.

Silvie LOVES treats. If she doesn't get healthy ones regularly, she'll beg junk food from anyone she meets! She turns up her nose at the carrots, zucchini sticks, and rice cakes I used to give my other dogs as snacks, so I give her a vet-formulated fatty acid wafer as a treat following her insulin. She's allowed a few small, high-fiber, naturally preserved biscuits in the afternoon, which helps prevent a dip in her blood sugar.

When we just don't have time to cook for her, we rely on a naturally preserved, high quality veterinary prescription formula food for diabetic dogs. Although she'll clean her plate, she let's me know, with a slightly mournful look, that she prefers home-cooking!

SWITCHING TO FRESH FOOD AND HOME-COOKED MEALS

1. Start small. Begin by replacing 25% of commercial food with fresh foods. For every cup of commercial food you cut back, replace it with about 1½ cups of fresh, whether it's pancakes or scrambled eggs, a tuna sandwich or a pasta salad, a meat and potatoes dinner or Chinese stir fry.

2. Keep it up for a month or two, then evaluate. Is your dog enjoying the change? What are her favorites? How's her weight, attitude, skin, and coat? Are you ready to take the next step?

3. Try mixing some nutritional boosters into her meals, and add calcium and a vitamin-mineral source.

4. Start with stews: 2 cups rice, barley, or other grain, 2 cups mixed veggies, and 2 cups lean meats (including some organ meat. Add a little garlic and olive oil, fresh parsley or turmeric and, at feeding time, 1 or 2 fish oil capsules and 1 tablespoon bone meal or a few teaspoons calcium carbonate.

5. Dried beans and other legumes are cheap and nutritious sources of protein. Overcook beans and grains to help make them easier to digest. Raw rolled oats and barley can be fed raw, and so not be compromised by the heat of cooking.

6. Carrots, apples, and broccoli stalks make tasty snacks, help exercise your dog's teeth and gums, and satisfy her need to chew.

7. When you first switch to a fresh foods diet, you may see pieces of whole foods appear in your dog's stool. After a few weeks, you should see less undigested food passing through. If not, try cooking those items a little longer, or purée them in a food processor or blender.

8. If your dog is a little fussy, try a tasty topping to spark her interest, including tomato sauce; milk, cream, or butter; a sprinkle of parmesan or other hard cheese; nutritional yeast flakes; broth; oils such as fish oil or vegetable oil.

9. For more detailed information and recipes, look for vet-recommended canine cookbooks, or contact a veterinary nutritionist at your local veterinary school, at www.acvn.org, or at petdiets.com to formulate a diet plan.

foods to avoid

Fried, processed, chemical-laden foods

Large amounts of onions

Pork fat (bacon, fat from pork chops, ham)

Grapes and raisins (until further studies indicate they are safe)

Chocolate

Another way to receive AAFCO's approval is to formulate a diet that meets their minimum and maximum nutrient levels *on paper*. These standards offer a wide range to the manufacturer, and are designed to be adequate for the "average" animal, which may not be optimal for your dog. In addition, due to bioavailability issues, you can't be positive that the nutrients in the bag are actually getting into your dog's system in adequate amounts.

Some companies meet AAFCO's requirements through a sort of back door policy. If they have one diet that has been approved through feeding trials, they can formulate a new diet that on paper is similar to their other product, and get the green light that way. The bioavailabilty of the nutrients could be all over the map, but the stamp of approval still goes.

Each dog food label should contain a statement of nutritional adequacy, but beware of wording that can be downright misleading. For instance, most veterinarians think labels bearing the words "animal feeding tests" are still the best choice, but beware that the fine print may indicate the food is only *comparable* to a diet that has been through feeding trials. If the label says "intended for intermittent or supplemental feeding only," it means **there is no data to show that this food is balanced to meet your dog's needs**—and it probably isn't.

Most importantly, keep in mind that AAFCO standards are minimal at best. If you are intending to feed your dog to *optimize* his health, you will want to look beyond minimum standards for nutritional adequacy.

THE MANUFACTURING PROCESS

Most manufacturers purchase a huge volume of raw materials, such as grains or precooked meat meals from rendering plants. Some companies buy their raw materials from the same source time after time; others purchase the cheapest available, and quality varies greatly.

The processing of dry commercial food starts with long hours of cooking slaughtered carcasses at the plant. The rendered carcasses are ground into "meal," and mixed with other ingredients: grains, fiber sources, emulsifiers, stabilizers, colorizers, flavor enhancers, and preservatives, to name a few. The mixture passes through a high-pressure steamer that "puffs" the product into kibble shapes. There is no way to prevent these extreme processing methods from damaging and altering the nutrients in the food, so manufacturers add back synthetic vitamins and minerals to make up for the loss. Unfortunately, there are no reliable standards for the maximum amount of nutrients that can be added back. A problem can result if certain mineral levels get too high and interfere with the absorption of other nutrients.

High processing temperatures also destroy the enzymes that occur naturally in food and, although your dog makes digestive enzymes to break down the food he eats, his pancreas might need to work overtime to make up for the loss.

Dry food processing involves spraying fats onto the kibble after it's formed. The quality of the fat sources used varies; none are too appealing. Some manufacturers purchase used restaurant grease for this purpose. Others use tallow, which comes from the fat that bubbles to the top of the vat and is skimmed off when carcasses are rendered. Outdated grocery store meats and, amazingly enough, their packaging are sometimes added to the rendering vat—by law, the tallow may contain up to $2^1/2\%$ polyethylene from plastic wrapping and other packaging material!

Many companies also apply a powder known as "animal digest" to their food. Digest is basically meat or poultry tissues that have been chemically or enzymatically altered to make a new compound that apparently enhances the flavor of their foods so dogs will eat it.

Canned dog foods contain fresh or frozen meats and meat by-products: organ meats, stomachs, blood,

lessons from an angel

During my pre-veterinary school years, I was fortunate enough to work with Dr. Paul Chaffee, a very kind and compassionate zoo veterinarian. He believed the lessons best learned and never forgotten were those that came from direct experience. I was sitting in his office one day, enjoying a rare opportunity to bottle-feed a baby orangutan, when Dr. Chaffee hung up the phone.

"A young bobcat's just been brought into the veterinary clinic up the road. Someone hand-raised her, but she's become vicious, and now they're dumping her," he said sadly. This wasn't the first time Dr. Chaffee had had to deal with such a case. "I think I know what's troubling her. I've instructed the vet to anesthetize her and take an X-ray of her whole body. Pick her up and bring her back with the X-rays, and we'll see what we can do." As I headed out the door, he added, "They call her Angel."

On her trip back to the zoo, Angel snarled and hissed in her cage, even though she was sedated. Dr. Chaffee nodded solemnly over Angel's X-rays. "Just what I suspected. Count up the fractures, Katy. This poor girl's been raised on stew meat."

Hard to imagine, but I counted 22 separate fractures. Every move she made, every touch, however gentle, caused excruciating pain. It was confirmed that Angel's diet had been 100% raw meat. Dr. Chaffee sat me down with a nutrition text, and instructions to figure out why the meat diet caused the problem.

Dr. Chaffee had just introduced me to the devastating effects of **nutritional secondary hyperparathyroidism**, a metabolic derangement caused by high phosphorus and no calcium in the diet, which was consistent with the meat-only diet Angel had lived on most of her life. Havoc had been wreaked on Angel's entire skeleton, and the withdrawal of minerals from her bones due to the deficient diet during growth left each bone weak enough to break from her own weight.

Angel became my project, and I gradually nursed her back to health, supplementing her when she was weak and helping her learn to eat a balanced diet in the form of live rodents. In time, her bones mended and she began to thrive. Eventually Angel was released to a large, private sanctuary in the California foothills. —*Katy*

and bone. These foods are processed similarly to canned goods for human consumption. In either case, the high temperatures damage nutrients. Canned products contain fewer grains, and therefore may be closer to a dog's natural diet. They are more likely to contain whole meat pieces, and dogs usually favor canned products over dry kibble. Because the canning process itself preserves the food, there is less need for chemical preservatives.

Fresh-frozen, raw foods diets are available by mail order, or through a health food store or pet store. Some of these are made from human grade meat and even organic ingredients. Some frozen, raw diets carry claims that they are complete and balanced for all life stages; others are intended as supplemental only, so be sure to check the label. A few companies produce wholesome, organic grain and dried vegetable mixes for supplementing. You provide the meat, and add their ingredients to make a complete and balanced meal.

PRESERVATIVES AND OTHER ADDITIVES

Preservatives are necessary to maintain the freshness and nutrient balance of dry dog food. Other additives are meant to increase flavor for your dog, and improve the appearance *for you*. To date, little research has been done on the effects of long-term consumption of these chemicals on a daily basis.

Studies do show that commonly used synthetic antioxidants (ethoxyquin, BHA, BHT) can increase the toxicity of *other* chemicals, perhaps making them more likely to induce cancers. In 1997, the FDA asked dog food manufacturers to reduce ethoxyquin levels, out of concern that a multitude of health problems might be related. Although never proven, many manufacturers have since removed it completely. Some holistic veterinarians have reported that dogs eating ethoxyquin-preserved diets developed seizures, which promptly disappeared when the diet was

changed to a naturally preserved food. Interestingly, ethoxyquin was originally developed as a rubber hardener and herbicide!

At any rate, synthetic antioxidants are known to affect your dog's own natural antioxidant system, cell membranes, and metabolic processes. The use of more expensive natural antioxidants, such as tocopherols (vitamin E) and ascorbic acid (vitamin C), is *by far* preferable in commercial dog food products.

HIDDEN INGREDIENTS

What is your dog eating that *isn't* on the can or bag label? Antibiotics and other drugs, for one. Over a third of the antibiotics produced in the U.S. are fed to livestock raised for consumption. Although these animals aren't supposed to be slaughtered until the drug levels are low in their systems, monitoring is minimal. It's not uncommon for sick animals, chock full of antibiotics, to be condemned for human consumption and make their way into pet foods.

In addition to providing raw materials for pet foods, rendering plants process carcasses for the cosmetics and fertilizer industries. Conscientious renderers might weed out the euthanized pets, diseased animals, or the recalled, contaminated meat products dumped at their plants. But pet food manufacturers can do little more than trust that such material doesn't wind up in the ingredient known as "meat meal." Some companies adopt a "don't ask" policy when it comes to their suppliers. This has sparked the term "dead, diseased, and dying," to refer to some of the animal tissues that may end up in some commercial products.

The fact is, sound quality control measures for pet food manufacturers are neither required nor regulated. Some do a very good job of self-regulating, purchasing high quality, even human-grade ingredients, monitoring their suppliers, testing their finished products, and submitting to voluntary inspections by the United States Department of Agriculture (USDA). Others buy the cheapest raw materials they can, do what is minimally necessary, and avoid outside evaluations at all cost.

The bottom line? What we *think* (or hope) we are serving our dog for dinner may not actually be what is in her bowl. When feeding commercial diets we rely for the most part on the integrity of the company we are buying from to produce the cleanest and safest product they can.

SELECTING A COMMERCIAL FOOD

Whether you feed a commercial food alone or use it in conjunction with fresh foods, variety is still important. Find a few high quality commercial diets and rotate them, or change foods if your dog does not seem to do well on the current one. While it's tempting here to name brands that are superior in quality, the fact is, companies and formulas change. We feel it's better to know *how* to choose a food and assess your dog's vitality.

- In general, companies that produce a cheap food are using cheap and, therefore, inferior quality ingredients. Avoid these brands! Also avoid generic and store brands. These, too, are often made with cheaper, poorer quality ingredients.

- Choose products that use organic or human-grade ingredients, or meats produced without hormones and antibiotics, when possible.

- Canine nutrition is an evolving science, and many holistic dog publications regularly report new discoveries and healthy feeding practices. Stay informed.

- Don't be afraid to call manufacturers directly, and shy away from companies unwilling to talk about their production methods and suppliers.

- Look for foods that are labeled as "natural." While this does not attest to the quality of the food, it does mean that it cannot contain synthetic preservatives and other chemicals, unless listed in a prominent way on the bag or can.

- When possible, avoid foods with a long list of synthetic additives that contain no nutritional value. **While most dogs eating commercial food *appear***

this product *has* been tested on animals

Many people who share their lives with dogs are opposed to the idea of using dogs for scientific experiments. Few people realize that the dog food they buy is a direct or indirect result of just such experiments. Some manufacturers conduct their own experiments, some contract other companies to do it for them.

Vivisection is among the most troubling of animal welfare issues. When it involves dogs, many people find that the concern strikes even closer to their hearts. It is virtually impossible to purchase a commercial dog food that is not, in some way, a part of the industry that experiments on our friends. The only way to avoid spending your dollars in support of this industry-wide practice is to feed a diet made exclusively from fresh foods. If that is difficult for you to do, you may wish to at least investigate the kinds of research practices your dog food company conducts or funds, and make them aware of your concerns. —*Jan*

Food allergies, gastrointestinal troubles, and thyroid disease appear to be increasing in dogs, and some feel that repeated exposure to the wide variety of chemicals present in many commercial foods may be a contributing factor. Daily bombardment of your dog's system may damage cells, perhaps even creating a greater risk of cancer.

healthy despite consuming these additives daily, the consequence of long-term consumption of multiple chemicals just isn't known.

- Look for whole meats as opposed to chicken, beef, or fish *meals*. Especially avoid "meat meal," "meat and bone meal," or "by-product meal."

- Don't rely on diets that list by-products as the first protein source. They're okay for the occasional meal, but less desirable than meat and poultry muscle meats.

- Buy from a store where the food does not sit on the shelf for long. Remember, when companies run feeding trials, they're not using food that has been sitting on shelves or improperly stored.

FEEDING COMMERCIAL FOODS

- Rotate every few months between 3 or more quality brands. Transition gradually between diets by mixing varieties for a week or two.

- Add foods from your own meals, in quantities from 10% to 25% of your dog's daily intake.

- Consider canned foods, as they generally have higher nutritional value, fewer additives, and less grains and fillers. Claims that your dog needs dry kibble to keep teeth clean just aren't true.

- Check the expiration date, and if it smells rancid or off when you open the bag or can, return it immediately. ("Naturally" preserved foods have shorter shelf lives than chemically preserved varieties.)

- Store open bags in airtight containers. Use tins for storage, or put the whole bag into the container, rather than dumping in the food. Open, refrigerated cans should be discarded after 3 days.

SUPPLEMENTING COMMERCIAL DIETS WITH FRESH FOODS

When preparing your own meals, make a little extra to share with your dog. Don't give him the ingredients you wouldn't want to eat yourself: trimmed fat, foods that aren't quite fresh, excessive sugar and chemicals.

Most commercial foods are already high in carbohydrates, because carbs are inexpensive. For balance, try adding vegetables, fruit, fish, poultry and other meats, or an occasional egg. Many dogs can't tolerate pork fat, so steer clear of bacon and ham products. While most can handle dairy products, avoid those if your dog has gas, bloating, or loose stools. Fish should always be cooked, as certain species such as salmon or steelhead can contain a hidden parasite capable of inducing a life-threatening canine gastroenteritis when fed raw.

Fatty acid supplements are always beneficial, and many dogs like the taste of fish, flax, and olive oils. If your dog isn't overweight, a teaspoon to a tablespoon of olive oil added to a meal is healthy and satisfying. (See page 301 in the Nutritional Materia Medica.)

Remember to scale back on the amount of kibble or canned food, or you'll be feeding too many calories, which will quickly turn to fat.

COMMON PET FOOD ADDITIVES

Processing Aids:	Emulsifiers and lubricants; anticaking, firming, and drying agents; oxidizing and reducing agents; stabilizers and thickeners; chemically modified plant material; polyphosphates
Appearance and Taste Enhancers:	Coloring agents; animal digest; sweeteners; artificial flavoring; texturizers; grease
Preservatives – Chemical:	BHT; BHA; ethoxyquin
Preservatives – Natural:	Rosemary or clove oil; ascorbic acid (vitamin C); tocopherols (vitamin E)
Miscellaneous Natural Additives:	Probiotics (for digestion); yucca extract (to reduce fecal odor; may also help reduce inflammation in arthritis); chicory extract (stimulates healthy intestinal bacteria); nutraceuticals

LABEL INGREDIENTS: WHAT THEY REALLY MEAN

Label reads:	What It Means:	Comments:
Meat (chicken, fish, beef, lamb, venison)	Flesh from slaughtered mammals; includes muscle meat, heart, and tongue.	Contains 60% moisture, so more common in canned foods; superior to meat meals (see below).
Poultry and Meat by-products	Parts of slaughtered animals, other than the meat; may include lungs, spleen, kidneys, brain, liver, blood, bone, intestines, head, and feet. (Excludes feathers, except in amounts that are unavoidable in good processing practices.)	While unappealing to most of us, these are parts eaten by dogs in the wild, and inclusion in dog food is considered suitable for the species. These should NOT be the only source of protein in a food.
Meat meal, Meat and bone meal, Meat by-product meal, Poultry by-product meal	Rendered animal tissues, supposedly exclusive of hair, hoof, horn, hide trimmings, manure, feathers, or stomach contents, except when unavoidable in good processing practices.	**Avoid whenever possible!** Quality is questionable and harder to control. Named meals (chicken, fish, etc.) are preferable to unnamed meals (such as meat or meat and bone).

DOG FOOD LABEL TERMS	
What's on the package:	**What it REALLY means:**
All Chicken or 100% Chicken	May have trace amounts of preservatives; is not nutritionally balanced if it contains only meat; usually intended as a supplement.
Chicken Dinner	At least 25% chicken if you include water, but only 10% chicken by weight of the product.
Chicken and Liver Entrée Chicken and Liver Platter Chicken and Liver Recipe Chicken and Liver Formula	At least 3% chicken and 3% liver by weight of product, excluding water for processing; more chicken than liver, because chicken is listed first.
With Real Chicken	Contains at least 3% chicken.
Chicken Flavor	Doesn't have to have ANY chicken in it—as long as there is digest or enough ingredient to "impart a distinctive characteristic" to the food.

Recommended Reading

Canine Nutrition and Feeding: What Every Owner, Breeder, and Trainer Should Know. Lowel Ackerman. Alpine, 1999.

Chinese System of Food Cures, Prevention and Remedies. Henry Lu. New York: Sterling, 1996.

Home-prepared Dog and Cat Diets: The Healthful Alternative. Donald Strombeck. Des Moines, IA: Iowa State University Press, 1999.

Small Animal Nutrition. Sandy Agar. United Kingdom: Butterworth Heinemann, 2001.

feeding large breed puppies

Puppyhood is the most nutritionally demanding time of a dog's life, and dogs likely to reach 70 pounds or more must meet an even greater demand. They are growing fast and for a long period, and their bones are less dense than those of their smaller dog friends. That makes them susceptible to skeletal diseases that may begin in puppyhood, but plague them for life.

While you can't control the genetic factors that influence development, you CAN control dietary factors by following these guidelines.

- Evaluate your puppy's Body Conditioning Score (page 15) every 2 or 3 weeks. Keep his weight as close to ideal as possible.

- Avoid "free feeding" programs. Feed 3 times a day until 12 to 16 weeks of age, then 2 times a day after that.

- Avoid supplements that contain excessive amounts of calcium or vitamin D. Some popular brands of treats contain both. Treats used in training should be very small, so the extra amounts don't impact overall dietary percentages.

- Many puppy foods have too much fat, calcium, or protein for large, growing puppies. If feeding a commercial kibble, look for labels marked "complete and balanced for all stages of life," with protein levels between 25% and 28%. Formulas labeled specifically for "Large Breed Puppies" are generally better suited to help your puppy maintain the proper Body Conditioning Score.

- If you add fresh foods to your puppy's diet, limit high calcium foods such as dairy products, and avoid too much fat.

alternative therapies
AND CONVENTIONAL MEDICINE

A S CONSCIENTIOUS as you are about caring for your dog, sometimes your best efforts can't prevent an illness or injury from throwing her out of balance. One afternoon you notice your friend is a little stiff when she gets up after a long nap. Or she snaps at a bee that annoys her while she's sunning out on the porch, and comes in with a swollen lip. Perhaps you catch your breath as you find an unfamiliar lump on her jaw while the two of you are lounging in front of the TV.

It may be that you have always relied on conventional veterinary medicine to deal with problems, but lately you're drawn more and more to the world of holistic health care options and hands-on healing therapies. So when your friend needs you to find just the right treatment for an injured paw or a life-threatening illness, how will you decide which course of treatment is best? What do alternative therapies offer that conventional medicines do not?

Conventional Medical Treatments	Alternative Therapies
Antibiotics	Nutrition
Steroids	Homeopathy
Antiinflammatory drugs	Herbs
Pain relievers	Flower essences
Hormones	Massage and other bodywork
Surgery	Energetic therapies
Vaccination	Acupuncture and acupressure
Chemotherapy	Chiropractic
Chemical parasite control	Lifestyle changes

HOW ARE THEY DIFFERENT?

When conventional medical treatments deal with specific physical symptoms without truly affecting the course of the disease nor addressing the underlying problem, it is called **palliative** treatment. Alternative therapies generally seek to go a step beyond palliative treatment. That is, they may help relieve discomfort but also treat the underlying *cause* of the symptoms, and supply nutritional and energetic support to facilitate the body's natural healing process.

But wait—when your dog isn't feeling well, getting rid of the symptoms is what you're after, isn't it? Maybe—or maybe not. The symptoms of disease are just a small part of the whole picture. They may even serve a useful purpose. When an animal gets sick, many symptoms are, in fact, part of the body's natural healing process. When your dog is limping after a hard day at play, the soreness she feels is her body's way of telling her to rest so that her muscles or ligaments can recover. Or if she runs a slight fever in response to the kennel cough she picked up, it's a sign that her immune system is responding to the invading organism that's causing her illness. That fever may even be helping to destroy the offending bacteria.

Alternative therapies aim to comfort your dog by easing the symptoms in a way that does not interfere with the healing process. But when conventional medicine targets a symptom without addressing the underlying cause, the disease may actually be suppressed, only to emerge again later in a similar or perhaps even more debilitating manner.

For example, if your a dog has red, itchy skin, the conventional approach might be to prescribe prednisolone, a form of cortisone. Chances are the drug will relieve the itchiness, regardless of what is causing it. Your dog will feel better for a while and the redness will go away. But when the drug wears off—or in some cases when allergy season strikes again the next year—the problem will return.

While many commonly used conventional medications come with an array of side effects, most alternative treatments do not. The cortisone shot that, within hours, may stop your friend from scratching also suppresses the adrenal glands and the immune system. It can thin the skin, weaken muscles, make her prone to urinary tract and skin infections, and lead to joint degeneration. Natural therapies may provide nutrients that enhance the immune response and support organ function while they alleviate the illness at hand. That's not to say that cortisone and other conventional medicines don't have their place—they can save a life in a crisis. But the side effects can be a high price to pay for a few months of itch relief.

Why do the medicines used in the alternative approach tend to work so differently from conventional treatments? A key reason is that these remedies are generally made from naturally occurring substances, used in their whole form—just as nature made them—that the body can more readily accept. Herbs and many supplements contain a wide assortment of supportive minerals and vitamins that may actually help the body process the "medicine." With homeopathy, healing is delivered on an energetic level, to resonate with the body's healing energy—there is literally no physical form of the substance present to cause any side effects.

Conventional medicines, manufactured in a lab, are designed to play a very specific role in a chemical reaction in the body. Unfortunately, they often affect other bodily processes as well, and some of those effects are less desirable. Even when drugs are made by isolating one active ingredient found in a plant, because these medicines are so highly concentrated their effects on the body—good or bad—are very powerful. In addition, many contain chemical additives that are used either to extract the active ingredient from the plant or as carrying agents. The side effects of these drugs often have nothing to do with the medicine itself, but rather are caused by these additives.

DIFFERENT TREATMENTS, DIFFERENT RESULTS	
Conventional Medical Treatments	**Alternative Therapies**
treat a specific body part or organ system	treat the whole individual
eliminate symptoms	treat underlying cause of symptoms
may cause side effects that can undermine overall health	rarely cause side effects
contain artificial or isolated ingredients that have powerful effects—good and bad	are made from whole, natural ingredients that act gently to support overall health
attempt to fight off disease	aim to support overall health

Does this mean you should avoid conventional treatments altogether? Definitely not. In the event of a serious illness or severe trauma, Western medicine may see your friend through a crisis. Blood tests and X-rays are valuable diagnostic tools that can guide you to the right treatment—conventional, alternative, or a combination of the two.

THE HOLISTIC APPROACH

In order to make the right treatment decision, it's helpful to understand how medical practitioners view health care from a holistic perspective. Holistic medicine treats the whole individual, rather than looking primarily at a specific complaint or diagnosis and prescribing a treatment to alleviate that particular condition. The holistic approach examines how the ailment is part of a bigger picture. What is there in the overall physical and emotional health of the patient that predisposes her to this illness? What can we do to improve her general well-being so that she will be less likely to become sick again? Alternative therapies are often employed by the holistic practitioner because these gentle therapies can benefit all aspects of the physical,

as well as the emotional and spiritual aspects of the individual.

A holistic response to your dog's itchy skin would seek to stimulate her body's ability to actually heal the skin, address her discomfort, both emotional and physical, and support her overall well-being. This might include removing any ingredients from her diet that could aggravate her condition, or using nutritional supplements to improve skin health. A homeopathic remedy that matches her symptom picture may be given to stimulate her vital force. Herbs, acupuncture, and acupressure might be employed as another way to support her body in its efforts to heal. An expanded exercise and grooming program might be instituted. While you may not see the immediate relief offered by a cortisone injection, your dog will experience a more permanent improvement in her skin condition as well as her mind, body, and spirit.

The holistic approach places a high priority on minimizing invasive, intrusive procedures and protocols whenever possible. Where conventional medicine emphasizes antibiotics to treat an abscess, for example, holistic care might emphasize homeopathy, herbs, poultices, and acupressure. In another case, a conven-

washoe's story

Mr. Kudor's much loved seeing-eye dog Washoe suffered from a particularly severe form of epilepsy. The gentle Golden Retriever's life hung in the balance when his bone marrow shut down, a rare side effect of an anticonvulsant drug.

My colleague had pulled Washoe through the worst of it by discontinuing the offending drug and increasing his other medications to control the seizures. But two transfusions later, Washoe was still weak and tired, and his seizures were returning more violently and frequently. Mr. Kudor asked whether any alternative therapies could help. Having just completed my acupuncture training, I was anxious to give it a try.

Washoe loved his sessions, and sprawled out on his blanket and thumped his tail whenever I approached with my box of needles. It wasn't long before the seizures decreased from twice a month to once every two or three months, and they were milder. In addition, Chinese herbs and Mr. Kudor's TLC had bolstered Washoe's energy. The integrative approach had been successful, and we were all pleased to see Washoe's lively, buoyant nature return. —*Katy*

tional veterinarian might recommend leaving your dog in the hospital for a day of testing or treatments. A holistic vet may suggest that you stay with your dog to reduce his stress while technicians draw blood, administer injections, or give intravenous fluids. He may even show you how to administer treatments at home rather than require your dog to spend the night in the hospital.

INTEGRATIVE MEDICINE

A comprehensive approach to health that enhances the best of conventional medicine by combining it with gentle, time-honored alternative therapies is termed **integrative** or **complementary medicine**. In this approach, you get the best of both worlds. When you understand the limitations and benefits of both conventional and alternative procedures, you can expand your horizons and make wise choices for your dog by integrating the two systems.

WORKING WITH YOUR VETERINARIAN

A holistic approach to veterinary care is centered on love, empathy, and respect. A holistic doctor asks, "How can I help this animal live a healthier, fuller life?" He places a high priority on preventive medicine and on supporting each animal in her own healing process. A holistic vet is usually trained in one or more forms of alternative medicine such as chiropractic, homeopathy, or acupuncture and Traditional Chinese Medicine, and usually has a keen interest in diet and nutrition. You may find that he shares your way of thinking about your dog as an emotional and spiritual being. The organizations listed at the end of this chapter can help you find an alternative veterinary practitioner in your area. Keep in mind that some are happy to do phone consultations.

There may be an herbalist, homeopath, or chiropractor in your area who works primarily with humans, but also has extensive knowledge of animal health. Be cautious. Treating animals is considerably different from treating people. Of all the healing professionals you will work with, your veterinarian, holistic or not, has the training to detect whether or not your dog is in a critical situation, and to recognize complicated conditions that might be missed by a someone who is not licensed to practice veterinary medicine. Fortunately, many vets are happy to work in conjunction with alternative practitioners to maintain and enhance your dog's health.

Finally, if a veterinarian doesn't call himself "holistic," it doesn't mean he doesn't think in a holistic way. It is important that he is receptive to your approach and open to exploring new ideas with you. Many conventional vets are willing to look beyond conventional medicine and use an integrative approach. If your current veterinarian is someone you trust, and you are comfortable with his staff and the hospital, don't be afraid to discuss your new direction with him. You may be pleasantly surprised to find that he is willing to join you and your dog on this new path.

Holistic Veterinary Organizations

American Holistic Veterinary Medical Association
(410) 569-0795
www.ahvma.org

International Veterinary Acupuncture Society
(970) 266-0666
www.ivas.org

American Veterinary Chiropractic Association
(918) 784-2231
www.animalchiropractic.org

Academy for Veterinary Homeopathy
(866) 652-1590
www.theavh.org

American Academy of Veterinary Acupuncture
(303) 772-6726
www.aava.org

Veterinary Botanical Medicine Association
www.vbma.org

Greta (left), German Shepherd. 1986–1995. Adopted at 1 year old from the Berkeley Humane Society in Berkeley, California.

Guido (center left), Chow/Labrador cross. Found in 1998 at 8 weeks old in Oakland, California.

Rudy (center right), Akita/Shepherd cross. 1987–2000. Found at 1 year old with a fractured leg and pneumonia, Berkeley, California.

Haru (right) Australian Shepherd/Brittany Spaniel cross. Found in 2002 at 3 months old in Oakland, California.

homeopathy
LIKE CURES LIKE

HOMEOPATHIC REMEDIES are easy to administer, they have virtually no side effects, and they can play a valuable role in the treatment of most any illness or injury. But they are different from the medicines most of us are accustomed to using, in the way they're made, the way they work, and how they are administered.

Homeopathy is based on the principle that "like cures like." This means that a substance that would *cause* symptoms if given in its natural state can be used to help *eliminate* those same symptoms when used in a homeopathic form. A good example is Ipecac. Ipecac syrup is used to induce vomiting when a poisonous substance has been ingested. However, the homeopathic version of Ipecac helps to eliminate the symptom of vomiting. How can this be?

How Remedies Are Made

The answer lies in the process used to create the remedies. Homeopathic medicines are actually highly dilute forms of their original substance. A pharmacist places a small amount of the original substance in water or alcohol to make a solution, and then pounds or shakes the solution vigorously—a process known as **succussion**. A small amount of this solution is then placed in more water or alcohol, and again pounded or shaken vigorously. The process is repeated over and over again until the desired dilution is reached. The result is a **potentized solution** that contains at most only a very minute amount of the original substance. In the final step, tiny sugar pills are impregnated with the potentized solution to make remedies that can conveniently be administered to the patient.

Each remedy has a number and a letter—actually the Roman numerals X, C, or M—assigned to it to signify just how dilute the solution is. These numbers and letters tell us the **potency** of the remedy. An X indicates dilution to a ratio of 1:10, or 1 drop of the original substance combined with 9 drops of alcohol or water for a total of 10 drops. A C potency indicates a dilution of 1:100, or 1 drop of original substance combined with 99 drops of inert liquid.

Let's return to our example of Ipecac. To make a homeopathic remedy from the Ipecac plant, a portion of the root is combined with water or alcohol to create a **mother tincture**. The mother tincture is then diluted according to the potency desired. To make a 1X potency of Ipecac, 1 drop of the mother tincture is placed in 9 drops of water—for a total of 10 drops—then pounded or shaken vigorously, or succussed, to release the energy of the Ipecac into the solution. This gives us our 1:10 dilution. If we take 1 drop of that solution and add it to 9 more drops of water, repeating the process, the result is a 1:100 dilution of our mother tincture. We call this a 2X potency. If a 6X potency is needed, the process is repeated a total of 6 times to create a 1:1,000,000 solution. Notice that in this case the 6 in 6X tells us how many zeros are in the ratio that describes the dilution.

You can begin to see how a 6X remedy, with only 1 part Ipecac out of 1 million parts water, would leave us with very little of the Ipecac actually present. Now consider that remedies are often diluted even further. 12X or even 30X potencies are very common. At 30X we would have only 1 drop of mother tincture of Ipecac for every 1,000,000,000,000,000,000,000,000,000,000 drops of our solution!

But wait—it gets even more interesting. Potencies identified with the letter C have been diluted in much the same way as the X potencies, except that for each dilution, 1 drop of mother tincture has been added to 99 drops of inert liquid, for a 1:100 dilution. A 30C potency means that we'd need to add twice as many zeros as in the 30X potency, above. When referring to even higher dilutions, the Roman numeral M, or more commonly 1M, is used to identify a 1,000C potency. Experienced practitioners use higher potencies still, with designations like 10M or LM.

All these zeros can be mind-boggling. Don't worry, there's no need to try to keep track of them. What's important is to understand that homeopathic remedies are extremely dilute forms of their original substances—so dilute, in fact, that there's little chance *any* of the original substance is actually present.

The obvious question then is, "How can they work?" The prevailing opinion among homeopathic practitioners is that the remedies themselves carry the energy of the original substance. This energy stimulates a response on an energetic level in the individual who takes the medicine. When that individual is ill, and has symptoms that are similar to those that might occur if that substance were taken in its pure form, the remedy stimulates the patient's life force, or **vital energy**, to begin the healing process.

Turning again to our Ipecac, we know that undiluted it can cause vomiting. If your dog gets carsick, giving him homeopathic Ipecac may help to eliminate the symptom of vomiting.

Because there is virtually none of the original substance remaining in the remedy, there is nothing to react with the body in a way that would cause side effects or toxic reactions. Homeopathic remedies are safe to use in the treatment of any animal, of any species. In fact, *the same homeopathic remedies work with all species.* While most conventional medicines, and even some herbal preparations, are species specific, the homeopathic remedy that relieves nausea or any other symptom in humans will also be effective and safe for use in dogs, cats, birds, reptiles—you name it.

Storage and Handling

Now that you know how homeopathic medicines are made, you can understand why they are also fairly delicate. Because we are dealing primarily with the energy of a substance, it's entirely possible for "energy" from another source to de-potentize a homeopathic remedy and render it ineffective. Things to watch for include highly aromatic substances (like mint, menthol, camphor, or cigarette smoke), magnetic fields, electromagnetic radiation, or extreme temperatures.

MAINTAINING REMEDY POTENCY

Protect them from:

Strong odors	Mint (some teas, chewing gum)
	Menthol (cough drops, inhalers, some ointments or rubs)
	Strong food odors
	Cigarette, cigar, or pipe smoke
	Incense
	Perfume or essential oils
	Scented soaps, shampoos
Strong energy fields	Television
	Computer
	Microwave
	Refrigerator
Extreme temperatures	Your car
	Direct sunlight

Careful storage and handling can minimize the risk of de-potentizing your medicines. Avoid storing your remedies in your medicine chest if it also holds products like Tiger Balm, BenGay, or mentholated cough drops. Don't keep them in or near the refrigerator, because food odors may pose a problem, and also because most refrigerator motors contain a powerful magnet. Your television set and computer monitor also emit energy fields that could ruin your remedies. A cool, dry cabinet or drawer, away from foods and other odors, is your best choice. With careful storage these medicines will remain useful indefinitely.

There are two basic guidelines for handling your remedies:

1. **Be sure there are no strong smells present**—in the room, on your hands, or on your patient—when you administer a remedy. Rinse your hands with cold water, but don't wash with soap, since most contain fragrances. Also, avoid using things like Tiger Balm or aromatherapy on you or your dog when giving your dog homeopathic remedies as they will not work in the presence of these substances.

2. **Handle the remedies as little as possible.** Once your hand touches a pellet either administer it or throw it away. If one tiny pellet becomes contaminated with a foreign substance or fragrance, it may de-potentize the remaining pellets if it is returned to its container.

Selecting a Remedy

Once you've decided to use a homeopathic remedy for your dog, a new set of questions arises. Which remedy should I use? What potency? How many pills should I give and how often?

Before you can answer any of these questions, you should know whether your dog is dealing with an acute or a chronic problem. An **acute** condition arises suddenly, is likely to be resolved within a short period of time, and is most often caused by external factors that can be clearly defined. All injuries are acute. Sudden onset illnesses, like kennel cough or an upset stomach, are also considered acute. **Chronic** illnesses are of longer duration, and are generally caused by an inherent imbalance in the functioning of the animal's organic or emotional system. Common examples include cancer, heart disease, and diabetes.

Some disorders may be either acute or chronic, depending on the pattern of **frequency** or **duration** with which they appear. If your dog becomes anxious during a thunderstorm, his anxiety is acute. However, if the anxiety stems from a variety of seemingly unrelated causes, and appears frequently over a period of several months, chances are he has a chronic anxiety disorder. In still other cases an acute illness or injury may lead to chronic illness. If your dog takes a nasty spill and sprains his knee, the initial symptoms may be treated on an acute basis. If, as a result of an injury, he develops degenerative arthritis in the knee, that will be treated as a chronic illness.

Selecting the right homeopathic remedy works a little differently from choosing a conventional medicine in that we're generally more interested in symptoms than in knowing what the diagnosis is. That does not mean that homeopathy only cures symptoms without addressing the cause of disease—quite the contrary. When chosen properly these remedies stimulate healing at the deepest level. But the symptoms *guide* us to the remedy that will promote the best healing response.

When treating an acute problem, often there are only a few symptoms that are most pronounced; in cases with a multitude of symptoms, usually one or two will be of greatest concern. In any event, the most severe or debilitating symptoms are addressed first.

Let's look at an example. If your dog is bitten in a scrap with another dog, you may observe a number of

---

acute or chronic?

If your dog seems prone to frequent, acute illnesses, there may be an underlying chronic disease state at the root of what only appear to be separate problems. Treating each illness as an acute event will provide palliative relief—that is, it suppresses the symptoms—but may mask the true illness. An experienced veterinary homeopath can help you sort through the many levels of symptoms and treat the underlying cause for a more permanent cure. —*Jan*

	ACUTE	CHRONIC
Duration	Generally self-limiting; symptoms last for days or weeks.	Not usually self-limiting; may last for months, years, or lifelong.
Cause	External, narrowly defined	In most cases there is no clear external cause; may be caused by an inherent imbalance, genetic disorder, or permanent organ damage.

symptoms, each treatable with a different homeopathic remedy.

You might notice: …and consider using:

Emotional distress	**Aconite**
Bleeding	**Phosphorus**
Pain	**Arnica**
Puncture wounds	**Ledum & Hypericum**

How will you know which remedy to choose? In the course of treatment you may use all of these remedies. **But the symptom that puts your dog *at greatest risk*, or that is causing the *most immediate distress*, is the one to treat first.** In this case, if your dog is showing signs of shock (panting, cool extremities or ear tips, pale gums) a dose of Aconite will help calm him and bring his system back into balance. If he is bleeding profusely, Phosphorus, along with direct pressure at the site of the wound, may help stop the bleeding. Of course, you'll also want to get veterinary assistance as soon as possible. But administering homeopathic remedies before you head to the hospital, and while you're on your way, can help stabilize him and begin the healing process right away.

naming names

If the names of homeopathic remedies seem like a foreign language to you, take heart. Begin by learning just the few you'll use most often. You'll find a list of the most common remedies on page 122. Once you become familiar with them they'll be like old friends that you'll turn to whenever trouble arises.

—*Jan*

If no single symptom is particularly severe, choose the most prominent, active symptoms—in this case pain and puncture wounds—to guide you to the correct remedy. In this case you'd probably use:

1. **Arnica:** Most often the first remedy for any injury, Arnica helps to minimize bruising and swelling, thereby minimizing pain. Give 2 to 3 doses 1 to 2 hours apart.

2. **Ledum** and **Hypericum:** Help to prevent infection in a puncture wound and promote healing. After treating with Arnica, give alternating doses of these two remedies until you've given 1 to 2 doses of each (that is, Ledum in the morning, Hypericum at noon, Ledum in the early evening, Hypericum at bedtime) for 2 or 3 days.

3. A topical application of **Calendula** and **Hypericum lotion** at the site of the wounds will also help prevent infection and promote healing.

When treating a chronic illness homeopathically, there will be a broad range of symptoms to consider, some of which may be surprising to you. In addition to what we usually think of as symptoms—pain, swelling, changes in urination or stool habits, respiratory difficulties, and so forth—you'll also consider your dog's temperament, body type, his personal habits and preferences. Does your dog love to sleep in the sun or does he look for a cool spot under the porch? Is he most playful in the morning or does he come alive at 11 o'clock at night? Does he prefer sleeping on his left side or his right? While these questions may seem to have little to do with your dog's illness, they will help you match his overall symptom picture, or energy pattern, with the remedy that will help him heal.

USING THE MATERIA MEDICA
A Materia Medica is a list of medicines, along with a description of the symptoms or illnesses that each

animal, plant, or mineral?

While most homeopathic remedies are made from plant or mineral substances, some are made from animal tissues or body fluids. Apis, made from the honeybee and Crotalus and Lachesis, made from the venom of poisonous snakes, are classic choices when symptoms resemble a bee sting or snakebite, respectively. There also is a class of remedies made from animal tissues called **organotherapy** that is used to treat conditions affecting the same type of tissue in live animals.

But with hundreds of remedies available, you can choose those that are not animal based, if you prefer. For example, Ledum, made from the marsh tea plant, is an alternative remedy for a bee sting. So instead of using snake venom to treat snakebite, or liver tissue to treat liver dysfunction, use the **symptoms you see** to guide you to a remedy. —*Jan*

medicine is used to treat. With hundreds of homeopathic remedies available, and dozens or, in some cases, hundreds of symptoms recognized for a single remedy, the Materia Medica is an essential tool for the serious homeopath and the home caregiver. While there are few such references designed for treating our animal friends, the simplified Homeopathic Materia Medica beginning on page 314 will help you interpret the remedies according to the symptoms you're most likely to observe in your dog.

Familiarizing yourself with the kinds of symptoms and characteristics listed in the Materia Medica will help you know what to look for when you begin to list the symptoms you see in your dog. The chart on pages 312-313 will help stimulate questions to consider, and guide you to the information you'll need to select your remedy.

Once you've charted your dog's symptoms, refer to Chapters 9 (Treating Illness and Injury) or 10, (When Your Dog is Seriously Ill.) for a list of the homeopathic remedies most likely to be appropriate. Look for the remedies that are most consistent with the *major* symptoms on your list. Next, turn to the Homeopathic Materia Medica (see page 314) and read through the description of the remedies you're considering. Chances are, one will stand out as most consistent with your dog's *overall symptom picture*. For more information on this process, see Selecting a Remedy for Chronic Illness beginning on page 305.

MULTIPLE LAYERS OF DISEASE

It sometimes happens that after the initial symptoms have improved or disappeared, a new set of symptoms will appear. This does not necessarily mean that your dog has developed a new disease. It may simply be that the most visible illness was one of several layers of disease, built up over many years of repeated trauma or toxic overload. Once you've helped your dog fight off the surface layer of illness, his body will be ready to deal with the next layer. For example, you may successfully treat him for a chronic skin rash, only to find him showing signs of joint pain a few weeks later. According to the principles of homeopathy, both symptoms can be caused by toxic residue in the body. It may take a series of treatments to help your dog rid himself of all levels of the associated illness. If new symptoms emerge, it's time to reevaluate his symptom picture, choose a new remedy, and proceed as before. Above all, don't be discouraged. It sometimes takes several turns through this process, and successively deeper levels of healing, to restore your friend to vibrant health.

With a long-term, chronic illness, it may take several weeks or even months to complete the healing process. Be patient. If your dog's condition does not improve, or if it worsens, don't hesitate to get veterinary advice. If you're new to homeopathy enlist the aid of an experienced veterinary homeopath.

Selecting the Right Potency

Once you've chosen the right remedy, the next step is to decide what potency to use. This leads us to a very intriguing aspect of homeopathy: *The higher the potency—that is, the more dilute a remedy is—the more powerful it is*. That's right. A very high

potency, in which the original substance has been diluted to a ratio of trillions or more, is more powerful—or deeper acting—than one that has been diluted to a ratio of a thousand or less. As you can imagine, there is much speculation among homeopaths about why this is true. One way to explain it is that the very high potencies carry a pure energetic imprint of the medicine and, therefore, heal your dog on a very deep energetic level.

When choosing the potency, consider these factors:

1. The severity of the injury or illness: A severe injury will require a higher potency than a minor one. 12C, 30C, or even 1M may be called for.

2. The strength or vitality of the animal: An otherwise strong, healthy animal will handle a high potency remedy well, while one that is old, frail, or very weak from a long-term illness should be treated gently with lower potency remedies, such as 6X or 12X.

COMMONLY USED HOMEOPATHIC POTENCIES*			
Low Potency	3X	For a dog who is very old or weak	For an illness or injury that is very mild
	6X		
	12X		
	30X		
	6C		
	12C		
	30C		
	100C		
	200C		
High Potency	1M	For a dog with a strong vital force	For an illness or injury that is severe

*Note: Some remedies, such as Hepar and Silicea, stimulate a different kind of response in different potencies. See the Materia Medica for specific guidelines.

is he getting better?

When you work with homeopathy, the first signs of healing may be dramatic, or they may be very subtle. It's not unusual to see a symptom disappear within hours or even minutes. Then again, the initial response may be so slight you'll question your evaluation. Perhaps your dog's energy seems just a bit brighter, or maybe he's simply resting more peacefully. You might see a clearer look in his eye, or you may just have an intuitive sense that he's improved. As subtle as those changes are, they're extremely valuable clues. Take this opportunity to tune in to your dog as only you can.

Careful observation of your dog's response to a remedy is important, because it provides valuable information about how to proceed with his homeopathic treatment. Even subtle signs of healing can be the first indication that the remedy you've chosen is a curative one, and that you should carry on as planned. If the healing response is dramatic, you'll know it's time to back off on, or reduce, the dosing frequency. Sometimes, particularly with acute illness or injury, your choice of remedy, potency, and frequency may change hour by hour—and it all hinges on your observations of your dog's response.

Developing good observation skills is part of learning to use homeopathy. The careful records you keep of the remedies you give and your dog's responses to them will become an important resource as you gain knowledge and experience. —*Jan*

If you're uncertain whether a remedy is the right match for your dog's symptoms, begin with a lower potency, such as 12X or 6C.

When dealing with acute problems, and with injuries in particular, a single potency is often all you need. However, if improvement stops short of complete recovery, try one or two doses of a slightly higher potency to complete the healing process.

Since chronic illness is generally deeper seated, with origins that may have begun long ago, it is often necessary to increase the potency of your remedy, as well as the frequency with which you give it, as healing progresses. (See the recommendations under Dosing Frequency below.)

Dosing Frequency

Once you've selected the remedy and the potency, you'll need to decide how often to give the remedy. As before, this choice is based on the severity of the problem, and on whether it is acute or chronic. For **acute**,

if symptoms appear worse...

Very rarely, after a remedy has been administered your dog may show a slight increase in symptoms, even though her overall energy, attitude and appetite are good. This may indicate what homeopaths call an **aggravation**. Most often this is a sign that the remedy was given in a higher potency or with greater frequency than was necessary. When this happens, symptoms generally disappear in a few hours or, at most, a couple of days, followed by a clear positive healing response.

When using homeopathic medicines, herbs, and other natural healing modalities, occasionally new symptoms appear, such as skin eruptions, discharge or inflammation around the eyes, or digestive disturbances. This does not necessarily mean your dog is getting sicker. In fact, it may be what's known as a **healing crisis**, a sign that the body is healing itself by eliminating toxins or by releasing an old "memory" of a previous illness.

If you see signs of an aggravation or a healing crisis in your dog, **stop giving the remedy until the symptoms subside**. Once they do, evaluate whether or not he appears healthier than before treatment. If so, resume giving the remedy but at a lower potency. If he seems about the same, it may indicate the remedy was not a good match for his symptom picture. Reevaluate the case, and look for another option. If symptoms are severe, consult your veterinarian. —*Jan*

severe conditions, such as extreme pain, shock or high fever[1], you may give a remedy every 30 to 60 minutes, or as often as every 15 minutes. (A remedy given less than 10 minutes after the last dose will generally not provide any additional benefit.) More moderate problems may require a dose only once or twice a day. If the animal was frail or debilitated before the acute problem arose, choose the minimum frequency that will get results. In all cases, **once you begin to see improvement it is important to "back off," or reduce the frequency of administration.**

Keep in mind that the function of these medicines is to stimulate the body to heal itself. Once that healing process has begun, the remedy has done its job. However, if you do not see improvement within 24 hours, you may have chosen the wrong remedy. Reevaluate your dog's symptoms and consider trying another. Consult your vet if the symptoms are severe.

For **chronic cases**, begin with a minimal frequency. Once a day is usually a good place to start; for a very old or weak dog, try once every other day. The right remedy will bring about some improve-

[1] Severe conditions such as shock, infections, and high fever may be life threatening and require treatment by a veterinarian. Homeopathic remedies can help to sustain your dog until you can obtain professional assistance.

ment in 2 to 3 days—or sooner. If your dog has been sick for a long time, initial signs of healing may be very subtle, or slow to emerge. If you see no improvement in 4 to 5 days, increase the frequency. If there is still no improvement after 2 or 3 days, try a higher potency. If, after a week of increasing the frequency and potency, your dog still does not respond, consider a different remedy and talk to your vet.

Once healing has begun, and your dog shows moderate signs of improvement, continue the remedy at the same frequency. If your dog improves dramatically, back off, or reduce the dosing frequency. Once

your friend appears to be healed, or nearly so, stop giving the remedy. If you see a relapse, resume treatment. If, however, your dog stops improving but is not fully recovered, increase the frequency. If you have been treating him 3 times a day and improvement ceases but you still see signs of illness, change to the next highest available potency but go back to a much lower frequency, such as every day or once every other day. Continue this pattern throughout the healing process: When improvement levels off, increase the frequency or potency; when symptoms have been alleviated stop giving the remedy.

In some cases, after weeks or months of good health the original symptoms may reappear. A single dose of the curative remedy will often restore your dog to feeling his best.

knowing when to stop

Those who are new to homeopathy often continue giving a remedy long after it's done its job. **Once a remedy *stimulates your dog's healing capacity*, it's time to back off on the dosing frequency, or stop giving the remedy altogether.** There is usually no reason to carry on with the dosage indefinitely. In fact, to continue to administer a homeopathic medicine after the healing process is complete or well on its way, may cause the original symptoms to reappear. When you stop giving the remedy, the symptoms should subside. Thus, unless directed otherwise by an experienced practitioner, monitor your dog's progress and discontinue treatment when it is no longer needed. —*Jan*

How to Administer a Remedy

Giving your dog a homeopathic remedy can be part of a quiet, relaxing time for both of you. Just follow these simple steps:

- After rinsing your hands, have your dog lie down in a comfortable spot, and spend a few moments stroking and talking to him until you are both relaxed. Make a point of gently touching him around his mouth so that he associates this contact with your loving attention.

- Open the bottle and gently tap the number of pellets you need—usually 2 or 3—into the cap, returning any extras *from the cap* back into the vial. (Remember, once you touch a pellet *do not* put it back in the vial.) Then pour the remaining pills from the cap into the palm of your hand, and pick those up with the thumb and forefinger of your other hand.

• With your free hand, stroke the side of your dog's face and gently lift his lip, placing the pellets on his gums. (If he is very relaxed you may be able to drop the pellets directly from the cap onto his gums, and thus avoid touching the pellets altogether.) Allow his lip to fall back against the gums and continue to gently stroke his face and body.

Chances are your dog will continue to lie quietly, enjoying your attention and barely noticing the sweet-tasting pills in his mouth. Ideally, the pellets will dissolve against his mucous membranes as they release their healing energy into his system. However, if he chews and swallows the pellets, don't worry. They will still do their job. Even if they remain on his gums only a few moments before he shakes his head and spits them out, there's an excellent chance his system will receive the benefit of the healing energy.

If your dog won't allow you to handle his mouth, an alternative method is to crush the pellets and dissolve them in a small amount of milk. If he doesn't lap all of it up in one sitting, that's okay. The amount of medicine he receives in one dose is unimportant. Simply remove what's left so that he doesn't inadvertently repeat the dose when he goes back for a sip later on. (See Dosing Frequency on pages 84-86).

HOW MANY PILLS?

With conventional medicines, quantity, of course, makes a crucial difference. But remember that homeopathic remedies carry the *energy* of a substance, so the number of pills you administer at a given time doesn't really matter—as long as you give 1 pill that has not lost its potency. Giving 2 or 3 or more potentized pills at a time won't change the effect. Customarily we give more than one pellet with each dose because some of them, for whatever reason, may have lost their potency. If you give 2 or 3 pellets you can feel confident your dog is getting the medicine as you intend.

PUTTING IT ALL TOGETHER

With homeopathic remedies we can stimulate the body's vital force to resolve illness or injury at its deepest level. Based on the principle that "like cures like," homeopathy asks us to dispense with many of the assumptions we make about how medicine works. Made from highly dilute forms of substances that may cause certain symptoms, homeopathic remedies stimulate our dogs' natural healing capacity to actually eliminate those symptoms, rather than simply mask or suppress them as is the case with some more conventional forms of medicine. These highly dilute remedies are very sensitive, and can be de-potentized by something as simple as a whiff of mint. Even so, they are extremely effective, safe, and valuable components of your natural healing regimen.

Selecting a homeopathic remedy is based not so much on diagnosis as on the symptoms your dog displays. As you practice evaluating signs of illness, as well as individual characteristics, personality traits, and preferences, you'll discover how easy it is to match that information with a homeopathic remedy that shares a similar symptom picture. Once you've chosen a remedy for your dog, as well as a potency, or dilution, that corresponds to her level of vitality and the severity of her illness, her response to that remedy will tell you when to modify the potency, the frequency with which you administer it, or the remedy itself. In the end, chances are homeopathy will help your friend achieve a greater level of health so that she is not only symptom free, but also more vibrant and resilient than before.

Recommended Reading

Dr. Pitcairn's Complete Guide to Natural Health for Dogs and Cats. Richard Pitcairn and Susan Hubble Pitcairn. Emmaus, PA: Rodale Press, 1995.

Homeopathic Care for Cats and Dogs: Small Doses for Small Animals. Don Hamilton. Berkeley: North Atlantic Books, 1999.

Homeopathic Pharmacies

If you're unable to find a remedy or potency in a local retail store, order it from a homeopathic pharmacy, such as:

Dolisos America, Inc., Las Vegas, Nevada. 1-800-DOL-ISOS (1-800-365-4767); www.dolisosamerica.com.

Hahnemann Laboratories, Inc., San Rafael, California. 1-888-4-ARNICA (1-800-427-6422), www.hahnemannlabs.com.

Homeopathy Overnight, Absecon, New Jersey. 1-800-ARNICA-30 (1-800-276-4223), www.homeopathy-overnight.com.

herbs
NATURE'S MEDICINE

USING HERBS to treat illness is the purest, simplest way to use medicine just as nature intended. It can be as easy as picking a sprig of parsley from your garden and adding the leaves to your dog's dinner. Using the whole leaf, root, flower, or seed ensures that a variety of compounds that occur naturally in the plant are available as the body needs them. As a result, one plant may offer a broad range of healing properties. In many cases a single herb not only contains substances that treat a specific problem, but also provides nutrients and phytochemicals that support the body's immune system and ability to function in many other ways. These benefits are especially valuable when treating older dogs or those who are in a weakened condition. In comparison, a drug that is manufactured in a lab to have a specific action in the body—even if that drug is *derived* from a plant—simply cannot provide the broad range of benefits available in a single herb.

Let's look at the herb mullein, or "donkey's ears," as an example. This common roadside weed contains a remarkable array of compounds: saponins that have potent antiinflammatory effects and also work as expectorants; a complement of antiviral and antibac-

terial components; and a protectant that soothes mucous membranes. The compounds work synergistically to ease coughing, reduce inflammation, inhibit viral and bacterial infections, and lubricate the irritated lining of the trachea. Other compounds present in the plant are said to help protect the liver and provide a calming effect. A strong mullein tea or tincture twice a day may be all your dog needs to support him through a bout of kennel cough, as opposed to an array of antibiotic, cough suppressant and expectorant drugs.

Herbs can also be combined, as when treating urinary problems, for example. Some senior dogs, especially females, are prone to recurrent urinary tract infections. Chronic use of antibiotics to prevent or treat these infections can tax an older dog's system even further. In addition, when a bladder infection is allowed to smolder, urinary stones sometimes develop.

The American cranberry (the fruit of which is dried and ground into a powder) has the extraordinary property of preventing bacteria from binding to the walls of the bladder. If the bacteria can't adhere to the bladder lining, they will have trouble causing an infection. Cranberry is also chock full of beneficial antioxidants that support the immune system. Dandelion—the flowers, leaves, and roots—is a perfect partner to the cranberry in this situation. Dandelion's mild diuretic action gently flushes water through the kidneys. This cleansing effect discourages those bacteria from colonizing the urinary tract lining, and flushes out deposits that could lead to stone formation. The potassium and minerals naturally present in dandelion help replenish those lost when fluids are released from the body, while vitamins A and C provided by the herb support the immune system in fighting off infections. Dandelion will also help cleanse the liver of toxins and improve digestion, potentially eliminating problems that contribute to the onset of the urinary tract infections in the first place. Finally, dandelion calms your dog so she'll get the rest she needs. As you can see, using a combination of medicines from nature's pharmacy addresses the immediate problem *and* supports her entire being for the long term.

When working with herbs, as with any healing modality, always remember to support the healing process with good nutrition. If you wish to rely primarily on herbal treatments, consider working with a professional who can guide you. And when a problem is severe, your veterinarian will be your best guide.

EASTERN OPTIONS:
Traditional Chinese and Ayurvedic herbalism

Many of the herbs used in China for more than 6000 years have also been used by Native Americans, and are commonly used by Western herbalists today. But few Westerners are accustomed to the Chinese system of classifying herbs according to their basic actions and ability to rebalance disharmony. Descriptions such as "dampness" or "wind" conditions may seem poetic from a Western perspective, but keep in mind that thousands of years before doctors had science to explain conditions such as diabetes or kidney failure, traditional herbalists developed a precious legacy that modern healers are just beginning to understand.

Chinese herbal medicine is based on the concept of synergy. In most cases an herbal prescription contains four classes of herbs, precisely balanced and blended to work together. The **imperial** herb provides the main therapeutic action, while the **ministerial** herb enhances the imperial's action, its absorption, and its distribution in the body. **Assistant** herbs counteract negative side effects, and **servant** herbs coordinate and enhance the overall effect.

HERBS COMMONLY USED IN SMALL ANIMALS

For immune support......	Astragalus, echinacea, reishi, Oregon grape root
For nausea and motion sickness...	Ginger, peppermint, chamomile
As gentle diuretics......	Dandelion leaf, parsley, horsetail
For liver problems......	Milk thistle, turmeric, dandelion root
For arthritis......	Boswellia, devil's claw, yucca, alfalfa

Adapted from *Herbs for Animals*, www.vbma.org.

Ayurvedic medicine, practiced in ancient India and parts of the Middle East, focuses on recognizing an individual's basic constitution, and uses herbs, diet, and lifestyle modifications to bring the constitution into balance.

A new, modern herbalism is emerging today that uses the ancient wisdom of both the Chinese and the Ayurvedics. Today's modified formulas often omit the body parts of animals, common in some traditional formulas. And production within the United States has developed with an emphasis on organically grown herbs and an assurance of quality of ingredients.

Using Herbs Safely

In general, herbs used for humans and dogs are the same. Unlike cats, who metabolize many herbal as well as drug compounds very differently, dogs digest, absorb, and eliminate herbs much like we do. There are, however, a few important considerations to keep in mind.

- Pay close attention to the *amount* of herbs you give your dog. An animal with a smaller stature will require a smaller dose. Most toxicity problems result from doses that are inappropriate for the dog's size, or when a patient decides to help herself to a preparation that wasn't kept out of reach.

- Use a trusted source when buying packaged herbal formulas. Herbal products don't have the same government controls that drugs do. This means that quality will vary, and studies have shown that dangerous substances like heavy metals, or even synthetic drugs that aren't listed on the label, can wind up in an herbal formula. Be particularly careful with products that come from other countries. A professional herbalist or your holistic veterinarian can direct you toward manufacturers with good track records.

- Herbs interact with certain drugs. This *can* be of benefit—you may actually be able to reduce the amount of a prescription medication by giving a gentler herb along with it. However, if your veterinarian has prescribed drug therapy, be certain you check with him before you add herbs. *Failure to adjust the drug dosage, or changing it too much, could be disastrous.*

- If your dog suffers from kidney, heart, liver, or thyroid disease, or if she is pregnant or nursing, always consult your veterinarian before administering herbal preparations.

- Herbs are generally not meant for long-term use; some that are quite safe when given for a few days or weeks can be very hard on the liver if given for months at a time.

- Finally, just as with humans, dogs can be allergic or hypersensitive to herbs or other plant substances. Vomiting, diarrhea, loss of appetite, excessive scratching, or sunburn are signs that the herb should be discontinued. If symptoms continue after withdrawal of the herb, consult your vet.

The table on page 92 contains a list of commonly used herbs that should be avoided or used with caution when treating your dog. If you are considering using a tablet or prepackaged formula that contains several herbs, read the label carefully to be sure that *every* item it contains will be safe.

HERBAL PREPARATIONS: What form will you use?

If you have the time and space to grow your own herbs you are fortunate to have access to the freshest medicines available. If not, quality herbs can be found at

HERBS TO USE WITH CAUTION—OR AVOID

Herb	Special Considerations	Recommendations
Black walnut (*Juglans nigra*)	A fungus has been known to invade the hull (after falling from the tree). Consumption of the walnut hull has caused death in some dogs who have consumed black walnuts in their environment.	Although common in "natural" worming compounds, side effects of vomiting, diarrhea and potential serious digestive upsets are common enough to suggest that you avoid its use, or use it only under the direction of an experienced veterinary herbalist.
Comfrey (*Symphytum officinale*)	Even at proper doses, alkaloids present in comfrey may cause liver failure in small animals if used for weeks or months, or if an undetected liver problem exists.	**For professional use only**, or only under the direct supervision of a veterinary herbalist.
Ephedra (*Ephedra sinica*) Ma huang	Can adversely effect unrecognized heart or respiratory disease; may elevate blood pressure.	Should never be used alone, and only with great caution in herbal combinations, under direction of an experienced veterinary herbalist.
Garlic (*Allium sativum*)	Anemia due to garlic or onion ingestion has been reported, but only in dogs given massive doses for prolonged periods. See Materia Medica for safe dosage.	Although toxic effects are rare, garlic should not be given to anemic dogs, or to puppies less than 8 weeks of age. *Use with caution* in Akitas and Shiba Inus, who may be more prone to the toxic effects of the onion family.
Gingko (*Gingko biloba*)	Can inhibit blood clotting, and may cause excessive bleeding during surgery.	Avoid use before any surgical procedure; avoid use with other drugs that can effect clotting (such as aspirin).
Pennyroyal (*Mentha pulegium*)	This oil is frequently used in herbal flea preparations. Read labels carefully. Pregnant or nursing dogs and puppies should not be exposed even to topical applications or herbal collars.	Avoid the oil—it is very strong and can cause death. Use the whole herb topically only, and with great caution.
Red clover (*Trifolium pratense*)	Contains coumarin, an anticlot, or blood-thinning, compound.	Do not use in dogs with clotting problems, when there is active bleeding, or if surgery is anticipated.
St. John's wort (*Hypericum perforatum*)	Use with caution in light-skinned dogs, particularly if short-coated or white-haired.	May cause sun-induced skin rash when given to dogs with very light coats and fair skin.
Tea tree oil (*Melaleuca alternifolia*)	Cats and small dogs have shown hyper-sensitives to topical tea tree oil.	Avoid use on small dogs. Use only topically and in diluted form on medium and larger dogs.

most health food stores or through a variety of mail order companies. Herbs are available in a variety of different forms. Most common are **tinctures** (also called **extracts**) **whole herbs** (fresh or dried), and **capsules** or **tablets**.

Tinctures are highly concentrated liquids made by soaking whole herbs in a solvent—usually alcohol or glycerin—so that the essential components of the plant are extracted into the solvent. Because they are so highly concentrated just a few drops are often all that's needed. The tincture may be added to your dog's food, or placed directly into her mouth. However, they often have a strong taste that your dog may find unpleasant, so it's usually best to add them to her tasty dinner.

Fresh herbs may also be sprinkled over her food. Culinary herbs, such as tumeric, parsley, and ginger have wonderful healing properties and also add flavor. However, the healing properties of many herbs are more easily absorbed by the body if they are first made into a tea and then mixed into the meal. There are two ways to make a tea. One is called an **infusion**, the other is a **decoction**.

- An **infusion** is made by pouring boiling water over the whole herb (fresh or dried), covering, and allowing the herbs to steep for at least 15 or 20 minutes. Once it has cooled, the tea is ready to use. Leaving the whole herbs in the water for several hours or overnight will provide maximum potency. An infusion should be used to prepare the more delicate portions of the plant, such as **leaves**, **buds**, and **flowers**. **For most herbs use about 1 teaspoon of the dried plant (or 1 tablespoon fresh) per 1 cup of water.**

- A **decoction** is made by simmering herbs in water for 15 or 20 minutes. Simply place the herbs in water, bring to a boil, reduce heat, cover, and simmer for the allotted time. As with an infusion, leaving the herbs to soak in the water for several hours or overnight will provide optimum potency. A decoction is the preferred method when using the tougher, more dense portions of the plant, such as **roots**, **bark**, or **seeds**. **About 1 teaspoon of dried herb (or 1 tablespoon fresh) per 1 cup of water** is a good rule of thumb.

Capsules containing a single human-sized dose of finely powdered herbs are now widely available, even in grocery stores. This is a convenient way to buy your herbs, however the dosage may be greater than you really want or need. Pull the capsule apart to release the amount of herb that is appropriate for your dog. Sprinkle into her dinner or, if you are giving the entire capsule, hide it in a treat, such as a piece of cheese. If your dog is particularly good at eating the treat and spitting out the herb, try spreading a bit of peanut butter on soft bread and wrapping it around the capsule, or dip the bread in a little honey, molasses, or clam juice.

Herbs compressed into **tablets** can be given whole or broken into smaller doses. **Chinese patent herbs**, or herbal combinations, are formed into tiny balls that are given whole. Like capsules, tablets can be hidden in a treat. If you prefer to mix them into a meal, be sure your dog doesn't pick them out and drop them to the side. If she does, crush them first to be sure she gets *all* of her medicine.

DOSAGE AND DURATION

The recommended dosage is generally proportionate, based on your dog's body weight, to a human dose. If your dog weighs 40 to 45 pounds, or about a quarter as much as the average human, then she should get about a quarter of the human dose for that particular herb. (See the table on page 94 for recommended dosages.) It's always safest to begin with smaller doses, but since small animals may actually metabolize herbs more quickly than larger animals, your dog may need a larger dose than you'd expect. If

GENERAL RECOMMENDATIONS FOR HERBAL DOSAGES					
	Up to 15 lbs	**15 to 35 lbs**	**35 to 65 lbs**	**65 to 100 lbs**	**Over 100 lbs**
Tincture	3 to 5 drops	5 to 10 drops	10 to 20 drops	20 to 30 drops	30 drops
Loose dried herb (for fresh herbs use about three times as much)	1/8 teaspoon	1/8 to 1/4 teaspoon	1/4 to 1/2 teaspoon	1/4 to 3/4 teaspoon	1/2 to 1 teaspoon
Tea (infusion or decoction)	1 to 2 teaspoon	1 to 2 tablespoons	2 to 3 tablespoons	1/4 to 1/2 cup	1/2 cup
Capsule (amounts listed are for a 500 mg capsule)	1/4 to 1/3 capsules	1/3 to 1/2 capsules	1/2 to 1 capsules	1 to 2 capsules	2 capsules
Tablet (500 mg)	1/4 tablet	1/2 tablet	1 tablet	2 to 3 tablets	2 to 4 tablets
Chinese Patent Pills	1 pill	1 to 2 pills	2 to 3 pills	3 to 6 pills	6 to 10 pills

Adapted from *Emerging Therapies,* Susan G. Wynn and IVAS Course notes, Robert Silverman, 1997

you do not see the desired response at the low end of the recommendations, it is usually quite safe to increase the dose toward the higher end of the scale. If your dog shows signs of digestive upset or loss of appetite, stop giving the herb for a day or two, and then start again at half the previous dose.

Most herbal preparations work best when given 2 to 3 times a day. One to 2 weeks of therapy is usually long enough to know if an herb is appropriate for your dog. If you aren't seeing any improvement, change the herb or check your dosage and talk to your vet.

NOTE: The doses in the chart above are intended as starting points for most herbs in most situations. Your veterinary herbalist may recommend higher doses in some circumstances. For more detail, see the Herbal Materia Medica beginning on page 345. Because herbs interact with drugs, consult your vet if your dog is on perscription medications.

Recommended Reading

All You Ever Wanted to Know About Herbs for Pets. Mary L. Wulff-Tilford and Gregory L. Tilford. Irvine, CA: BowTie Press, 1999.

Natural Health Bible for Dogs and Cats. Shawn Messonnier. Roseville, CA: Prima Publishing, 2001.

acupressure, acupuncture,
AND THE PRINCIPLES OF TRADITIONAL CHINESE MEDICINE

aCUPRESSURE is an excellent form of therapy that employs your fingertips to apply pressure to various points on your dog's body. Acupressure works in much the same way as **acupuncture**, but instead of using needles, all you need are your hands, your focus, and your healing intention.

More and more people are using these techniques to treat animals and relieve pain. However, many people aren't aware that acupuncture is part of a 3,000-year-old holistic healing system called **Traditional Chinese Medicine**, or **TCM**. According to this healing system, each animal's "life force," or **qi** (pronounced "chee"), moves through pathways called **meridians**, and can be accessed at specific points where a pathway courses close to the body's surface. TCM doctors insert acupuncture needles into these points to regulate, redirect, and rebalance the life force. Herbal medicines, food therapy, and acupressure are also used to rebalance qi in a holistic approach that activates the animal's own energy to support healing.

In TCM, imbalances in health are carefully monitored before they create disease. When you visit a veterinarian who practices TCM, she will ask you questions, and will touch, smell, and closely observe your dog. His pulses and tongue appearance will provide further information regarding any health imbalance.

If your dog does become ill, this traditional approach can be a powerful tool that may be successful in a way that more contemporary approaches are not. Scientific inquiry has identified the release of numerous neurochemicals, hormones, and pain-relieving substances into the bloodstream and spinal fluid in response to the placement of acupuncture needles. This explains why this healing method can be used to treat so many problems, from pain to internal medical conditions, and even itchy skin.

While acupuncture is considered a deeper treatment technique, acupressure is an excellent variation that you can apply at home. Acupressure does not replace sound veterinary care, but it can be used to support healing, reduce muscle spasms, strengthen the immune system, and relieve pain. By learning the basic technique and a few very useful and powerful points, you can use your own energy to restore and rebalance that of your animal friend.

Finding A Point

The illustration below shows the location of a number of commonly used acupressure points. Because these points are found along meridian pathways that cross and interact, they can be used to treat a number of different conditions.

When searching for an acupressure point, use the chart on pages 98-102, along with the illustration on page 103, to find the general area on your dog. Then use your fingertips to gently circle the immediate area. You are looking for a depression, or a small indenta-

tion, in the muscle or in areas between muscles, bones, and ligaments. Closing your eyes may help you feel for the point. You may actually "feel the energy" at the point location. Learn to trust your intuition when your senses tell you you're in the right spot. Keep in mind that acupressure points are never on bony prominences or **mountains**, but are down in the **valleys** adjacent to the mountains.

USING ACUPRESSURE TECHNIQUE

There are a variety of acupressure techniques used by professional practitioners. Before you begin with the basics, take a moment to quiet your mind and focus your attention on your dog and the results you wish to achieve. Choose a familiar location where you'll both be comfortable. Acupressure can be done with the patient standing, sitting, or lying down. Most dogs enjoy the treatment so much that they will voluntarily find a favorite position on their own.

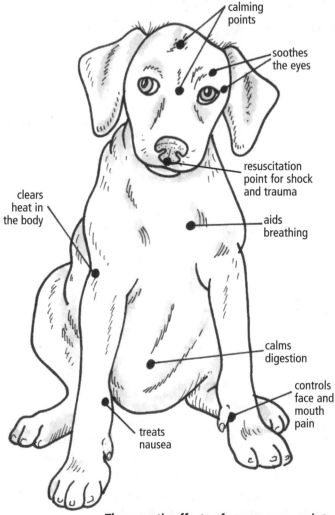

calming points

soothes the eyes

resuscitation point for shock and trauma

aids breathing

clears heat in the body

calms digestion

controls face and mouth pain

treats nausea

Therapeutic effects of acupressure points

THE BENEFITS OF ACUPRESSURE

Helps manage chronic pain, improves mobility, and can relieve muscle spasms

Can increase sense of well-being, provide short-term pain control and relaxation

Can alleviate nausea (from drugs, anesthesia, or illness) and help control vomiting

Can increase strength and promote tissue healing

Can enhance circulation and increase blood flow

Can positively affect immune response and various organ functions

a system of channels and organs

In TCM, vital energy flows through a system of channels, or meridians. Eleven organs interact intimately with these channels. The term "organ" has a much broader meaning in TCM than the anatomical organs we think of in Western medicine. It includes a concept of organ functions, and the energies that flow to and from the organ. Accessing these channels by stimulating a specific point can have an effect on the organ connected to the channel, or it can effect body functions or tissues along the meridian itself. While our diagram doesn't show the meridians of energy flow, the capital letters that demark an acupressure point refer to the meridian on which the point is located. There are 7 yang meridians: Stomach (ST), Large Intestine (LI), Urinary Bladder (BL), Gall Bladder (GB), Small Intestines (SI), Triple Heater (TH), and Governing Vessel (GV). These channels tend to run along the top and outer sides of your dog's body and limbs. The 7 yin meridians, Spleen (SP), Lung (LU), Kidney (KI), Liver (LIV), Heart (HT), Pericardium (PC), and Conception Vessel (CV), tend to course on your dog's underside and inner thighs and forelegs.

dry, damp, hot, cold

Most people are familiar with the idea of the balance between yin and yang, two opposites that are in fact dependent on each other—like night and day. The balance of health in TCM can be further broken down into other, equally important but more detailed components. An ear infection, with a wet, soupy discharge, could indicate excessive "dampness." Constant thirst might signal a "dry" condition. "Heat" might be found in a sprained ankle or an inflamed ear. Observe your dog: Is he always cold, burrowing under his covers? Or does he pant and want to go outside the moment you turn on the furnace? In TCM, you can use a number of techniques to help rebalance the harmony of the body. The chart on pages 98–102, Common Acupressure Points, will guide you to points used to treat heat conditions or dampness.

Start with gentle stroking and light massage. You don't need to be an expert to know what will quiet your dog and help him relax. He'll tell you! When he's ready, you can use the gentle circling technique to locate the first acupressure point with your index finger.

Once you've found the point, use your index finger or thumb to apply steady, even pressure, keeping your thumb or finger straight but not rigid. Slowly increase the pressure, but not so much that your dog tenses, resists, or seems uncomfortable. Hold for 5 to 15 seconds, then release. Treat the same point on both sides of the body. Depending on the condition, you will probably treat several different points in one session. Remember to breathe, and stay focused on the problem as well as the restoration of health you hope to achieve. Always close a session with light stroking, from head to tail.

TREATING TENDER POINTS

As you begin to explore your dog's body with acupressure and massage, you will likely come across zones of maximum tenderness that will react with a twitch response when you apply pressure. These are called **trigger points**, and will often correspond to points you'll find on the acupressure chart. These tender areas indicate either an imbalance or an area of trauma to the muscle. They may also arise when a muscle is overused. A typical trigger point, often present in older dogs, is located on the top of the back directly behind the shoulder blades. Many senior dogs have hind-end weakness or pain associated with arthritis. As a result, they overuse the front end to lift themselves up from a lying-down position, causing muscle strain behind the shoulders, and the development of associated trigger points.

Gently massaging a trigger point will cause the muscle to relax, *but too much pressure or vigor will increase pain and cause muscle contractions*. Stay focused and observe your dog carefully. Use your acupressure technique to gently release the points. While holding the even pressure, you may rotate your thumb or finger in a counter-clockwise motion for a few seconds before releasing. At your next session, check the trigger points you found last time to see what progress you've made. (See illustration on page 183 for common trigger point areas.

COMMON ACUPRESSURE POINTS			
	Names	Location	Uses
LU1	Central Storage	In a depression at the front of the chest (see page 197) in the breast muscle, slightly below shoulder joint level.	For coughs, bronchitis, supports the lungs.
LU7	Broken Sequence	On the inside front leg, just above the bony prominence on the inside wrist, in a small depression. See also page 197.	For respiratory or wrist problems; helps stiff neck.
LU9	Great Abyss	On the inside front wrist at the crease formed when you flex the paw. See also page 197.	For respiratory or wrist problems.
LI4	Adjoining Valleys	In the web between the front dewclaw and first inside toe. If your dog doesn't have a dewclaw, find the point along the inside toe, where a dewclaw would be. See also page 197 and 207.	For pain in face, mouth, foreleg, and moves qi when used with LIV3.

LI11	Crooked Pool	Lift the foot, flex the elbow, and you'll find a crease forms on the outside of the elbow. Feel for the depression at the end of the crease, just in front of the bony prominence. See also page 207.	Clears "heat" from the upper body. Important point for allergies and infections.
SP1	Hidden White	On inside of hind dewclaw, just above the nail.	For uterine bleeding, shock, clears "heat."
SP4	Grandparent and Grandchild	In a depression on inside of hind footbones, at top end of dewclaw bone attachment, or at level shown on illustration page 231.	For uterine bleeding, or bleeding associated with gastrointestinal tract; diarrhea.
SP6	Three Yin Junction	On the inside hind leg, just behind the tibia bone, in a small depression. See page 231 for best view.	Important point that supports qi and yin.
SP9	Yin Mound Spring	High on the inside thigh (hind leg), just below the knee joint, in a depression behind the tibia bone, in front of the major thigh muscle.	For "damp" conditions, urogenital disorders, and knee pain.
SP10	Sea of Blood	On inside thigh muscle, in front of and above SP9, in the large muscle in front of femur bone.	For female reproductive problems, dermatitis, allergies, and itch.
ST1	Receiving Tears	Immediately below the eyeball, where the lid meets the eye, directly below center of the pupil.	For eye problems—be careful, this point is very close to the eye.
ST2	Four White	Just below ST1, directly under the center of the eye.	For conjunctivitis and eye discomfort.
ST36	Foot Three Mile	On the outside hind leg, just below the knee, in a clear depression in the middle of the muscle toward the front of the leg. See also page 207.	Boosts qi, aids digestion. Important point with many uses.
ST44	Inner Courtyard	On the hind foot, find the web between the innermost toe (closest to the body center) and the next toe. Find the depression just up from the web.	For face, mouth, dental, and foot problems; clears "heat" from these areas.
SI3	Back Stream	On front paw, in the depression on outside of paw bone, above where it joins the outside toe.	For neck, shoulder and back pain. Sprains and other trauma.
SI19	Palace of Hearing	In a depression in front of the ear, near TH21 and GB2. See close-up page 151.	For ear infections or pain, deafness.
HT7	Spirit's Gate	On the outside back of the lower front leg. Bend the wrist, and feel for the large hole formed slightly above and behind the wrist crease. It's a large depression that your finger wants to move right into.	Calming point. Good for stabilizing the emotions and some heart problems.
PC6	Inner Gate	On front leg, find the sole pad behind the wrist. Move up the leg to the depression between two tendons that run up the back of the leg. See also page 197 and 207.	Calming point. Excellent for nausea and vomiting; used with some heart problems.

KI3	Great Stream	On inside hind leg, above the ankle (hock), in a large pocket (opposite BL60, outside of leg in same location). Close-up view page 231.	Support kidneys, nourishes yin and the body's fluid.
KI7	Repeated Current	On inside hind leg above the ankle (hock), in front of Achilles tendon, at the level below where muscle belly ends and rope-like tendon structure begins.	Support kidneys. Good for back pain and weak legs.
BL1	Eye's Bright	In a depression just above innermost corner of the eye.	For eye problems: tearing, dry eye, conjunctivitis.
BL2	Bamboo Leaf	In a notch, above BL1 and innermost corner of the eye, at brow level.	Eye discomfort.
BL13	Lung's Hollow	On the back, between the shoulder blades. Gently stroke between the shoulder blades from front to back.	For support with pneumonia, bronchitis.
BL15	Heart's Hollow	On either side of the spine, in the small indentations behind where top of the 5th rib meets the vertebra. Count ribs from the last (13th) and move forward.	Supports the heart; calming and cooling point.
BL20	Spleen's Hollow	Similar to BL15, but just behind where 2nd to last rib joins the vertebra. See also page 207.	Good for gastrointestinal problems. Supports qi.
BL21	Stomach's Hollow	See description page 209.	For vomiting, stomach problems, use with CV12. Clears "dampness."
BL22	Triple Heater's Hollow	One indentation forward of BL23 on the lower back, on either side of the spine.	Supports the kidneys; removes "dampness."
BL23	Kidney's Hollow	On the middle of your dog's side, locate the last rib, then go straight up to the spine. Find the point in the indentation beside 2nd lumbar vertebra.	Supports the kidneys. Used for back troubles.
BL25	Large Intestine's Hollow	In an indentation along the back next to 5th lumbar vertebra, find BL23 and count back 2 indentations along the back muscles.	For back pain, constipation, and other intestinal disorders.
BL28	Bladder's Hollow	Slightly to the side of midline on the back, level with the sacrum. To locate sacrum, see page 184.	For urinary dysfunction.
BL39	Entrusting Yang	Find BL 40. Then work your finger around the outside of the leg, staying at the same level, in a small depression next to the biceps tendon.	For back and bladder problems.
BL40	Entrusting Middle	On the back hind leg, in the very center, right behind the knee. Your finger will easily find the hollow that forms there when the leg is bent.	For back problems, stiffness, pain. Clears "heat." Helps the hip and knees.

BL54	Reaching the Limit	Exact location not agreed upon, but most feel it is in the depression at the top of the triangle that surrounds the hip joint (formed with GB29 and GB30, see page 103).	For hip pain, arthritis and dysplasia.
BL60	Kunlun Mountain	In the depression just above the ankle (hock) joint, on the outside of the leg (between two bumps).	For hindlimb, lower back, and especially ankle pain. Also for difficult labor.
TH5	Outer Pass	As you run your hand down the outside front leg, you will feel an indentation between the bones that stops at TH5, about a sixth of the distance from wrist to elbow.	For arthritis pain, stiff neck, and ear problems.
TH17	Shielding Wind	Just below the ear, in a well-defined depression.	For ear problems
TH21	Ear Gate	In front of the ear, above SI19. See close-up page 151.	For ear pain, infection, deafness.
TH23	Silken Bamboo Hole	In a well-defined depression at outside corner of the eyebrow, directly above outside corner of the eye.	For eye disorders, including dry eyes and conjunctivitis. Also for seizures.
GB1	Pupil Seam	In a well-defined depression a short distance from outside corner of the eye.	For eye problems.
GB2	Reunion of Hearing	In a depression in front of the ear, close to and beneath SI19. Massage with SI19 and TH21.	For ear disorders; helps with seizure control.
GB14	Yang White	Above the center point of the eye, at the level of the brow, in a very small depression.	Eye problems; seizures.
GB20	Wind Pond	In the nape of the neck, at the base of the skull, immediately behind the back of the ears, find a shallow spot. It will be easier to find it on your dog if you find it on yourself first, by moving your head up and down.	For eye redness; seizures; clears "heat" and "wind."
GB29	Between the Bones (and many other names)	Exact location and name not agreed upon, but the depression in front of the hip joint (forming a triangle with BL54 and GB30) is considered effective.	For hip pain, arthritis, and dysplasia.
GB30	Encircling Leap	In the depression behind the hip joint.	For hip and arthritis pain.
GB34	Yang Mound Spring	In a small depression on the outside hind leg, below the knee joint. Find a small bony prominence (see page 103) and let your finger slip down and slightly forward.	For muscle and tendon problems.
LIV3	Great Impact	On the inside hind paw, above the innermost toe (not dewclaw.) Exact location in dogs is not agreed upon, but find a slight depression about a third of the way between the top inside toe and the bottom of the ankle joint. See page 103 and 231. Use broad strokes on the side and front of paw area.	Moves qi (especially with LI4). Helps irritability and liver, eye, reproductive disorders, and some arthritis problems.

LIV14	Gate of Hope	On the side of the body behind and slightly above the elbow, at the level of the milk gland line, between the 5th and 6th ribs.	For liver support (point may be sensitive in liver disorders). Also for mastitis.
CV4	Hinge at the Source	With your dog on her back or side, find the umbilical scar, and the front of the pubic bone, on her abdominal midline. You'll locate the point halfway in between these landmarks.	For urogenital disorders, including abnormal uterine bleeding and urinary incontinence.
CV6	Sea of Qi	On the midline of the belly, a little behind the umbilicus.	Supports the kidneys; supports qi; resolves "damp." Good for urogenital problems.
CV12	Middle Stomach Cavity	On the midline of the belly, halfway between the end of the sternum bone and the umbilicus. See page 207.	Helpful for digestive tract and vomiting.
GV4	Vital Gate or Life's Fire Gate	On the midline of the back, between the 2nd and 3rd lumbar vertebrae.	Warming point. Good for kidneys, back, and overall energy and vitality.
GV14	Big Vertebra	On the midline of the back, where the neck vertebrae meet the vertebrae of the back. Lifting the head up and down, find the hinged place, just in front of the "big vertebra." Press your finger into the deep hole there.	Helps with stiff necks. Supports immune system.
GV20	Hundred Meetings	On top of the head, in a notch just forward of boney protruberance on the midline, between the ears. Use back and forth motion in the notch.	Calms the spirit, clears the mind.
GV26	Center of the Upper Lip	At the junction where the hairless part of the nose meets the upper lip. See pages 96 and 197.	An emergency point, for resuscitation from respiratory arrests, sunstroke, or collapse.
	Yin Tang	On the midline of the forehead, between the eyebrows.	Calming point. Good for eye soreness and redness, and nasal problems.

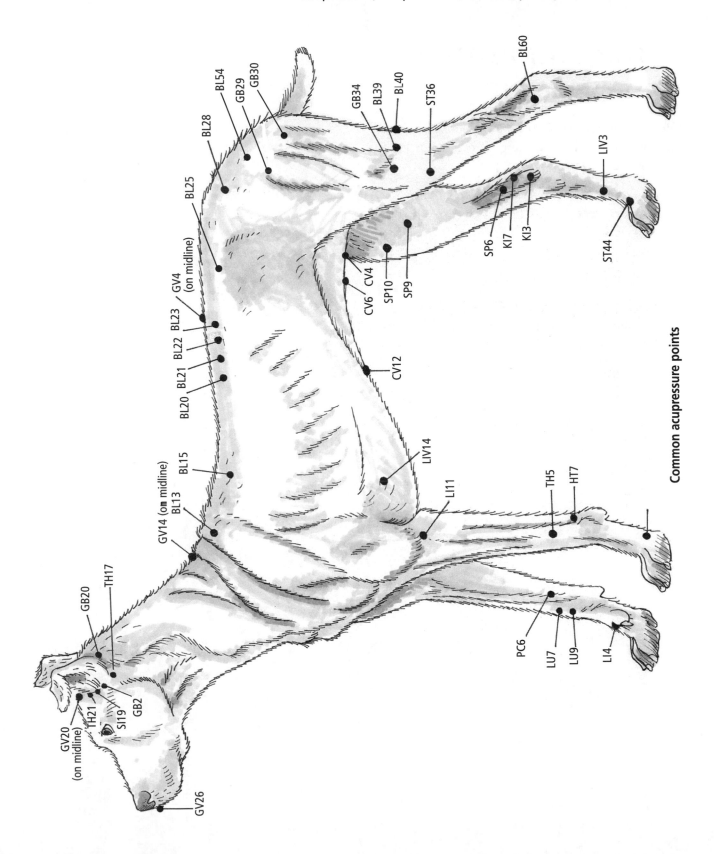

Common acupressure points

Recommended Reading

Canine Acupressure: A Treatment Workbook. Nancy Zidonis and Marie Sodenberg. Parker, CO: Equine Acupressure, 1995

Four Paws, Five Directions: A Guide to Chinese Medicine for Cats and Dogs. Cheryl Schwartz. Berkeley: Celestial Arts, 1996.

The Healing Touch. Michael Fox. New York: New-Market Press, 1990.

The Well-Connected Dog: A Guide to Canine Acupressure. Amy Snow and Nancy Zidonis. Tallgrass, 1999.

chapter 8

bodywork, energy medicine,

AND OTHER THERAPIES

bODYWORK AND ENERGY MEDICINE are two categories of healing therapies often used by holistic practitioners and caregivers. **Bodywork** includes techniques like massage, acupressure, and Tellington Touch to move or stimulate parts of the body. **Energy medicine** occurs at a more subtle level. It involves moving, stimulating, clearing, or otherwise influencing the energy field or energy flow through the use of visualization, Reiki, Therapeutic Touch, or even prayer.

You can explore the benefits of any of these methods with a little information and practice. Your dog will be a valuable teacher as she gives you feedback about the effectiveness of your skills, and plenty of appreciation for your efforts.

Energy Medicine

Energy medicine by definition works with the patient in a nonphysical way through the concept of the interconnectedness of body, mind, and spirit. The art of healing has long been performed in cultures around the world through a variety of spiritual practices that include prayer, chanting, meditation, and visioning. Shamans, priests, and medicine men and women have passed their special gifts down through the ages. Present-day healers develop new techniques as they study the old. And while modern science has almost entirely overshadowed these arts in our culture, researchers have begun to demonstrate the measurable therapeutic value these ancient healing traditions have to offer.

VISUALIZATION

The practice of visualization is just what it sounds like it is—visualizing, or seeing, an event that you hope will occur, based on the belief that your thoughts create reality. Many people believe that the more detailed and precise your visualizations, the more powerful they are. For example, if your dog is recovering from a broken leg, you might simply hold her in your thoughts as you drive to work or do the laundry, and imagine her running happily across the meadow behind your house. Another approach would be to sit quietly in meditation and, in your mind's eye, hold an image of her broken bone, then see each step of the healing process in minute detail as it occurs. You might imagine the bone cells multiplying and coming together across the fracture, or envision healing blood cells carrying nutrients to the site. If you repeat the process on a regular basis you may in fact create a reality on an energetic level, and facilitate the physical manifestation of that reality.

One of the advantages of visualization, as well as other forms of energy work, is that your dog does not need to be present for you to do the work. This can be a valuable tool if you're out of town and she's home alone, when she's hospitalized and you can't be with her, or even while she's in surgery. Visualization can enable you to be a part of her healing process even when only your heart is with her.

Try this:

- Think of some way in which you'd like to see your dog feel more at peace. For example, if she gets nervous when you go to the vet, visualize her being more relaxed in that setting.

- Set aside 10 minutes in which you won't be disturbed. Find a quiet, comfortable spot, close the door, and turn off the phone. Close your eyes, take a few deep breaths, and try to clear your mind of distractions.

- In your mind's eye, create an image of your dog in as much detail as you can muster. See the color of her fur, the swish of her tail, and the sparkle in her eye. Call to mind the way she smells (that's right, visualization involves *all* the senses).

- Now, with all that detail still in place, imagine you are on your way to see the vet. Start from the moment your dog typically begins to get nervous. If she senses something's up the minute you pick up the car keys, begin there. If she's happy in the car, but begins to tremble when you turn into the hospital parking lot, start at that point.

- Throughout this visualization your dog is happy, relaxed, even wagging her tail. Remember to include as much detail as possible. Notice the feel of your dog's breath on your hand as you snap on her leash. See the reflection in the windows as you walk up to the hospital building. All the while, keep coming back to the image of your dog enjoying the event—playful, energetic, with a bounce in her step. See her greet the nurse with a joyful lick, and wiggle with happiness when your vet enters the exam room. Be sure to note your own feeling of relaxation throughout the visualized visit.

- Repeat your visualization at least 3 or 4 times each week. If the problem is severe, or if your next veterinary appointment is just a couple of weeks away, try to do the exercise 2 or more times a day.

- When the time comes to actually take your dog in for her check-up, be sure to hold your visualization in mind before and during the visit. Be careful that you don't succumb to the old expectation that she'll be fearful. Let your visualization become your new memory of her experience of it.

You may not see a dramatic difference at her next appointment—then again, you might. Be open to the possibility. A wise osteopathic doctor has a sign hanging in his waiting room, that says, "We don't expect miracles. We count on them." You may find that your positive expectation is the best way to make miracles happen for you and your dog.

THERAPEUTIC TOUCH

Therapeutic Touch comes from the ancient practice known as "laying on of hands," in which the healer seeks to rebalance the energy field of the patient. In the early 1970s therapist Dora Kunz and Delores Krieger,

the power of your intentions

Some clients arrive at the clinic full of hope and optimism, even though their dog is very sick. "I just know you can make her well!" their eyes seem to say. Others seem only to be going through the motions of seeking veterinary help. They say things like, "Well, I know there probably isn't anything you can do, but...." Half-heartedly they turn their sick friend over with every expectation that the outcome will be grim.

Oddly enough, there seems to be a correlation between the recovery rate of sick animals and the expectations of their guardians. While no formal studies have been done to document this, time and time again I've seen amazing results—as though a very sick or severely injured dog is inspired to heal by the sheer conviction of his person that a recovery is possible. Then again, when a caretaker seems to have given up hope, it seems more likely that our best efforts to make the dog well will be unsuccessful.

I can't offer a clear accounting of why—or even if—the expectations of guardians do, in fact, affect the healing capacity of their animal friends. I can only guess that the power of their intention—just like the power of visualization or prayer—somehow influences the creative, healing energies of their dogs, and perhaps even my own healing energies and those of our nurses, as well. When the family is full of hope and maintains the deep conviction that their cherished companion will pull through a crisis, it seems to serve as a catalyst for the positive energies of an entire hospital staff to come together in a powerful way. If my observations are correct, the phenomenon is most certainly a testament to the amazing bond between a dog and the humans who love him. —*Katy*

Ph.D., R.N., developed a systematic approach to the technique, and were instrumental in the acceptance and implementation of Therapeutic Touch in nursing programs and hospitals throughout the United States. Since then, its benefits have been widely recognized in relieving stress, stimulating the immune system, and promoting healing. One study documented a significantly higher level of hemoglobin in the blood of patients who received Therapeutic Touch as compared to a control group that did not, even though the therapy was administered by nurses who had no prior experience with it.

Interestingly enough, Therapeutic Touch doesn't actually involve touching the body at all. Rather, it involves moving the hands *over the patient's energy field*—about 3 to 5 inches away from the physical body—assessing any irregularities and restoring balance where they exist. Frequently, dogs receiving the therapy relax into a deep sigh, or give a gentle wag of the tail, even though no physical contact has been made.

"Touching" a patient's energy field may sound like a foreign concept for those of us imbued with Western notions of physical reality. But with a little experimentation and practice, almost anyone can feel what might be described as subtle variations in the air around the body. These variations provide valuable clues to your dog's health problems, and may even help you locate an elusive injury. Once you've assessed her condition, you can apply the technique to help get blocked energy moving again, or treat your friend to a deep relaxation even when she's feeling fine.

Try this:

- Have your dog lie quietly on his bed or other comfortable spot. It's customary among Therapeutic Touch practitioners to ask their patients' permission before beginning a treatment. Since your dog deserves the same respect accorded human patients, go ahead and do the same for her.

- Take a moment to clear and quiet your mind. (See page 109, Healing the healer.)

- Rub your hands together briskly several times to stimulate their sensitivity. When they feel a little warm and tingly, hold one hand over your dog, palm facing him, and slowly move it closer and closer to her body, gliding it gently in the direction of her fur. Do this several times, till you are about 3 to 6 inches away from her body. You may find that the air feels slightly denser as you get within a few inches of her coat. That density you feel is a layer of her energy field, or **aura**.

- Continue to float your hand over her body just where the density increases, until you begin to feel subtle differences in the texture of the energy—

there may be a place where the air feels particularly thick, or where the density seems to diminish. You may even find that your hands tingle when they glide over a particular spot. Don't be misled by changes in temperature due to body heat; the sensations you're interested in are related to disturbances in the energy pattern around the body, not temperature.

- Be observant of your dog's responses. Chances are she'll relax, her breath may become slower and more even, she may even go to sleep. However, if she seems disturbed by your efforts, respect her feedback. Check to be sure that your mind is calm and quiet. Try moving your hands further away from her body, or moving them more slowly. Some very sensitive dogs feel your energy acutely; in other cases the energy is so disrupted in a particular area that she's unable to tolerate more than a very mild energetic touch. In any case, if your dog gets up and moves away, **don't** persist. Take note of her sensitivity, and consider the possibility that it's a sign of illness or injury. Reassess your techniques and try again another time.

- If your dog relaxes into your treatment, as most will, continue to move your hands over her energy field in the direction of her fur, as though you're smoothing any disturbances. Move your hands gently, just as if you were softly stroking her, even though your hands are a few inches away. Pay special attention to those places where you felt a disturbance. Imagine that you're encouraging movement where energy is blocked, drawing out excessive energy, or adding energy where it's depleted. Always move the energy out toward the tip of her tail, or down through the bottom of her feet.

- Finish your session by gently smoothing over her entire aura. Sit quietly a moment with her.

Therapeutic Touch is a technique that you can explore with a minimum of training. However, the more you practice the more skilled you will become. Everyone has the capacity to feel energy, but for some it takes time. Continue to practice, and explore opportunities to attend workshops or study with a skilled therapist. Many nursing schools now teach the technique. Your local hospital may be able to guide

healing the healer

Whether they involve touching your dog with your hands, your thoughts, or your prayers, most alternative healing modalities are based on an understanding of the interconnectedness of all beings. That means that what each of us does, what we think, and even who we are affects every other being on the planet. This understanding applies to the most loving, well-intentioned healing thoughts, emotions, and actions, but it also applies to the negative ones. When you touch your dog with love, he will receive love, and that's healing. If you are angry or unhappy or anxious when you touch him—whether it's a physical touch or just a thought—you will impart that negativity.

Does that mean you should never touch or think about your dog when you're feeling bad? Of course it doesn't. One of the wonderful gifts our dogs give us is their loving presence when we're having a rough time. In that capacity, they impart their love to us, and so *they* become the healers. There's no reason we should not accept this gift from them.

However, when you take on the role of the healer, you open a channel in which energy is exchanged between you and your dog. It's worthwhile to take the time to be sure the "medicine" you give him is pure.

Before you begin a healing session with your dog,

- Sit quietly and assess your state of mind. Make a conscious intention to set aside any negative thoughts or emotions for the moment. (Imagine putting them in a box and tucking it away where you can return to it later, if necessary.)

- Create a mental picture of a place where you feel safe and comfortable. A beautiful nature spot works well, or a favorite corner of your home. Feel your connection to the ground beneath your feet or your seat, and imagine that you are rooted deep into the earth. Feel the tension flowing out of your body.

you to training opportunities. Or contact Nurse Healers-Professional Associates International, an organization dedicated to providing information and educational resources for Therapeutic Touch, at www.therapeutic-touch.org.

REIKI

This hands-on healing technique has its roots in Japan. Reiki, which means "universal life force," seeks to rebalance the life force energy that has been blocked. It is especially useful for easing pain, promoting natural healing, restoring emotional well-being, and treating a variety of conditions in both people and animals.

While the techniques used in Reiki are similar to Therapeutic Touch, its practitioners, called Masters, place a greater emphasis on the transmission of information and energy from a Master to his students. If

---

cleansing the healer

Once you accept the notion of clearing your dog's energy field to help him heal, you may wonder, "Okay, but what am I supposed to do with all that bad energy?" On the surface, the question suggests an overly literal interpretation of the process. It may be, but the analogy holds—if you make the effort to clear your dog's energy field, it makes sense to then clear your own. Strange as it may seem, while there's little chance you would acquire an illness from your dog by trying any of these techniques, some healers report noticing a mild reflection of their dogs' symptoms in their own bodies *if* they don't do some simple cleansing rituals afterward. And while the phenomenon is rare, some sensitive people seem more prone to absorbing the energy of others, almost like a sponge. So make a habit of doing a quick energetic cleanse, for your own well-being and as a nice closure to your healing session. Try one of the following techniques:

- Run some clear, cool water over your hands, as you visualize any impurities being rinsed away from your energy field.

- Burn some incense sage (also called white sage), cedar, or a stick or cone of all-natural incense, and use the smoke to "smudge" your body—allow the smoke to flow all around you, over your hands, your legs, your head, as you visualize it clearing away the negativity.

- Sit on the ground or on a comfortable chair, and visualize a radiant, white light flowing in through the top of your head and out through the soles of your feet deep into the earth, cleansing your energy field of negativity as it passes through you.

this form of therapy interests you, contact a Reiki Master in your area who can provide treatment for your dog, or training for you.

TELEPATHIC COMMUNICATION

While not necessarily a form of healing, telepathic communication with your dog is enormously enriching to your relationship. Chances are that the two of you already communicate telepathically, whether you're aware of it or not. Have you ever noticed that she sometimes shows up at your side *before* you've acted on your thought to go find her? What about all the times you looked at her and "just knew" what she was thinking? These incidents reflect the innate capacity most of us have to be sensitive to another's thoughts, even if our culture tends to scoff at the idea.

Learning to share information telepathically with your dog is accessible to anyone. The biggest obstacle most people face is a reluctance to trust their intuition, and to recognize the information that routinely passes unspoken between the two of you. Be open, and listen to the thoughts that seem to just pop into your head. Pay attention to the conversations you sometimes carry on with your dog, even though you assume you're the only one who's talking.

Working with an animal communicator: In recent years, many individuals have honed their skills in telepathic animal communication, and offer their services to help others better understand their dogs. Whether your dog is behaving oddly or seems distressed or fearful, these practitioners may be able to offer helpful insights. However, it's unlikely they can answer very specific questions, nor should they attempt to make a veterinary diagnosis or make health care decisions for you.

PRAYER

An emerging field called **psychoneuroimmunology** explores how the intricate interconnectedness between the neurologic and immune systems of the body can induce self-healing in response to one's thoughts and emotions. This is a fancy way of saying that when we pray for ourselves, or know that someone else is praying for us, we are able to tap into and mobilize our own healing energies.

But if you choose to pray for your dog, will she know you are praying for her? And does it matter? The results of a recent study that explored the power of prayer for humans may be able to answer that question. The study involved approximately 400 heart patients, half of whom were prayed for by distant prayer groups, while the other half were not. The doctors, nurses, and patients themselves had no idea who was in the "prayed for" group and who was not, but the results showed some astonishing differences. Those patients who were prayed for were 5 times *less* likely to need antibiotics, and 3 times *less* likely to develop fluid in their lungs. Since then, many studies have shown that the subjects of distant healing intentions heal faster, or otherwise benefit physically. Other studies have found that seedlings grew faster, wounds in mice healed more quickly, and AIDS patients enjoyed better health when someone prayed or meditated on their behalf.

How is this possible? Some researchers suspect the existence of a type of energy field we don't yet understand. Remember, it was not so long ago when we had no understanding, or even an awareness, of electromagnetic waves or X-rays.

Perhaps a scientific understanding of *how* we heal with our intention is not really necessary in order to explore the use of prayer or meditation as a part of our relationship with our animals. After all, everyone can relate to the concept of healing through tender loving care. Focusing your intention on your dog's health through prayer is just another way to provide that care.

Bodywork

Anytime you touch your dog with love, healing happens. When you apply your touch according to a particular system of care, you can enhance the benefits enormously. Bodywork has been found to relieve stress or depression, improve circulation, enhance immune function, promote healing, and even help the body release endorphins to ease pain. In addition, it's well known that animals of many species thrive better when they are touched than when they are not. (In fact, young primates—including humans—will die if they are not held.) That may be one reason why both parties—the practitioner and the recipient of therapy—often report a greater sense of well-being after a treatment.

MASSAGE

Massage involves the physical manipulation of tissues. It can range from a very gentle movement of the skin and tissue just beneath, to a more invasive action that affects deep muscle tissue or even organs. Massage improves circulation, breaks up adhesions, stimulates the immune system, promotes emotional and physical relaxation, and alleviates depression. The enhanced circulation alone contributes to the healing of injured tissue by bringing nourishment to the area and flushing out toxins. And the quiet time and focused attention you give your dog will be rewarding for both of you.

Try this:

NOTE: If at any time during this exercise you feel your dog become tense, soften your touch or decrease the movement of tissue. This exercise should be relaxing for your dog. If it's not, you may have discovered an injury or painful site, or you may simply be working too aggressively.

- Take a few deep breaths to calm your mind. Have your dog lie comfortably on her side. Talk quietly to her, and stroke her gently until she is relaxed.

- Run your hands gently over her body. Move in the direction of her fur, from her head to her tail and down each leg. Notice the different sensations you feel under your hand. Where does the skeleton lie just beneath the skin? Are there places where the muscles feel firmer than others?

- With the palm of your hand flat against her shoulder, make firm but gentle movements so that her skin moves slightly over the muscles. Move your hand back and forth or in circles, then repeat the motion in different places all around her body. Notice where the skin slides easily, and where you feel resistance.

- Use your fingertips to gently explore the length of her spine. Begin at the base of her skull, and slowly "walk" them down her neck and back, one finger on each side of the spinal column. Without applying pressure, try to feel where each vertebra begins and ends. Gently massage the soft tissue on either side of the spine.

- Run your hands down the length of her hind legs, and feel the large muscles just above the knee, on the front and back of the leg. Massage those muscles, running your hand softly along their length, and moving them very gently from side to side. Continue down below her knee, then run your fingers along the tendons and the skin between the tendon and bone. Gently rub each pad on her feet and the tender tissue between the pads. Repeat the process with her forelimbs, beginning with the muscles above her elbow.

- Using the tips of your fingers, massage the small muscles of her forehead, cheeks, muzzle, and ears.

- Finish with slow, gentle strokes from the top of her head to the tip of her tail, and down the length of each leg. Sit quietly with her for a moment.

Regular massage sessions will give you valuable information about your dog, where she is tense, what kinds of touch she likes, and what she doesn't. She'll come to look forward to her massage, and learn to enjoy your intimate touch and undivided attention as a welcome, relaxing experience.

ACUPRESSURE AND TRIGGER-POINT MASSAGE

Acupressure is an extension of the ancient Chinese practice of acupuncture. It utilizes the same concept of energy flow within the body, and seeks to stimulate the points where the energy meridians lie just beneath the skin. However, instead of inserting needles, acupressure involves using the fingers to apply pressure to those points. An obvious advantage is that, while needles must be inserted only by a trained medical professional, you can apply the **principles** of acupuncture using the **technique** of acupressure at home. To date, no studies have been done to establish that acupressure is in fact as effective as acupuncture, however practitioners report positive responses in the patients they treat. Refer to Chapter 7 for guidance on how to begin using acupressure. Your veterinary acupuncturist can also help you choose specific points to benefit your dog.

Trigger-point massage uses a hands-on technique similar to that employed in acupressure, however treatment begins by scanning the body for areas of maximum tenderness that need healing and releasing. These painful areas are often the result of previous injury, irritation, or stress. While trigger-point massage therapists are trained and particularly adept at locating and releasing these points, developing the sensitivity you need to apply the techniques yourself just takes practice. If you're willing to spend a little time touching, feeling, assessing, and comparing the differences in the feel of the tissues beneath your fingers, you'll soon be able to help your dog overcome

stiffness and soreness, and perhaps even help her regain that spring in her step.

Try this:

- Prepare yourself and your dog for a massage session, as above.

- As you scan your dog's body with your fingertips, try closing your eyes to increase the awareness in your hands. You are searching for areas, usually no larger than a dime, where the tissue feels harder and firmer than the surrounding tissue, or stringy and slightly swollen. These points are often at sites where muscles attach to bone.

- Refer to the Common Trigger Points chart on page 201 to familiarize yourself with the places where you are likely to locate a problem. If your dog occasionally favors a front leg, for instance, you may find a tender area over the triceps region.

- Be careful to use only a light touch when you're locating points. They can be extremely sensitive, and even a good-natured dog may yelp (or even bite!) if the area is squeezed or pressed too firmly. When you find a sensitive spot, your dog may turn to look at you or at the spot you're touching. Some trigger points cause **referred pain** in other parts of the body, so you may see her shift her focus to an entirely different area.

- Once you've located the tender points, release them by using acupressure technique: firm but gentle pressure for 5 to 15 seconds, then a somewhat lighter pressure for a few seconds more.

Once you've "released" an area, you've helped increase the blood circulation and lymph drainage. By relieving muscle tension, you increase range of motion to the area. Sometimes after a session new trigger points will become more evident in other areas that need work, so be sure to start each session anew, and let your fingers tell you where your dog needs your touch.

TELLINGTON TOUCH

In 1978 Linda Tellington Jones developed a system of working with problem horses by using a combination of bodywork and movement exercises. The system was based on her work as a practitioner of Feldenkrais, the human bodywork modality named for its founder, Moshe Feldenkrais. Linda later adapted her approach to work with other companion animals, and has since established an extensive network of training materials, workshops, and practitioners of what is known as Tellington Touch, or TTouch.

TTouch uses the hands in a variety of ways to stroke, massage, and lift various parts of the body. The most basic technique involves making small circles with the fingers and hands, so that the cells are stimulated in a very subtle way.

TTouch can be used to calm your dog in a stressful situation, relieve discomfort after surgery or an injury, or help a fearful dog become more confident. It can also calm and focus a dog who is distractable or has difficulty learning new tasks.

Try this:

- With your dog standing or sitting comfortably at your side, use your fingertips to make small circles on her body. Begin at the top of her head and work your way down along her neck, over her shoulders, and around her torso. Be gentle, using just enough pressure to slide the skin over the tissues beneath. (Practice making a few circles on your own forearm or, to be sure you're being gentle enough, on your face.) Move slowly, taking a second or two for each circle. If your friend seems uncomfortable, use less pressure or work more slowly.

- Spend a little time making your circles all around your dog's head, including the top of her skull, her cheeks and, if she's comfortable with it, her lips.

- Holding the skin softly between your thumb and forefinger, very gently make tiny circles on the flaps of your dog's ear. Begin at the base of the ear and work your way along each edge toward the tip. Then return to the base and follow imaginary lines again and again from base to tip, until you have covered the entire surface of the earflap. Continue around the base of the ear.

- Apply TTouch to the pads of your dog's feet and, again using your thumb and forefinger, gently work with the tender skin between the pads.

- Stand or sit behind your dog and hold onto her tail. Make slow, gentle, circular motions with the tail, first in one direction and then the other. Then, very gently pull the tail straight out, in a continuous line from her spine. Be sure not to bend or pull the tail beyond a point that is comfortable for your friend.

Flower Essences

Dr. Edward Bach was an English homeopathic physician, chemist, botanist, and lover of nature who recognized the profound effect the mind and spirit could have on healing, and was concerned that the medical profession was not more attentive to the attitude and personality of the patient.

In 1930 Dr. Bach turned to the nontoxic flowers of wild plants and trees of his own English countryside for their healing energies. His study centered on the effect the plants had, not on the physical plane, but on what he called the **emotional body**. He developed a special process through which water absorbed the energy of the plants. He then used the water to balance the energy of his patients. He identified 38 **flower essences**, and proposed that it might be possible to transfer the life force from the plants to help balance a patient's vital force. Like homeopathic preparations, flower essences are vibrational, or energetic in nature, and physically dilute—so dilute in fact that there is no measurable amount of the flower present in the remedy.

Today, the medical profession recognizes the body-mind-spirit connection that so interested Dr. Bach. Science has now shown us how a person's or animal's mental and emotional state can trigger the release of hormones and neurotransmitters, for example, that will indeed effect the body's ability to heal. The study of energetic medicines is still in its infancy, however. Despite the lack of scientific evidence, many people have found flower essences to be effective, eliciting dramatic, positive changes in their dog's behavior.

PREPARING FLOWER ESSENCES

- Place 2 to 3 teaspoons of brandy or vinegar into a 1-ounce colored glass bottle. Fill the rest of the bottle with spring water.

- Use the chart on pages 116-117 to choose the remedies you need, and add 3 to 6 drops of each one to your bottle. You can combine up to 6 remedies. Be sure to shake each stock bottle before you withdraw the remedy, and shake your mixture when you are done. Even if you are using just a single remedy, dilute it as above or use it directly from the stock bottle. Be careful not to touch the tip of the dropper against any other surface.

- Store your remedies in a cool place, out of sunlight and away from microwave ovens, computers, or heat.

USING FLOWER ESSENCES

Dosage: Before using your remedies, shake them well, in a vertical direction. Start with a few drops 2 to 3 times a day as needed. You can decrease or increase the frequency, depending on your dog's response.

Different ways to administer flower essences:

- Place the drops directly into your dog's mouth, the way you would administer a homeopathic remedy.

- Part the hair at the base of her neck and place a few drops on her skin.

- Massage a few drops into the areas of bare skin under the earflaps.

- Apply the essences to your own hands and give your pet an all-over massage.

- Add a few drops to her drinking water each day. Discontinue if she objects to the taste.

- Mix a few drops into her food.

- Add 10 to 12 drops from the stock bottle to a small spray bottle of spring water. Spray a mist directly onto your dog, on her bed, or into her travel crate.

ABOUT RESCUE REMEDY

This is a Bach flower remedy that you can purchase as a premixed combination of flower essences. It contains Cherry Plum, Clematis, Impatiens, Rock Rose, and Star of Bethlehem, and was designed to be used as a single remedy. It is the most well known of the flower essences, probably because it is so effective, with so many uses (see page 123). Choose Rescue Remedy to help calm your dog before or during any traumatic or stressful event, including a trip to the veterinarian's office.

COMMON FLOWER REMEDIES AND THEIR USES	
Rescue Remedy	A combination of 5 flower remedies. Use in any stressful situation, emotional or physical, or when your dog shows signs of anxiety or fear.
Star-of-Bethlehem	Use when your dog experiences a loss (as of an animal or human friend), when comfort is needed, or when he is suffering from emotional or physical trauma.
Walnut	For the dog having a hard time adapting to change, such as moving to a new home, having a new person in the household, or adapting to your new work schedule.
Red Chestnut	For dogs who worry about other animals or their guardians; when a dog senses impending danger, such as an earthquake or storm.
Pine	For the dog who tries so hard to please, or who has experienced a lot of rejection in life; also for the dog who lacks confidence and acts guilty whenever you are upset, even about something unrelated to him.
Impatiens	For the dog who is very nervous or easily agitated, especially one who shakes when nervous; also for dogs experiencing any type of pain.

Holistic Practitioners

CHIROPRACTIC CARE

The word **chiropractic** comes from the Greek roots *cheir* and *praxis*, which translate to mean "hand" and "practice," or a medical practice done with the hands. The philosophy behind this treatment is based on the relationship of the spinal column not only to your dog's nervous system and back, but also to her biomechanics and movement, and circulation. Therapy is aimed primarily at manipulation of the vertebral column as a way to alter the progression of a disease process. Chiropractic care can help alleviate many problems, particularly those that involve the muscles, joints, and nerves.

The American Veterinary Chiropractic Association (AVCA) provides post-graduate courses to train and certify both veterinarians and human chiropractors for the special needs of animals. Contact the AVCA for the name of a chiropractor in your area who is qualified to treat animals.

MASSAGE THERAPY

While you can certainly give your dog a soothing, healing massage at home, a certified massage therapist has the expertise to provide a more precise level of care. There is a large variety of massage modalities and specific schools of therapy available. Most practitioners are willing to explain how their techniques differ from others, and the merits of various forms. Therapies that are used with animals by holistic practitioners include acupressure massage, trigger-point

SUGGESTED FLOWER REMEDY COMBINATIONS FOR SPECIFIC TROUBLES

Difficulty traveling	Walnut, Aspen, Elm, Mimulus (add Scleranthus if there is also car sickness), Rescue Remedy
Fearfulness	Aspen, Mimulus, Rockrose, Red Chestnut, Larch, Rescue Remedy
Lack of confidence	Centaury, Pine, Larch
Nervousness	Aspen, Mimulus, Sweet Chestnut, Rescue Remedy
Excessive barking	Chestnut Bud, Vervain, Heather, Cerato
Grief	Star-of-Bethlehem, Walnut, Honeysuckle, Gentian
Loneliness due to isolation (as when you must leave your dog in a kennel or at the veterinary hospital)	See above for grief; also Chestnut Bud, Aspen, Rescue Remedy
Poor socialization (doesn't get along well with others)	Beech, Holly, Willow, Chestnut Bud, Walnut
Chronic illness	Centaury, Gorse, Olive, Honeysuckle, Crab Apple, Gentian

massage or myotherapy, craniosacral therapy, and Bowen therapy.

OTHER MODALITIES

Holistic veterinarians and animal healers may use other forms of alternative therapies, including acupuncture, magnetic therapy, laser or low-energy photon therapy, aromatherapy, and Contact Reflex Analysis. Keep in mind that most branches of alternative medicine do not have published data on effectiveness in dogs. However, these are generally gentle therapies considered safe when properly practiced. Your holistic veterinarian is your best resource for helping you sort out which might hold promise for your dog's particular condition or health status.

Recommended Reading

Animals as Teaches and Healers: True Stories and Reflections. Susan Chernak McElroy. New York: Ballantine Books, 1997.

Getting in TTouch with Your Dog: A Gentle Approach to Influencing Behavior, Health, and Performance. Linda Tellington-Jones. Trafalgar Square, 2001.

Kindred Spirits: How the Remarkable Bond between Human and Animals Can Change the Way We Live. Allen M. Schoen. New York: Broadway Books, 2001.

Kinship With All Life. J.Allen Boone. San Francisco: Harper SanFrancisco, 1954.

The Power of Prayer and the Practice of Medicine. Larry Dossey. San Francisco: Harper SanFrancisco, 1993.

Therapeutic Touch: A Practical Guide. Janet Macrae. New York: Alfred A. Knopf, 1988.

When Animals Speak: Advanced Interspecies Communication. Penelope Smith. Hillsboro, OR: Beyond Words Publishing, 1999.

American Veterinary Chiropractic Association, Bluejacket, Oklahoma, for information regarding chiropractic therapy for dogs. 1-918-784-2231, www.animalchiropractic.org.

2 part two

Tashina (left), Great Dane/Shepherd cross. 1992–1998. Adopted by Jan Allegretti at 10 weeks old in Forestville, California.

Savannah (right), Great Dane. Adopted in 1999 at 5 years old from the Mendocino County Animal Care and Control Shelter in Ukiah, California. Savannah is an editorial and healing consultant to Jan and special spiritual adviser to her community.

part two

treating injury and illness
the holistic medicine chest

Before you Begin:

Part Two is designed to help you learn to read the state of your dog's emotional and physical health and then guide you toward selecting an alternative therapy or therapies that will address some of the problems you may observe. Remember that a holistic approach integrates many disciplines, including conventional medicine. Thus Part Two is also designed to help you work in concert with your vet with the objective of doing what is right for you *and* your dog. Let's begin by considering a few basic guidelines that pertain to all home therapies.

- **Don't wait for a crisis.** Trust your intuition when you feel your dog is somehow "off." An underlying health imbalance can manifest in subtle ways or even look like something you once accepted as normal for your dog. Minor skin problems, quirky behaviors, sensitive digestion, or even stiffness is a good place to start when experimenting with a new therapy. Developing finely tuned observation skills will not only help you choose the right treatment, it will also be of utmost importance when you are evaluating for improvement.

- When you first notice changes in your dog, consider employing herbs, homeopathy, and acupressure. **If you suspect a serious illness or injury, get a diagnosis from your vet.** Ask questions. Be sure you understand the diagnosis and any treatments your vet might recommend. Home therapies can help to minimize complications of many conventional treatments. Or, in some cases, you may find them valuable alternatives to conventional treatments.

- **Remember that your veterinarian is there to help you,** to answer your questions, and provide assistance.

Setting Up a Holistic Medicine Chest:

Learning to work with alternative medicines is easier than you might expect. A surprisingly small number of items will help you handle a wide range of injuries and illnesses (see the lists on pages 122-124). Start with just a few remedies and become familiar with how they work. Then add new ones as the need arises.

HOMEOPATHIC REMEDIES

Remedy	Symptoms for acute injury or illness (For chronic illness see the Homeopathic Materia Medica beginning on page 305.)
*Aconite	Shock, stress, anxiety, chills or overheating. Use in any injury where symptoms of shock are present. May be alternated with Arnica, if indicated. Also useful to calm a fearful or anxious dog.
Apis	Stings, from any insect, especially bees or wasps. Also, any swelling that is hot.
*Arnica	Think of Arnica first in the treatment of any injury, including bruising, strains, or sprains, as from trauma or over-exertion. Also reduces pain and promotes healing after surgery. Reduces swelling, bruising, and soreness. Has been called "homeopathic aspirin."
Belladonna	Fever, overheating. In case of fever, use every 10 to 15 minutes till fever begins to drop, then reduce frequency to every hour. As with all remedies, discontinue when patient begins to improve on his or her own. In case of heatstroke or nonresponsive fever, consult your veterinarian
*Crotalus	Snakebite, or symptoms that resemble a snakebite. Contact a veterinarian as soon as possible for further help.
Hepar	In low potencies helps to open and drain localized infections, such as abscesses. In higher potencies helps reduce drainage and formation of pus.
*Hypericum	An excellent remedy for any affection of nerve tissue, or tissue having lots of nerve endings, such as nails and toes. Also for back pains that involve pinched or irritated nerves, particularly in the lower back. Reduces pain, quiets nerve responses. Also helps prevent infection in wounds. Use alternately with Arnica for cuts and lacerations. Use alternately with Ledum for puncture wounds.
Ipecac	Nausea, vomiting.
Ledum	Helps to heal and prevent infection in puncture wounds; use alternately with Hypericum. Also, for any injury near the bone, e.g., tendons, ligaments, periosteum. Also, any swelling that is cool.
*Nux vomica	Digestive discomfort, particularly a bloated, gassy condition, as from overeating.
*Phosphorus	Helps stop bleeding. Use along with compression
Rhus tox	Skin irritation, itching, rash, especially those that resemble Poison Oak or Poison Ivy. Also, joint soreness that gets better with movement. Has been called the "rusty gate remedy."
Silica	Helps the body eject foreign particles, such as splinters or foxtails. *Caution: Not to be used in animals with implants such as plates or pins in bones, or where foreign matter has been enclosed by the body and rendered benign.*

*Most essential components of your Medicine Chest.

HERBS AND OTHER NATURAL REMEDIES

Remedy	Symptoms
Activated charcoal	Can be fed with yogurt or broth to absorb orally ingested toxins. Available as powder, tablets, or capsules.
*Calendula tincture and *Hypericum (also known as St. John's Wort) tincture	One bottle each of these herbal tinctures will last for years, and will be among the most versatile and frequently used items in your medicine chest. With just a few drops of each, you can make a lotion or an ointment to speed healing and soothe a wide range of skin affections. For a lotion, add 6 drops of calendula tincture and 6 drops of hypericum tincture to ½ cup of water. Shake vigorously. Apply to burns, cuts, lacerations, and scrapes to cleanse, aid healing, ease pain, prevent infection, and promote drying. Where risk of infection or aggravation of the injury exists, saturate a cottonball with lotion, place on the wound, and leave in place for 24 hours, re-wetting the cotton as needed without disturbing contact. For an ointment, use the same formula added to a vegetable gel (such as shea butter or Un-Petroleum Jelly). Stir vigorously for one minute. Apply to dry, crusty scrapes, burns, or irritated skin. Aids healing and moisturizes.
Chamomile	Taken internally, has a calming effect and aids digestion. Topically, it soothes the skin and helps heal abrasions and burns.
Dandelion	Detoxifying, calming, strengthening. Aids in function of the liver, urinary tract, and reproductive system. Good source of trace minerals.
*Echinacea	Supports the immune system.
Garlic	Supports the immune system and is useful in fighting bacterial, viral, and fungal infections. May deter fleas, ticks, and internal parasites.
Potato	A coarsely grated potato makes an excellent poultice to draw out swelling or foreign particles, such as splinters and foxtails. Apply gratings directly to the point of entry, cover lightly with plastic wrap to keep moisture in. *Be sure wrap does not bind around limbs.* Secure with VetWrap or elastic bandage.
*Rescue Remedy	Use along with any other remedy for stress, trauma. Helps to stabilize, physically and emotionally. Best applied to gums or mucous membranes, but may be applied anywhere on the body.
Sage	For an ointment, mix 2 teaspoons of powdered herb to ½ cup of vegetable gel such as shea butter or Un-Petroleum jelly. Aids in healing scrapes and minor cuts while repelling flies.

*Most essential components of your Medicine Chest.

WRAPS, TAPES & TOOLS	
Remedy	**Symptoms**
Adhesive tape	The waterproof variety is best. Use extreme caution if tape is wrapped around a limb—if the bandage slips, circulation may be impaired.
*Cottonballs	Cottonballs made from real cotton, organic if possible, are best for applying lotions or cleaning and dressing wounds.
Plastic wrap	The kind of wrap you use in your kitchen is useful for keeping moist dressings moist or dry dressings dry.
*Glass jars	Use these to make and store your calendula-hypericum lotion and ointment.
Tweezers	Handy for removing ticks, splinters or a foxtail from the skin.
*VetWrap	Most convenient and safest way to secure wound dressings. It sticks to itself so it holds without tape, and is flexible with plenty of stretch. (If you have trouble finding it, try your local farm supply, feed store, or tack shop.)

*Most essential components of your Medicine Chest.

dr. katy's additions to the medicine chest

Aloe vera plant — You can grow your own, so it's there when you need it. Clip the fleshy leaves to squeeze out the healing gel. Soothes damaged skin, whether from burns, abrasions, or sun exposure.

Yunnan Pai Yao — Available at Chinese pharmacies and some health food stores, this formula has amazing powers to curb bleeding, assist clot formation, support tissue healing, and reduce pain. Give 1 to 3 capsules. Can be repeated 2 to 3 times a day. For short-term use only.

Pill Curing — Another time-tested Chinese formula, good for overeating, flatulence, nausea, or sluggish digestion. Comes in little vials of disc-shaped compressed herbs. Give 1/3 to 1 vial. Can be repeated in 12 hours.

Sterile gauze — Great for when a wound is contaminated with dirt and debris. Open the packet and use the gauze to pick off the debris and gently wipe away the dirt. Can be moistened with a dilute Betadine solution (readily available at pharmacies — one of the best non-soap wound cleaners to further remove bacteria).

behavioral and emotional problems

When your dog joins your family, he comes with a complex set of behavioral patterns already in place. Even a very young puppy is hardly a blank slate. While he has much to learn about the world and appropriate ways to act in our society, he was born with a host of instinctive behaviors that, while more or less mysterious to us, are powerfully ingrained. Many of those we see as troublesome, including some forms of chewing, digging, submissive urination, and even aggression, have been built in over generations of evolutionary development. In another, wilder society, they might even be incremental to a dog's survival.

When we bring dogs into our lives, it is our responsibility to help them understand which behaviors are acceptable and which are not. Even when our dogs are well educated in these matters, when faced with stress, illness, or injury, they may fall back on those instinctive behaviors as the only way they know to protect themselves, or to express their distress.

Treating behavioral and emotional problems with understanding, and with an eye toward correcting the *cause* of the problem rather than only seeking to eradicate symptoms, is part of the holistic approach.

Recent research has revealed a genetic component to problem behavior in certain breeds. However, when breed predisposition can be ruled out as a contributing factor, and there is no obvious pathology involved, behavioral and emotional difficulties may be symptoms of one, two, or all three of the following underlying causes:

Lack of education: Your dog does not know his behavior is inappropriate or, more often, does not know what behavior *is* appropriate.

Stress: Your dog reverts to instinctive behaviors in an effort to relieve stress by protecting himself, or by using expressive behaviors in an effort to alter his environment or to ask you to alter it for him. In some cases negative experiences during puppyhood, an impoverished early environment, or other earlier trauma may cause some dogs to experience stress even when there's no apparent immediate cause.

Physical problems: Your dog's behavior is a response to pain or the consequence of a physical disability. Diet, environment, or genetic factors may also contribute to an array of behavioral and emotional problems.

In most cases, addressing any or all three issues will usually help you get to the root of the problem, because often, more than one of these factors combine to create troublesome behavior or inappropriate reactions. For example, if your dog snaps at the child next door, it may be due to his arthritic hip (a physical problem) that causes him pain, which leads him to act out. Or, he may behave aggressively toward a strange dog coming down the sidewalk because he is frightened (stress), and has not been taught a more appropriate response (lack of education).

PREVENTION

Most behavioral and emotional problems can be avoided with a sound preventive program. Whether your dog joins your family as a puppy, an adult, or as a senior citizen, a few basic guidelines will help put him on track to be a model citizen, emotionally secure and a pleasure to be around.

- Make sure your house is a safe haven for your friend. Create an environment in which there's a minimum of opportunity for inappropriate activities, and a minimum of emotional stress. This may mean installing or repairing a fence or gate, or taking his need for companionship, play, and quiet time into account.

- Enroll your dog in a socialization class. The first four months of a puppy's life are a critical time for him to develop his personality and gain social skills. Even an older dog will benefit from a refresher course. Knowing what's expected of him will help him to please you on a regular basis, which in turn will help him feel more secure and make your life easier. Safe interaction with people and other dogs will encourage him to enjoy their company rather than become anxious or aggressive. It will also help you become attuned to the ways you influence his behavior, consciously or not.

- Expose your dog to a broad range of experiences in a safe, controlled manner so that he'll learn to adapt to whatever comes his way (see pages 6-10).

- Use praise, food treats, toys, love, understanding, and more praise as you teach your dog appropriate behavior. Physical punishment or other harsh treatment causes stress, and may ultimately result in severe emotional problems or even more undesirable behavior. Teaching him with enthusiastic appreciation for his efforts will inspire him to respect your leadership, seek your approval, and honor you with his trust.

What to Look For:

- **Aggression:** Your dog snaps at strangers or children, or growls at another dog without provocation. Aggression is often based on fear, an effort to avoid pain, or reflects the dominance behavior of his ancestry. It is the most dangerous and worrisome of all behavior problems.

- **Soiling in the house:** Your new friend arrives home from the shelter and promptly urinates or defecates inside the house. This might simply be due to lack of education. However, if your previously tidy dog suddenly begins to soil inappropriately he may be ill, or a change in his routine could be causing him stress.

- **Destructive behavior:** Your dog chews your furniture, or destroys other objects, or even gnaws on his paw. Most often this is a response to stress or anxiety, often coupled with an education problem—perhaps one in which a guardian has unknowingly helped the behavior to develop. Evaluate what could be making him feel insecure or frightened. Chronic pain also causes stress, so consider a thorough check-up to rule out a physical cause.

- **Anxiety:** Your dog is frightened by a single trigger, such as a loud noise or a visit to the vet's office. Sometimes it's reasonable to show signs of fear, as when an automobile backfires as it passes in front of the house. If your dog becomes startled, then wags his tail and relaxes when he realizes there is no legitimate threat, that's okay. But if he cowers in the closet, and stays there shivering for the rest of the afternoon, he's suffering from an anxiety disorder.

- **Lack of manners:** Next to aggression, destruction, and urinating on the carpet, a simple lack of manners may seem like little more than an inconvenience. But if your dog all but knocks you down with his exuberance when you come home at night, or steals your dinner off the table when you get up to retrieve a fork, he may be on his way to making your life miserable.

What You Can Do:

🐕 **Be aware of the subtle things you do to encourage or discourage behaviors in your dog.** Every time you interact with him you teach him something. When you're happy he learns that whatever is going on in that moment is a good thing. He may associate your goodwill with an external event or, more commonly, with his behavior in the moment. If you're angry or anxious, he's likely to make a similar connection.

🐕 **Review your dog's environment and his routine. Has there been a change that may be causing him stress?** Has there been an addition— human or other—to the family? Have you recently begun spending more time away from home? Take steps to eliminate the source of stress, if possible. If not, reassure him by building an extra measure of your focused, positive attention into his regular routine.

🐕 **Ask yourself whether you or other family members are inadvertently contributing to the unwanted behavior.** For example, if you are leaving your young dog home alone all day, with few toys and no companions, you are setting up a situation for destructive behaviors. If he's been barking excessively, and you give him a chew toy to get him to be quiet, you're probably rewarding the behavior you'd like to discourage.

🐕 **Examine your dog's diet to be sure she's getting the proper balance of nutrients.** A diet that is too high in protein can cause anxiety or hyperactivity. A lack of variety increases the chance of developing a food allergy that could effect his behavior. Chemical additives in his food—or pesticides or other chemicals in his environment—might cause aggression or hypersensitivity. Review

Chapter 3 for dietary issues, and Chapter 2 for environmental causes.

🐕 **Consider the possibility that your dog is acting out due to a health problem.** If he's soiling in the house, it may indicate trouble with his urinary or digestive tract. If he's behaving aggressively, it's possible he's in pain. Poor health and chronic pain can make even the best-natured dog cranky. Depending on the nature of the behavior, a veterinary exam could save you months of corrective training that could have been remedied with a simple medical procedure.

🐕 **Take some time to write down the potential causes of behavioral and emotional trouble**—lack of education, stress, and physical problems (see page 125). Include any genetic factors, negative experiences during puppyhood, or an impoverished early environment that may also play a role. For each category on your list, jot down any contributing factors in your dog's case. The more insight you have regarding the root cause of the difficulty, the better you will be able to understand it from your dog's perspective, and help him overcome it.

🐕 If you've begun to see behaviors that are unacceptable, **seek help from a variety of trusted sources (veterinarians, trainers, canine behavioral counselors, and recommended books) right away.** If the problem has roots in your dog's ancestral history, there are powerful instincts at play, and overcoming them will take education and persistence. If it's the result of a frightening experience he had last week, or an annoying set of behaviors that's cropped up recently, chances are your dog has received some *negative* education—that is, he has *learned* to behave in an inappropriate manner. Behavioral patterns that are allowed to go uncorrected for lengthy periods are much harder to deal with.

🐕 **Join a training or socialization class with your dog.** The instructor can give you valuable pointers regarding how you interact with him—and insights into what you may be teaching him without even realizing it. You'll be given exercises you can work on at home with your friend. The extra time you spend together will be fun for both of you, and will give him lots of opportunity to gain your approval. The interaction with other dogs and people in the controlled class setting will help him gain confidence and social graces.

If your dog has a behavioral problem, it is your responsibility to protect him from injuring himself or others. Dogs who chase cars may get hurt, and endanger drivers who try to avoid them. Aggressive dogs allowed off-leash, or even *on* leash but not under control, can be disastrous not only for other dogs, but for those who try to break up a fight. Take care to control your friend until you are able to help him become a more polite member of society.

Even the less hazardous episodes of misconduct can begin a cycle in which your frustration with your dog causes you to behave in ways that effect him, which in turn causes him to behave in progressively more inappropriate ways. **Don't let minor annoyances grow into major aggravations that sully your friendship, or even drive you to consider relinquishing your guardianship.** Work with him on your own, in a class, or with a private trainer to teach him positive ways to deal with his anxiety or gain your attention.

Soiling in the House

Although more common in puppyhood and during the senior years, house-soiling can happen at any life stage. If your dog is having accidents in the house, don't assume it's a behavioral problem until you've thoroughly investigated the possibility of a physical one. A compromised gastrointestinal or urinary tract could be the cause. Neurologic problems and senility may also be to blame. When physical or medical problems are not the cause, the following suggestions can help correct inappropriate urination or defecation.

What You Can Do:

🐕 **Examine your dog's emotional state.** House-soiling can be related to anxiety, and if it only happens while you're away, it's probably **separation anxiety.**

🐕 **Try to identify the triggers for your dog's emotional upset.** Learn about **desensitization and counter-conditioning** exercises from a veterinarian or behaviorist to help ease his anxiety and correct the behavior. (See page 131, Change the Feelings, Change the Behavior.)

🐕 Accidents may be the result of cognitive dysfunction syndrome, or **senility. If your dog is elderly, offer him more opportunities to go outside and praise him lavishly for eliminating outdoors,** as you did when he was a pup. **Also, promptly clean soiled areas with enzymatic cleaners** (available at pet stores) to remove the odor that may attract him to the area again. (For more information see page 274.)

🐕 **If your dog dribbles urine in times of high excitement, help him by remaining calm yourself.** Try a more reserved greeting when you arrive home, or perhaps even ignore him for a few minutes. It will help him tone down a little, and minimize the chance of triggering the dribbling.

🐕 Dogs communicate their submissiveness to one another through body postures such as cowering, rolling over, and avoidance of eye contact. Sometimes they'll even urinate to make the point. **Never punish or reprimand your dog for submissive urination; it will only make matters** worse. To help him out, greet him in a less threatening manner by averting your gaze at first, and by kneeling down so that you're at his level. Puppies with a tendency to submissive urination usually outgrow it after the first year with sensitive, patient training.

🐾 **Be aware that subtle, negative facial expressions, a stern tone of voice, or one that shows frustration can be upsetting for a timid dog.** Remain calm and nonthreatening when you interact with him.

🐾 **Homeopathy** may help calm a fearful or nervous dog. Try **Aconite** for incontinence associated with fear or anxiety. **Staphysagria** may help an emotionally sensitive dog who is mortified at the slightest correction.

🐾 **Try calming herbs such as chamomile or valerian root** in lieu of stronger drug therapies.

🐾 **A combination of the flower remedies Cherry Plum, Chestnut Bud, Larch, and Pine** may help relieve emotional distress. In some cases, Rescue Remedy is helpful.

🐾 If your dog is male and unneutered, there's a good chance the house-soiling problem is related to **territorial marking. Neutering your dog can not only solve the problem, but also improve his health in other ways.** If you wait too long to consider this option the behavior may become a learned one, and more difficult to stop with neutering alone.

🐾 **Most important, be patient.** The problem may resolve itself as your dog matures and gains confidence. In the meantime, avoid triggering the behavior: Remain positive, calm, and nonthreatening. *Above all, avoid ANY form of punishment.*

Noise Phobias

If your dog responds to a loud noise such as a firecracker, the backfire of a car, or a thunderstorm by cowering, pacing, trembling, or attempting to escape, he likely suffers from a fear reaction that is so strong, it's actually considered a phobia.

What You Can Do:

🐾 During times when you anticipate he'll be exposed to loud noises, such as on the Fourth of July, offer him a **protected area** to go to where he may be shielded from the noise. This can be difficult, because dogs have such keen hearing, and you may live in a place where you can't remove him from the noise altogether. But a familiar, sheltered area may help him feel more secure.

🐾 The homeopathic remedy **Aconite** may help reduce anxiety or fearfulness. Give 30 minutes before an event that triggers the anxiety, if possible, and every 15 to 30 minutes as needed.

🐾 Try dosing him with the common herbal sedative **valerian root**, a few hours or a day before an anticipated event, even a predicted thunderstorm. Combine valerian with **melatonin** for a more potent effect. (See page 352 for dosing.)

🐾 Some people report success with **Flower Essences**, or Bach Flower Remedies. Consider Rock Rose before and after the event, Larch for fearful dogs that cower around noise, Mimulus for any fear, and Cherry Plum for those that become hysterical and try to escape.

🐾 **Seek help from a behaviorist** who can teach you about **desensitization** and **counterconditioning** techniques if home therapies aren't enough. (See page 131, Change the Feelings, Change the Behavior.)

Destructive Behaviors

Whether your dog is digging up the rose bed or chewing up your new carpet, destructive behaviors are a costly and infuriating problem for guardians. Realizing that digging and chewing are perfectly normal canine behaviors in the wild is little comfort when you are looking at a shredded family heirloom! And unfortunately, the tendency is to use punishment to discourage the behavior, usually with little success.

First, try to determine the motivation behind the destructive behavior—there are many possibilities. A dog may dig in the yard in search of a pesky gopher, or he may just be trying to create a cool area to rest. If the hole he's digging is near the fence, he may be trying to escape, especially if he is bored or, in the case of an unneutered male, picking up the scent of a dog in heat.

Chewing may occur because your dog just doesn't have enough outlets for all his energy. Or, some of the most destructive behaviors surface when a dog experiences separation anxiety from being confined or separated from family members.

What You Can Do:

- Provide adequate exercise and playtime, developing routines your dog can count on. A daily walk, a game of Frisbee, or a romp with his dog friends provides structure that is important. These outlets for energy may keep him more relaxed when you are away during the rest of the day.

- Provide appropriate toys and objects for chewing. When he focuses on an inappropriate item, replace it with a chew toy and offer generous praise for chewing the correct object. Your dog is intelligent and, with positive reinforcement, can quickly learn the rules.

- If you suspect your dog is exhibiting signs of separation anxiety, seek professional help. *Your dog is not destroying items to punish you;* he is suffering from a true anxiety disorder and is miserable when he resorts to demolishing his environment. He needs support from you, but it must be the right kind of support. Learning the proper desensitization and counterconditioning techniques, combined with your genuine concern and love, can successfully bring him back to a healthier state.

Aggression

Of all the potential behavioral problems that can develop in your dog, aggression is by far the most dangerous and worrisome. No one can say for certain what has caused the rise in reports of canine aggressiveness in recent years, but three factors seem to be human encouragement of aggressive behavior through breeding practices, impoverished early environment, and deliberate training.

There is more than one type of aggression in dogs. This can be confusing to guardians. For instance, when a friendly and obedient companion snarls only at the veterinarian's office, it's probably an example of **fear aggression.** Perhaps a previous trip to the vet involved a painful procedure. And while he may never show aggressiveness in his usual environment where he feels safe and secure, the smells, sounds, and sights of the veterinary hospital trigger his response.

Dominance aggression harkens back to the social dynamics of the wolf pack. Once your canine companion has decided he's top dog over you, following simple advice about obedience and training isn't always enough to break the aggressive pattern. A canine behavioral counselor or veterinary referral is your best bet if your dog is showing this form of aggression.

Predatory aggression is by far the most disconcerting because this largely instinctual behavior comes without a warning. In the wild, of course, wolves wouldn't think of warning their prey with growls or threats. When a domestic dog expresses his predatory instinct it's most often in a modified form—for exam-

change the feelings, change the behavior

The next time your dog does not behave the way you want him to, ask yourself, "How does he *feel* about what I'm asking him to do?" Animal behaviorists tell us that your dog may *want* to do what you ask, but his feelings (such as fear or anxiety about the situation) might prevent him from being able to do so.

Let's take Max, for example. Max knows the sit-stay command perfectly, but he's fearful of children. When asked to stay when a small child approaches, he gets up and walks away. If Max is punished or scolded for this, the next time a toddler approaches he might stay as commanded, but since he no longer feels able to avoid the child he may nip at her instead.

Animal behaviorists use techniques called **counterconditioning** and **desensitization** to help dogs overcome many behavioral problems. Counterconditioning simply means teaching your dog to associate something good with a situation he thought was only bad. If Max was to receive a treat every time he was in the presence of a small child, he might think, "How great it is that I get treats whenever kids are around!" and then no longer be afraid. This type of conditioning can be used to instill all kinds of good behavior.

If Max was so fearful of children that he couldn't even think of taking a treat when a little person was near, his behaviorist might begin by giving him the treat whenever a child was in sight, perhaps even in another room. The distance between the toddler and Max could be shortened slowly over time, so that Max would become less *sensitive* to the situation. This is called desensitization training.

Fear or anxiety can lead to phobias, destructive behavior, aggression, or other unwanted behavior. Learning to recognize and respect the importance of your dog's emotions, and learning from a knowledgeable source how to use the principles of counterconditioning and desensitization, are two things you can do to bring your dog's behavior into harmony with those around him.

ple, your retriever may chase the cat with no intent to harm her—but a dog bred for a strong predatory nature can kill a small child.

What You Can Do:

🐕 **Neuter your male dog.** Although this would not likely have any effect on fear-biting or predatory aggression, it can help most other aggressive behaviors.

🐕 **Confine and control your dog** (with a leash and preferably a head halter, or a muzzle if necessary) until you can seek appropriate help.

🐕 **Remove triggers for aggression,** if possible, until you understand how to proceed. This may mean avoiding handing out bones when your dog is with others or, if he's dominating human members of the family, not allowing him on the couch where he might demand control. Keep small children, animals, and unfamiliar people away from a dog with aggressive tendencies, even if he has never attacked or nipped at anyone before.

🐕 **Seek help from someone trained to deal with canine behavioral problems.** Your veterinarian is your best resource for connecting you with a professional expert. Getting advice from well-meaning people who do not fully understand the potential risks of living with an aggressive dog can be very dangerous.

🐕 **Consult a veterinary homeopath.** Homeopathic practitioners describe **rabies miasm** as a cause of aggression in dogs due to repeated use of rabies vaccination. While this concept is considered controversial, a homeopath may be able to offer help.

herbs for behavioral troubles: do they really work?

Like most vets, I have conventional antianxiety drugs and other behavior-modifying medications at my fingertips, but I try to use gentler, alternative therapies whenever possible. I'm often asked to suggest an herb for an anxiety problem or unwanted behavior, when what is really needed is training, some good behavioral counseling, and an understanding of how dogs react emotionally to their environment. Herbs, homeopathic remedies, and nutritional supplements can be used successfully, but rarely as the sole approach. Looking to herbs alone is not unlike looking for the quick-fix provided by harsher treatments. Valerian root or hops or chamomile may provide some calming effects, and you might find gingko helpful for a senile dog's troubles. An experienced homeopath may recommend a constitutional remedy to help bring ease and balance your dog's emotions and behavior. But if the external cause of the behavior is not addressed and corrected it's unlikely that any homeopathic remedy, herb, or supplement will be able to make the problem go away. A holistic approach sometimes means undertaking a greater commitment when it comes to working out behavioral problems. —*Katy*

cuts, bruises, bites, and stings

Into the life of every happy, healthy, adventurous dog, a few cuts, bruises, bites, and stings must fall. Most will be minor injuries that you can easily manage yourself. When a deep laceration or other serious injury occurs, your dog's vitality and healthy immune system will help her respond well to veterinary care for a speedy recovery. Soon she'll be bounding across the fields again, off on another joyful adventure.

Cuts and Punctures

FIRST AID

If the wound is severe:

- Your first priority is to control any profuse bleeding. Stay calm (breathe!) and apply a pressure wrap, if needed.

- Give a dose of **Phosphorus** or **Yunnan Pai Yao** from your Medicine Chest. If the bleeding does not subside within a few minutes, repeat the Phosphorus every 10 to 15 minutes while you're in transit to the vet.

- If your dog is in shock or the wound is severe, dose with **Rescue Remedy** or **Aconite** before heading off to the vet. Repeat every 15 minutes as needed.

For less severe wounds:

- Gently clean the cut or puncture wound with a mild soap and cool water; flush any debris or dirt away from the deeper tissue with a sterile saline solution, such as an eye wash preparation. If your dog has tangled with another dog or cat, or if the wound is visibly contaminated with debris, flush with water for 5 minutes, and use a dilute Betadine solution on the last flush.

- Apply a cool water compress or soft ice pack for a few minutes every hour *immediately following* the injury to minimize swelling. If the area is too sensitive to touch, apply the compress *around* the wound.

- Not all wounds need bandaging, but if there's a little gaping and the wound is on a limb: Rinse the area with **calendula-hypericum lotion** (see page 123), then soak a cotton ball with the lotion and apply it to the wound; cover with a small square of plastic wrap (like cellophane) before bandaging so the cotton ball doesn't dry out. If it does become dry, simply rewet it with more lotion without disrupting contact with the wound.

- Take care that your wrap doesn't impair circulation, and remove it after about 24 hours to inspect the wound. If there is no sign of infection and the tissue has begun to heal, rinse frequently with **calendula-hypericum lotion** throughout the day (every few hours would be ideal), until the wound is covered with dry tissue.

- If the skin is torn away, exposing muscle, tendons, or other tissue beneath, chances are you'll need veterinary help. Above all, avoid getting soap or hydrogen peroxide into the deeper areas of the wound, as they can destroy cells and delay healing. Rinse instead with **sterile saline** or sterile eyewash if you have it, or water, followed by **calendula-hypericum lotion**. Some vets have found that **honey** applied to wounds where the skin has been torn away speeds healing. Apply a generous coat, cover with a sterile bandage, and change daily.

NUTRITIONAL SUPPORT

- **Antioxidants** (such as vitamins A, C, and E, and others listed in the Materia Medica) twice daily until healing has occurred.

- **Bromelain** (pineapple extract) can help reduce swelling and inflammation.

HOMEOPATHY

- Give **Arnica** first—just 1 or 2 doses—to ease swelling and pain or bruising of damaged tissues.

- Follow with **Hypericum** to ease pain, promote healing, and help prevent infection.

- If the wound is a puncture, as from a splinter, thorn, or animal bite, give alternating doses of **Hypericum** and **Ledum**.

If the wound becomes infected or an abscess forms, choose one of the following:

- **Hepar** in a very low potency (such as 3X or 6X) to promote drainage, or a high potency to promote absorption.

- **Silicea** if there is a chance any foreign material remains in the wound.

- **Belladonna** if infection or abscess feels very hot and red, and your dog is agitated.

HERBS

- If there's a fair amount of initial bleeding or bruising, give **Yunnan Pai Yao** capsules by mouth twice daily for 5 days to enhance tissue healing after injury. You can empty the capsule and use the powder to make a flush for the wound as well, or pour the capsule directly onto mouth or tongue lacerations.

- Give **garlic** and **Oregon grape** orally for their antibacterial effects daily for 5 days.

- As an alternative to Betadine, you can flush the wound daily with a tea of **goldenseal, goldthread, yarrow**, or **echinacea** until you are sure that the risk of infection has passed—usually a few days. When the wound looks clean and there's no odor or discharge, stop the flushing and allow it to heal over. The tea can also be taken orally (1 to 3 dropperfuls, 3 times a day, mixed with food) to help the body combat bacteria.

- OR, flush with **calendula-hypericum lotion** during the first days, while the wound is open and moist. When it becomes dry, switch to **calendula-hypericum ointment** (see page 123) to keep the tissue soft as it heals.

- **Comfrey** or **plantain leaves** make good compresses to speed healing. To make a warm compress, pour boiling water over the leaves and steep for 15 minutes; dip a washcloth into the warm (not too hot) tea, and apply to the wound for 3 to 4 minutes, several times a day.

- **Calendula-hypericum ointment** or **aloe vera gel** are good choices once the wound is closed.

- If the wound becomes infected, or if an abscess forms, continue to apply **calendula-hypericum lotion**.

See your vet if the condition does not improve within 24 hours, or if swelling or pus is present.

OTHER

- If your dog tangled with wildlife, check to see that his rabies vaccination is up to date, and ask your veterinarian about a booster shot if it isn't.

- While tetanus is rare in dogs, it can occur with deep punctures, and is preventable with appropriate antibiotic therapy. Consult your veterinarian.

- A dog bite wound may look small on the skin surface, but the muscles and tissues underneath may have been macerated and severely damaged, leaving them prone to infection. If your dog seems depressed, is running a fever, has painful swelling beneath a puncture site, or the wound weeps a smelly discharge, check with your vet. A drain may need to be inserted beneath the skin to allow infected material to escape from the body.

- In the aftermath of a dog fight, have your veterinarian evaluate your dog, especially if he's lost a lot of blood, if there is any question about whether a bite entered a body cavity, or if there is a rapid deterioration in his condition.

Bruises

Whether your dog takes a body slam playing with another dog, or stumbles down an embankment while chasing butterflies, any blunt trauma or crushing of the tissues is likely to cause a bruise. The telltale color of skin bruising can be lost in his luxurious coat, but a developing bruise will cause tenderness and swelling. Part the hairs for a closer look.

FIRST AID

- Applying an **icepack** from the start will help slow bleeding beneath the tissue.

- After 12 to 24 hours, alternate between hot and cold applications to stimulate circulation.

HOMEOPATHY

- **Arnica**—Give immediately after the injury to minimize or prevent bruising. Also effective for older injuries.

- **Bellis**—For old bruises, or for those that are extremely painful.

HERBS

- **Yarrow**—Excellent for bruises. Use the dried or fresh leaves to make a poultice.

- **Chin Koo Tieh Shang Wan**—A popular Chinese formula that contains 20% pseudoginseng root with other herbs to help invigorate the circulation and move blood and toxins from damaged tissue, thus decreasing pain and swelling. Give 1 to 5 pills twice daily, depending on your dog's size, for up to 2 weeks following the injury. **Yunnan Pai Yao** is a good alternative.

Insect Bites and Stings

- Gently cleanse the area with a mild soap and water.

- Make a paste of baking soda or a poultice to apply immediately to the site.

NUTRITIONAL SUPPORT

- **Bromelain** helps with inflammation and edema; **quercetin**, a bioflavanoid, inhibits the release of histamine and other inflammatory chemicals in the body. Look for products that contain a combination of both, along with other bioflavanoids. Dose down from human dosage proportionately, according to your dog's size, and give twice daily for 2 to 3 days.

HOMEOPATHY

- **Apis** if swelling is hot, red, and very painful.

- **Ledum** if swelling is cool or hot (an effective non-animal alternative to Apis).

- If an abscess forms as a result of a bee sting, give **Hepar** or, if you think there may be a sting in the wound, **Silicea**. Consult your vet for all abscesses, or if your dog becomes lethargic.

HERBS

- Poultice with **calendula, chamomile, comfrey**, or **slippery elm**, or a grated potato.

- **Aloe vera gel** is soothing. If you've got the plant, simply break off a leaf, split it open, and squeeze the thick gel directly onto the area.

- Bee stings and insect bites can become infected. To help prevent infection, give your dog **garlic** and **Oregon grape** twice a day for 3 days. A clay poultice (bentonite clay powder mixed with alcohol-based grapeseed extract) is also useful.

OTHER

- If your dog is prone to allergy, be sure to keep **quercetin** on hand and dose at the first sign of a sting. If your dog is *highly* allergic, her face may swell to the degree that she's almost unrecognizable. Call your vet for advice, but in the meantime a human antihistamine (such as benadryl, at a dose 1/4 to 1/2 the human one, depending on size) will help stop the swelling and provide comfort.

Spider and Scorpion Bites

Spider and scorpion bites are painful, and a well-placed bite from species such as the black widow, brown recluse spider, or southwestern scorpion can be serious—in some cases, even lethal. Suspect a poisionous spider or scorpion bite when the area is very swollen and painful, red, black, purplish, or oozing. Your dog will likely be depressed or in pain.

It's always best to notify your veterinarian when any poisonous bite is suspected. The danger of shock, gangrene, and toxic bacterial infections mean professional care is required.

See pages 135-136, Insect Bites and Stings, for appropriate therapies.

Snakebites

Poisonous snakebites are even more serious than spider and scorpion bites, because the venom can rapidly alter blood pressure, clotting, heart rhythm and, in the case of coral snakes, breathing. Shock and collapse can occur immediately or hours after the bite. If you're unsure what bit your dog, and you're in rattlesnake country, you can sometimes recognize the telltale fang marks at the site of swelling, but failure to identify them doesn't rule out snakebite.

If a rattlesnake, coral snake, copperhead, or water moccasin bites your dog, do not wait until the onset of symptoms to seek help. Antivenin, to neutralize the toxins in your dog's body, should be given within the first few hours for best effect.

FIRST AID

- If you're in a remote area without vet support, try to stay calm and keep your dog calm. Talk to her in a soothing voice, don't let her move, and call for veterinary help as soon as possible. If you can, carry her, or send someone for help so that she doesn't have to walk or be jostled. Keep her warm to combat shock.

- Don't apply a tourniquet or freeze the area; there's no evidence that cutting at the site and sucking out the venom will help. Cool compresses *may* help, but if your dog seems uncomfortable when the area is touched, don't press the issue.

- Give homeopathic **Crotalus** or **Lachesis** immediately. Repeat dosage every 20 to 30 minutes until you arrive at the veterinary hospital.

NUTRITIONAL SUPPORT

- Give an **antioxidant blend** supplement for 2 weeks after the bite.

- **Quercetin** as an additional antioxidant.

- **Medicinal mushrooms** for long-term immune support while your dog is healing.

---

homeopathic first aid for snakebite

Rattlesnake bites are serious business. If you live in rattlesnake country, it makes good sense to have a supply of homeopathic Crotalus or Lachesis on hand. A tiny vial of one of these remedies tucked into your pocket or backpack anytime you're out hiking, or within easy reach in your Medicine Chest, can give you a head start on helping your dog recover from a potentially life-threatening encounter. While not a substitute for veterinary care, it allows you to begin treating your dog while you travel to the hospital. If you've hiked to a remote area without access to veterinary care, you'll be grateful you have a way to help her fight the effects of the venom.

- Crotalus atrox, Crotalus horridus, and Crotalus cascavelle are remedies made from the venom of three different species of rattlesnake. Try to determine which kind of rattlesnake is prevalent in your area and order the remedy made from the same species. If you're not sure, Crotalus horridus is a good choice. These remedies are generally not available in stores, but can be ordered through a homeopathic pharmacy.

- Lachesis is the remedy made from the bushmaster snake, but is widely used as a remedy for rattlesnake bite. It's easier to buy than Crotalus, since many stores that carry homeopathic remedies include Lachesis in their inventory.

- If neither Crotalus or Lachesis is available, give Ledum or, if your dog is very agitated, Belladonna. If you begin to see changes in the tissue around the bite, switch to Arsenicum.

—Jan

HOMEOPATHY

Crotalus or **Lachesis** (see page 137).

PREVENTION

With over a dozen species of poisonous snakes in the United States, the best preventive measure you can take for your dog is to know the habits and habitats of the poisonous species in your area.

Be alert whenever your dog is in snake country, and be aware that even a well-trained dog might not respond to your command to come when intrigued with (or confronted by) a rattler.

For the safety of your dog and the rest of your family, it's a good idea to keep brush piles away from the yard and home; woodpiles should be fenced off-limits, if possible.

Porcupine Encounters

Some dogs just can't resist these interesting creatures, and preventing an encounter will be best for all parties involved. If your dog does tangle with one, chances are

---

antivenin for snakebites: does your dog need it?

I live in rattlesnake country, and every year I tend to a dozen or more dogs who've had the misfortune of tangling with one of these creatures. Rattlesnakes aren't normally aggressive, but sometimes a dog will accidentally step on one, or just can't resist investigating the rattler's clear warning signal.

Antivenin is an expensive, and sometimes hard to obtain, neutralizer to the snake's venom, and it can increase your dog's chance of surviving a nasty bite. Many dogs survive rattlesnake bites without the use of antivenin, but deciding who *doesn't* need it is a difficult call to make! The amount of swelling and tissue reaction around the bite isn't a reliable indicator of how much venom entered your dog's system. Many variables affect survival: how deep or how close the bite is to an artery; your dog's activity level since the bite; and the time of year and age of the snake (the toxic substances are found in higher concentrations in young snakes and in all snakes during springtime). Your dog's overall health and constitution can make a difference, too.

Your vet is your *best resource* to help you decide whether administration of antivenin is warranted; signs that a hefty amount of venom has entered your dog's system can show up in blood tests, in how your dog's heart sounds, or in his blood pressure reading. The earlier the intervention, the better the chances that therapy will be helpful. Antivenin can't save all dogs, but with a serious bite, it's your dog's best chance.   —*Katy*

most of the quills will be imbedded in the face and neck, mouth, and front legs.

- Start with a dose of **Rescue Remedy** and **valerian** to help calm your dog.

- Give a dose of **Arnica** to help with the pain and tissue injury.

- A pair of pliers works best for removing the quills. Grasp the quill close to the skin, and try to pull out slowly in the direction the quill is pointing.

- Wash the punctures gently with a mild soap, and apply **calendula-hypericum lotion**.

- Give alternating doses of homeopathic **Hypericum** and **Ledum** for the puncture wounds, to promote healing and prevent infection.

- Be sure you thoroughly check your dog's mouth, including the tongue and roof of the mouth, for hidden quills. You may feel broken quills under the skin. Homeopathic **Silicea** may help his body expel the fragments. However, if the sites fester the quill fragments may need to be removed surgically.

- Consult your veterinarian about removing the quills under anesthesia if there are large numbers in the mouth and your dog is in too much pain to allow you to remove them (she may bite you unintentionally!) or if there are quills broken and imbedded near a joint (these can cause permanent lameness if not dealt with properly).

the eyes

Some of your most treasured moments with your dog are those quiet times when her eyes meet yours and light up in a smile. Or you see her looking peacefully across the meadow and notice the simple sweetness in her gaze. Her eyes tell you so much—about her mood, her desires, even her character. They're the windows to her soul and the doorway to her emotions. They also reflect her physical health, and are in need of your own watchful eye to be sure they sparkle for many years to come.

A dog's eyes are very similar to our own, but there are important differences that make those soft brown (or blue or amber) eyes uniquely canine. For example, a dog possesses a third eyelid, also called the **nictitans**, that can flick over the eyeball to protect it from injury whens she runs through the tall grass. Like ours, the surface of the eye, or **cornea**, is kept moist and clear of irritants and chemicals by the tears produced in the **lacrimal glands** of the eyelids. The inner lid, or **conjunctiva**, has a generous blood supply. It can become reddened, or blush, easily when toxins, heat stress, or infections are present in the body.

The inner structures of the canine eye work the same as the human eye. The **iris** functions like the diaphragm of a camera, dilating and constricting to let in more or less light. And the **lens**, suspended on tiny ligaments behind the iris, changes shape to bend light as it hits the back of the eye, helping the eyes focus. Your dog's **retina** has the same light receptors, the **rods** and **cones**, that you do, although you have more cones in your eyes and can therefore distinguish colors that your dog cannot. Dogs don't see only black and white, as was once thought; they can see many shades of gray. Studies indicate they can distinguish some colors that are very different from one another, such as green and purple, but red, orange, yellow, and green all look pretty much the same to your dog.

The ability to perceive vision depends on a healthy nervous system. The fibers of the **optic nerve** on the retina cross over behind the eye and enter the brain, where the information is processed.

MAINTAINING HEALTH

- Your dog's eyes are sensitive organs. Avoid the same dusty conditions or exposure to chemical irritants as you would for yourself. Use a sterile saline eye irrigating solution, readily available at grocery and drugstores, to wash out dust and debris. Make your own by mixing $1/2$ teaspoon of sea salt into a cup of boiled water. Be sure to cool it completely before use.

- Keep your dog's head inside the vehicle when travelling at high speeds. If your dog must have her face in the breeze, check into Doggles, available online. Surprisingly, some dogs are happy to tolerate this protective canine eyewear!

- Be aware of the hazards for a dog running at full speed in dry grass and brushy areas. Plant seeds, burrs, and foxtails are easily trapped behind your friend's third eyelid. Carefully remove foreign material with a pair of tweezers or forceps and a steady hand. Abrasions that may have occurred will usually heal on their own in a few days, if the foxtail is promptly removed.

does your dog need glasses?

Your dog's ability to focus isn't quite as good as your own. Objects closer than a foot or two are likely to be a little blurry. Some dogs are a tad farsighted, while others are more nearsighted. Genetics play a role, as dogs bred for working at a distance, like herders, and sporting breeds, such as the retrievers, are more likely to be farsighted. In other words, their distance vision might be good, but up close they'd need glasses.

Your dog's depth perception is best when she's looking straight ahead, whether she's following the neighbor's cat or a Frisbee in flight. If she sports a particularly long nose, it will cut down on her close-up vision by literally getting in the way. Your dog's eyesight at a distance might not be as sharp as yours, but with her tapetum, the special layer of cells overlying her retina, she's got the edge over you with better night vision.

- Many, *many* eye diseases are hereditary. Be aware that, while some breeders have their dogs' vision certified by a specialist, certain purebred dogs may be more prone to eye disease than their mixed breed cousins.

- Protect puppies from the claws of perturbed felines! You may need to supervise meetings between puppies and cats until a peaceful relationship is established. Innocent and inquisitive pups can lose their vision permanently by a well-placed claw in the eye.

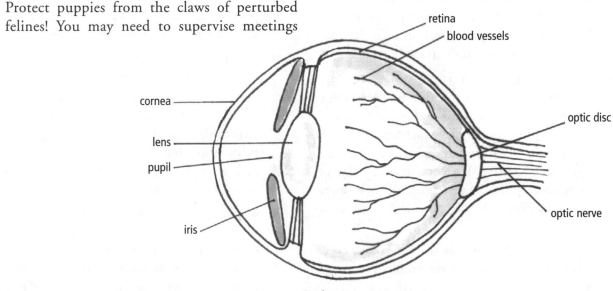

Canine eye anatomy

SIGNS OF TROUBLE

If you suspect a problem, consider this: many dogs have lost their sight because proper treatment was delayed by just a day—or even a few hours. Eye injuries should *always* be considered serious. Don't take chances with your dog's sight. Learn the signs of eye discomfort. In particular, when more than one sign is present, consult your vet to determine the extent of the injury.

Special instruments are needed to fully evaluate all of the structures of the eye. Dilation of the pupil will help your vet see the retina, optic nerve, and blood vessels, aiding in his diagnosis. More difficult eye problems or those needing specialized surgery can be referred to a veterinary ophthalmologist.

What To Look For:

- **Discharge.** Mucus or gray discharge is common with mild irritants or allergies. Yellow or green indicates infection.

- **Redness of inner lids.** The conjunctiva should be pink, but not red. Redness can indicate infection, heat stress, or toxins.

- **Redness of the eyeball.** Redness of the white part of the eyeball itself is more serious—it can mean glaucoma or a deeper infection or inflammation. Contact your veterinarian for an exam.

- **Cloudiness.** Look closely. Is the surface of the eye (the cornea) cloudy, or is it the lens, behind the colored iris? If the cornea is clouded over, you will not see the remaining structures of the eye, and a serious injury (chemical or physical) might have occurred. If accompanied by signs of discomfort, contact your veterinarian. For more about lens cloudiness, see page 143, Cataract or Not?

- **Difference in pupil size.** This can mean one eye is inflamed, or indicate a nerve problem or even a tumor.

signs of eye discomfort

Pawing at the eye

Rubbing the eye on the ground

Squinting

Tearing

Holding the eye closed in bright light

Red eyes accompanied by lethargy

- **Squinting.** Squinting *always* means discomfort. It can be associated with a scratch, a foreign body, infection, cornea injury, or an ulcer—anything that causes eye pain. Continual squinting for more than a day should be evaluated by your veterinarian.

- **Pawing at the eye.** This indicates itchiness or discomfort. Check for an obvious injury or foreign body. When accompanied by eyeball redness or heavy squinting, seek immediate veterinary support—glaucoma is a possibility, and prompt attention may save your dog's eyesight.

- **Photophobia.** It means, literally, "aversion to light." In practical terms, it simply means that your dog's eyes are painful or become irritated when exposed to bright light. There's a good chance she's suffering from this symptom if she is squinting, but only when she's in direct light, or if she seems to prefer to be in the darkened areas of your home.

- **Bulging of the eye.** When the eye bulges, it may mean an increase in pressure within the eyeball itself (glaucoma), or it may be a tumor or abscess behind the eye. ***Any delay in treatment for glaucoma will most assuredly mean loss of vision.***

cataract or not?

A cataract is a clouding of the eye's lens. Vision is dimmed in the early stages; when advanced, it leads to blindness. Diabetes is the most common cause of cataracts in dogs, but they may also be hereditary or a result of aging. Cataracts should not be confused with *nuclear sclerosis*, also called *lenticular sclerosis*, a normal part of canine aging that causes a bluish-gray tint or cloudiness in the lens. Nuclear sclerosis rarely disrupts a dog's sight, although it may make her close-up vision a bit blurry. How can you tell the difference? Shine a flashlight or other bright light into your dog's eyes from a distance, at night. If the cloudiness in the lens is due to nuclear sclerosis, the light will cause a flashback from the retina (like you often see when an animal appears in your car's headlights). A cataract, on the other hand, is dense enough that no light will get through to the retina, and little or no flashback will appear.

NUTRITIONAL SUPPORT

- **Vitamin A** is important for normal vision. **Vitamin E** and **zinc** are important in the proper function of vitamin A. Fresh vegetables or a natural multivitamin-mineral supplement are good choices for home prepared meals; pet foods usually add back *more* of these nutrients than your dog needs, but since freshness can vary, it won't hurt to supplement.

- Consider including **berries** that are purple or blue (such as huckleberries, black currants, or blueberries) in your dog's diet. The antioxidants and flavanoids in these berries are reported to help prevent cataracts. Try sprinkling dried berries over her meal. (Note: If your dog is diabetic, you may not want her to have the extra sugar contained in these fruits. You can substitute bilberry extract instead.)

- Although there aren't any statistics for dogs, **lutein**, found in dark, leafy greens such as kale and spinach, helped reduce the incidence of cataracts in human studies.

HOMEOPATHY

These remedies can be given orally.

Apis–Redness and swelling of the eyelids or conjunctiva; conjunctivitis.

Arnica–First remedy for any injury to the eye. Eases pain and speeds healing.

Euphrasia–A soothing remedy for irritation to the eye where there is profuse tearing; conjunctivitis.

Symphytum–An important remedy for any injury to the eye.

HERBS

- **Bilberry extract** contains high levels of important flavanoids, and very high anthocyanoside levels. If your dog has vision trouble, a degenerative eye disorder in the early stages, or has a hereditary predisposition to eye problems, this herb could be helpful. It's usually available as a 25% vaccinium or bilberry extract. **Give 20 to 100 mg 3 times daily, depending on size.**

- To make a **simple herbal eyewash** for eye irritations, superficial abrasions, or conjunctivitis, start with one of the following:
    - ½ teaspoon goldenseal, chamomile, or eyebright, **or**
    - 4 to 8 drops Oregon grape decoction or extract **or**
    - 4 drops calendula tincture and 4 drops hypericum tincture **or**
    - 3 crushed pills of Huang Lian Su Pian

    Pour 4 ounces of boiling water over one of the herbs above and steep until cool. Strain through an unbleached coffee filter. You can freeze in ice cube trays to use as needed or refrigerate for up to 4 days. *As with all medications, if the redness worsens or irritation develops, discontinue use.*

- If your dog has red eyes, tends to be hot, and has a red tongue, try the Chinese herbal **Long Dan Xie Gan Wan** for 2 to 3 weeks to rebalance her health.

- Herbs such as **Oregon grape** or **echinacea** support the immune system when your dog has conjunctivitis from bacterial infection. But keep in mind most cases of conjunctivitis in dogs are due to trauma, dirt, or allergies.

- **Eyebright** formulas for topical and oral use are sometimes helpful for conjunctivitis.

ACUPRESSURE

The point **Adjoining Valleys LI4** (see pages 98 and 103) is a Master Point, and very useful for eye pain. The illustration on page 145 shows the many local acupressure points that may soothe the eyes. With your dog seated in front of you, apply gentle pressure to a number of these points, gently massaging each one in a small circle. You'll know it's helping when your dog begins to relax.

Dry Eyes

Dry eyes result from a deficiency of tear film, leaving your dog's cornea dry, inflamed, and uncomfortable. Although it can be a temporary disorder associated with a drug reaction, infection, or injury, it's usually attributed to a malfunctioning immune system in older dogs. In any case, it can lead to painful ulcerations on the surface of the cornea. Dogs with dry eyes often have other immune system disturbances such as environmental allergies. If your vet has already diagnosed this problem, chances are he has measured your dog's tear production and prescribed cyclosporine eye drops to arrest the immunologic reaction in its tracks, but therapy is usually considered a lifelong proposition. Supportive care at home may not stop your dog from needing his eye drops, but you may find you need to use them less often. Once you've started home support, have your vet monitor your dog's tear production for improvement.

NUTRITIONAL SUPPORT

- Be sure your dog is getting the **vitamins A and E** he needs, as well as **zinc**. Choose a multivitamin-mineral supplement fortified with antioxidants and bioflavanoids.

Common acupressure points surrounding the eyes

- If you're home-cooking, Chinese food therapy suggests foods that are neutral and cooling (see pages 43-44) and that benefit the liver energy, such as poultry, bulgar wheat, green peas, and salad greens.

HOMEOPATHY

- **Aconite**—Useful primarily when the condition is temporary, where no tissue changes have occurred. Eyeball is red, cornea inflamed; photophobia.

- **Belladonna**—Eyeball is fiery red, cornea inflamed; photophobia and squinting; dog is agitated.

- **Conium**—Corneal inflammation, ulceration, opacity; conjunctivitis; photophobia.

- **Euphrasia**—Conjunctivitis with heavy discharge; corneal ulcers and opacity; photophobia.

- **Merc. cor.**—Corneal ulcers and inflammation; photophobia; pain worse at night; minimal discharge.

- **Silicea**—Use after tissue changes have occurred to help clear corneal opacity.

HERBS

- Even with your veterinarian's treatment, your dog's eyes may occasionally get red and inflamed. It's a perfect time for an **eyebright** tea compress. Make an infusion using a tea bag or the dry herb. Strain through cheesecloth or an unbleached coffee filter, and apply a moist compress using a gauze pad or soft clean cloth. A **chamomile** compress can be made in the same way, and is also soothing.

- In Traditional Chinese Medicine, dry, itchy, red eyes are associated with deficiency of the liver blood and yin fluid. Look for Chinese herbals with Rehmannia—especially Rehmannia Tea (or Ming Mu Di Huang Wan or Eye's Bright, Rehmannia Pills) and give orally for support.

ACUPRESSURE

Gently massage acupressure points around the eye each day. If time is short, concentrate on **Receiving Tears ST1** and **Eye's Bright BL1**.

- **Eye's Bright BL1**
- **Receiving Tears ST1**
- **Bamboo Leaf BL2**
- **Four White ST2**
- **Yang White GB14**
- **Yin Tang**

Points found elsewhere on the body (see illustration on page 103) include:

- **Three Yin Junction SP6**
- **Great Impact LIV3**
- **Adjoining Valleys LI4**
- **Foot Three Mile ST36**

HOLISTIC VETERINARY TREATMENTS

The eyes often provide a window to greater imbalances elsewhere in the body, and your holistic veterinarian is likely to use homeopathy, Traditional Chinese Medicine, herbs, or nutritional therapy to help restore health at a deeper level. Eye problems often correct themselves when the underlying imbalance is identified and healing is achieved. Every effort is made to reach a balance in health so that other problems, perhaps more serious than your dog's eye condition, won't surface later.

OTHER

Your vet may prescribe artificial tears or eye ointments to keep your dog's eyes well lubricated while she sleeps.

Blindness

Blindness can result from many causes. Unfortunately, the early symptoms of diseases such as glaucoma are often missed, and your dog may lose vision before a diagnosis is made. At the first sign of suspected vision problems, see your veterinarian. Glaucoma, cataracts, uveitis (inflammation of the internal eye) and retinal diseases can be the result of hereditary influences or environmental causes, and if one eye is blind, you'll want to do your best to keep the other one healthy. An ophthalmologist can prescribe drops that may prevent blindness in the good eye, and surgery to remove cataracts is now available. If your dog does become blind in both eyes, the way you support her at home can make all the difference in the world to her quality of life.

- **Fencing and gates.** These safety measures take on new importance when you have a dog with poor vision. Be sure to keep her in an enclosed area. If she wanders out of the yard into strange territory, it may be difficult for her to avoid danger or find her way home.

- **Leave things where they are.** Blind dogs have a remarkable sense of their surroundings and can bound through the house with glee, as long as things are left as they are. Rearranging the furniture or leaving objects in pathways can confuse and stress your blind friend.

- **Tickle her senses.** You'll find that a blind dog gets more joy than ever from the fresh scents in her environment. Watch how keen her hearing becomes. Notice how she responds to your touch. Offer games and activities to bring out her talents.

- **Don't make her an invalid!** All she really needs is a seeing-eye person, right? Don't relegate her to the back yard. Find safe places for romps and take her on plenty of leash walks to keep her physically fit and happy.

the ears

the next time your dog perks up his ears to a sound you can't hear, take a moment to appreciate the wonderful range his hearing affords—almost two full octaves above your own—while tiny ear muscles help him rotate, drop, and elevate his ears with precision and responsiveness. And what a wonderful form of communication it is, as your dog announces his feelings and intentions to friend or foe, just by the position of his ears.

Dog ears come in such variety! Two cartilages form the external ear; the larger of the two varies to let a Bloodhound's ears flop while a German Shepherd's stand erect. The smaller ear cartilage helps connect the ear to the skull, and while our ear canals dive horizontally inward, a dog's ear canal drops vertically first, then makes an L-shaped turn inward.

At the end of the ear canal is the eardrum, or **tympanum**. Beyond this membrane lies the bony middle ear, where the sound resonates. There's a tube that connects the middle ear to the back of the throat, and nerves connect the inner structures of the ear to the brain.

The inner lining of the ear canal is actually just skin. This is an important point, because what we think of as **ear** diseases in our dogs are really **skin** problems that start in the ear canal.

In Traditional Chinese Medicine, the ear is considered a meeting place of all the channels of qi flowing through the body. It's no wonder that some acupuncturists use *only* the acupuncture points mapped out on the ear for their treatments. With over two hundred points to choose from on each, the ear holds many ways to access the qi.

MAINTAINING HEALTH

- Keeping your dog's ears clean is important. A gentle swab of the outer canal (just the areas you can see) with witch hazel or calendula-hypericum lotion works well. Pet stores and veterinary clinics also carry nonchemical, vinegar-based products that are gentle and effective.

- Overzealous cleaning or plucking of hairs can lead to irritation, and any irritation in the canal can change a healthy environment to one that invites bacteria and yeast to multiply. At your annual check-up, ask your vet to demonstrate the best cleaning method for your dog's ears, since each dog has such different ear anatomy. One simple rule: ***Never to go deeper into the canal than you can see.*** Otherwise, you may actually push debris further into the canal and damage the eardrum.

- If you live where foxtails or dry grass is a problem, shaving the hairs around the base of the ear can help.

SIGNS OF TROUBLE

Ear diseases in dogs are caused by bacterial infections, right? Perhaps you've even given antibiotic drops, and the ear problem cleared up...until the next time. The truth is, bacteria is not the *cause* of most ear problems, but anything that changes the normal health of the ear canal can leave an opening for bacteria and yeast to grow and multiply. Remember, your dog's ear canal is lined with skin,

COMMON CAUSES OF EAR DISEASE

Foreign bodies, such as grass seeds (foxtails)

Fleas and flea allergy

Growths (benign and malignant)

Environmental allergies (grasses, pollens, dust mites)

Substances in foods (food allergy)

Ear mites (less frequent in dogs than in cats)

Inherited seborrhea (common in Spaniels)

Glandular problems, particularly an inactive thyroid gland

Yeast infections (often secondary to the above problems)

Chronic dampness and humidity (as from swimming)

Reactions to drugs

Irritation from excessive hair plucking or improper ear cleaning

Immune system disorders

Prolonged use of antibiotics (promotes yeast overgrowth)

and skin diseases are usually to blame for unhealthy and unhappy ears. So whenever you notice your dog has an ear discharge, odor, or sensitivity, don't stop at the ear. Look further. Evaluate your dog's skin and coat, check for parasites such as fleas, or trouble spots on the skin. (See page 165.) If your dog has a food allergy, you might see ear troubles coupled with mild gastrointestinal symptoms, such as belching, flatulence, and soft stools.

What to Look For:

- **Scratching.** Your dog will scratch his ears when they're itchy or uncomfortable.

- **Shaking the head.** If your dog shakes his head repeatedly, chances are his ear is painful or irritated, as from a foxtail or infection. If he's also holding one ear lower than the other, that's probably the ear that's bothering him the most.

- **A head tilt.** Tilting the head to one side means either a very painful ear or an inner ear problem, often from an infection that has extended across the eardrum. In either case, your dog needs a veterinary evaluation.

- **Repeatedly ducking or bobbing the head while swallowing** may indicate a foxtail in the ear, tonsil, or throat.

- **Sensitive to touch.** Infected ears are painful. If a foxtail or plant seed is lodged deep in the canal, your dog might cry out when the base of the ear is even gently touched. In some areas of the country, the *spinous ear tick* can cause great discomfort when it crawls into the canal and feeds there.

- **Redness.** Tiny blisters, redness, and swelling of the skin and tissues of the ear are all common symptoms associated with allergies, but redness can also result from yeast infections and constant scratching.

- **Offensive odor or discharge.** Strong odors usually mean infection. If a wet, soupy discharge is present, and the ear is painful to touch, it's time for a veterinary check-up.

- **Bloody discharge** from one or both ears. This indicates a serious disruption and your veterinarian should see your dog as soon as possible.

- **Heavy accumulation of wax.** A small amount of brown wax is normal for some dogs. Excessive brown wax is often seen with skin problems effecting the ears. Black, waxy discharge may mean yeast or ear mites. Ear mites can sometimes be seen with a magnifying glass as tiny, white, moving dots.

🐾 **Crusts or scabs on the tips of the ear.** Flies can cause irritation to the ear margins. Diseases that affect circulation to the ear tips cause a similar appearance.

What You Can Do:

🐾 If your dog suddenly starts showing signs of discomfort, and you suspect he may have a foxtail, examine his ears immediately to see if the pesky plant seed is visible. (Remember that if he's carrying one ear lower than the other, the dropped ear is most likely the site of the problem.)

🐾 If you spot a foxtail that's *easily within reach*, try to remove it before it travels further into the ear canal. Take care, though, not to reach deeper into the canal than you can see, or you'll risk pushing the foxtail toward the eardrum.

🐾 If you do remove a seed, but your dog continues to show signs of discomfort, there may be one or more additional foxtails lodged deeper in the canal. See your vet for assistance.

NUTRITIONAL SUPPORT

- A healthful diet will help to maintain healthy ears. Food allergies play a huge role in creating ear troubles, and the fewer chemicals and unnecessary additives in your dog's diet, the better. Veterinarians report far fewer allergic and other ear problems when dogs eat home-prepared meals.

- If you're feeding commercial foods, check the label for ingredients. Common offenders for allergy-related ear troubles are soy, dairy, wheat, beef, and fish. Changing to a naturally preserved diet can help when chemical sensitivities are suspected. Experiment with different brands that contain different ingredients. However, most commercial foods have so many ingredients in common that you're better off trying a homemade diet with rabbit or venison as a meat source or a vegetarian diet to see if the ear problems resolve.

- Since many ear problems are allergy related, nutritional support for allergies with supplements such as **fish oils** (for omega-3 fatty acids) and **antioxidants** will help.

HOMEOPATHY

- **Arsenicum** – Skin is dry and scaly or raw, with watery, offensive discharge.

- **Belladonna** – Severe pain that comes on suddenly; ear feels hot; skin is red and inflamed; dog is very agitated.

- **Calc. sulph.** – Watery, yellow discharge.

- **Hepar** – Ear infection, with foul-smelling pus.

- **Pulsatilla** – Infection with impaired hearing; thick discharge, with inflammation.

- **Sulphur** – Deafness due to infection and discharge; disease made worse by the suppression of symptoms.

HERBS

- If your dog has the unfortunate experience of a foxtail deep in the canal where you can't see it, you'll need your vet's help to remove it. Keep your dog comfortable with a little warm **olive oil** or **calendula-hypericum ointment** to soften the sharp points.

- Ear mites, though common in cats, are rare in dogs, but they sometimes appear when a dog or puppy enjoys sleeping with an infected cat friend. If you're sure ear mites are present, pyrethrum eardrops are probably the most effective over-the-counter product to use. Made from natural plant compounds, successful treatment means daily use for a week, rest for a week, then another week of treatment. Be sure to check your cat as well.

- Some people have had success with **olive oil** applied to the canals for mites. For added potency

medicating your dog's ears

1. Gently lift the earflap with one hand, and hold it up in a vertical position.

2. Squeeze or drop the medication into the canal while you continue to hold the earflap vertically, allowing the medication to run down into the horizontal portion of the canal.

3. Massage the ear at its base. If you hear a squishing sound, you'll know the medication successfully entered the deeper portion of the canal.

4. Release the ear, and let your dog shake his head. If you're using an ear cleaner, gently wipe away any debris before instilling any other drops.

5. Once all the medication has been applied, clean the outer part of the canal and the inside portion of the earflap with a small amount of witch hazel or rubbing alcohol.

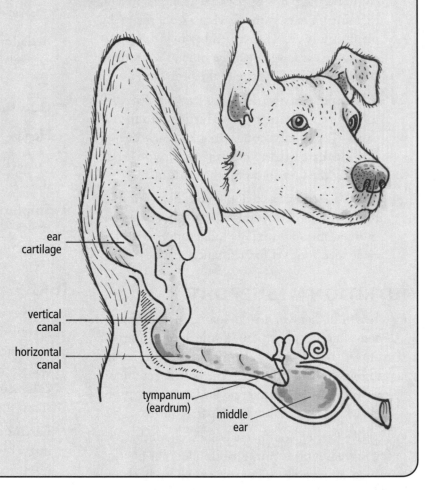

ear cartilage

vertical canal

horizontal canal

tympanum (eardrum)

middle ear

infuse 1 ounce of oil with 1 teaspoon of dried oregano or rosemary and let it sit for 2 days, then strain the oil to remove the herbs. The oil will smother the adult mites, but the eggs will hatch weeks later, making this approach a little frustrating. Having your veterinarian treat the mites is often the best choice, followed by your home care to promote healing of the tissues. Puncture a **vitamin E** capsule and sqeeze the vitamin into a little olive oil; add a few drops of **grapeseed extract**, then apply the mixture to the ear and massage gently. This soothes the ear and keeps bacteria from taking over. Another approach combines the oil infusions of **garlic** and **mullein flower** with vita-

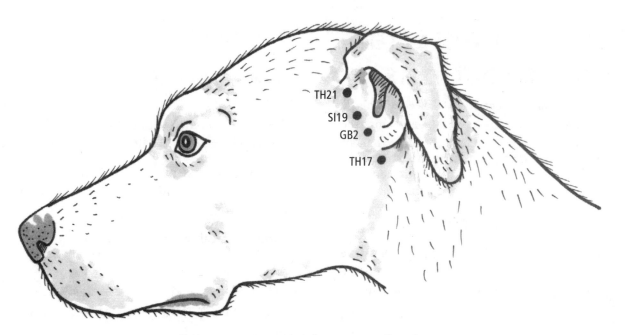

Common acupressure points surrounding the ear

min E oil and grapeseed extract to keep ear mites at bay if your dog is likely to be reexposed. Just swab a little of the salve onto the inner flap of the ear and drop a little into the canal.

- **Calendula-hypericum lotion** may be helpful in treating yeast infection. Apply a small amount well inside the ear and massage gently.

- If flies are irritating the margins of your dog's ears, **sage ointment** will help repel the flies while it softens the scabs and speeds healing. (See page 125.)

- People are often tempted to reach for immune-enhancing herbs when their dog has chronic ear troubles. This may not be wise if your dog's ear disease is a result of allergies, when the immune system is already overreacting.

ACUPRESSURE

The illustration above shows the location of common acupressure points around the ears that can help when your dog is uncomfortable. If he is very sore, it's best to wait until he can tolerate the light pressure.

- **Ear Gate TH21**
- **Palace of Hearing SI19**
- **Reunion of Hearing GB2**
- **Shielding Wind TH17**

Additional points on the front leg that help with pain, heat, and itching include:

- **Adjoining Valleys LI4**
- **Crooked Pond LI11**
- **Back Stream SI3**

OTHER

- **Dilute vinegar** is a simple treatment you can use routinely on your dog's ears. Since yeast tends to overgrow at the drop of a hat, 6 to 10 drops of the solution each week can keep prolific yeast at bay. Just mix apple cider or distilled white vinegar equally with spring water to get the dilution you need. Combine it with a few drops of rubbing alcohol to dry out ears after swimming.

Chronic Bacterial Ear Infections

Most chronic bacterial infections will need antibiotic therapy to prevent serious invasion of bacteria into the middle ear, and to decrease the chance of permanent scarring of the canal, which will leave the ear permanently obstructed.

NUTRITIONAL SUPPORT

- **Probiotics** will support your dog's system while on antibiotics, and may even help him fight the infection. **Digestive enzymes** are also helpful.

- If your dog is prescribed a trimethaprim-sulfa antibiotic (Primor, Tribrissen) be sure to supplement with **B vitamins**, particularly folic acid, during the course of therapy.

- If you suspect the bacterial infection is the result of a food allergy, try the **8-Week Food Allergy Trial** (see page 210). Don't expect immediate results; improvement can take 6 to 12 weeks.

- Give an **antioxidant blend** daily during a serious bout. Make sure it contains at least 100 IU of vitamin E.

HOMEOPATHY

As with any chronic illness, a remedy to treat chronic ear infection should be selected by considering the entire symptom picture. See guidelines in the Materia Medica.

- **Arsenicum** – Inner ear is raw and painful; thin, foul-smelling discharge.

- **Belladonna** – For palliative treatment of acute flare-up of pain with agitation, in chronic cases; swollen glands.

- **Hepar** – Foul-smelling discharge; impaired hearing.

- **Hydrastis** – Discharge of mucus and pus; deafness.

- **Mercurius** – Foul-smelling discharge, thick, yellow, bloody; worse at night.

- **Pulsatilla** – Hearing is impaired; discharge is thick, and may be foul-smelling or odorless; pain is worse at night.

- **Sulphur** – Deafness due to infection.

HERBS

- **Calundula-hypericum** lotion or ointment, applied to the ears.

- **Garlic** given orally to fight infection.

- **Oregon grape** or **echinacea**, given orally to support the immune system.

- **Mullein leaf** tea, added to meals.

- **Long Dan Xie Gan Wan** is a classic Chinese formula when ears are damp and hot. Give 1 to 3 pills 2 to 3 times daily for 2 weeks. Cut the dose in half if loose stools develop.

ACUPRESSURE

See illustration on page 151. The following points are also useful for ear infections:

- **Crooked Pool LI11** – To clear heat.
- **Shielding Wind TH17** – For many ear disorders.
- **Yin Mound Spring SP9** – To clear dampness.
- **Big Vertebra GV14** – For all infections.

OTHER

- **Checking thyroid function.** Hypothyroidism is a disorder that can lead to chronic skin and ear disease. When less than optimum levels of thyroid hormone are present, a number of body systems can be affected, and a chronic ear problem might be the first sign. If your dog is middle-aged or older, or purebred, discuss thyroid testing with your veterinarian. (See also The Glandular System beginning on page 235.)

- **Flower essences** may be a comfort to your dog when he is miserable from ear infections. Try Agrimony if he seems restless. Crab Apple is cleansing, and a good choice if your dog is hiding and withdrawn. Olive and Gentian are both helpful for a dog who is exhausted due to chronic illness.

Massage is a good way to help your dog feel more comfortable. Ear infections drain the energy, and the chronic pain causes tense muscles in the neck, jaw, and shoulders. A gentle upper-body massage, staying away from the painful ears, can relieve stress and help him relax until he is fully healed.

Chronic Yeast Infections

NUTRITIONAL SUPPORT

- Remove any sources of yeast in the diet, as well as sugar. Check labels on treats for corn syrup or other sources of sugar. Raw foods diets are sometimes helpful.

- Provide daily **antioxidant** support.

- Supplement daily with **probiotics**.

- Make sure you are managing any underlying allergies that can cause chronic yeast problems.

- 1 fish oil capsule per 10 to 15 pounds body weight daily can help with the itching and inflammation. If you suspect a fish allergy, substitute flax oil or hemp oil supplement.

HOMEOPATHY

- **Alumina** – Severe itching; scratches till it bleeds.

- **Candida albicans** – A remedy made from the yeast organism.

HERBS

- Rather than herbal ear drops, the **dilute vinegar** solution, described on page 151, is your best bet for yeast problems. It can also be used as a rinse.

- **Calendula-hypericum ointment** relieves itching and helps the body fight the infection.

ACUPRESSURE

See page 152, Chronic Bacterial Infections.

HOLISTIC VETERINARY TREATMENTS

Your holistic veterinarian will provide nutritional counseling and prescribe Chinese herbs or a homeopathic remedy based on your dog's constitution, and may also employ acupuncture and chiropractic manipulations to treat chronic ear infections. Some holistic practitioners find low-energy photon therapy to be a useful complement to other treatments. Your vet will likely explore in depth the possibility of allergies, and offer ways to rebalance your dog's immune system. Above all, the holistic approach will work toward reaching a level of health that *prevents* chronic ear troubles.

OTHER

- If your dog is prone to yeast infections, use live-culture plain yogurt for your regular ear-cleaning regimen. Soak a cotton ball in the whey that sits on the top of the yogurt, then gently squeeze some into the ear canal and pat around the inner earflap. Wipe out excess with a clean cotton ball.

- Flower essences (see page 153).

Acute Ear Infections

Sudden signs of ear discomfort can signal a foreign body or infection. Until you can see your vet, the following options will make your dog more comfortable:

- Warm olive oil will help moisten any sharp-pointed plant material that could be lodged in the canal.

- If your dog is not in too much pain, try a gentle **calendula tea** as a flush, or **calendula-hypericum lotion**.

- If the outer ear is red, swollen, or blistered, **aloe vera** is a soothing treatment.

- Apply acupressure at **Big Vertebrae GV14** and **Crooked Pool LI11**, and if your dog is not in too much pain, a gentle massage at **Wind Pond GB20** can help.

- If your dog is anxious, a little **valerian tincture** or **tea** every 3 to 4 hours can be calming.

WHAT TO EXPECT FROM YOUR VETERINARY VISIT

If your dog has ear problems, with pain and discharge, you'll want your veterinarian to do a thorough exam. This may mean she'll need to anesthetize your dog to fully visualize the vertical and horizontal canals without causing undue pain and stress. Fast your friend for 12 hours prior to your visit, just in case.

Expect your vet to take a thorough history from you. Remember, to get to the bottom of the problem, the more information she has the better. Bring along any eardrops or other prescriptions that you've used in the past.

She may also take a sample from the ear canal to examine under the microscope. This will help identify whether bacteria, yeast, or mites are present. If a serious or stubborn infection due to pseudomonas bacteria is suspect, a culture will help ensure the right antibiotic is used, and avoid prolonged exposure of your dog's system to an ineffective one. A thorough irrigation of the canal while your dog is sleeping can remove discharge and debris and make him feel more comfortable, but you'll need to know how to maintain the ears at home, too. If you're not sure, ask for a demonstration. Also ask her to discuss her views on the underlying disorder, or any dietary changes or further testing she might recommend. If she advises surgery (lateral ear resection), be sure you've explored all the options before you agree to this procedure. If your dog has allergies, failing to address them will make such a surgery worthless.

Once treatment is under way, it's often tempting to discontinue it after several days, particularly if your dog's symptoms disappear, and you're concerned about the use of antibiotics. This can be very dangerous, as it can allow the most resistant bacteria to take over. Continue treatment for the duration of the prescription, and be sure to keep the follow-up appointment. Examining the ear canals after treatment is the best way for your vet to evaluate the effectiveness of therapy. Even when it appears that all is well, an examination with an otoscope may reveal that the case hasn't fully responded to treatment.

the trouble with tank

Tank was just a puppy when I first met him. The German Shepherd had grown into a handsome gentleman, but by the time he was two years old he'd already been to the clinic a half dozen times, always for a red, itchy ear that didn't have any visible irritant in it—just a little extra wax. Still, Tank was miserable, and his guardian struggled diligently with this strapping boy to get the ear medications down into the canal where they belonged—not an easy task with Tank!

On one memorable visit, as I stood scratching my head after I again found nothing in the ear, I remembered that food allergies, which usually cause problems in *both* ears, could occasionally appear in only *one* ear. The rest of Tank's skin was fine, but that didn't rule out the possibility of an allergy. Tank had been eating a variety of commercial diets, but none contained fish. We decided to try him on a naturally preserved, high quality fish and potato diet—a more affordable alternative to a home-cooked plan for this ninety-pound chow hound! I knew that if my theory was correct, that Tank was allergic to one of the ingredients in his diet, and if we gave him a diet made from ingredients his system had not "seen" before, there was a good chance we would solve his ear troubles.

Tank's dad was pleased that I hadn't prescribed another difficult ear treatment, but after a few weeks he still wasn't sure if the new diet was helping. Tank's problem had been intermittent, and so it was hard to tell whether there was real improvement—*until* the day, that is, that the new diet ran out over a long weekend, and Tank ate a supermarket brand for a few days. The poor boy's ear turned red and angry almost overnight, but at least we'd found our answer.

I still see Tank now and then, but never for ear troubles! —*Katy*

the mouth

While you might think the main function of your dog's mouth is to shower you with licks and kisses, or alert you to the mail carrier's approach, it has other important functions, too. It's the entrance to her gastrointestinal and respiratory tracts. The saliva she secretes bathes the mouth cavity, helps her chew, and helps protect her oral membranes from bacterial invasion. And of course, her teeth and tongue help her to eat, groom, and defend herself.

The best way to become familiar with your dog's mouth is to get up close and take a good look, maybe while she's happily panting away after a brisk game of Frisbee. If she hasn't lost any, she'll have 42 teeth (pups have just 28). Her incisors, or front teeth, grasp and nibble. Her large canines are adapted for capturing prey, and her back teeth do the grinding and chewing.

MAINTAINING HEALTH

- **Feed a natural diet** to promote oral health and discourage tartar accumulation. Remove items from the diet that tend to stick to the teeth. Raw foods diets can be helpful.

- **Brush your dog's teeth regularly.** Brushing is the best way to combat nasty tartar and plaque build-up. This is especially important for small dogs, where the teeth tend to be crowded together. And since most small dogs aren't active chewers, the tartar tends to build up quickly.

- **Encourage recreational chewing.** There are many dental toys and chew devices to choose from. If your dog is an aggressive chewer, stay away from the hardest varieties that might bruise the gums or even break teeth. Raw knuckle bones are recommended by some holistic veterinarians, but never feed cooked bones. Rawhide chews, especially those made outside the United States, are often loaded with artificial coloring and preservatives that can cause rashes and allergic reactions on the inside of the mouth and lips. U.S.-made veterinary brands, coated with enzyme cleaners to clean the teeth, are the safest rawhides.

- **Beware of false advertising.** A variety of foods and treats are marketed with claims about whitening teeth, freshening breath, and reducing tartar. Most have no published data to support their claims, with the exception of products that carry the Veterinary Oral Health Council (VOHC) seal of approval. Feeding dry food does NOT keep teeth clean.

- **Clean tooth crowns**, or visable portions of the tooth, at home with an inexpensive dental scraper available in pet catalogs. Don't confuse this cosmetic cleaning with the deeper professional cleaning needed if your dog develops periodontal disease. The damaging bacteria hide out under the gumline, and general anesthesia is needed to thoroughly clean and scrape the area.

- While most dogs enter adulthood with healthy mouths, gum disease often begins to creep in after about 3 years of age. **A veterinary dental exam** is an important part of the annual checkup for middle age and older dogs.

- When your veterinarian detects a level of gum or tooth disease that requires deeper cleaning, extractions, or oral surgery, **don't delay** in following through with these procedures. Unattended gum disease can lead to infections in other organs such as the liver, kidney, and heart, and may even cause teeth to fall out if the condition becomes advanced. Abscessed teeth, another complication of untreated gum disease, are painful, and are an additional way for unwanted bacteria to invade your dog's system.

- **Keep your dog's immune system in top shape.** Gum disease causes bacteria to enter the bloodstream through the lymph system and the small blood vessels of the mouth. A healthy immune system can clear the bacteria from the blood, while a stressed immune system might allow bacteria to set up shop in various organs. An unbalanced immune system can also launch an exaggerated response to the bacteria of the mouth, and will destroy normal oral tissues.

SIGNS OF TROUBLE

To do a thorough oral examination, both you and your dog will need to be comfortable with the process. Start in puppyhood to make this task easier, and always remember to reward your friend for his cooperation.

When doing an oral exam, get a good look at the hidden areas, such as under the tongue, in the back of the throat by the tonsils, and in the pockets under your dog's lips. Share the discovery of any growths in the mouth or on the tongue with your veterinarian.

Prompt surgery and treatment of malignant tumors can save your dog's life.

Also note any missing or fractured teeth, and keep a record or have your veterinarian note it in the chart at your next visit. Progressive tooth loss is a sign that you need to reevaluate and upgrade your home care regimen.

What to Look For:

- **Red, inflamed gums.** Healthy gums are pink and smooth, not cobblestone in appearance, nor red or swollen.

- **Tartar build-up.** Your dog's teeth should be white, or just a little yellow. Mild plaque can be seen as a filmy yellowish build-up at the base of the teeth. Heavy tartar is thick and rock-hard. It can be brown, yellow, or even greenish in tint, and will break off in chunks when pried loose with your thumbnail.

- **Bad breath.** Inspect your dog's mouth thoroughly when you detect a new odor, even if she seems normal in every other way. Mouth odors can result from infected teeth or gums, foreign material such as bone splinters or plant debris, or even mouth tumors. Bad breath is also caused by problems not related to the mouth, including food allergies, digestive disturbances, kidney disease, and diabetes.

- **Draining tracts or facial swelling.** This suggests a more serious problem, such as a tooth root abscess or a tumor in the jaw or facial bones.

- **Pain when chewing.** Chewing should be a pleasant experience, so any pain or difficulty is abnormal. If your dog chews only on one side of her mouth, inspect the other side closely for problems.

- **Worn teeth.** When you see worn incisors, immediately check your friend for chronic skin irrita-

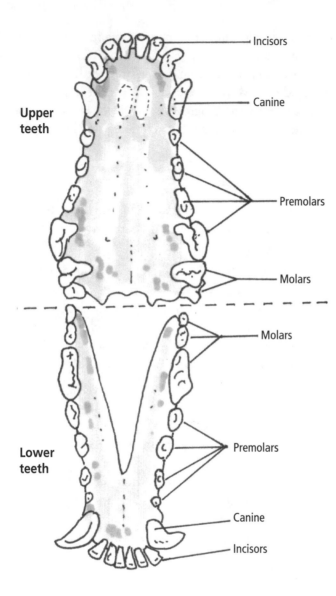

Upper teeth

Incisors

Canine

Premolars

Molars

Lower teeth

Molars

Premolars

Canine

Incisors

tions. The most common reason for a dog's front teeth to be worn is that she is constantly chewing on herself.

🐕 **Loose or infected teeth.** If your dog has multiple loose or infected teeth, it's a sure sign that an underlying health imbalance needs to be addressed.

🐕 **Gums that bleed easily when touched.** Your dog's gums might bleed a bit when she works on a favorite chew toy or knuckle bone, but when you gently probe her mouth and rub or brush the gums with a soft toothbrush, there should be no bleeding.

🐕 **A healthy tongue coating.** Your dog's digestive juices create that thin, white film on the back of her tongue. Traditional Chinese Medicine practitioners routinely use changes in the tongue coating to detect health imbalances.

NUTRITIONAL SUPPORT

• **Feed minimally processed whole foods**, including some raw foods, regularly. Raw carrots make a perfect crunchy snack, and the carotenes they contain help keep oral membranes healthy.

• A **raw knucklebone** can provide chewing exercise, and the saliva produced during chewing will help keep the mouth bacteria under control. While most holistic vets approve of this approach, veterinary dentists point out the real risk of tooth fractures, even from raw bones. Whatever you decide, don't let it be a "bone of contention" in multiple dog households! Provide a separate place in the house or yard for each dog to enjoy her chew treats.

• **Antioxidants**, especially **vitamins C and E**, help strengthen periodontal tissue. Vitamin E can be squeezed from the capsule directly onto mouth abrasions or small sores. Your friend can get vitamins A, B, and D from fresh foods, or they can be supplemented.

• **Probiotics** and **digestive enzymes** should be considered for dogs with chronic mouth troubles. It may take a month or two to see any improvement.

• **Zinc** helps keep oral tissue healthy, and a daily vitamin-mineral supplement should ensure your dog gets all she needs. Your veterinarian may carry a zinc-vitamin C gel that can be applied directly to your dog's gums to fight mouth bacteria.

- The proper levels of **calcium** and **phosphorus** are extremely important in keeping the bony portion of the tooth socket from deteriorating. Bone loss causes tooth loss, and if you're feeding a home-prepared diet, be sure you are supplementing adequately with these nutrients. (See pages 53-54.) Some commercial diets, especially those with meat and bone meal as ingredients, can be *too* high in calcium and phosphorus. Some nutritionists warn that excess levels contribute to tartar accumulation.

- The nutritional supplement **coenzyme Q10** (also called CoQ10) helps resolve gum disease and some periodontal problems in their early stages. Puncture the capsule and apply it directly to the gums, or give it with food. Give 10 to 60 mg a day, depending on your dog's size. For maximum benefit, give with a meal.

- **Chinese food therapy** calls for foods that cool the stomach, because the Stomach meridian carries qi through the mouth. In Traditional Chinese Medicine, the kidney essence must be strong for strong teeth and a healthy immune system, so foods to strengthen the kidney are important, too. Feed barley, millet, corn, and thoroughly cooked brown rice for grains. Eggs, lentils, string beans, and small chunks of raw beef are also options. Avoid processed dry foods altogether when teeth or gum problems exist. If that's not an option, choose "natural" brands, with highly digestible proteins and little fat, and supplement these with cooked grains.

- The nutritive value of **alfalfa** and super green foods, such as **spirulina**, is helpful for animals with poor digestion or those who have been on a poor diet.

HOMEOPATHY

- **Apis** – Gums are red and inflamed.
- **Arsenicum** – Gums bleed easily; bloody saliva.
- **Calc. fluor.** – Teeth are weak, brittle, decayed, loose.
- **Mercurius corrosivus** – Loose teeth, unhealthy gums, terrible breath.
- **Phosphorus** – Gums bleed easily.
- **Pyrogenium** – Infection with terrible odor.
- **Silicea** – A boil on the gum, or abscess at the root.

HERBS

- Chinese Watermelon Frost ointment has soothing qualities for treating mouth sores. Try this and Angelica 14 as an oral Chinese herbal formula for human use to relieve mouth pain.

- For fighting infections, use immune enhancers such as **goldenseal, echinacea, Oregon grape, green tea extract** or **garlic**.

- For long-term immune enhancement, use **medicinal mushrooms**.

ACUPRESSURE

- **Adjoining Valleys LI4** – A Master Point for the face and mouth.
- **Crooked Pool LI11** – Relieves heat and cools the mouth.
- **Great Stream K13** – Nourishes the yin, or cooling element.
- **Big Vertebra GV14** – Relieves heat conditions and strengthens the immune system.

OTHER

- **Try offering a mouth massage.** Sure, it sounds strange. But many dogs love to have their mouths and gums rubbed and massaged. Using light to moderate pressure, make circular motions around your dog's lips, jaw, chin, and cheeks. If she's com-

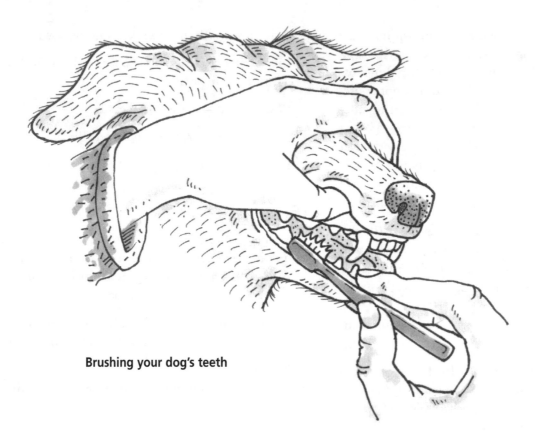

Brushing your dog's teeth

fortable with your fingers in her mouth, move on to the gums. It helps improve mouth circulation and tissue strength, and you might be surprised by how relaxed your dog will become!

- **Get by with a little help from your friends.** If you are having trouble brushing or examining your dog's mouth, ask a member of the staff at your veterinary clinic to show you some techniques. Review pages 16-17 for some helpful tips on brushing. If you're an Internet browser, go to www.pet-dental.com to download a quick movie on how to do a dental exam, or another on how to brush your dog's teeth.

- **Prepare for dental procedures.** Chapter 10, When Your Dog Is Seriously Ill, addresses a number of ways to support and comfort patients when sur-

gery is needed. The same recommendations will be helpful when your dog will be anesthetized to have her teeth cleaned, or for oral surgery.

Periodontal Disease

Periodontal disease is the term for inflammation or infection of the tissues that support the teeth. Bacteria hide effectively in the sticky plaque under the gumline, and years of accumulation create a snowball effect—damage from the bacteria create pockets where *more* bacteria can hide, and eventually the damage is severe enough to weaken the bone. Teeth fall out and, what is worse, bacteria get picked up in the bloodstream. All of a sudden what started out as bad breath has mushroomed into a major stress to the immune system, and potential for further health problems.

While careful attention to your dog's dental health will often prevent periodontal disease, sometimes life just sneaks up on us. Once a serious problem exists, you'll want to find ways to support your dog in addition to the dental procedures your veterinarian is likely to perform.

NUTRITIONAL SUPPORT

- **Home-prepared diets**, with raw foods included, can greatly improve your dog's oral health. If your dog is recovering from oral surgery, tofu is a soft, easy-to-chew protein source you can feed while the tissues are healing.

- **Vitamin supplements** (A, B complex, C, E) with **mineral support** (zinc and selenium) along with a bioflavanoid complex.

- **Lactoferrin** – An immune-modulating supplement derived from colostrum. When applied to your dog's gums, it works to slow the proliferation of mouth bacteria by binding the iron they need for growth. Mix the contents of a capsule with a little milk or cream and massage directly onto inflamed areas.

- **Coenzyme Q10** – a powerful antioxidant found in every cell of the body. Age and a stressed immune system can deplete your dog's own supply. Give 10 to 60 mg a day, depending on size, with food. Improvement is usually noticeable in just a few weeks. Discontinue if you see no improvement.

HOMEOPATHY

- **Carbo veg.** – Gums bleed easily, are retracted, infected; offensive breath.

- **Iodum** – Ulcers in the mouth; excessive salivation, with terrible odor; gums bleed easily.

- **Mercurius** – Gums are spongy and sore to the touch; teeth are loose; abscess at the root of the tooth; offensive breath.

- **Merc. cor.** – Gums are purple, swollen and infected; terrible odor.

- **Silicea** – Abscess at the root of the tooth; offensive breath; infected gums.

HERBS

- For immune enhancement, try **echinacea** for short-term use, **medicinal mushrooms** for long-term support.

- For their antioxidant properties, **grapeseed extract** or **green tea extract** following dental surgery.

- **Yunnan Pai Yao** helps control bleeding after major tooth extractions.

- Antibacterial herbs, **goldenseal, Oregon grape,** or **myrrh** for topical use on healing gums. Make a strong tea and add honey to improve taste.

- Human mouthwashes that contain the herb sanguineria, or bloodroot, applied topically in small amounts.

- **Non-alcohol aloe vera gels** are soothing, but should be used sparingly, as swallowing too much can cause intestinal upset.

ACUPRESSURE

- **Adjoining Valleys LI4**

- **Crooked Pool LI11**

- **Big Vertebra GV14**

- **Foot Three Mile ST36**

- **Inner Courtyard ST44**

HOLISTIC VETERINARY TREATMENTS

A holistic practitioner will likely see your dog's periodontal disease as a symptom of a more subtle health imbalance. The focus of treatment will be to build overall health, rather than just attacking the disease at hand. Whether through acupuncture, herbal formulas, glandulars, or homeopathic remedies, alternative therapies will be chosen for your dog's individual constitution. Acupuncture is an excellent way to address post-surgical pain should your dog need extractions or other oral surgery. Some holistic vets report benefit from photon light therapy for patients with periodontal disease and gingivitis.

OTHER

Daily brushing and a healthy diet are the mainstays of maintaining a healthy mouth, and should always be a part of home care whenever periodontal disease has occurred. However, if your home support is to be effective, it helps to start with clean, healthy tissues. A professional cleaning under general anesthesia is the best way to accomplish this.

the skin

the skin is considered the largest organ of the body. It is literally the barrier between your dog and her environment, protecting sensitive tissues from physical and chemical trauma. It's also a sensory organ, allowing her to perceive heat, cold, and the loving pressure of your touch. Together, the skin and coat help her regulate body temperature. The skin is intimately related to the other systems in the body, and it reflects the health of the internal organs and immune system.

If your dog is healthy, she has a whole new set of skin cells every twenty-two days to replace those that grow old and die. The rate of hair growth varies by breed and season, but there are always some hairs being lost as new ones come in, and most dogs shed their coat completely twice a year. Healthy skin is supple and elastic, and whether your dog's fur is wiry, silky, long, or short, when she's in peak condition her coat should be dense and shiny.

If you notice your dog seems to shed excessively during trips to the veterinary clinic, that's a stress response. When stress hormones are released, your dog literally lets go of all the hairs that are almost ready to be shed. In the wild, it actually makes her a bit more slippery when she's being pursued by a predator.

MAINTAINING HEALTH

- Healthy skin and coat require a full complement of nutrients, especially protein, vitamins, and fatty acids. Feeding **a wholesome diet** is the best way to ensure your dog's skin stays healthy and her coat is shiny. A poor diet is one of the most common causes of unhealthy skin.

- **Routine brushing** will keep your dog's coat free of plant burrs and debris. The brushing action also stimulates the release of protective oils.

- **Control fleas.** These creatures cause more skin disease than any other external factor, and will aggravate any preexisting skin problem. (See pages 21-25 for more information on flea prevention and control.)

- **Control skin infections.** Some dogs need regular shampooing to prevent skin infections, while others stay clean enough just playing in wet grass. Excessive bathing robs the skin of natural oils, and may actually encourage skin trouble. Develop a routine that's appropriate for your dog's particular skin type and condition.(See page 167, Shampoo Therapy.)

- **Avoid overvaccination.** Unnecessary stimulation of the immune system can create problems down the line.

- **Minimize your dog's exposure to chemicals.** The more **allergens**, or foreign proteins, that your dog encounters over a lifetime, the more likely her immune system will respond inappropriately with allergies. Any chemical that contacts your dog's skin has the potential to cause skin irritation.

the skin as a detoxifying organ

The skin lies between your dog and the rest of the world. But it's not exactly a suit of armor—it's porous, so material *can* pass through it. Substances are absorbed into her body through the skin, while others are released.

Much as the liver, bowels, and kidneys work to remove unwanted material from the body, the skin is a vehicle for releasing substances as well. Over time, the by-products of metabolism and the healing of injured tissues, chemical additives in food, and pollutants in the air and water all find their way into your dog's body. They may accumulate in tissues, or move through her via the blood and lymph systems. If those unwanted substances are not filtered out by the organs of the digestive tract or excretory system, they may accumulate. The overload causes skin eruptions, digestive upset, respiratory problems, or other debilitating diseases.

To feel, look, and function at her best, your dog needs to remove toxic materials from her body. One way is to pass them through her skin. When an excess of toxic materials is released through the skin, it may cause an eruption of one kind or another, which carries a mixed message of sorts for you. While it's good to know that your dog's body is cleansing itself of unwanted material, it suggests a need to consider why her system is facing an overload in the first place. It's also a sign the other members of her "toxic removal system"—the liver, bowels, kidneys, and blood—could use a little extra help.

Evaluate your dog's diet, environment, and recent health history. Has she been exposed to food additives, chemicals, or pollutants that could be avoided? Is she dealing with a major illness, injury, or emotional stress and in need of nutritional or herbal support? Modify her environment and lifestyle as needed, then see pages 168-169 for ideas to help your dog to **detoxify**, and rid her body of the by-products of life. —*Jan*

SIGNS OF TROUBLE

If your dog is itchy, uncomfortable, and chewing at herself all night on the bed next to you, she's got a skin problem. Allergies are one of the most commonly diagnosed itchy skin problems in dogs. When uncontrolled, allergies lead to bacterial or yeast infections in the skin, and chronic odors and painful skin sores. Some skin diseases are subtle, and if there's no discomfort involved, they may even go unnoticed. The small patches of hair loss seen in the early stages of Demodex mange look insignificant. An advanced case of Demodex, on the other hand, can leave a dog hairless and miserable.

What to Look For:

- **Skin lesions:** Look for tiny red bumps, small pustules (these look like white-headed pimples), and tiny black dots at the base of hairs. Red bumps are common with allergies, pustules often suggest bacterial invasion, and the tiny black dots come from plugged hair follicles.

- **Skin odors:** In Traditional Chinese Medicine, odors are important indicators of health imbalances. Even if the skin and coat look fine, if you notice a strong odor, especially soon after a bath, the skin or internal environment is not in a healthy balance. If you're using homeopathic medicine, the odor may be a clue to finding the remedy that would be most helpful.

- **Hair loss:** Loss of hair is due to destruction at the level of the hair follicle (as in the case of Demodex mange) but it may also occur because a dog is persistently chewing and biting at the skin. Some dogs are "closet" chewers—they'll hide this behavior from you, especially if they've learned you don't approve. Check the front teeth (incisors) for heavy wear. Chronic chewers can wear these teeth right down to the gumline.

- **Patterns of diseased skin:** If the areas that are most raw and irritated are the feet, armpit, and groin, this suggests an inhaled allergy problem. If the rump, base of the tail, and back of the legs are a mess, a fleabite hypersensitivity is likely. And if the only area of trouble is the hairless, soft skin of the abdomen, suspect an irritant (such as a plant, carpet cleaner, etc.) that may be causing a contact dermatitis on this sensitive region.

- **Blackened or thickened skin:** This is *always* an indication that a skin condition has become chronic. The blackened areas come from a change in pigment due to continuous irritation. They may be permanent, even after the problems are controlled.

There's often a sense of urgency when your dog is suffering from skin troubles. You want her to be comfortable, and you want results in a hurry—for her sake. The conventional medical response is to relieve the symptoms, but this can sometimes interfere with a more complete healing for your dog. If cortisone or antihistamines relieve her itch, you may be satisfied and look no further, thus missing the possibility that a change in her diet could prevent the need for these medications.

There are ways to assist the body in healing itself by using gentle alternative therapies, but natural healing often takes time. This is a dilemma for holistic healers. The ongoing symptoms of skin disease can create enough discomfort for your dog (and hence, for you!) that you may be tempted to abandon slower-working natural therapies in favor of a quick-fix approach.

Take heart. It's possible to address your dog's immediate symptoms *and* pursue a holistic approach to heal the problem at its source. Get in the preventive mode and look for deep-seated internal or elusive external triggers to skin disease, while you support overall health and maximize your dog's comfort. And, if need be, use a combination of conventional and alternative therapies when troubles arise.

Don't be afraid to try multiple approaches. Not all therapies work well on each dog, mainly because deficiencies and underlying health imbalances vary tremendously. When you find something that works for you and your friend, stick with it. When things aren't working, consult your veterinarian or a veterinary dermatologist.

NUTRITIONAL SUPPORT

- Many guardians have found that a **change to a home-prepared diet or a raw food diet** completely eliminated their dog's long-term skin troubles. This solution can produce lasting results within a few days, weeks, or months.

- A dietary sensitivity can exacerbate any skin problem. By feeding a **variety of foods**, or rotating between up to 10 or 12 different quality brands, you are less likely to see dietary allergies. Once a dietary sensitivity is suspected, try the **8-Week Food Allergy Trial** (see page 210). The next best option is a naturally preserved veterinary formula designed for allergies.

- Some dogs with skin disease, especially those with hair loss or crustiness on the skin, show improvement with **enzyme supplements**.

- Adding **fatty acid supplements** to the diet is excellent for all inflammatory skin conditions. Fish oils are best for supplying omega-3 fatty acids, but if your dog is allergic to fish, try flax. Be sure to allow at least 2 months to see improvement. If a dry kibble is the basis of your dog's diet, add corn, olive, or sunflower oil (1 teaspoon per 10 pounds of body weight) to replace omega-6 fatty acids that may be lost in processing and storage.

- **Antioxidants** are indicated whenever there is skin inflammation or allergy. Give vitamin E (200 to 400 IU, depending on size of the dog).

- Seasonal hair loss, particularly around the flank area, can be treated with **melatonin** supplements, at $1/4$ to $1/2$ the human dose. Boxers and Dachshunds who have sparse hair year round may also respond.

- **Vitamin A** suppresses overactive skin glands (called sebacaceous glands), a disorder that leads to crusts and scales and smelly skin in some Cocker Spaniels, Labrador Retrievers, Miniature Schnauzers, and Shar-Peis.

- **Zinc** is involved in several immune mechanisms and can also benefit some skin conditions, especially those with heavy crusting of the footpads, elbows, heel area, and face. Breeds likely to show signs are Siberian Huskies, Alaskan Malamutes, Doberman Pinschers, and Great Danes.

HOMEOPATHY

- **Arsenicum** – Dry, rough, scaly patches; hives; swelling; itching.

- **Calc. sulph.** – Infections or eruptions that produce thick, yellow discharge.

- **Hepar** – Abscesses or infections.

- **Ledum** – Itching around the feet and lower limbs.

- **Rhus tox.** – Tiny red blisters, intense itching; hives; eruptions may become infected.

- **Silicea** – Abscesses; eruptions that itch, may be worse during the daytime; skin problems that are worse after vaccination.

- **Sulphur** – Dry, scaly patches, easily becomes infected; intense itching.

- **Thuja** – Polyps, warts, ulcers; skin eruptions that may be caused by vaccination.

- **Urtica urens** – Hot spots; hives.

HERBS

Topical applications:

- **Aloe vera** – For burns, abrasions, hot spots.

- **Calendula** – Antiinflammatory, antibacterial, antifungal.

- **Calendula-hypericum lotion** – To dry out wet, oozing eruptions or to cool a hot spot.

- **Calendula-hypericum ointment** – To soften crusts or moisten and soothe dry, scaly patches.

- **Green or black tea** – As a compress, to dry out moist sores.

- **Witch hazel** – Also a good astringent.

Single herbs used internally:

- **Astragalus** – Gentle immune support and anti-inflammatory.

- **Evening primrose oil** – A good source of fatty acids.

- **Licorice** – Antiinflammatory.

Chinese herbal formulas:

- **Lien Chiao Pai Tu Pien** – For itchy rashes, redness; also for hives.

- **Long Dan Xie Gan Wan** – For itchy, moist eruptions, especially in the groin.

SHAMPOO THERAPY

This may be the most overlooked natural therapy for dogs with skin disease. Shampooing removes dander, loose hair, bacteria, yeast, and debris that might be causing allergies. Some dogs need shampooing to remove the dead skin cells that sit on the surface of the skin and provide a breeding ground for bacteria and yeast. If your dog is prone to skin infections, regular bathing may decrease or eliminate the need for oral antibiotics or antifungal medication. With the right shampoo and rinse, you can moisturize and soft-

---

internal cleanse for chronic skin problems

Combine:

2 parts **burdock root**

1 part **dandelion** (equal portions of root and leaf)

1 part **red clover** (flowering tops)

1 part **garlic** powder

(Use organic ingredients if possible.)

Add 1 tablespoon of the mixture per 40 pounds body weight to each meal.

At serving time add **cleavers** - ⅕ teaspoon glycerine-based tincture or 2 tablespoons strong tea per 40 pounds body weight.

Flaxseed oil, evening primrose oil, borage seed oil, fish oil, or a prepared multi-essential fatty acid supplement should be fed concurrently with this formula.

Adapted from Gregory Tilford, herbalist, 1999 AHVMA Annual Conference Proceedings

---

en dry skin to reduce itchiness. If your dog is extremely allergic, look for "hypoallergenic" on the label to avoid making his discomfort more severe.

Use the table on page 170 when you're shopping for shampoo and avoid products made with artificial colors, fragrances, and other chemicals. While the occasional bath with a human shampoo is fine, it's not the best choice for routine use. The pH of a dog's skin is more alkaline than ours, and routine bathing with human shampoos can dry the skin.

Start with weekly baths until the symptoms are under control, then gradually lengthen the time between bathing until you find a routine that works best

cleansing the body from the inside out

Skin eruptions, hot spots, or other irritation often point to an overload of toxins. Your friend may benefit from an internal cleanse, which involves stimulating and supporting one or more of the body's cleansing organs: the liver, the bowels, the kidneys, and the blood. This can be done through the careful use of nutrition, homeopathy, herbs, and bodywork.

Nutrition. One of the most common ways to cleanse the body is through a fast. Avoiding food for 24 hours or more gives the digestive tract a break. When the intestines are allowed to become empty of food, the mucus and debris that otherwise build up on the intestinal lining begins to slough off and pass out of the body through the bowel. As a result, the intestines do a better job of absorbing nutrients.

While withholding meals is probably not an idea your dog would suggest on her own, if you join her in her fast—and reap the benefits as well—you may find that her eyes brighten and her energy increases before you even complete the fast. A small bowl of broth 2 or 3 times a day will prevent her from feeling deprived. One day without meals is probably as long a period as you should attempt without professional guidance.

Homeopathy. These gentle medicines promote cleansing in part by mirroring the toxic substances the body has absorbed, and by awakening the energy of certain organs to help remove the unwanted materials. **Arsenicum album, Mercurius, Silicea, Sulphur,** and **Thuja** are among many

for your dog's skin. If you're shampooing frequently, follow up with a leave-on moisturizing rinse. For itchy dogs, an oatmeal rinse after the bath works wonders.

OTHER

Evaluate your dog's **emotional state**. Dogs will sometimes lick and chew, not because of skin disease, but because they are anxious, bored, lonely, or stressed. Many people like to use **Flower Essences** along with other alternative therapies when dealing with a chronic skin problem.

- **Crab Apple** – For unhealthy coats, dermatitis, and strong odor; for dogs who overgroom and aggravate their skin lesions.

- **Chestnut Bud** – For dogs who chew on themselves, even when the skin looks healthy.

- **Walnut** – For dogs who are highly sensitive to environmental toxins or grasses and pollens.

- **Agrimony** – For dogs who just can't seem to get comfortable, who are sensitive to flea bites, and who tend to be emotionally sensitive.

homeopathic remedies that support the action of the organs that remove waste from the body. It's no accident that the symptoms associated with them resemble the symptoms of an individual who is having skin eruptions and intestinal difficulties, as are common when the liver, kidneys, and digestive tract are not functioning at their best.

Herbs. Herbal teas, tinctures, and powders can help you cleanse all the body's cleansing organs. **Burdock** cleanses the blood, stimulates liver and gall bladder function, and supports the kidneys. **Milk thistle** is known for liver support, while **dandelion root** supports liver and kidney function, and **red clover** helps purify the blood. **Ginger** cleanses the colon, and **cleavers** acts as a gentle diuretic and stimulates the lymphatic system to carry waste material out of the body.

Bodywork. A gentle, healing massage is one of the most rewarding ways to stimulate removal of waste from the body. As you move your hands over your dog's fur, manipulating the muscles and stimulating circulation in the lymph system and the skin, you encourage the movement of fluids that is an important part of the cleansing process.

When you help the body mobilize *all* of its cleansing mechanisms, you may find that the skin is no longer burdened by a build-up of waste material that can only be released through unsightly, uncomfortable, and unhealthy skin eruptions. When the liver, kidneys, and intestines are functioning optimally, your dog's eyes will be bright, her coat will shine, and her skin will be clear. —*Jan*

Hot Spots

"Hot spot" is the familiar term for a moist dermatitis that erupts after trauma to the skin. It can become a weeping, painful, infected mess. The edges are often red with an oozing center, sometimes covered with a yellow plaque. Hot spots can spread rapidly, and though they occur on any part of the body, the common locations are the side of the face, top of the neck, rump, or base of the tail. The initial trauma to the skin is often the result of itching and scratching due to fleas, tick bites, an abrasion, or perhaps an underlying hypersensitivity or allergy. Golden Retrievers, Saint Bernards, and Rottweilers seem particularly susceptible.

- If your dog has long hair, clip away the hair on and around the hot spot. Gently cleanse the area with a hypoallergenic or soap-free cleanser. Rinse with cool water.

SHAMPOOS: INGREDIENTS TO LOOK FOR

Problem:	Ingredients to look for:	Comments:
Itchy skin and allergic skin disease	Oatmeal	Soothes itchy skin.
	Aloe vera	Reduces inflammation.
Dry skin	Lactic acid, carbolic acid, urea	Naturally occurring moisturizers.
	Olive oil, vegetable oil, coconut oil, lanolin	Emollients to soothe dry skin.
	Biotin, pantothenic acid, essential fatty acids	Skin nutrients; may also thicken the coat.
Chronic bacterial skin infections	Benzoyl peroxide	Although not truly a natural product, its use can help avoid the need for oral antibiotics. It penetrates hair follicles and skin glands. Can be drying or cause irritation.
	Aloe vera	Has antibacterial properties, but is not as good for deep infections.
	Tea tree oil	Use with care—may cause irritation for sensitive dogs. Use only in a diluted form.
Chronic yeast and fungal infections	Acetic acid, boric acid	Also good for bacterial problems.
	Sulfur	Works well, but strong odor is not tolerated by some people.
	Selenium	An ingredient in Selsun Blue human shampoo.
	Vinegar	When diluted, makes a good after bath rinse for yeast infection.
For external parasites	Sulfur	Too drying for frequent use.
	Pyrethrins	Natural plant compound; effective against fleas.

- Frequent application of a compress or lotion is very important, and may need to be applied every few hours initially, then 3 to 4 times a day. Apply compresses for 3 to 5 minutes, or longer if the condition is severe.

- For recurrent hot spots, be sure fleas are under control, and evaluate your dog's diet for possible allergies.

NUTRITIONAL SUPPORT

- If your dog is of a breed that is particularly susceptible to hot spots (Golden Retriever, Saint Bernard, or Rottweiler) a vitamin A supplement (no more than 5,000 IU a day in a large dog) and additional omega-3 fatty acids may help prevent recurrences.

HOMEOPATHY

If hot spots are acute, try the following remedies, in low potency:

- **Belladonna** – Sudden onset; skin is very hot and red; dog is agitated.

- **Calendula** – Soothes heat; promotes healing.

- **Sulphur** – Coat tends to be rough and dirty.

- **Urtica urens** – Itching is intense.

If condition does not improve within 3 or 4 days, or if the condition is chronic, discontinue remedy and consult an experienced homeopath.

HERBAL SUPPORT

- **Calendula-hypericum lotion.** Apply with a cottonball as often as 5 times a day or every 30 minutes, as needed. If your dog is too sensitive to be touched in the affected area, try putting the lotion in a mist sprayer for a more gentle application.

- **Oatmeal soaks.** If your dog is constantly scratching at the hot spot, an oatmeal soak is an excellent way to break the itch cycle and provide relief. Simply stuff a cotton sock with oatmeal and soak it in hot water until a gooey emulsion forms. Let it cool, and lay it gently over the area.

- **Tea bag soaks:** Green and black tea have astringent properties that will help dry the hot spot. Apply a soaked tea bag directly to the skin, or make a compress out of a strong tea and a clean cloth. Especially helpful for those weepy, watery hot spots.

- **Aloe vera gel.** See page 172, Burns.

Advanced or Deep Hot Spots

When a yellow discharge develops at the center of the hot spot, the edges are red and inflamed, the area affected is growing larger, and your dog's discomfort is worse, chances are bacteria (usually the staph type) have taken hold. Sometimes hot spots emerge from a deeper, internal bacterial condition (called deep pyoderma), which is more serious.

- **Immune support.** With deep or advanced hot spots, support the immune system to help combat the infection. Good choices are echinacea, astragalus, or medicinal mushrooms. Add antioxidants, including vitamins C and E and grapeseed extract. Probiotics added to each meal will also help.

- **Burrow's solution.** A sulfur-based astringent that helps dry the hot spot, soothe the skin, and fight bacteria.

- **Check the diet.** Always reevaluate the food you're feeding if your dog has any recurrent or deep-seated skin problem.

- **Stay on top of the situation.** These infections can get out of hand quickly. Treat often, keep the hair next to the area clipped, and if your dog is miserable, feverish, or the hot spot continues to spread, seek veterinary support. Antibiotics are sometimes needed to get the deep staph infection under control.

HOLISTIC VETERINARY SUPPORT

If home treatment is not effective, consider an evaluation by a Traditional Chinese Medical practitioner or homeopath to address deeper underlying imbalances.

Burns

Burns that involve a large area of skin should receive immediate veterinary attention to control pain and prevent serious infection from invading the body. Smaller burns can be treated at home.

NUTRITIONAL SUPPORT

- For larger burns, add extra protein and energy (calories) to the diet to promote healing.

- If you aren't already giving a **multivitamin supplement**, do so during the burn's healing phase, along with an **antioxidant** blend.

- Give **coenzyme Q10, vitamin E** to support healing.

HOMEOPATHY

If burn is severe, use **Arnica** as a first remedy to ease inflammation and tissue damage. Follow with **Hypericum** to quiet nerve endings, promote healing, and help prevent infection. **Calendula** will help speed the regrowth of skin.

HERBS

- **Aloe vera** is your primary treatment for most burns. Consider growing your own plant for quick access to this excellent home first-aid cure. Simply cut a fresh leaf and spoon out the gooey center; apply directly to the burn twice a day until healed. The fresh gel is best, but if you can't locate a plant, use an alcohol-free commercial product that is at least 99% gel.

- **Calendula-hypericum lotion** is also an excellent, cooling treatment for burns. Apply the lotion 3 to 5 times a day or as often as every 30 minutes to ease the pain, prevent infection, and promote healing. If the injury is in an area that can be bandaged, saturate a cottonball with the lotion, place it on the wound, and leave it in place for 24 hours, re-wetting the cotton as needed without disturbing contact. If the tissue becomes dry and crusty, switch to **calendula-hypericum ointment.**

- **Echinacea, astragalus**, or **medicinal mushrooms.** If a large area of skin is involved, add one of these to the diet for immune support.

- **Sage ointment** soothes the skin and promotes healing. Also discourages flies that might otherwise bother the wound.

Flea Infestations

If your dog is infested with fleas, start by evaluating her overall health. Healthy dogs who aren't stressed or living in overcrowded conditions don't develop severe infestations in most parts of the country, so if you're battling a batallion of fleas, ask yourself how you can better care for your friend. If she's scratching excessively from an occasional flea, then you're likely dealing with an allergic situation. You may want to review the discussion on preventing and controlling flea problems on pages 21-25.

Skin Allergies

Our dogs are more allergy-prone than ever before. Not only are they exposed to the age-old causes of allergies like pollens and grasses, fleas and food, now there's cigarette smoke, cleaning products, air fresheners, smog, perfumes, and a host of other environmental chemicals for their bodies to handle. It's no wonder that at least 15% to 20% of dogs today suffer from allergies.

The holistic approach to skin allergies means understanding them as imbalances of the immune system, rather than just trying to manage the symptoms. But rebalancing your dog's immune system isn't always an easy task. That's why *preventing* allergies is such an important goal. And when an allergy does appear, if you see it as an early warning sign that the immune system has gone awry, prompt attention to it might prevent more problems later on.

Don't get discouraged if your dog has skin troubles. Consulting a veterinary dermatologist for up-to-date therapies may be just what your dog needs to get her on track.

In addition, consider these useful tips:

- Wash bedcovers weekly in hot water to kill flea eggs, and also to remove particles you can't see that could be contributing to the allergy.

- Treat your dog to one of the new hypoallergenic mattresses and pillow covers to help control allergies.

- Reduce the level of dust mites, pollens, and molds in your home with a HEPA (high-efficiency particulate air) filter. Change all air filters on a regular basis.

- If your dog suffers from environmental allergies, make a comfy T-shirt and pick up a set of booties for her to wear when she goes out. Or, rinse her feet well after walks, and dry them thoroughly.

NUTRITIONAL SUPPORT

- **Omega-3 fatty acids** may be the most important supplement you can use for allergic skin disease. Give an elevated dose (1 fish oil capsule per 10 pounds body weight, daily) for the first 2 to 4 weeks. An allergic dog will benefit from fatty acid supplementation year-round, or at least during her allergy season.

- **Vitamin E**, included in many omega-3 supplements, is important whenever fatty acids are added to the diet. High doses (200 to 400 IU, depending on size) of vitamin E provide antioxidant support.

HOMEOPATHY

Homeopathy can be a very effective remedy for the treatment of allergies. However, it involves the use of a constitutional remedy, and is best managed by a trained homeopath to avoid the suppression of symptoms.

HERBS

- Topical application of your **calendula-hypericum lotion** or **dilute witch hazel spray** helps when itchy spots flare up.

- **Lien Chiao Pai Tu Pien.** This TCM formula helps when skin break-outs, itchiness, restlessness, and odor develop. Use it no longer than 1 or 2 weeks.

ACUPRESSURE

- **Adjoining Valleys LI4** – Especially good if face is itchy.

- **Wind Pond GB20** – Usually quite calming.

- **Three Yin Junction SP6** and **Broken Sequence LU7** – Especially if skin is dry.

If your dog's skin is too uncomfortable he may not enjoy the treatment, so stay focused on his attitude and emotional state as you work with the points. Be gentle, and continue only if he remains relaxed and comfortable.

OTHER

If your dog is taking cortisone (also called prednisone or steroids) for environmental allergies, chances are good that with the right combination of holistic therapies and support, you will be able to wean her off the drug. (See Side Effects of Cortisone, at right.) If you're willing to use antihistamines, they will give her some relief during the deeper healing process. Antihistamines have fewer side effects than steroids, but they may have to be given 3 to 4 times a day if your dog is extremely itchy. Three antihistamines commonly available without prescription are diphenhydramine (Benadryl), clemastine (Tavist) and Chlorpheneramine (ChlorTrimeton). One may work better than another for your dog, so if you don't get a good response try a different one. Trim the human dosage down to fit your dog's size (by weight), and if she gets too sleepy, cut back. Remember, if you are trying a holistic approach, a little itching might be tolerable if it means avoiding the potential side effects of drugs while you're heading toward a truly healthy state. But don't let your dog itch to the point of discomfort or distress.

Consider a small dose of cortisone "as needed" to relieve occasionally severe symptoms rather than keeping her on it full-time. ***But never, ever stop long-term cortisone abruptly***, as this can cause shock and even death, and always consult your vet before making dosage or medication changes.

Demodex Mange

Demodex canis is a microscopic mite, present in small numbers on all dogs, living deep in the hair follicles and sebaceous glands of the skin. Hair loss and skin sores arise when the number of mites gets out of hand, usually because of genetic or immune system problems. Young dogs frequently suffer small areas of hair loss, especially on the face. These mange spots

SIDE EFFECTS OF CORTISONE
Increase in thirst and appetite
Increase in panting (at higher doses)
Thinning of the skin
Decrease in the elasticity of the skin
Thinning of the hair coat
Poor regrowth of the coat after clipping or grooming
Dry skin due to decrease in oil production
Calcium deposits in the skin (rare, but uncomfortable)
Increased risk of liver dysfunction or pancreatitis
Increased risk of urinary tract or skin infections
Increased risk of obesity
Can worsen pre-existing diseases such as heart disease or diabetes
Suppression of the immune system

will spontaneously disappear 90% of the time as the dog matures.

If, however, the disease becomes widespread, it can be particularly debilitating. Your veterinarian will likely prescribe dips or daily oral medications, but often the word "control" rather than "cure" is used. Natural therapies can be used in conjunction with conventional treatments for a more complete response, or to hopefully achieve a permanent cure.

NUTRITIONAL SUPPORT

- A **home-cooked** or **raw foods diet,** or feed the highest quality commerial diet possible.

- Add a daily **vitamin E** supplement as well as **omega-3 fatty acid** supplement and a **mixed carotenoid** (contains vitamin A and beta-carotene) supplement.

the skin | 175

- Provide a daily **vitamin-mineral** that contains vitamin C, selenium, and zinc.
- **Digestive enzymes** and **glandular therapy** are recommended by some holistic veterinarians.
- **Garlic** and **medicinal mushrooms** for immune support.

HOMEOPATHY

- **Arsenicum** – Dry, scaly, itchy, skin; pustules. Patchy hair loss.
- **Sulphur** – Dry scaly skin; easily infected; itching; oozing; pustules. Hair loss. Symptoms recur.

HERBS

- **Calendula-hypericum lotion** – Soothes skin and promotes healing.

- **Chamomile rinse** – A good topical therapy.
- **Astragalus** – As a single herb or as part of a Traditional Chinese herbal formula.

OTHER

- Stress, both physical and emotional, will tax the immune system, so take care to minimize both. **Flower Essences** are helpful when emotional stress is involved. **Massage** helps relieve both physical and emotional stress.
- Acupuncture helps balance the skin and support the immune system. Your veterinary acupuncturist can guide you in the use of home acupressure.

back, limbs, and paws

Your dog's body is built around a system of bones and muscles that offer support, protection, and mobility. The long bones of the legs and intricate bones of the feet and spine keep him upright and create the graceful—or husky, as the case may be—profile that you admire so much. His ribcage, pelvis, and skull protect the internal organs and brain from injury. Like a well-oiled network of hinges and pulleys, the joints and muscles work smoothly to allow him to wag his tail, chew a cookie, or propel him across a grassy field. The muscles deftly convert chemical energy into the mechanical energy that moves the bones and joints with fluid grace. A vast network of nerve fibers direct and guide the motion, and an equally complex lattice of blood vessels supply nourishment and oxygen for every activity. When your dog's muscles are well developed and his joints and ligaments are strong and healthy, the freedom of his movements and ease of his stride are readily apparent. His manner is relaxed and joyful.

MAINTAINING HEALTH

Your dog's assembly of muscles, tendons, ligaments, cartilage, and bone is commonly called the **musculoskeletal**, or **locomotor**, system. Proper development is key to maintaining a comfortable gait and a free, flowing stride throughout life. Generations of selective breeding practices have led to some disturbing tendencies to develop breed-related orthopedic problems that can be devastating to dogs, even at an early age.

To help maintain the good health of your dog's musculoskeletal system, careful attention to diet and exercise are essential.

- During puppyhood, a balanced diet—formulated for your dog's growth expectancy—in amounts that do not lead to obesity, helps prevent bone and joint diseases that result from too-rapid growth.

- Avoid oversupplementation of calcium and fat, especially for growing puppies. If you are feeding him a home-prepared diet, check with your veterinarian or a veterinary nutritional service to ensure balanced meals for this lifestage. (See page 70, Feeding Large Breed Puppies.)

- Avoid obesity by monitoring weight and Body Conditioning Score (see page 15) and offer daily opportunities for exercise.

- Ensure that your dog receives adequate protein for building muscles, and adequate calcium for strong bones. While commercial foods have proper calcium and phosphorus ratios, home-prepared meals, particularly if meat-based, need added calcium to prevent bone disease.

- Maintain a routine of regular exercise to keep joints flexible and muscles and ligaments strong, and in turn help prevent injury.

SIGNS OF TROUBLE

Sometimes lameness is caused by something as simple as a thorn in the paw, while other times the cause may be elusive. Is your friend just a little sore from too much Frisbee over the weekend, or showing the first signs of bone cancer? Careful attention to the events leading up to the lameness, and a thorough examination of the back, limbs, and paws will help establish where the problem lies, and provide clues to how serious it might be. Age and breed should be taken into account as well. For instance, a **luxating patella**, or a knee cap that pops out of place, is common in young, small breed dogs like Pomeranians. **Panosteitis**, or painful bone inflammation throughout the body, is seen primarily in young, large breeds such as German Shepherds or Great Danes. Bone tumors or arthritis are more common in mature dogs; strained muscles and torn ligaments are most common in very active dogs.

There are literally hundreds of causes of musculoskeletal problems. An unexplained lameness, or one that persists, may need your vet's evaluation and, in many cases, require X rays. In cases that are particularly difficult to diagnose, blood tests, microscopic evaluation of joint fluid, neurologic tests, muscle or nerve biopsies, arthroscopy, or even magnetic resonance imaging (MRI) may be needed.

What to Look For:

If your dog is limping, there could be a problem with or injury to:

- muscles of the back or legs
- nerves in the spine or limbs
- tendons or ligaments
- bone, cartilage, and joint structures
- soft tissue pads of the paws

The following symptoms may indicate pain or weakness due to a musculoskeletal problem:

- He has trouble getting up after sitting or lying down.
- He is unwilling to jump into the car.
- He quickly loses interest in playtime.
- Your good-natured dog has become cranky with his dog friends when they play together.
- Your friend has trouble finding a comfortable position when he lies down, especially at night. He may appear restless, pace, or pant excessively.
- He seems intent on licking or chewing on one of her limbs.

INVESTIGATING THE PROBLEM

Begin by asking yourself a few key questions:

- Did the trouble come on slowly or show up all of a sudden? Sudden lameness is often the result of overuse or injury, while symptoms that develop gradually might indicate nutritional imbalance, arthritis, dysplasia, or other disease.

- Where has your dog been? If he's been swimming in the ocean or a lake, he may have cut or bruised a paw on something below the water's surface. If he's been running through dry grass, a plant seed, or foxtail, may have punctured the tender area between his toes and begun to migrate through the tissue. Exposure to certain ticks can lead to Lyme disease.

- Has she engaged in vigorous activity? An unusually long run on the weekend can lead to muscle, joint, or tendon soreness, especially in the dog who is a couch potato the rest of the week. Jumping for a Frisbee can cause ligament tears. Chronic overuse can lead to degenerative arthritis.

- Next, watch your dog move: Is the problem worse in the hind quarters or in the front? Is he limping or just stiff? Are stairs difficult? Do you see signs of weakness or balance problems as he moves?

Examine your dog with your hands. Feel for swelling (hot or cool?) or signs of pain or external trauma, such as abrasions, lacerations, or puncture wounds.

- Start at the bottom, inspecting each paw carefully for small punctures, foreign matter, or discolorations that suggest a stone bruise.

- Move up the limb, bending each joint in the direction it normally moves when your dog walks. Look for signs of pain or swelling, listen for cracking sounds that may suggest arthritis, and evaluate the amount of mobility your dog can handle comfortably. Compare it to an unaffected limb, if necessary.

- Press lightly on all the bones and muscles of the leg and spine (including the neck area), feeling again for swelling. Watch your dog's response for signs of pain.

- If your dog seems weak in one or more limbs, have him stand beside you on a flat surface, then turn each foot over one at a time by gently bending the toes under, so he stands on the top of the foot. If your dog does not correct the placement quickly, there may be a disruption of nerve impulses to the limb.

- Any signs of limb paralysis or lack of sensation, intense pain, a joint that is hot or swollen, or bowel or urinary incontinence indicate a need for immediate veterinary evaluation.

NUTRITIONAL SUPPORT

- When planning meals, include **foods that contain sulfur**, such as asparagus, eggs, and a little garlic, to help support repair and rebuilding of tissue. Or supplement with **MSM**.

- **Chondroprotective agents** (glucosamine, chondroitin, glycosaminoglycans) protect joint cartilage, help heal damaged areas, and help with joint lubrication.

- **Omega-3 fatty acid supplements** reduce inflammation in muscles or joints.

- **Antioxidants** help eliminate free radicals released into the joint due to injury. Free radicals can further damage the joints.

- If your dog is showing signs of weakness or difficulty with coordination, and has been on a poor diet, **vitamin B-complex** can help support the neurological system.

COMMON CAUSES OF LAMENESS

Congenital anomalies*

Osteochondrosis (OCD, a form of joint disease)*

Elbow or hip dysplasia

Panosteitis (inflammatory bone disease)*

Arthritis (due to joint degeneration, immune system disorder, or Lyme disease)

Trauma (to muscle, bone, joint, or nerve)

Infection (in bone, joint, tissue, or full body)

Nutritional imbalance*

Tendonitis (especially in the shoulder)

Cancer (bone, muscle, joint, or nerve)

Neuritis (nerve inflammation)

Dislocations or fractures

Sprains or strains

Myositis (muscle inflammation)

* primarily in dogs under 12 months of age

HOMEOPATHY

- **Arnica** – Always the first remedy—and often the only homeopathic remedy needed—for injury, especially sprains, strains, bruises, or overuse. Excellent for minimizing or reducing pain, swelling and bruising, and for speeding recovery in any injury. Also helpful to begin treatment of any painful condition. If you suspect your dog has sustained an injury, or has simply played harder than usual, a single dose of Arnica immediately after the event may prevent soreness.

- **Bryonia** – For joints that are swollen and hot, and painful when pressure is applied; stiffness. For pain that seems to worsen with movement.

- **Calc. carb.** – Skeletal problems that are related to calcium deficiency, from either a poor diet or the body's inability to absorb calcium.

- **Calc. fluor.** – Skeletal problems in underweight, unhealthy dogs.

- **Calc. phos.** – Skeletal problems, particularly in young, growing dogs. Promotes healing of fractures.

- **Hypericum** – For any break in the skin, to ease pain and help prevent infection. Alternate with Arnica for cuts and lacerations. Alternate with **Ledum** for puncture wounds. Also helpful for injuries or disease that involve the nerves, including injuries to the back, especially where there is pain in the lumbosacral area. Eases pain in areas that are very sensitive, like an injured nail.

- **Ledum** – Helps heal injuries to the tendons, ligaments, periosteum. (tissue that surrounds the bone). Also, any swelling that is cool. Alternate with **Hypericum** to heal and prevent infection in puncture wounds. Alternate with **Arnica** for sprains.

- **Rhus tox.** – For pain or stiffness that gets better after moving around.

- **Ruta** – For pain in the lumbosacral area, especially when there is also weakness or pain in the hind limbs.

- **Silicea** – Helps the body eliminate foreign matter, such as foxtails or imbedded glass or thorns.

- **Symphytum** – Helps mend broken bones.

HERBS

- The spices **turmeric** (powder) and **ginger** (best if fresh) have been reported to have antiinflammatory effects. Both can be sprinkled right onto your dog's meal. Especially for older, weak dogs.

- **Dandelion root** tea or tincture added to the diet will supply valuable nutrients to aid healing.

- Use hot tea (not hot enough to cause a burn) made from **ginger root** (decoction) or **thyme leaves** (infusion) for a hot compress to promote circulation. (NOTE: Heat should not be used during the first 24 hours after an injury.)

ACUPRESSURE

Whenever your dog is stiff, lame, or uncomfortable, check for trigger points (see page 183), For tendon and ligament injury, and to strengthen hips and knees, massage **Yang Mound Spring GB34** and **Entrusting Middle BL40**. See additional points recommended throughout this section.

OTHER

- When lameness or pain is present, do not push your dog to exercise until you have located the problem and can determine whether exercise will benefit or exacerbate the condition.

- Make sure your dog's bed is well insulated, nicely padded, and out of drafts.

- A morning massage can work wonders to relieve stiffness and increase circulation.

- If your dog is overweight, help him lose the pounds to relieve stress on the joints, and to reduce the chance of injury, arthritis, or metabolic problems. A recent veterinary study showed that as much as 40% of lameness problems could be cured by simply achieving weight reduction goals, with no other forms of therapy.

- A **potato** poultice, made from shredded raw potatoes, will help reduce inflammation and draw out foreign matter such as foxtails.

HOLISTIC VETERINARY TREATMENTS

Acupuncture is one of the most successful of complementary therapies when it comes to the musculoskeletal system. **Laser therapy** at acupuncture sites, **electroacupuncture, moxibustion** (heating of acupuncture points by holding a burning stick of Artemesia vulgaris, or mugwort, above each point), and gold bead implantations at acupuncture points are all methods used by veterinary acupuncturists. Spinal manipulation and other **chiropractic therapies** are also used widely for problems of the back and limbs.

Sprains and Strains

A sprain is an injury to a ligament, the fibrous tissue that connects one bone to another, supporting the joint. A strain is an injury to the muscle-tendon unit (see illustration on page 181), usually occurring when the muscle is stressed beyond it's capability. These injuries can be mild to severe. If your dog won't walk on the injured leg, you'll want to have your veterinarian evaluate the situation. With sprains and strains,

the option of surgery

Surgery on the musculoskeletal system is a way to correct genetic conditions, fractures, ligament tears, disc problems, and even some arthritis trouble. Holistic support following surgery will help your friend be more comfortable, mend more quickly, and gain further mobility. Ask your holistic veterinarian about acupuncture, chiropractic, physical therapy, and other bodywork for your dog following surgery.

there's likely to be swelling at the joint or tendon, and your dog may wince when you press on the area. (See also page 182, When a Joint is Swollen.)

- Apply ice packs immediately, for about 10 minutes. Repeat several times during the first 24 hours. Keep your dog *off* the leg as much as possible.

- After 24 hours, begin alternating hot and cold treatments every few hours. With mild sprains support isn't necessary, but an elastic bandage sometimes provides comfort, as long as it's not wrapped so tightly that circulation is impaired.

- If pain or swelling is severe, or your dog is unwilling to put weight on the injured leg, get veterinary assistance.

NUTRITIONAL SUPPORT

- Give your dog a good **multivitamin-mineral complex** to promote nutritional balance and support tissue repair. The B vitamins are important during any stressful situation, and zinc, manganese, calcium, and other minerals are important in tissue healing.

- **Antioxidants** help eliminate free radicals released into the joint due to injury. Free radicals can further damage the joints. Supplement with **vitamin E**.

- **Bromelain** and **papain** help reduce pain and bruising at the site of the sprain or strain.

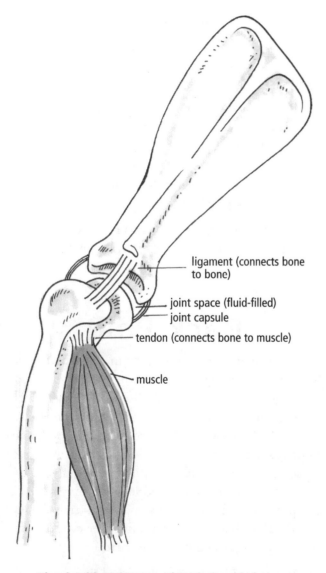

ligament (connects bone to bone)

joint space (fluid-filled)
joint capsule

tendon (connects bone to muscle)

muscle

The shoulder joint: note the relationship between tendons, muscle, ligaments, bone, and joint.

HOMEOPATHY

- **Arnica** – The first remedy in treatment of an injury.

- **Bellis** – Sprains that are extremely painful, but get better with movement.

- **Ledum** – For sprains and strains with swelling that is cool. Excellent for injuries to tendons, ligaments, periosteum. Alternate with **Arnica** if swelling persists and injury is very painful.

- **Ruta** – For sprains or injury to the cartilage.

- **Symphytum** – For injuries to the tendons, ligaments, periosteum.

HERBS

- A salve, poultice, or infusion of **comfrey** leaves applied topically to the sprain or strain speeds healing due to the herb's ability to promote cell growth. (Warning: Do not use internally due to potential for toxicity.)

- **Chin Koo Tieh Shang Wan** is known as the "traumatic injury pill," this popular Chinese herbal patent formula contains 20% pseudoginseng root to help stop hemorrhaging into the tissues.

- Make a poultice from **slippery elm bark** to help reduce swelling.

- Apply a **ginger** compress to stimulate circulation and reduce inflammation.

ACUPRESSURE

Gentle acupressure on local points around the area of injury can help move stagnated blood and increase circulation at the site of the injury. Other helpful points include:

- **Great Impact LIV 3**

- **Yang Mound Spring GB34**

when a joint is swollen

If your dog comes home holding up a paw, and you see a swelling at one of the joints, there are a number of possible causes. The "wrist" (or carpus) and "ankle" (or hock; see illustration on page 187) have a very complex anatomy, with 5 bones, 8 tendons, 11 ligaments, and a multi-layered joint capsule in each joint. Mild injuries will usually cause minimal lameness, so if a joint is swollen and your dog won't bear weight on the limb, it's serious enough to consult your vet. If there is a bone fracture, a severe sprain, or a torn ligament, early surgical repair is advised, before your dog has a chance to damage the joint further. This offers the best chance for a full recovery, thus avoiding chronic pain or lameness later in life. A swollen, painful joint can also be a sign of a bacterial infection or even Lyme disease. A simple procedure to drain a small portion of joint fluid for analysis will provide a quick diagnosis.

- **Kunlun Mountain BL60**
- **Foot Three Mile ST36**
- **Entrusting Middle BL40** – For hip and knee injuries.

HOLISTIC VETERINARY TREATMENTS

Magnetic field therapy can be used to create a favorable environment for tissue repair. It's been reported to increase blood flow to the area, bringing important nutrients and reducing pain and swelling. **Low energy photon therapy** (or **laser therapy**) can also stimulate the body's natural defense systems in the treated area. **Acupuncture** is an excellent therapy to move qi and blood, reduce pain, and increase circulation to the area.

OTHER

- Rest your dog for 7 to 10 days, then begin light exercise, such as leash walks, during the following 7 to 10 days. Complete healing can take as long as 3 weeks, so vigorous exercise should be kept to a minimum until you're sure your dog's tissues can handle the stress.

- If lameness or swelling recurs once exercise is resumed, consult your veterinarian for further investigation.

Back Pain

There are many problems that can cause back pain. Some breeds are particularly prone to disc problems (see page 251, Intervertebral Disc Disease) while others may suffer from arthritis in the back joints, particularly the lumbosacral (LS) region, (where the last lumbar vertebra meets the pelvis). Dogs suffer from muscle strains in the back just like we do. If your dog has a weak back or weak hind legs, she may get muscle spasms or tension in her upper back (right behind the shoulder blades) from pulling herself up rather than efficiently using her hindquarters.

- While exercise is generally a good thing, when the back is sore, rest is best. Be sure your dog has a

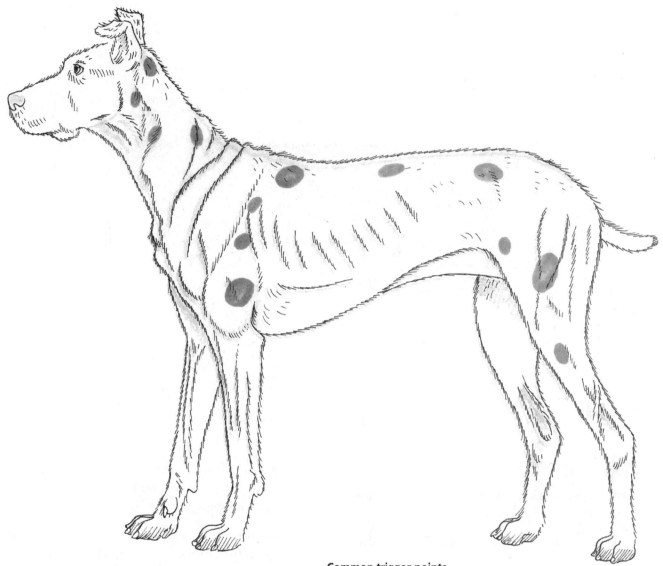

Common trigger points

comfortable, warm, and firmly supported place to sleep.

- If your dog is slow to rise, is having difficulty jumping into the car, or seems uncomfortable after a long walk or run, it could due to pain in the LS region of the back. You'll find the soreness just forward of where the hips and pelvis meet the spine. If this area is tender, a full 6 weeks of rest

may be needed. Your veterinarian can help you rule out other problems with X-rays.

- Most dogs with back pain enjoy a little heat therapy. Try hot water bottles or a heating pad turned to the lowest setting, with a towel or light blanket sandwiched in between your dog's back and the heat source.

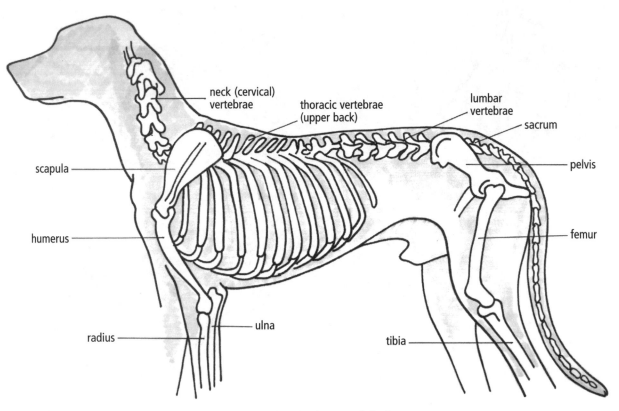

The spine and major bones of the legs

NUTRITIONAL SUPPORT

- **Antioxidants** – Vitamins A, C, and E, or a good antioxidant blend.

- **DLPA** (dl-phenylalanine) – May help if pain is minor.

- **Fat and calorie-controlled diet** – If your dog is overweight, the stress on the back can be a major cause of recurrent injury and pain.

- **Vitamin B-complex** – To support the nerves, especially in times of stress.

HOMEOPATHY

- **Arnica** – Begin treatment with Arnica, particularly if soreness is due to an injury.

- **Conium** – Loss of motor control, particularly when it begins in the hind limbs and spreads forward. Numbness in the toes.

- **Gelsemium** – Legs appear heavy when walking. Dog gets tired easily. Impaired control of the muscles; trembling and weakness. Pain in the back and hind limbs.

- **Hypericum** – Excellent for any injury involving the nerves, or to quiet the nerves so that surrounding muscles can relax. Pain in the LS region.

- **Ruta** – For pain in the LS region, particularly when pain extends down the back of the hind legs.

- **Bryonia** – Pain at the nape of the neck.

HERBS

- **Chamomile**, **valerian**, or **kava kava** for muscle relaxation.

ACUPRESSURE

Whenever your dog appears sore in the back region, scan her body for trigger points (see illustration on page 183). Tender points may be found over the muscle groups of the legs as well, so do a thorough scan for any sensitive areas. Avoid deep pressure, using your dog's expressions and body tension to guide you.

- **Entrusting Middle BL40** – Relieves pain anywhere along the back.

- **Yang Mound Spring GB34** – For muscle spasms, especially along the sides of the back.

- **Encircling Leap GB30** – Helps with lower back and hip mobility.

- **Back Stream SI3** – For neck and back pain, and muscle spasms of the neck and shoulder area.

HOLISTIC VETERINARY TREATMENTS

Acupuncture and **chiropractic care** are among the most useful alternative therapies for back pain. Usually a series of treatments, followed by periodic tune-ups, can keep your dog feeling comfortable, even if he's a senior citizen. **Moxibustion**, the burning of an herb above the acupuncture points, is often used by acupuncturists to treat cold, stiff backs, with or without the use of acupuncture needles.

Paw Injuries

Most dogs lead active lives, so abrasions and lacerations to the pads of the feet are fairly common.

- Control bleeding with direct pressure. Most lacerations on the foot pad will not bleed profusely. If a deeper laceration has torn an artery or vein, direct pressure, with or without a bandage, and the homeopathic remedy **Phosphorus**, or the Chinese herb **Yunnan Pai Yao**, can help control the bleeding until you reach the vet.

- Clean the wound thoroughly, using a Betadine solution diluted to the color of weak tea. Follow up with **calendula-hypericum lotion** and a bandage (change daily until the wound is closing nicely).

- Give **Oregon grape, echinacea**, and **astragalus** orally for their antibacterial action, and **grapeseed extract** for its powerful antioxidant effect.

- Alternate homeopathic **Arnica** and **Hypericum** to ease pain, promote healing, and help prevent infection. If the wound is a puncture wound, after the first day alternate Hypericum and **Ledum**.

- Consult your veterinarian if the wound develops a drainage of pus or a foul odor, or becomes more (rather than less) painful over time. Homeopathic **Hepar** will help with infection. Low potencies (3X to 6X) will encourage the wound to drain; higher potencies (30C) will encourage absorption and drying of the infection.

NOTE: Most foot pad lacerations don't need to be sutured to heal effectively. In fact, surgery is rarely more effective than simple wound management, bandaging, and confinement.

Nails and Nailbed Problems

Nails and the soft tissue around them are subject to trauma, especially if nails are allowed to grow to excessive lengths.

- **Torn or injured nails:** Clip or file the injured nail, removing loose pieces if possible. Bleeding is usually minimal. Cleanse with a dilute Betadine solution and follow with **calendula-hypericum lotion** and bandage for 1 to 2 days. Give the homeopathic remedy **Hypericum** to help ease pain, promote healing, and prevent infection.

- **Non-healing wound at base of nail:** There are 11 different malignant tumors that can occur at the base of the nail. Most cause swelling and redness, and either a small growth or just an ulcerated area that appears much like a wound. Any non-healing wound at the base of the nail must be checked by your veterinarian.

- **Deformed nails:** When all or most of the nails are deformed, brittle, and damaged, chances are a nutritional deficiency, an immune system disorder, or a dystrophy (a degeneration related to an inherited trait) is involved. Try supplementing with **vitamin E** and **selenium, zinc, vitamin A,** and **biotin** (or gelatin). Consult your veterinarian for nail analysis if the condition does not respond.

Arthritis

While we tend to think arthritis affects only senior dogs, as many as one in five dogs have signs of arthritis, and it can strike any dog at any age. Whether your dog experiences a nagging morning stiffness, discomfort after heavy exercise, or the more debilitating and painful forms of crippling arthritis, alternative therapies can help manage his condition. Your goal is to address any underlying cause that may be contributing to the arthritis, maximize your dog's mobility, and minimize her discomfort through gentle and supportive measures.

Conditions that lead to arthritis include:

- Improper nutrition, particularly mineral imbalances or inadequate protein.

- Poor conformation and other genetic factors, often from poor breeding practices.

- Invasion of the joint by a bacteria or other organism (such as Lyme disease).

- Previous joint, ligament, or bone injury in the region of the joint.

- Overwork, leading to chronic joint trauma, especially in growing animals.

- Obesity, which causes trauma from the excessive load on the joints.

- Immune system problems, including specific immune system diseases or hypersensitivity reactions to antibiotics or vaccinations.

NUTRITIONAL SUPPORT

- **Vitamins A, C**, and **E.**

- **Zinc, selenium,** and **manganese** – To help the body utilize antioxidants.

- **Chondoprotective agents** (glucosamine, chondroitin, glycosaminoglycans).

- **Green-lipped mussel** (*Perna canaliculi*) – A rich source of antiinflammatory compounds as well as glycosaminoglycans, vitamins, and minerals.

- **Sea cucumber** – Natural chondroitin source, with added natural vitamins and minerals.

- **Omega-3 fatty acids** – Suppresses the inflammatory reaction that occurs in arthritic joints.

- **SOD** (Super oxide dismutase) – Another antioxidant with antiinflammatory properties.

- **DLPA** (Dl-phenylalanine) – For minor pain.

HOMEOPATHY

NOTE: Arthritis is a chronic condition. Be sure to evaluate your dog's entire symptom picture and select a remedy using the guidelines for chronic illness (see Materia Medica).

- **Arnica** – Begin with Arnica, then follow with the remedy that matches your dog's symptoms.

- **Bryonia** – Pain and stiffness in nape of neck and lower back. Joints are hot, swollen, and painful, but get better from pressure.

- **Calc. carb.** – Bony enlargements at the joint.

- **Calc. fluor.** – Pain gets worse when your dog begins to move, then gets better with continued movement.

- **Causticum** – Pain in joints, with deformity of the joint. Nighttime restlessness.

- **Ledum** – Hot or cool swelling in the joints. Joints make a cracking sound when moving.

- **Rhus tox.** – Known as the "rusty gate" remedy, for pain and stiffness that gets better with motion.

HERBAL SUPPORT

- **Antiinflammatory herbs** – Boswellia, yucca, ashwaganda, licorice, turmeric, ginger.

- **Nutrient herbs** – Alfalfa, dandelion root, parsley.

- **Tonic herbs** – Ashwaganda, gingko (particularly important for older animals).

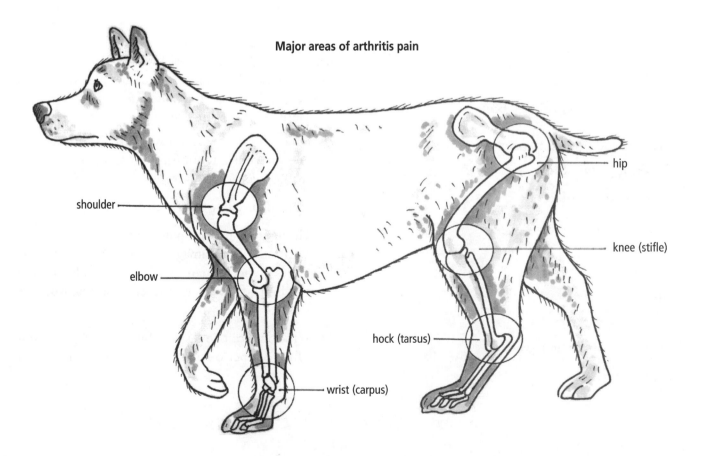

Major areas of arthritis pain

shoulder

elbow

wrist (carpus)

hip

knee (stifle)

hock (tarsus)

ACUPRESSURE

Use acupressure points around injured or painful joints to encourage circulation. Massage tender trigger points with the acupressure technique. Refer to the illustration on page 183 for commonly affected trigger points. Your veterinary acupuncturist can assist you with point location.

For hip pain: The points below are found in a triangle around the hip joint (see illustration on page 103). Hold each point, or use a small circular motion, for 15 seconds each day.

- **Between Bones and Hip GB29**

- **Encircling Leap GB30**

- **Reaching the Margin BL54**

For knee pain:
- **Yin Mound Spring SP9**

- **Foot Three Mile ST36**

- **Yang Mound Spring GB34**

For neck and front limb pain:
- **Back Stream SI3**

- **Crooked Pool LI11**

- **Outer Pass TH5**

OTHER

Physical therapy:
- **Massage**

- **Range-of-motion exercises**

- **Swimming**

HOLISTIC VETERINARY TREATMENTS

Acupuncture (including electroacupuncture, laser, gold bead implants, and moxibustion; post surgical therapy) and **Chinese herbal medicine** have all been found to be helpful for releiving arthritis pain. A trained **homeopath** can help you address your dog's needs based on his overall symptom picture. **Physical therapy** (including chiropractic, massage, whirlpool, and range-of-motion exercises) helps with your dog's mobility.

Fractures

Although a broken bone may not be life-threatening, it's an emergency that requires immediate veterinary attention to manage pain and decrease the chance of permanent disability. When there's also a laceration or break in the skin at the fracture site, early vet care to properly clean the wound and remove hair and debris can be vital in preventing bone infection later on.

Until you reach the vet:

- Stay calm. Use **Rescue Remedy**, breath deeply, and use your intentionality to send your dog the message you're there to help!

- Control bleeding with pressure.

- Give **Arnica** in high potency (1M if available) to help with tissue damage and mitigate pain. If your dog is in shock, **Aconite** (also 1M) can help stabilize him. If bleeding is severe, use **Phosphorus** (30C).

- If the limb can be easily stabilized (by taping a roll of newspaper or plastic tubing to the leg), you

conventional therapies — what you should know

Conventional therapy for arthritis may involve surgery, but more often nonsteroidal antiinflammatory drugs (NSAIDs) or steroidal antiinflammatory agents (cortisone) are prescribed. There is no doubt that NSAIDs, which include aspirin, carprofen (Rimadyl), etodolac (Etogesic), and piroxicam (Feldene) carry risks associated with long-term use, as do cortisone drugs, which have more immediate side effects. All of these medications have the potential to cause:

- Kidney damage
- Liver damage
- Stomach or intestinal ulcers
- Diarrhea
- Depression
- Loss of appetite
- Cortisone and some NSAIDs may cause degeneration of the joint with prolonged use.

While effective in suppressing inflammation and providing pain relief, if there is a preexisting problem with your dog's kidney or liver these drugs can spell disaster. Even if your dog's organs are functioning normally, blood tests should be evaluated periodically during prolonged use (once in the first few weeks, and every 3 to 6 months thereafter) to watch for early signs of damage. It is advisable to stop NSAIDs a week prior to any scheduled surgery, as they may also inhibit blood clotting or affect the kidneys in some patients.

With all this in mind, it is worthwhile to try holistic options before subjecting your dog to these hazards. If he is already on an NSAID, you may find his dose can be gradually reduced or even discontinued when you embark on a program of holistic treatment.

When pain is unresponsive to other forms of treatment, NSAIDs and cortisone have their place, of course. By alleviating joint inflammation and pain, they can increase your dog's mobility and willingness to exercise, and thus get him through a crisis. Just be sure to discuss side effects with your veterinarian, and ask him to monitor your dog's condition with blood tests.

may find that support helps decrease your dog's pain. Be careful! If attempting stabilization causes more discomfort or anxiety, let your dog protect the limb himself as best he can until your vet can help.

- Use **Arnica** for the first days after veterinary treatment while the injury is still painful. When pain subsides, switch to **Symphytum** to help mend the bone.

Bone Cancer

While still relatively rare, bone cancers and cancers of the cartilage are developing more frequently in dogs than in the past, especially in certain breeds such as Rottweilers. Fortunately, treatment options are also increasing. If your dog is diagnosed, ask your veterinarian about all the options available to you. For more information on home support, see Chapter 10, When Your Dog Is Seriously Ill.

meet squid

Her name is Squid. She's a glossy, compact, black Labrador who always has a smile on her face. Her passion is Frisbees. Ginny's passions are biking, running, paddling—and her beloved companion Squid.

I met Squid after she had damaged a ligament in one of her knees. While the conventional solution for such an injury is surgery, Ginny wanted to save this as a last resort.

Three years later Squid was still playing Frisbee with gusto and joy. Her secret? An initial round of acupuncture treatments, followed by 4 to 6 acupuncture tune-up sessions yearly, plus 2 daily supplements (containing omega-3 fatty acids, glucosamine, antioxidants, boswellia, alfalfa, and other herbs and nutrients). And, oh yes, plenty of love and plenty of exercise with Ginny!   —*Katy*

the respiratory and circulatory systems

EVERY MINUTE OF HER LIFE, your dog's lungs and heart supply her with life-giving oxygen from the air she breathes. The airways and lung tissue that make up the **respiratory system** work in concert with the **circulatory system**. Oxygenated blood travels from the lungs to the heart, which then pumps it through a vast network of blood vessels to all the vital organs and tissues of the body. Even today, scientists find mystery in the complex physiology of these two integrated systems, with their abundant array of hormonal and chemical transmitters that direct and modulate so many vital processes. It all comes together in a beautiful dance, so that with each breath oxygen enters every cell in your dog's body, bringing her the gift of life.

MAINTAINING HEALTH

- Regular exercise is one of the best prescriptions for healthy heart and lungs. If your dog is a couch potato, start slowly, working gradually into a routine that is enjoyable for both of you.

- Obesity stresses the heart and interferes with proper breathing. There are no short-cuts here: A chubby dog needs a healthy, low-fat, calorie-restricted diet along with regular exercise.

- "Garbage in-garbage out" applies to your dog's lungs, perhaps even more than to your own. Your dog lives his life closer to the ground, where heavier-than-air pollutants such as car exhaust and second-hand smoke are more concentrated. This means your friend may be at higher risk for cancers, chronic bronchitis, and respiratory infections. Protect your dog from bad air quality whenever possible.

- Nutrients important for the heart include potassium, magnesium, and the amino acids taurine and carnitine. American Cocker Spaniels are prone to taurine deficiency and may benefit from a daily supplement.

- Coenzyme Q10 protects heart cells from degeneration, and fatty acid supplements are also beneficial. Both are helpful for dogs diagnosed with heart murmurs or with a family history of heart disease.

- If your dog lives in an area where heartworm disease is prevalent, take measures to prevent infestation of these mosquito-borne parasites. (See page 21.) Other, less common parasites can also infect the lungs. Discuss prevalence with your holistic veterinarian before you agree to routine deworming measures.

- Keep teeth clean and gums healthy. (See pages 16-17 and 160) Periodontal disease increases the risk for heart and other organ infections.

- Heart disease afflicts more dogs today than ever before, in part due to poor breeding practices that leave some dogs at greater risk of heart disease. All elderly dogs should have regular veterinary checkups to evaluate the heart and lungs, but at-risk breeds should be monitored even more closely. (For a list, see page 194.) If your dog is purebred, ask your veterinarian whether a baseline electrocardiogram, or EKG, is advised.

SIGNS OF TROUBLE

Become familiar with your dog's normal breathing patterns when she's sleeping and when she's active. Changes in breath sounds or the amount of movement as the chest rises and falls can indicate problems in the lungs or airways. Because an accumulation of fluid in the lungs often accompanies heart problems,

Finding your dog's heartbeat: note the heart's location, sandwiched between the lungs. The easiest spot to feel the heartbeat is just behind the left elbow.

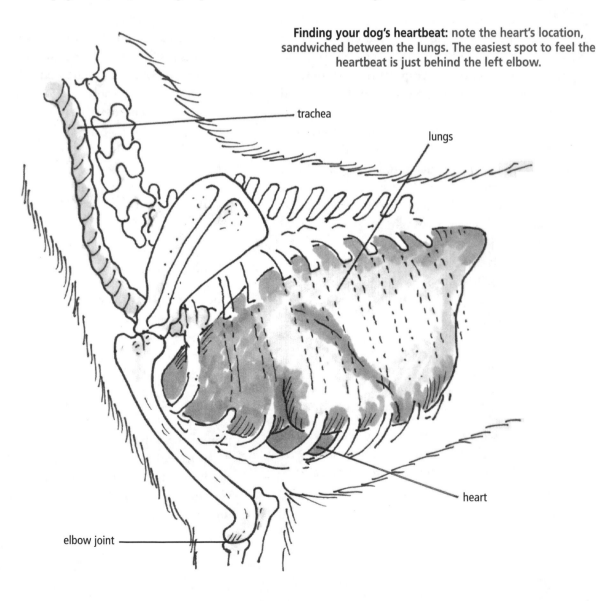

trachea

lungs

heart

elbow joint

changes in breathing can also mean problems in this organ as well. Learn to feel for your dog's heartbeat. It should have a regular rhythm, or what vets call an "irregularly regular" rhythm. In this case, the heart beats a little faster on the in-breath than on the out-breath. Normal heart rate is between 70 and 160 beats per minute, with large dogs at the low end and small dogs and puppies at the high end.

What to Look For:
- **Increased respiratory effort.** Does your dog seem to work harder than usual with each breath she takes? Does her chest rise and fall more sharply? Are the respirations more rapid? Not all changes in respiration are related to the lungs and heart. Electrolyte disturbances, anemia, pain, and many other diseases affect breathing patterns.

- The rapid, shallow, open-mouthed respiration that occurs when your dog pants is part of her cooling mechanism. It occurs normally after exercise, or when your dog is anxious. However, if **panting becomes excessive, or is accompanied by unusual sounds**, there could be an obstruction in the airway or other serious disorder.

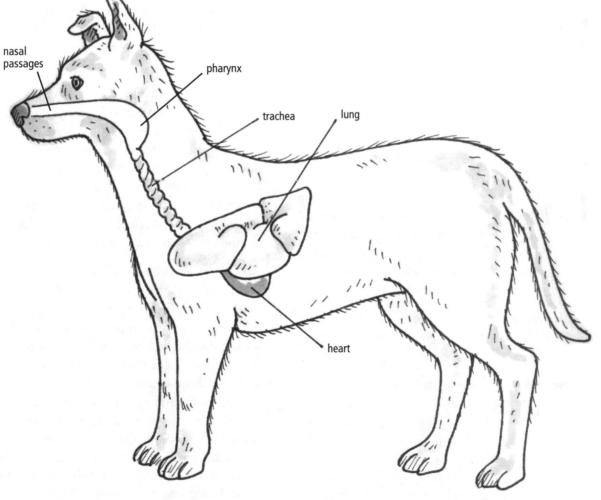

The respiratory system

SOME BREEDS AT HEIGHTENED RISK OF HEART DISEASE

Miniature Poodles

American Cocker Spaniels

Boxers

Golden Retrievers

German Shepherds (heart cancer)

Portuguese Water Dogs

Doberman Pinschers

Newfoundlands

Cavalier King Charles Spaniels

Most miniature breeds (heart valve problems associated with aging)

Miniature Schnauzers (heart rhythm disturbance)

- **Acute sneezing**. When your dog suddenly begins to sneeze violently, a foreign body, such as a foxtail or other plant material, may be lodged in a nasal passage. If not removed, a foxtail can travel deep into the respiratory tract and cause serious illness. If sneezing persists for more than 2 to 3 hours, your vet may need to extract the material while your dog is under general anesthesia.

- **Chronic sneezing** can represent an allergy, a respiratory infection, or a polyp or tumor in the nasal cavity.

- **Reverse sneezing**. This sound is often misinterpreted as a cough. Your dog extends her neck and makes forceful sounds on both inspiration and expiration, and may continue to do so for several minutes. Fortunately, the cause is usually related to nasal and throat irritation. Although it may sound serious when it happens, it rarely is. (Stroking the throat, or offering a bit of honey or slippery elm to coat the throat, can speed recovery.)

- **Coughing**. Does the cough sound harsh or softer? Does it rack your dog's body or is it mild and intermittent? Harsh, prolonged coughing suggests involvement of the airways, where as a soft, infrequent cough is more common with a lung or heart problem. If your dog coughs when she's excited, it's likely due to an irritated windpipe, as in a case of kennel cough or the tracheal collapse that can occur in miniature breeds. Production of green or yellow phlegm usually indicates infection somewhere along the respiratory tract. If your friend coughs only at night, or first thing in the morning before her circulation is in full swing, and the cough does not produce any phlegm, it could be a sign of heart disease.

- **Weakness or fainting**. Does your dog seem weak most of the time, or only during or after exercise? Does she tire easily on a walk, or refuse to go the full distance? Weakness is a common warning signal that the circulatory system isn't up to par. Fainting, or a temporary loss of consciousness, can occur when the brain is not getting enough blood flow. Prolonged weakness or fainting indicates a complete veterinary evaluation is warranted.

- **Abnormal mucous membrane color**. A blue tint to the color of the mucous membranes suggests your dog is not getting enough oxygen; grayish membranes may mean poor circulation. These are serious conditions, but don't be confused by the blue or gray color that is normal in some dogs, such as Chow Chows. The best way to evaluate mucous membranes is to lift up your dog's lip, directly over the large canine teeth in the front of the mouth. Look at the color of the gums above the teeth. Gentle pressure with your finger for only a second should create a whitish spot, and normal color should return a second or 2 after you remove your finger. If the pink color doesn't return in 2 to 3 seconds, and your dog has any other symptoms of distress, contact your veterinarian.

Respiratory Disease

When respiratory disease is present, your holistic veterinarian will look at patterns of disease, and work with you to address your dog's overall health, not just the part of the respiratory system that's showing the most symptoms. In situations such as pneumonia, where conventional therapy with antibiotics is clearly of value, home therapies can *complement* your veterinarian's prescribed treatment, enhance your dog's well being, and strengthen his system to hasten healing.

NUTRITIONAL SUPPORT

- **Modify your dog's diet to maintain optimal body weight.** Obesity will make any respiratory problem worse.

- If your dog has been exposed to kennel cough or other contagious disease, add **garlic** and **turmeric** to his meals to boost immunity and help ward off infection. Add foods high in **antioxidants**, or an antioxidant blend supplement. Make sure to include **vitamins A, C, and E**.

HOMEOPATHY

- **Aconite** – Sneezing; hoarse, dry cough; labored breathing; small amount of watery nasal discharge; symptoms come on after a chill; worse after midnight.

- **Arsenicum** – Sneezing; cough worse after midnight; watery nasal discharge; small amount of frothy sputum; body feels cold to the touch.

- **Bryonia** – Dry hacking cough, dry mouth, dry stools, excessive thirst. Cough is painful, with sputum the color of rust; difficult respiration.

- **Calc. sulph.** – Thick, yellow discharge from the nose or from a cough.

- **Hepar** – Productive cough; sneezing; thick discharge from the nose; worse in dry, cold air.

- **Kali bich.** – Sneezing; coughing with sticky, yellow sputum; ropy, green or yellow nasal discharge.

- **Lycopodium** – Deep, hollow cough; crusts and plugs in nose; ulcerated nostrils.

- **Phosphorus** – Bleeding from the nose; chronic nasal discharge; dog is chilly, trembling, and thirsty.

- **Sepia** – Heavy green nasal discharge; cough with much sputum; cough associated with irritation in the larynx.

HERBS

- **Ginger** – To loosen congestion, stimulate circulation and warm the body, and help fight infection.

- **Mullein** – Soothes mucous membranes; cough suppressant, natural antiviral and anti-inflammatory.

- **Marshmallow** – Soothes irritated membranes; antibacterial.

- **Thyme** – To help loosen congestion.

- **Wild Cherry Bark** – Commonly found in syrup form. Use the child's dose to help with hacking cough associated with bronchitis or kennel cough.

ACUPRESSURE

If your dog is exposed to kennel cough, acupressure can tonify lung qi and support the immune system to protect against infection. A number of lung points are located on the inside, and slightly to the back, of your dog's lower front legs. (See illustration on page 197.)

Stroking this area can stimulate a number of points simultaneously.

To treat chronic coughs or lung problems, consult your holistic veterinarian. An acupuncturist will use physical symptoms, the quality of your dog's pulse, and the color of his tongue to make a TCM diagnosis and prescribe the points you might use at home.

- **Central Storage LU1**
- **Broken Sequence LU7**
- **Great Abyss LU9**
- **Adjoining Valleys LI4**
- **Big Vertebra GV14**
- **Foot Three Mile ST36**

Pneumonia

NUTRITIONAL SUPPORT

- Dogs affected with pneumonia tire easily, and sometimes even lack the energy to eat. Offer small meals frequently, and hand feed if needed. Increase protein levels to support immune system and healing.

- Supplement with **antioxidants**. Vitamin E is especially important for treating lung disease. Vitamins A and C and bioflavanoids are also very helpful.

- **Bromelain**, an enzyme found in pineapple, helps break up mucous secretions, enhances antibiotic absorption, and has antiinflammatory action.

HOMEOPATHY

- **Antimonium tart.** – Audible mucus in respiratory tract but little expectoration.

- **Arsenicum** – Dry cough; difficulty breathing, worse when lying down; dog is very chilly.

- **Bryonia** – Painful, dry cough; difficulty breathing; dog is thirsty.

- **Lycopodium** – Pneumonia that has been untreated for some time; very difficult breathing; sputum is heavy grey or bloody pus.

- **Phosphorus** – Breathing is rapid and difficult; dog is very chilly, hypersensitive; symptoms are worse in cold air; becomes exhausted from coughing.

HERBS

- **Echinacea, goldenseal, Oregon grape, garlic** – For immune support and to help fight infection.

- **Astragalus, ginseng** – As a tonic.

- **Dandelion** – For mild diuretic action and as a tonic; encourage daily doses of a strong tea throughout recovery.

- **Thyme** – Helps loosen congestion.

ACUPRESSURE

- **Big Vertebrae GV14**
- **Hundred Meetings GV20**
- **Great Abyss LU9**
- **Foot Three Mile ST36**

Heart Disease and Circulatory Problems

We see more dogs with heart disease today due to, among other things, longer life span, poor breeding practices, and the use of drugs that damage the heart. Nevertheless, we are better able to manage heart disease and maintain our dogs' quality of life by using safer and better medications, and integrating holistic medicine as a part of their care.

Fortunately, dogs don't suffer from hardening of the arteries. Cholesterol problems and strokes are rare. High blood pressure can affect older dogs, especially those suffering from diseases of the kidney or adrenal glands. Heart murmurs, the abnormal heart sounds that result from a disturbance in the flow of blood in the heart, are common in small breeds as they age. This is due to a slowly progressive, degenerative condition of the heart valves.

If your dog is diagnosed with a heart murmur, chances are your veterinarian won't recommend therapies unless there are obvious symptoms of disease. This is often a great time to *support* the heart and circulation, and address your dog's health as a whole, warding off or slowing the advance of disease in the process.

NUTRITIONAL SUPPORT

- There is no single diet that is appropriate for all dogs with heart disease. Overweight dogs should have their calories restricted, as obesity stresses the heart.

- Excessive weight loss is a common problem with advanced heart disease or serious circulatory problems. Your dog might be just too tired or weak to finish a meal. **Hand feed** small portions throughout the day until your dog becomes stronger. To encourage eating, warm the food and add flavor enhancers such as salt-free tomato sauce, olive oil, salmon pieces, or a little honey.

- Watch excess salt in a heart patient's diet. Avoid high sodium foods, including all processed meats, packaged or canned foods, dairy products, processed dog treats, breads, and chips. Senior dog foods are usually low in salt, but be sure the food is right in other ways, including calorie content

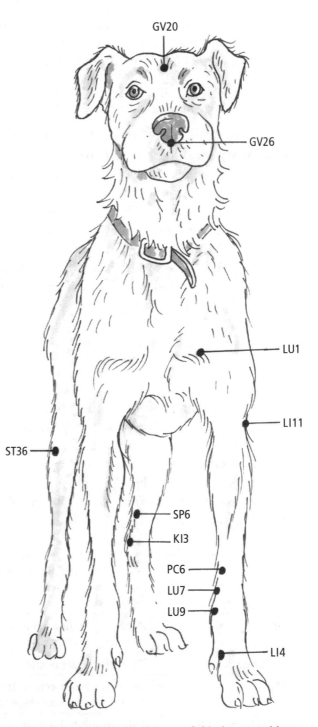

Common acupressure points: useful in heart and lung conditions, or to increase energy

and wholesomeness, before you settle on one of these as your basic diet. Stricter limitations on salt intake are needed in advanced heart disease.

- Consider feeding supplements that are particularly good for your dog's heart. (See below.)

- If your dog is diagnosed with **dilated cardiomyopathy**, try megadoses of **L-carnitine**. In some dogs with this disease, the heart muscle is lacking carnitine, so supplementation might improve heart function dramatically. For Cocker Spaniels give 1 gram every 8 to 12 hours; for Doberman Pinschers, Great Danes, Boxers, and other large breed dogs give 2 grams every 8 to 12 hours. Watch for mild diarrhea when megadoses are used. Should this occur, cut back the dose a little for a few days, then try slowly increasing it again. Before you begin any new supplements, check with your vet.

- Because **taurine** deficiency may also lead to heart disease, you might want to try megadoses of this nutrient as well. This is particularly advised if it's possible your dog's diet has been deficient in taurine (for example, if a vegetarian or commercial diet has been fed over a long period of time without rotating brands or formulas). Try 500 to 1000 mg 2 to 3 times daily.

- Supplement with **coQ10** to improve function of the heart muscle. Depending on the size of your dog, use 30 to 100 mg daily, unless your holistic veterinarian recommends larger doses.

- Dogs with poorly functioning hearts benefit from **antioxidants** to decrease oxidative stress on the heart. Use daily.

- **Fish oil** has been shown to improve survival in dogs with congestive heart failure, and helps address the weight loss and poor body condition that can develop. Use 1 to 4 capsules daily, depending on size.

HOMEOPATHY

Choosing a homeopathic remedy to support your dog's heart health is best done by an experienced practitioner. The following remedies suggest just a few examples of the many benefits this modality may provide.

- **Aconite** – A short-acting remedy that may be helpful in an acute event.

- **Carbo. veg.** – Poor circulation; lack of oxygen in the blood.

- **Crataegus** – A tonic remedy for the heart.

- **Digitalis** – Helps regulate heartbeat.

- **Naja** – Edema; valvular disease; shortness of breath.

HEART HEATH SUPPLEMENTS		
What	**Why**	**How Much Daily**
Taurine	Amino acid, heart nutrient; may be deficient in diet	250 to 1000 mg
L-Carnitine	Essential heart nutrient.	250 to 500 mg
CoQ10	Improves heart contraction, protects cells from degeneration.	60 to 180 mg
Essential fatty acids	Help regulate heart rhythm	1 to 4 fish oil capsules
Antioxidants (particularly vitamin E)	Protect against degeneration of heart muscle	200 to 800 IU vitamin E

HERBS

- Never begin herbal therapy on a dog in treatment for diagnosed heart disease without consulting your veterinarian first. While the herbs listed below can benefit your dog, caution is advised. Herbs may alter the amount of drug support your dog needs, and toxicity or worsening of the heart condition might occur if the dosage is not adjusted properly.

- If your dog has periodontal disease, the bacteria in the mouth can enter the bloodstream, causing further heart damage. Herbs to support the immune system, such as **astragalus** or **echinacea**, and those that have potent antibacterial action, such as **Oregon grape extract,** are good choices.

- **Hawthorne** – Heart tonic, helps stabilize blood pressure; antioxidant.

- **Coleus** – Gently helps to reduce blood pressure.

- **Garlic** – Improves circulation. (Can also affect clotting.)

- **Gingko** – For circulatory disorders; may increase cerebral circulation. (Can also affect clotting.)

- **Ginseng** – Helps with fatigue, helps combat stress. (Not for use in dogs with high blood pressure.)

- **Dandelion** – Helps balance fluids and electrolytes in the body.

ACUPRESSURE

Acupressure can help to strengthen, or tonify, the qi and heart as well as promote circulation. Use in cases of early heart disease to calm the heart spirit and balance the heart energy.

- **Spirit's Gate HT7** – Stabilizes the emotions.

- **Heart's Hollow BL15** – Balances the heart energy.

- **Inner Gate PC6** – Calms the spirit.

---

getting to the "heart" of it

Poets, monks, and ancient sages all refer to the heart in a way that suggests a connection to the spiritual and emotional being, rather than just as a physical organ responsible for pumping blood through our bodies. The connection between the heart and the emotions is seldom part of a Western medical approach, but certainly is recognized in Chinese, Native American, and the Auyervedic medical systems. These traditions suggest that to support the heart, you should support the emotional being as well. Heart disease is known to be more prevalent in depressed people, and we can see a similar pattern in dogs. Chronic heart valve disease is more common in the miniature breeds—the same breeds that tend to worry and fret more. When you provide a peaceful environment and pay attention to the emotional needs of your dog, you support the health of his heart as well.

If your dog has advanced heart disease, the most important point is **GV26**, or **Center of the Upper Lip**. (See illustrations on pages 96 and 103.) This point might help restore consciousness if your dog has collapsed. If your dog is unconscious, apply very firm digital pressure to GV26, but remove your hand as soon as you see her come around. Simultaneous firm pressure in the center of the bottom of the hind paw (a powerful acupressure point on the kidney meridian lies here) can also help restore consciousness.

OTHER

- Keep your dog fit through daily exercise.

- Avoid stress, both emotional and physical. For emotional stress, experiment with the Flower Remedies (see Chapter 8).

HOLISTIC VETERINARY TREATMENTS

- In addition to guidance on the use of herbal support and nutritional support, your holistic veterinarian may prescribe glandular therapy, offer an exercise plan, or discuss ways to avoid stress and support emotional well-being.

- Acupuncture has been shown to help correct heart rhythm disturbances, and can affect blood pressure and increase your dog's well being and energy level. The calming effect of acupuncture can benefit high-strung dogs or those under stress.

DRUG THERAPY AND CONVENTIONAL SUPPORT

If your dog has been diagnosed with a disease that ultimately leads to heart failure, chances are he's receiving one or more medications. **Diuretics** are

The canine heart

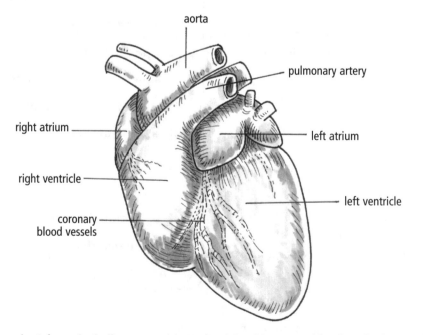

Your dog's heart is similar to your own: the right side pumps blood to the lungs while the left side pumps oxygenated blood to the rest of the body.

used to control fluid build-up in the lungs. **Vasodilators** improve the quality of life and increase survival time in patients with heart disease. **Digoxin** and related drugs are prescribed to help the heart beat more efficiently.

Your veterinarian should use the lowest possible doses of these drugs to control symptoms while minimizing side effects. Dogs with heart disease greatly benefit from blood monitoring, as this can help ensure that the lowest effective doses of medications are being used, and that the kidneys and other organs are not being compromised by the drugs. If your dog feels sick as a result of her meds, do not assume she can't take them. An adjustment in dosage may be all that is necessary. Remember, these are life-giving medications that should never be stopped abruptly without consulting your veterinarian.

The use of **ultrasound** is a noninvasive tool to help diagnose your dog's condition and monitor her progress. This can be done without anesthetics, causes no discomfort, and gives your vet a wealth of information.

If your veterinarian does not have access to ultrasound diagnostics, ask for a referral. Similarly, if he is not familiar with serum drug monitoring or cannot perform blood pressure measurements, and your dog is experiencing problems with the drug therapy or is not responding to treatment, ask for a referral to a cardiologist, or contact the Veterinary Heart Institute at www.vetheart.com.

the digestive system

the stomach, pancreas, liver, and intestines are the main organs that transform food into the life-giving energy and healthy tissues your dog needs. The **stomach** serves as a reservoir to store the food, adding hydrochloric acid and digestive enzymes to the mix before emptying the contents into the small intestine. Bile from the **liver** and enzymes from the **pancreas** are released through two separate ducts into the **small intestine**, where most nutrition is absorbed into the body. The **large intestine** acts as another reservoir, providing time and space for water and electrolytes to be absorbed from the intestinal tract. It's also home to most of the beneficial intestinal bacteria, which aid digestion and keep disease-causing bacteria from colonizing.

An even larger system of organs, nerves, enzymes, hormones, and body chemicals come together to complete the digestive process. Recent discoveries, such as how emotions impact the digestive system, and the complex role the immune system plays, offer exciting clues to how we can improve health in the future.

MAINTAINING HEALTH

When the gastrointestinal (GI) tract and related digestive organs are optimally healthy, the breath smells fresh, the appetite is good, and the stomach doesn't make a lot of gurgling or rumbling noises. Your dog doesn't have excessive flatulence, his stools are soft but firm, and he is full of energy.

- Start by **feeding a natural diet** that is as fresh as possible, with high quality, digestible ingredients, and free of chemical toxins and unnecessary additives. Feed portions that maintain optimum weight, and offer a variety of foods to reduce the chance your dog will develop a food allergy to an ingredient he eats day after day. Variety will ensure he gets a full complement of nutrients.

- Although many dogs thrive well enough on 1 feeding per day, eating **2 or 3 meals a day** will be easier on his GI tract if he's having problems. Some popular raw foods diet plans suggest **fasting** your dog one day a week. While fasting does offer some benefits to the GI tract, it may be emotionally stressful to your dog, especially if he is with you as you eat your customary meals—unless, of course, you choose to fast right along with him.

- **Nutrients and additives** in your dog's diet can have both a positive and negative effect on bowel function. If he is having digestive difficulties and you are feeding supplements, stop them for a few days and gradually reintroduce them one at a time. Your dog can develop an adverse reaction to anything he eats, and this is the best way to discover whether something you are giving him is having a negative impact on his system.

- **Periodically examine your dog's stool for form, consistency, and odor**. Stool health is one of the best indications that the digestive system is working properly. A highly digestible diet means there will be few stools; a bulky, high fiber diet means larger and more frequent stools.

- If your dog experiences digestive upsets or flatulence regularly, **experiment with changes in the diet.** If you are feeding raw food, try home-cooked meals to see if the symptoms abate. If you are feeding commercial dog food, select one with higher quality ingredients (See pages 66-67, Selecting a Commercial Food) or switch to home-prepared meals. Increasing or decreasing fiber content may also do the trick but, in general, it's best to keep fat content low.

- **When making major dietary changes, do so gradually** over a period of a week or more. While healthy animals adapt easily, a dog with a weak system or an imbalance may experience discomfort and diarrhea from an abrupt change. A sudden increase in high-fat ingredients may cause a serious disturbance to the pancreas gland.

- **Non-food factors** can also affect gastrointestinal health. **Avoid over-vaccination**; it may be responsible for some immune-mediated intestinal diseases. **Chronic emotional or physical stress** can also impact digestion.

- **Store harmful substances where your dog won't be likely to eat or chew on them.** Keep toxic substances and plants, drugs, and medicines out of reach. (See pages 26-28 for a list of potentially harmful substances around the home.) Be sure trashcans and compost piles are securely covered to avoid tempting your dog with all those intriguing smells.

- Include **probiotics** in the diet to help maintain a healthy balance of bacteria in the digestive tract, particularly if your dog has taken antibiotics.

- If you have a large or giant breed, especially one with a deep-chested body type like a Great Dane, Irish Setter, or Doberman, you need a thorough understanding of **bloat** and **stomach torsion**, or **gastric dilatation/volvulus (GDV).** Prevention is key, but if that fails it's essential that you know the early warning signs of this life-threatening syndrome, as well as the emergency steps you can take that may save your friend's life. (See pages 213-214.)

SIGNS OF TROUBLE

Dogs seem to have "iron" stomachs, because their apparently indiscriminate eating habits allow them to eat everything from an old carcass to a new carpet, often without even a hint of nausea. An occasional moderate digestive disturbance, especially if preceded by indiscretion in food choices, should not be a cause for alarm. In fact, vomiting and diarrhea are nature's ways of purging the system. Some dogs instinctively eat grass to help induce vomiting. However, severe vomiting or diarrhea that begins suddenly in an otherwise healthy animal may be a sign of poisoning, blockage in the digestive tract, or another serious disorder.

Chronic digestive disturbance, whether it happens on a daily basis or intermittently, might simply mean your dog needs a change in his diet. Keep in mind, though, that it *could* indicate something more serious like inflammatory bowel disease, ulcers, pancreatitis, or even cancer. In any case, knowing what to look for can help you determine how to proceed.

What to Look For:

See your veterinarian immediately if there is:

- **Blood in vomited material or in the stool.** This could be a sign of a dangerous obstruction, bleeding ulcers, a toxin, or an overwhelming bacterial infection.

- **Panting, shaking, or crying.** If your dog is exhibiting these or other distress symptoms, an obstruction or toxin needs to be ruled out.

An inability to keep water down. Your dog is unable to hold even water or other fluids in his stomach, and the problem has persisted for more than 12 hours.

Dry heaves, bloated belly, or severe discomfort. If you dog is vomiting but nothing is coming up, even if his abdomen is not distended, but he is obviously distressed, he may be suffering from bloat or stomach torsion (see pages 213-214). **Death can occur within a few hours—get your dog to a vet immediately.**

Dehydration. Severe vomiting or diarrhea that lasts more than a few hours can lead to dehydration, electrolyte imbalances, or even shock.

Straining to defecate, or painful defecation. Colon problems or obstructions are possible. Enlarged prostate can also impinge on the colon and cause these symptoms.

Other Signs of Gastrointestinal Problems:

Weight loss. While a bout with vomiting or diarrhea may cause his weight to drop off, it should be regained easily once his digestion and absorption of nutrients returns to normal. Significant weight loss along with other gastrointestinal symptoms suggests a problem that your veterinarian needs to investigate.

Chronic gas, burping, or excessive rumbling in the stomach.

Intermittent disinterest in food.

Mucus in the stools. The presence of mucus in the stool indicates an imbalance in the colon.

Color change in stools. Black or tar-like stools indicate bleeding in the upper part of the intestinal tract. Gray stools suggest liver trouble. Bright yellow or orange also indicates an imbalance.

Excessive odor. When accompanied by loose stools, a strong odor is often a sign of a parasite infection, such as giardia.

Large volume of stool. This may indicate an absorption problem. If your dog is creating an unusual amount of stool—whether in frequent bowel movements or by passing large quantities each time—it could indicate the quality of his diet is not up to par, or that he is not absorbing nutrients properly. Vegetarian diets create larger stools, and if you are adding fiber for any reason, increased volume is to be expected. But if stools are large and your dog is thin or losing weight, it's time to consult your veterinarian.

Investigate the Environment:

If your dog experiences a sudden case of diarrhea or vomiting, look for **foreign objects** that may have been chewed and ingested. Are any toys or socks missing? Do you see any telltale clues, like a frayed carpet? Smaller ingested objects can sometimes be encouraged to pass through by feeding pure cotton balls or small chunks of bread soaked in milk, to bind the offending object and protect the intestinal track

signs of dehydration

- Listlessness

- Weakness

- Lack of interest in surroundings

- Dullness in the eyes

- Dry mucous membranes or gums

- When you gently pinch the skin over the shoulder blades, it stays tented for a few seconds rather than immediately returning to normal.

from injury. But don't take chances. If you think your dog may have an obstruction, *always* notify your vet. Early intervention can be lifesaving.

🐕 Check also for **toxic substances or plants**, or any open containers of drugs or medicines. See pages 26-28 for a list of common household toxins (If you locate the source, call ASPCA hotline at 1-888-426-4435 for immediate advice on how to help your dog.)

🐕 Check for upended trashcans and signs of digging in the compost pile. **Garbage and compost** can contain life-threatening bacterial toxins. Watch your dog closely for deterioration in his condition. Rapid changes indicate a need for immediate veterinary attention.

Knowing what you can do at home, when the symptoms indicate no immediate emergency, can help your dog begin to feel better right away. For acute vomiting or diarrhea, begin with the suggestions that follow and use the rest of the chapter for further support. If the problem persists or does not respond to your best efforts, consult your veterinarian.

COMMON CAUSES OF ACUTE VOMITING OR DIARRHEA

Dietary indiscretion

Food allergy or dietary sensitivity

Parasites

Foreign body (toy, bone, etc.) obstructing the bowel or stomach outflow

Internal disorder affecting the pancreas, kidney, liver, or adrenal gland

Drug reaction (may be due to antibiotics, NSAIDs, steroids, heart medications)

Emotional stress

Acute Vomiting

NUTRITIONAL SUPPORT

- Sometimes the most important thing you can do for your dog when he's vomiting is simply to rest his gastrointestinal tract by **withholding food and water** for 6 to 12 hours. A longer fast may lead to dehydration if vomiting continues, and should only be done on your veterinarian's advice.

- To reintroduce food after the fast, start with **highly digestible, bland foods**, such as cooked rice, tapioca, or even barley or rice water in small portions. (See page 207 for a recipe for barley water.) If no vomiting occurs after 3 to 4 hours, gradually add more easily-digested ingredients. Try plain cultured yogurt, poached eggs, baked potatoes, bananas, or cooked lean poultry or meat. Resume your dog's usual diet gradually, over a period of 2 to 3 days.

- If your dog has acute, recurrent vomiting, **reevaluate his diet**. Greasy and fatty foods are hard to digest. If you're feeding raw meats, are they clean and fresh? Are you overfeeding? Or could it be a single ingredient that's giving him trouble?

- If your dog is prone to carsickness, withhold food 2 hours prior to traveling.

HOMEOPATHY

- **Arsenicum** – Retching or vomiting that's worse after eating or drinking; vomitus contains blood or green mucus. Drinks a large volume of water, but in small, frequent portions. An important remedy for digestive disturbances related to ingestion of toxins or decayed food. Call your vet immediately when vomitus contains blood.

- **Ipecac** – Persistent nausea and vomiting of undigested food, bile, blood, or mucus. May have hiccups.

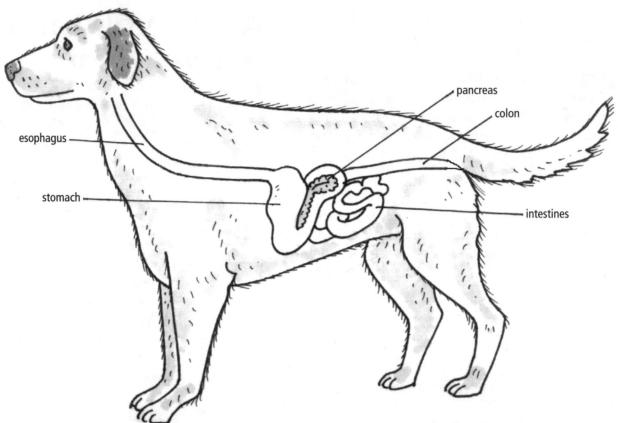

esophagus

stomach

pancreas

colon

intestines

The digestive tract

- **Nux vomica** – Nausea, retching, and vomiting, particularly after overeating; bloat (seek veterinary attention immediately).

- **Phosphorus** – Vomits water or undigested food; vomiting after surgery. Very thirsty. Better after cold water.

- **Veratrum album** – Profuse vomiting, made worse by drinking; very thirsty for cold water, but vomits immediately after drinking. Extremely hungry. Call your vet if vomiting is profuse.

HERBS

- If your dog is vomiting after he raided the cat food container, or gorged on something else inappro-

priate for his system, try a dose of **Pill Curing,** a popular Chinese herbal remedy for nausea and vomiting from overeating. Give $1/4$ to 1 vial, all at one time, depending on the size of your dog.

- Other gentle and effective ways to settle the stomach include a **ginger** or **chamomile tea**. Add a teaspoon of chamomile flowers to a cup of boiling water and steep for 10 minutes, or simmer a few thin slices of fresh ginger root in water for 15 or 20 minutes. Add honey to improve taste and help calm the stomach. Offer your dog small amounts, by the dropperful. (Tiny dogs need just a few dropperfuls; large dogs will need almost $1/2$ cup.) As an alternative to teas, use a few drops of chamomile or ginger tincture. To prevent carsickness, give tea ½ hour before traveling, and then every 2 hours as needed.

ACUPRESSURE

- **Inner Gate PC6** is an excellent way to help control vomiting and calm nausea. It will also calm your dog.

- **Foot Three Mile ST36** is good for any stomach problem, and can help increase physical strength and provide energy.

- **Stomach's Hollow BL21** and **Spleen's Hollow BL20** are found close together on the back, just in front of and behind the last rib where it connects to the spine. (See illustration below.) These points, and **Middle Cavity CV12**, on the belly, may be a little sensitive. Use light pressure and hold for no more than 10 or 15 seconds each.

OTHER

Always consider your dog's **emotional state**. Just like ours, his tummy can become upset due to excitement, nervousness, anger, or anxiety.

Evaluate your dog's home environment and lifestyle for causes of stress, and remove or minimize them if possible. **Rescue Remedy** and homeopathic **Aconite** will help ease occasional stress, but there are times when what he needs most is rest, physically and emotionally. Digestive upsets can be your first sign of an imbalance, and addressing his emotional health *now* could prevent serious physical problems later.

barley water

1 cup barley

3 cups spring or distilled water

1. Place barley and water in a large pot. Boil for about 3 hours.

2. Cool, strain (discarding the barley), and serve.

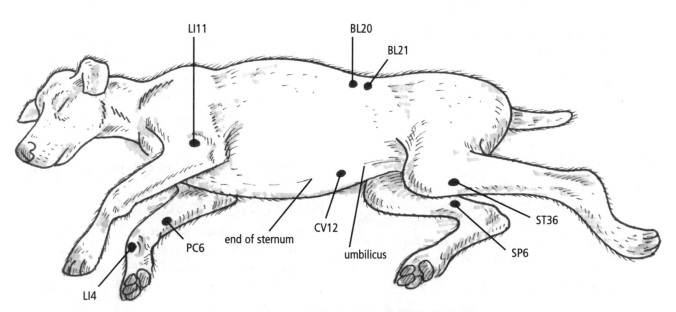

LI11   BL20   BL21

CV12   end of sternum   PC6   LI4   umbilicus   SP6   ST36

Common acupressure points for gastrointestinal troubles

Acute Diarrhea

NUTRITIONAL SUPPORT

- Just as with vomiting, resting the digestive tract is important when diarrhea occurs. Try a **24-hour fast**, offering small amounts of spring water or rice or barley water regularly.

- If your dog has watery or explosive diarrhea and is in danger of dehydration, electrolyte powders (made for humans) can be mixed in water and given in small sips throughout the first day of illness. The second day, follow food reintroduction guidelines listed for Acute Vomiting (see pages 205-207). Most diarrheas that are due to overeating, or ingesting something that upsets the GI tract, will be resolved in 3 to 4 days.

- Powdered bentonite mineral clay can be given orally to pull toxins out of the intestinal tract and slow the bowel a bit. Use ¼ to ½ teaspoon mixed with plain yogurt. Activated charcoal can be used in a similar fashion. Just cut back the recommended human dose in proportion to your dog's weight. Or offer carob powder, ½ to 2 teaspoons 3 times a day, mixed with water and a little honey. See also Medicine Chest.

- 2 or 3 doses of **probiotics**, given 6 to 12 hours apart, can help clear up diarrhea, especially if it occurs while your dog is taking a course of antibiotics.

HOMEOPATHY

- **Arsenicum** – Dark, bloody diarrhea, very offensive odor; worse after eating. Rectum protrudes. Body is cold. An important remedy when diarrhea is related to ingestion of toxins or decayed food. Report any bloody diarrhea to your vet.

- **Mercurius** – Diarrhea with straining.

- **Nux vomica** – Diarrhea after overeating; alternating constipation and diarrhea.

- **Phosphorus** – Passes large amounts of stool, then is exhausted afterward; stool passes involuntarily.

- **Pulsatilla** – Watery stool; mucus and blood in stool; worse at night.

- **Veratrum album** – Very painful, watery diarrhea, large amounts of stool, explosive. Dog is exhausted.

HERBS

- **Slippery elm** is a nutritive herb that soothes and heals inflamed intestines. Give 1 to 3 capsules, depending on size, twice a day, mixed in a little broth. Also beneficial as a tea or tincture.

ACUPRESSURE

- **Foot Three Mile ST36**, **Three Yin Junction SP6**, and **Middle Cavity CV12** are all useful in treating diarrhea.

- If there is foul smelling or yellowish diarrhea, and your dog feels hot, add **Crooked Pool LI11**.

OTHER

If your dog is eating a raw foods or a meaty bone diet, and acute diarrhea problems become recurrent, refer to Chapter 3 for cautionary information.

Acute Constipation

NUTRITIONAL SUPPORT

- Occasional **constipation** is likely due to dietary indiscretion, but if the problem is chronic, reevaluate your feeding program. Are you feeding an all-kibble diet? It may be too dry for your dog, especially if he is a light drinker. Are you giving too many indigestible bones? Is fresh water always available?

- While excessive fiber can occasionally be the cause of constipation, it's usually a *solution* to constipation problems, especially in older dogs. Add **fresh vegetables** to the diet, or try a daily spoonful of **pumpkin** or **bran**.

- Give **probiotics** to help balance the consistency of the stool.

- Add an extra portion of **vegetable oil** to the meals.

HOMEOPATHY

- **Aloe** – Sensitivity around anus and rectum. Flatulence.

- **Nat. mur.** – Stool is very dry; pain after passing stool; bleeding from the anus.

- **Nux vomica** – Frequent attempts to pass stool; passes small amounts of stool.

- **Sepia** – Stools are large and hard, or soft but difficult to pass; straining.

- **Sulphur** – Frequent unsuccessful attempts; stool is small and hard.

HERBS

- **Psyllium** (seed husks from the plantain plant) is one of the best remedies for constipation and general intestinal health. Give 1/2 to 2 teaspoons mixed in water or broth once or twice a day.

- **Flaxseed** – Freshly ground (1/2 to 3 teaspoons a day) flaxseed provides not only fiber for constipation, but is a great source of B vitamins and essential fatty acids.

- **Milk thistle** – The tea, added to meals, to support the liver and soften the stool.

ACUPRESSURE

Traditional Chinese Medicine recognizes more than 25 different patterns of disharmony that can lead to constipation. Your veterinary acupuncturist will help you choose specific points for your dog, based on the pattern of symptoms. Here are a few to try, especially as a way to prevent problems if your dog is prone to constipation.

- **Foot Three Mile ST36** and **Three Yin Crossing SP6** if your dog's tongue is pale.

- **Adjoining Valleys LI4** and **Crooked Pool LI11** if your dog's tongue is red.

OTHER

- Make sure your dog is getting enough exercise, and has plenty of opportunities and time for eliminations in a place he feels comfortable.

- Rule out pain as a reason for chronic constipation. Dogs will hold their stools if there's pain in the rectum, pelvis, hind limbs, or lower back area. Neurologic problems can also impair your dog's ability to eliminate stools.

Chronic Digestive Problems

Chronic problems of the digestive tract often have one or more symptoms: poor appetite, salivating (due to nausea), vomiting, diarrhea, weight loss, or stools with strong odor or abnormal color or texture.

NUTRITIONAL SUPPORT

- Loose stools or vomiting can be caused by a **food hypersensitivity**. It may be an allergy to something your dog has eaten a couple of times, or over a long period. It could be a reaction to a chemical additive or even a simple protein or grain. (While any dog can react to a given food or ingredient, Irish Setters are particularly prone to wheat sensitivity. Shar-Peis are known for multiple dietary allergies.) **Change ingredients** if you suspect this may be at the root of the problem. If your dog has a true hypersensitivity, it can take 3 to 10 weeks to see improvement after removing the offending ingredient from the diet. Once a hypersensitivity is confirmed (by seeing a good response to the diet change), gradually reintroduce foods, one at a time each week, to pinpoint the offending substance. See the **8-Week Food Allergy Trial**.

- Another **diet trial** that helps some dogs is a highly digestible, low-fat diet: 1 part cooked, skinless chicken breast or low-fat cottage cheese, mixed with 2 parts cooked white rice. Add a pancreatic/digestive enzyme and probiotic supplement that contains lactobacillus. You may see a reduction in the diarrhea within 3 to 4 days, and a balanced, long-term maintenance diet program can then be instituted. Be sure to add fresh vegetables and vary the ingredients for a long-term diet plan.

- Many dogs, for various reasons, lose the normal complement of beneficial intestinal bacteria that play a major role in defense against disease. To replenish normal intestinal flora and reestablish a healthier intestinal tract, offer your dog a **probiotic supplement** for at least a week. Some dogs benefit from long-term supplementation. If your dog has a food allergy, look for a probiotic without dairy, wheat, corn, or animal products.

8-WEEK FOOD ALLERGY TRIAL

¼ pound lamb or tofu
1 cup cooked white rice
¼ to ½ teaspoon olive oil
1 teaspoon bonemeal, ground oystershell, or calcium carbonate powder
1 daily vitamin supplement (human or canine)

- Recipe feeds a 10- to 20-pound dog for one day. Increase amounts accordingly.

- When deciding whether to use tofu or lamb, choose the ingredient that your dog has never eaten in the past. If your dog has eaten both in the past, try pinto beans, venison, rabbit, or turkey.

- Provide only spring water during the 8-week diet trial. Offer no treats or any other food sources, including beef-flavored heartworm preventives. If you see partial, but not complete, improvement at 8 weeks, extend the trial for 2 to 4 additional weeks.

- This diet is not meant for long-term use. If you continue to feed it longer than 12 weeks, supplement with fresh vegetables.

Adapted from *Home Prepared Dog and Cat Diets: The Healthful Alternative*. D. Strombeck. Iowa State University Press, 1999.

- A **prebiotic supplement,** or food supplement that *promotes* the growth of friendly bacteria in the intestinal tract, is also helpful. Look for fructo-oligosaccharide, or FOS supplements, and adjust the human dose proportionately to your dog's size. Some specialized veterinary diets contain chicory root to provide FOS; other natural sources include Jerusalem artichoke, asparagus, bananas, and garlic.

- **Apple cider vinegar** contains beneficial vitamins and minerals, and is a wonderful food for intestinal health. Most dogs don't mind a little in their water bowl when they're having digestive problems.

- The amino acid **glutamine** fuels intestinal cells and speeds healing. Raw spinach and parsley are good sources, and concentrated powdered supplements are also available. (See pages 212-213, Inflammatory Bowel Disease.

- Provide adequate levels of **essential fatty acids**. For chronic digestive problems with inflammation of the digestive tract, fish oil (unless your dog is allergic to fish) and flax oil are good choices.

- Provide a daily **antioxidant** blend supplement. Keep in mind that high doses of vitamin C can cause diarrhea, so reduce the dose if stools become loose.

- Chronic digestive problems will often be alleviated with **enzyme supplements**. Product quality can vary. Ask your holistic veterinarian for a recommendation.

HOMEOPATHY

There is a wide variety of symptoms associated with chronic digestive troubles, and many, many homeopathic remedies that may address them. Evaluate your dog's overall symptom picture and consult the Materia Medica to determine the remedy most appropriate for him. The following list includes some of the remedies you may want to consider.

- **Arsenicum**
- **Carbo. veg.**
- **Colocynthis**
- **Nux vomica**
- **Sulphur**

- **Thuja**
- **Mercurius**
- **Veratrum album**

HERBS

- The powerful antiinflammatory and antiallergic effects of **licorice** make this a good choice for stomach ulcers and inflammatory conditions of the intestinal tract. Choose the deglycyrrhizinated extract form (DGL) to protect against the cortisone-like side effects that can occur with long-term use of licorice, and reduce the human dosage proportionately to your dog's size. See Materia Medica for cautions and side effects.

- When intermittent upsets occur, a **tea** of **slippery elm, plantain, licorice, and marshmallow root** can be soothing. **Milk thistle** or **dandelion root tea** will support the liver and aid digestion. **Ginger root tea** will help balance the consistency of the stool. A few tablespoons twice daily works well for medium-sized dogs.

COMMON CAUSES OF CHRONIC VOMITING OR DIARRHEA
Irritable bowel syndrome and emotional stress
Inflammatory bowel or stomach diseases
Parasites
Food allergies
Problems with motility of the intestinal tract
Poor diet
Tumors of the gastrointestinal tract
Bacterial overgrowth in the small intestines
Chronic pancreatitis

ACUPRESSURE

The points listed under Acute Vomiting and Acute Diarrhea (see pages 207 and 208) can also be used in chronic cases.

For chronic constipation, try:

- **Adjoining Valleys LI4**
- **Large Intestines Hollow BL25**
- **Foot Three Mile ST36**

For best results, your veterinary acupuncturist can assist in choosing points based on a TCM diagnosis for your individual dog.

WORKING WITH YOUR VETERINARIAN

If your dog is suffering from chronic digestive disturbances, he deserves a methodical inquiry to pinpoint the underlying cause. Your conventional veterinarian is likely to suggest basic blood tests and a fecal examination for parasites. X-rays and ultrasound may also be used, as well as endoscopy, a procedure that uses a fiber optic light source to view the stomach and intestinal tract for abnormalities while your dog is anesthetized. Biopsies can be taken at the same time. Exploratory surgery is usually the last resort.

Your holistic veterinarian is likely to suggest dietary and other changes before proceeding with more invasive testing, as long as your dog's condition is stable. She can help you sort out food issues that may be contributory, and also explore emotional factors that can manifest as physical symptoms. Through homeopathy, acupuncture, herbal formulas, and food therapy, she will focus on rebalancing and supporting the body's life force toward a deep level of healing.

Inflammatory Bowel Disease (IBD)

There are a number of different diseases of the gastrointestinal tract that fall under the heading of inflammatory bowel disease, or IBD. In this disease, white blood cells line the digestive tract and inhibit nutrient absorption, causing severe weight and protein loss. Intestinal biopsies are the only way to confirm this set of diseases, although the symptoms of chronic digestive disturbance, weight loss, and abnormalities on your dog's blood tests may point to this diagnosis as a possibility.

IBD is a frustrating problem. Conventional therapy often calls for very strong drugs to treat the disease. However, holistic veterinarians have reported successfully weaning patients off their medication, and even curing some cases, with proper nutritional support and alternative therapies. The tips below will be of benefit if your dog suffers from IBD, and perhaps help you avoid or reduce the use of strong drugs. Of course, never attempt to discontinue medications without the advice of your veterinarian.

NUTRITIONAL SUPPORT

- Feed only a **rice-based, hypoallergenic fresh food diet**, preferably vegetarian. Tofu is an excellent protein source. (In some cases substituting fresh, cooked rabbit or venison will work in place of tofu.) If this is impossible, feed a veterinary formula (vegetarian or "novel protein" type) that is designed for food allergies. Avoid raw foods until your dog's intestinal health is restored.

- Provide daily **antioxidants**: For a medium-sized dog, vitamin E (400 to 800 IU), vitamin A (1000 to 5000 IU), and selenium (10 to 20 micrograms) are sufficient, but an antioxidant blend can also be useful. Vitamin C is hard for the diseased intestinal tract to handle, so leave it out until intestinal health is restored.

- Provide a daily source of vitamin **B complex**, as well as 10 to 15 mg of **zinc** and a complement of **trace minerals**.

- Supplementing with the amino acid **glutamine** or **fish oils** have helped some dogs.

- Give a daily **probiotic** supplement, such as lactobacillus acidophilus or a combination formula. Look for those that contain **prebiotics** (FOS) and **digestive enzymes** as well.

- **N-acetyglucosamine** may help heal the inflamed bowel lining.

HOMEOPATHY

Homeopathy can be an effective remedy for dealing with IBD, and there are many remedies that reflect individual symptoms of the disease. Use the guidelines in the Materia Medica to help you evaluate your dog's overall symptom picture to determine the remedy most appropriate for him, or seek the help of a trained homeopath. Consider the remedies listed earlier in this chapter for the symptoms most prevalent in your dog.

HERBS

- **Licorice** in the form of DGL extract supplement. (See page 211.)

- **Pill Curing** is especially helpful with nausea; can be used long term, or for intermittent bouts of indigestion.

- **Slippery elm**, and **chamomile** to help soothe symptoms.

- **Boswellia** to help reduce bowel inflammation.

ACUPRESSURE

The acupressure points used will vary with your dog's symptoms. You can refer to the points used for acute problems on pages 207, 208, and 209, but consulting an acupuncturist is best for chronic problems associated with IBD. You can always work with points along the Stomach and Spleen Meridians **SP6, ST36**, as Spleen Deficiency is a common TCM diagnosis when IBD symptoms are present.

Bloat and Stomach Torsion (Gastric Dilatation/ Volvulus—GDV)

These terms refer to distension of the stomach with air, food, or fluid (**bloat**, or gastric dilation), which can sometimes lead to a critical situation in which the stomach actually rotates inside the abdominal cavity (**stomach torsion**, or gastric volvulus). Once the stomach rotates, circulation is inhibited and the stomach tissue begins to die. This extremely painful and life-threatening condition occurs most frequently in purebred large and giant breed dogs with a deep-chested body.

To Help Prevent Bloat or Gastric Torsion:

- **Avoid large meals,** especially those that consist only of dry food. Instead, feed a high quality, easily digestible diet divided into at least 2 meals each day.

- **Avoid vigorous exercise that lasts more than 2 hours at a time.**

- **Avoid vigorous exercise, excitement, or stress for 30 minutes before or 2 hours after a meal.**

- Placing your dog's food dish on an elevated surface so that he does not need to stretch down to the floor when he eats may help.

- Because dogs who are generally nervous, fearful, or aggressive are at greater risk for bloat and torsion, it's important to minimize stress around feeding time, particularly if your dog has one of these temperaments. If possible, feed your dog in a quiet place where he can be alone.

- If your dog has a close relative who has suffered a GDV, discuss the pros and cons of a preventive surgery called gastroplexy with your veterinarian. In this procedure, the stomach is attached with internal sutures to the abdominal wall to minimize the possibility of rotation. The procedure can be performed at the same time as spaying or neutering.

If your dog does show signs of bloat, (non-productive vomiting, distress) *see your veterinarian immediately*. Administer Nux vomica at 15-minute intervals while you travel to the vet.

the liver

Your dog's liver plays a central role in the balance of most of his biochemical processes. It regulates the metabolism of fats, carbohydrates, hormones and vitamins, and it produces clotting factors that control bleeding, important blood plasma proteins for maintaining health, and bile to help digest food. It stores vitamins, iron, and other minerals, as well as energy in the form of carbohydrates, glucose, and fat. It neutralizes the toxic effects of medications and the potentially poisonous substances that may enter your dog's system. Because the liver is intimately involved in so many diverse metabolic activities, it is subject to injury from a wide variety of infections, toxins, and diseases. Fortunately, it has a phenomenal reserve and remarkable regenerative capabilities—as much as two thirds of the liver can be removed, and it will regenerate itself in just a few months. But while the liver's resilience is a *good* thing, it means that a lot of damage can occur before your dog shows signs of illness.

MAINTAINING HEALTH

- Avoid exposure to toxins and chemicals as much as possible. This is the single best way to protect the liver from damage.

- Ask your veterinarian to explain the side effects of all medications prescribed for your dog. If there's a chance of liver damage, ask if there is an alternative medication; if not, find out how to minimize the risk. For example, if your dog is being treated for seizures with phenobarbital, ask about switching to potassium bromide. (See also pages 250-251, Controlling Difficult Seizures.)

- Symptoms of liver disease can be vague. Consider an annual blood panel, especially if your dog is aging. If he is taking any drug on a long-term basis (such as phenobarbital or cortisone) and a screening panel shows any abnormalities, ask about a **bile acid assay**. This is a more sensitive test that will give more detailed information about how the liver is functioning.

SIGNS OF TROUBLE

Identifying the problem can be difficult. In *early* liver disease, your dog may show no detectable signs of illness. When the liver fails, the symptoms can mimic a number of other diseases.

What to Look For:

- Loss of appetite
- Weight loss
- Listlessness
- Poor coat condition
- Soft stools
- Gray stools
- Swollen abdomen

🐕 **Fluid retention**

🐕 **Jaundiced (yellow) mucous membranes**

🐕 **Weakness**

🐕 **Confusion**

🐕 **Convulsions or delirium in advanced illness**

If your dog is diagnosed with liver disease, your vet may do a liver biopsy to diagnose the cause (there are many!) and the severity of the problem. Conventional therapies are used to treat the underlying problem or reduce the symptoms. The holistic approach involves *supporting* the liver while it is healing, and creating an environment that will maximize the liver's enormous healing capacity.

If the diagnosis is liver cancer, the aim is to assist that part of the liver that isn't diseased, maintain health in the rest of the body, and provide physical

---

COMMON POTENTIAL LIVER TOXINS

Cortisone (steroid) compounds

Phenobarbital (anticonvulsant)

Chlorinated or phenol chemical compounds (older brands of pesticides, pine oil products)

Heavy metals (mercury from tainted deep-sea fish, lead from old paint chips)

Nonsteroidal antiinflammatory drugs (NSAIDs) such as aspirin, Rimadyl, Etogesic, or Feldene

Endotoxins (from food poisoning)

Leptospirosis infection (see page 34)

Aflatoxins (from grain-based foods that are contaminated with mold)

Poisonous mushroom or plant

---

and emotional comfort. You'll offer similar support if your dog is in crisis as a result of an acute liver injury. This can follow heatstroke, toxin ingestion, bacterial diseases, or a reaction to a drug. If the liver has been slowly deteriorating (as with chronic diseases associated with copper accumulation in the liver, common in Beddlington and West Highland Terriers), your supportive efforts will be much the same.

NUTRITIONAL SUPPORT

- In liver disease, there's a decreased ability to detoxify whatever goes into your dog's system. More than ever, you'll want to avoid synthetic chemicals in his diet, as well as flea or tick repellents that might be absorbed into his body.

- Raw meats contaminated with salmonella pose a more serious problem when the liver isn't functioning. Opt for cooked meats during healing.

- Create a diet that is low in fat, moderate in protein, and with easily digestible grains. A meal based on rice, with eggs, cottage cheese, soy, or chicken for protein, is a good choice. Be sure to include steamed vegetables for their array of nutrients, as well as vitamin B complex, olive oil or another source of fat, and the proper amount of calcium supplementation (see Chapter 3, A Wholesome Diet). In advanced liver disease, or in copper-associated liver problems, discuss your diet plan with your veterinarian, or contact www.pet-diets.com. Prescription veterinary diets (both canned and dry) are available, some with natural preservatives, to meet these requirements.

- Feed 3 smaller meals a day, rather than 1 or 2 larger ones.

- Be cautious about your choice of nutritional supplements. Some are not metabolized well when the liver is not healthy. The following supplements are safe, even when your dog has liver disease:

- **Vitamin C** – 250 to 500 mg per day, depending on your dog's weight and tolerance.
- **Vitamin E** – 100 IU per 10 pounds body weight daily. (Preparations that include selenium are acceptable.) Use only the d-alpha form.
- **Coenzyme Q10** – 10 to 30 mg per day.
- **Glutamine**
- **SAM-e** (or S-Adenosylmethionine) is perhaps the best nutritional supplement you can give for the liver. A healthy liver produces this important antioxidant, and without it, more liver damage occurs.
- Ask your veterinarian about **N-acetylcysteine** for liver support.
- **Glandular therapy** (feeding liver or freeze-dried liver extracts) may be beneficial in some mild cases of liver trouble, but is not recommended for copper-associated diseases. (See page 243, About Glandular Therapy.)

HOMEOPATHY

Liver disease should be treated as a serious, chronic condition that needs veterinary advice and support. Choose homeopathic remedies based on your dog's complete symptom picture. See Homeopathic Materia Medica for guidelines.

- **Carduus mar.** – Pain in the abdomen. Stools are hard, difficult to pass, may be bright yellow; constipation alternates with diarrhea. Jaundice.
- **Chelidonium** – Pain under lower edge of right shoulder blade. Jaundice due to liver obstruction. Liver enlarged, abdomen distended.
- **Cholesterinum** – Liver engorged. Jaundice. Particularly useful when disease is due to obstruction of the bile duct or fatty liver; cancer of the liver.

The liver relative to other organs

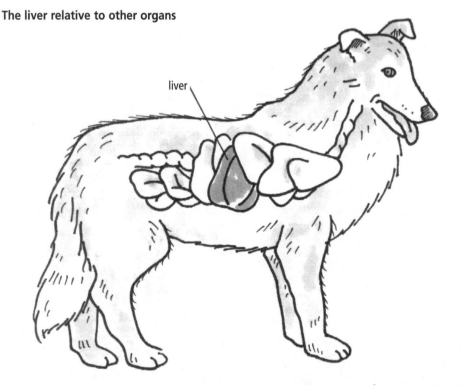

liver

- **Hepar** – Abdomen distended and painful. Hepatitis, liver abscess.

- **Nat. sulph.** – Vomits bile. Very large stools; flatulence. Hepatitis.

HERBS

- The extract of the **milk thistle** seed is your best choice for liver trouble. It protects liver cells from injury and supports the regeneration of new ones. Offer it at the first sign of a problem, or use it for support when your dog must take drugs that might damage the liver, such as cortisone or chemotherapy. It's believed that long-term use might help inhibit cirrhosis when the liver has been damaged.

- **Dandelion root** is an excellent liver tonic and particularly useful when bile clearance is a problem, or when a diuretic effect is needed.

- Other beneficial herbs for the liver include artichoke, turmeric, and the Ayurvedic botanical, picrorhiza root. You may find extracts of these herbs included in some milk thistle supplements.

- **Alfalfa** is helpful when the liver is in failure, as it provides a good source of vitamin K, as well as other vitamins and nutrients. Vitamin K-dependent clotting factors are produced in the liver, so a damaged organ may need this support. Other good sources include **green tea** and **dark, leafy greens**.

HOLISTIC VETERINARY TREATMENTS

Your holistic veterinarian is likely to employ a wide range of complimentary therapies to promote the healing of the liver, including Chinese medicine, homeopathy, therapeutic touch, and glandular therapy. As always, the goal will be to address lifestyle, diet, and your daily routine with your friend in an effort to provide the best possible support for his mind, body, and spirit.

the urinary tract and reproductive system

Your dog's urinary tract is a marvelously intricate system of organs, hormones, and chemistry. The **kidneys** are the primary organs responsible for regulating the internal environment of the body. They play an important role in water and electrolyte balance, in the elimination of the everyday waste products that result from metabolism, and in the removal of certain toxins. As the kidneys remove toxins and waste from the blood, they create the urine that will eventually carry the unwanted substances out of the body. Urine is stored in the **bladder** until it passes through the **urethra** and exits the body. Nerves reaching from the spinal column to the bladder and urethral **sphincter** muscles signal appropriate contraction and relaxation during urination.

The urinary tract is dependent on other organs and body systems to function properly. An imbalance anywhere in the body can affect the ability of the kidneys to do their job. For example, to keep the urinary tract in good condition we must also take care of the circulatory system—particularly the heart—as well as the adrenal glands.

MAINTAINING HEALTH

To help your dog's urinary tract stay healthy:

- Provide easy access to fresh water, and remember to clean the bowl regularly.

- Make sure your dog has easy access to a place where he can urinate whenever he needs to. Even if you think he is very good at holding it, making him wait will cause overdistension, or stretching, of the bladder, and can lead to chronic problems.

- Provide a balanced diet with fresh foods and plenty of variety. Supplement with omega-3 fatty acids.

- Minimize the stress in your dog's life as much as possible. Supplement with vitamin B-complex and an antioxidant blend if your dog is undergoing an emotionally or physically stressful period.

- Avoid dehydration, especially if your dog is a senior citizen. If he does not receive the water his body needs—whether from failure to drink, excessive diarrhea, or even if someone simply forgets to fill the water bowl—kidney damage may occur.

FUNCTIONS OF THE KIDNEY

Regulates the body's water and electrolyte content

Assists in regulation of blood pressure

Filters waste material from the bloodstream

Assists in the production of red blood cells

Converts vitamin D into a form that the body can use

- If your dog is elderly, it's wise to have his blood and urine checked by your veterinarian every 6 to 12 months to evaluate kidney function. As he ages he becomes more prone to undetected urinary infections or other disease processes that affect his kidneys. These conditions can be serious and may become chronic, so catching them early is key.

SIGNS OF TROUBLE

Any change in your dog's urinary habits needs your attention. Water intake and urination are so routine, it's easy to forget to take notice of them. But an awareness of your dog's habits when he's well, and tuning in to any changes, are key to catching and addressing a potentially serious problem in its earliest stages.

What to Look For:

- **Increased urination.** Does your dog seem to squat or lift his leg for a longer period of time than usual?

- **Frequent urination.** Even if he only passes a small amount each time, if he's asking to go out more often it's likely that something is not as it should be.

- **Increased thirst.** You can usually tell how much water your dog consumes throughout the day simply by noticing how often you fill his water bowl. **Even with moderate exercise and warm weather, he should not drink more than $1\frac{1}{2}$ to 2 cups per 10 pounds of body weight in a 24-hour period.** A dog who is unusually thirsty probably has either a urinary tract problem or other disorder that needs your attention. If his water intake does not return to normal within 2 to 3 days of home treatment, seek veterinary assistance.

- **Blood in the urine.** If you see signs of blood in the urine, consult your vet. Even if it appears to be just a small amount, it indicates a loss of integrity somewhere along the lining of the urinary tract. This might be due to inflammation from a bacterial infection that can be treated easily in a matter of days. Or it could mean damage caused by a toxin in your dog's system, or by a kidney or bladder stone. It might even be a sign of cancer. In any case, it's a reliable sign that treatment is needed.

- **Straining.** Does your dog seem to be having difficulty urinating? Does she try and try, with little result? When your friend goes out to relieve herself the urine should flow freely and easily. Eliminating urine is a vital function. Failure to do so results in a build-up of toxins in the body, and may be the result of a blockage in the urethra. If your dog appears unable to urinate at all, consult your veterinarian.

- **Pain or discomfort.** If your dog runs away and looks distressed after urinating, or seems intent on licking the penis or vulva, he or she may be feeling some burning in the urethra. Frequent urination is often a sign of bladder discomfort. If he seems uncomfortable when you apply gentle pressure in the lumbar area, just over the kidneys (see illustration on page 221), he may be feeling pain in the organs themselves.

- **Odor.** By itself, a strange odor to the urine is probably no cause for alarm. But if other symptoms are present, this might help you determine the right treatment.

- **Incontinence.** Is she urinating in her sleep, or squatting just before she can get outside? Does urine drip from the penis or vulva—and your dog doesn't seem to notice? The inability to control the flow of urine can be caused by problems related to the neurologic system, the hormones, the bladder, or the bladder sphincters and muscles of the urethra.

➤ **Marking.** Does your dog suddenly seem to have forgotten his housetraining? If he is urinating in strange places it may be a sign of emotional difficulties, senility, or a urinary tract problem. Unless there's an obvious reason for him to begin expressing himself in this way (such as a new puppy in the house or a major change in his routine), ask your veterinarian to run tests to check for a physical cause. If the results are normal, you can then explore the possibility of a behavioral or emotional cause.

➤ **Weight loss.** Unexplained weight loss is always a sign that something is awry. When it occurs with other urinary tract symptoms, it's an indi-cation that whatever is troubling him is taking a significant toll on his system.

➤ **Loss of appetite, with nausea or vomiting.** These symptoms may indicate kidney trouble, and are signs that your dog's condition might be serious.

➤ **Mouth sores and bad breath.** An odd smell or sores in your dog's mouth could be the result of a build-up of toxins as a result of kidney failure. If he's listless and disinterested in food, see your vet right away.

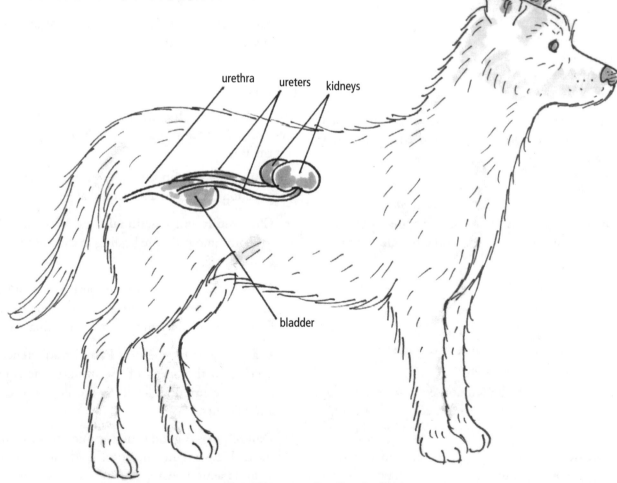

The urinary tract in a female dog

The start of a urinary tract infection might respond to home treatment if addressed quickly. A more serious condition—an established infection, urinary stones, toxins in the system, or even a tumor—will require assistance from your veterinarian.

NUTRITIONAL SUPPORT

- When urinary problems are present, as much as possible avoid dry commercial kibble in favor of wet foods and homemade diets.

- If you suspect a urinary tract infection, choose cooling foods, such as raw fruits and vegetables, tofu, bulgur, and yogurt, or those listed on pages 43-44, TCM Food Therapy.

- Urinary incontinence in a spayed female may be the result of a lack of estrogen. Try adding phytoestrogens, such as soy foods, or soy isoflavones to her diet.

- In rare cases, urinary incontinence may be caused by an allergy. Try feeding a **hypoallergenic diet** such as tofu and potato or rabbit and rice. (See the 8-Week Food Allergy Trial on page 210.)

- Supplement with **vitamin B-complex** and **antioxidants** in times of stress, and **glucosamines** if there is chronic irritation to the bladder lining.

HOMEOPATHY

The following remedies are common choices for treating urinary tract problems. Keep in mind that many of these are chronic conditions, and remedy selection should be handled accordingly.

- **Aconite** – May be helpful if used *at the first sign of trouble*, especially after exposure to cold or dampness. Straining, obvious discomfort after urination.

- **Arsenicum** – Scanty flow, incontinence, straining, discomfort during or after urinations; blood in urine.

- **Belladonna** – Sudden onset of symptoms. Straining; incontinence.

- **Berberis** – Frequent urination; mucus in urine. Painful urination or tenderness in the kidney region.

- **Cantharis** – Frequent desire to urinate, straining, blood in urine. Pain or discomfort during or particularly after urinating; kidney area is painful to the touch.

- **Equisetum** – Incontinence, particularly in puppies and aging females; scanty flow; mucus or in urine. Pain or discomfort, especially just after urinating; right kidney area is painful when touched.

- **Nat. mur.** – Excessive thirst. Frequent and copious urine; incontinence. Pain after urinating.

HERBS

When using herbs for urinary tract conditions, give them on an empty stomach, and in the form of teas and tinctures.

- **Astragalus** – Supports the immune system if an infection is present; also helpful as a general tonic.

- **Chamomile** and **marshmallow** – Work together to soothe and promote healing in the lining of the urinary tract.

- **Cornsilk** – Fresh from your garden or from the produce department, this is an excellent remedy for any chronic inflammation in the urinary tract.

- **Cranberry** or blueberry – Prevents adherence of bacteria to the lining of the urinary tract; helps prevent recurrent infections; excellent source of antioxidants.

- **Dandelion** – A good general tonic for the urinary tract. Helps fight infection and has a gentle diuretic action. An excellent source of vitamins and trace minerals that can be lost as a result of a urinary imbalance.

- **Echinacea** – Supports the immune system.

ACUPRESSURE

The bladder meridian ends on the hind foot, and the kidney meridian begins there. As a result, there are a number of acupressure points on the hind foot and lower leg that are very important for urinary health maintenance. Other important points include:

- **Vital Gate GV4**
- **Kidney's Hollow BL23**
- **Bladder's Hollow BL28**
- **Great Creek KI3**

OTHER

- If your dog is marking, or urinating in unusual places and you've ruled out a physical cause, it's safe to assume there is an emotional issue. For example, if you've recently gone back to work, or if you've introduced a new member to the family—canine, feline, or human—your old friend may be feeling like *his* place in the family is uncertain. Giving extra time, attention, praise, and affection will go a long way to reassure him, and may help alleviate the marking behavior. If marking persists, seek advice from a compassionate trainer or behavior specialist to help you get to the root of the problem. Above all, *be patient and understanding*. Keep in mind that if your dog is feeling insecure, punishing him is likely to make the problem *worse*, not better. (See pages 128-129, Soiling in the House.)

WORKING WITH YOUR VETERINARIAN

Blood tests will determine whether your friend's kidneys are removing chemicals from the bloodstream as they should. A urinalysis will help detect microscopic signs of blood in the urine, as well as bacteria, abnormal proteins, cancer cells, crystalline substances associated with kidney or bladder stones. An X-ray or ultrasound can also help detect abnormalities in the kidneys, ureters, or bladder.

With test results in hand, your vet will evaluate the symptom and continue investigating to find the underlying cause of your dog's urinary problem. She will also offer specific suggestions, including dietary recommendations, to help you address your dog's situation. If your dog is diagnosed with one of the illnesses listed below, you can do much to support his recovery.

Urinary Tract Infection

NUTRITION

- As much as possible, avoid dry commercial kibble in favor of wet foods and homemade diets, or add water to dry kibble to encourage water consumption. High quality meat-based diets help keep the urine acidic, which discourages infection.

- From the perspective of Chinese medicine, a urinary tract infection is considered a heat condition, so try to choose a diet that's rich in cooling foods to help bring your dog into balance. (See pages 43-44, TCM Food Therapy.)

HOMEOPATHY

- **Belladonna** – Frequent urination with large volume; straning with small volume; incontinence. Sudden onset, especially if fever is present.

- **Cantharis** – Much straining and discomfort; often associated with diarrhea.

- **Equisetum** – Bladder infection.

- **Sulphur** – Frequent urination; urgent desire. Signs of discomfort during and after urination. Skin and coat are greasy.

- **Thuja** – Frequent urination; sudden, urgent desire; incontinence; signs of severe pain or discomfort after urination. Often associated with exhaustion and weight loss.

- **Uva Ursi** – Frequent urination. Blood, pus, and mucus in urine.

HERBS

- **Astragalus** – Supports the immune system when an infection is present.

- **Cornsilk** – Reduces inflammation in the urinary tract.

- **Cranberry** or blueberry extract – Inhibits the adherence of bacteria to the lining of the urinary tract, and for antioxidant support.

- **Echinacea** – Supports the immune system.

- **Grapeseed extract** – Antioxidant support.

- **Marshmallow** – Soothes and promotes healing in the urinary tract.

- **Oregon grape** – Inhibits the growth of bacteria.

ACUPRESSURE

- **Bladder's Hollow BL28**

- **Entrusting Yang BL39**

- **Yin Mound Spring SP9**

- **Three Yin Junction SP6**

HOLISTIC VETERINARY TREATMENTS

Acupuncture can be very effective, especially at the first sign of symptoms, or for health conditions that could lead to recurrent infections. Follow with acupressure.

Urinary Incontinence—Physiological

Urine leakage can result from a variety of physical causes related to the neurologic system, the hormone system, the bladder, or the urinary sphincters. Treatment will vary according to the cause and the symptoms.

NUTRITION

- If your spayed female dog has been diagnosed with a weakness in the sphincter muscles of the urethra due to a lack of estrogen, your veterinarian may prescribe estrogen therapy or phenylpropanolamine (PPA) tablets. Adding soy foods, soy isoflavones, wild yam, or other phytoestrogens to the diet may make it possible to decrease the dosage of estrogen or PPA.

- Switching to a hypoallergenic diet such as tofu and potato or rabbit and rice may help if there is an underlying food allergy. (See page 210 for the 8-Week Food Allergy Trial.)

HOMEOPATHY

- **Arsenicum** – May be associated with poor overall condition, such as low energy, weight loss, weakness, as in older dogs; body feels cold.

- **Belladonna** – Continuous dripping.

- **Causticum** – Urinary incontinence when asleep. Tired, weak, poor condition overall, or weakness in hind legs and dribbling when walking.

- **Equisetum** – Primarily affects the bladder. Urinary incontinence during sleep; may be associated with bowel incontinence. Very young dogs and older female dogs.

- **Gelsemium** – Particularly in aging dogs.

- **Hypericum** – For incontinence associated with neurologic difficulties.

- **Pulsatilla** – Particularly for females.

HERBS

- **Alfalfa** – Helps with incontinence in some spayed females.

- **Six Flavor Tea** – Helps with incontinence, especially with early kidney dysfuction and a tendency to be heat intolerant.

- **Golden Book Tea** – May help when there's a strong desire to seek warmth.

ACUPRESSURE

- If incontinence is associated with hind-end weakness or stiffness, or with generalized weakness, try **Vital Gate GV4, Kidney's Hollow BL23,** and **Great Stream KI3.**

- If your dog is restless at night, and also tends toward constipation, try **Broken Sequence LU7, Hundred Meetings GV20,** and **Sea of Qi CV6**

HOLISTIC VETERINARY TREATMENTS

- **Acupuncture** in combination with traditional **Chinese herbal formulas.**

- **Chiropractic**, especially if incontinence is associated with weakness or neurologic problems.

OTHER

- If your dog is overweight, **adjust his diet** and activity level to bring his weight under control.

- Make sure your dog gets **plenty of exercise** to help tone muscles, improve circulation, and manage weight.

Urinary Incontinence— Behavioral

If your veterinarian has ruled out a physical cause for your dog's incontinence, the problem may be a behavioral one—that is, its cause is rooted in your dog's emotions. There are many possible causes of behavioral incontinence. Some young dogs lose bladder control when they are very excited or frightened, or when they have been punished verbally or physically. Older dogs who are very sensitive or who lack self-confidence may urinate in stressful situations. For more inormation, see pages 128-129, Soiling in the House.

Urinary Stones

NUTRITION

To effectively prevent recurrences, you'll need to know what type of stone your dog has, or what its mineral composition is, and the pH of your dog's urine. Your veterinarian will give you specific recommendations based on your dog's condition, but the table on page 226 offers some general guidelines for preventing the recurrence of common canine urinary stones.

AVOIDING THE RECURRENCE OF URINARY STONES

For all types of urinary stones:

- Encourage your dog to drink plenty of water. Avoid water that has been treated with chlorine (as tap water often is). The chemical taste may discourage your dog from drinking as much as she should.
- Avoid feeding a diet that is very high in protein.
- Avoid over-supplementation of minerals, which must be eliminated through the urinary tract and therefore become the basis for more stones.

If your dog had:	Avoid:
Calcium oxalate stones	• Excess vitamin C. • Excess salt. • High calcium and high oxalate foods such as broccoli, dairy, tofu, peanut butter, celery, kelp, spinach and most greens, sweet potatoes, wheat germ, or high-calcium treats. • Diets that include large amounts of meat, which tends to make the urine acidic.
Cystine stones	• High protein diet. • Urinary acidifiers such as vitamin C.
Struvite stones	• High protein diet. • Foods with high phosphorus or magnesium content. • Recurrent infections, which can lead to the formation of this type of stone.
Purine stones	• High purine foods such many seafoods, organ meats, and nutritional or brewer's yeast. • Low moisture foods. • Urinary acidifiers such as vitamin C.

HOMEOPATHY

- **Berberis** – Kidney region is painful to the touch; excessive licking of genital area indicating urethral pain.

- **Cantharis** – Pain or discomfort, particularly after urinating.

- **Hydrangea** – Painful urination, frequent desire to urinate; mucus in urine; dog is very thirsty. (Use 1X to 3X or the lowest potency available.)

- **Nit. ac.** – Urine is bloody, with offensive odor; elevated protein levels in the urine.

- **Uva ursi** – Frequent urging with blood, pus, and mucus in urine.

HERBS

For dogs with a history of urinary tract stones, herbs are useful to guard against urinary tract infections that lead to stone formation. Herbs can also help your dog expel small stones, or grit, from the bladder before they develop into larger stones that require veterinary intervention.

- **Cranberry** – Helps prevent or eliminate infection, but should be avoided with calcium oxylate stones.

- **Dandelion** or **parsley** – Act as gentle diuretics.

- **Marshmallow root** tea or tincture (in a glycerine base) or cornsilk – Soothe and lubricate membranes.

- **Oregon grape root** or **echinacea** – Helps ward off infection. Effectiveness may be diminished if given longer than 1 month.

HOLISTIC VETERINARY TREATMENTS

Traditional Chinese herbal formulas are available to restore imbalances that lead to urinary stones. Seek help from a qualified practitioner to prescribe a

acute kidney failure

This is an urgent, life-threatening event that requires immediate veterinary care. Most often it is caused by ingestion of a toxic substance such as antifreeze, or by a severe injury or infection. Symptoms include loss of appetite, vomiting, weakness, and lethargy. If the kidneys are not functioning, toxins build up rapidly in your dog's system. If the condition is not corrected at once, permanent damage to the kidneys is likely to occur.

Unfortunately, in the early stages of kidney failure the symptoms can be mild and vague even though intervention may be warranted. If your dog ingests antifreeze, for instance, your best chance of saving his life is within the first few hours; if you wait for even mild symptoms to manifest, it may be too late. If you suspect that your dog's kidneys are at risk, *it is imperative that you seek veterinary help as soon as possible.*

To support your dog with alternative therapies in addition to veterinary treatment, the homeopathic remedies **Arsenicum**, **Apis**, **Belladonna**, **Phosphorus**, or **Picric Acid** may be helpful. See the Materia Medica to determine which remedy best matches those symptoms you see in your dog.

formula based on your dog's symptoms, to help prevent recurrences.

Chronic Kidney Disease

Because of the many vital functions these organs perform (see page 219), kidney disease is a serious health problem. In most cases, your veterinarian will try to determine the underlying cause. When this is impossible, or when permanent damage has occurred, supportive care for the kidneys as well as your dog's entire physical and emotional being will be the focus of treatment.

There is an important distinction between *acute* (sudden onset) and *chronic* kidney disease. The acute variety is usually caused by toxin ingestion, severe infection, or a traumatic event that affects blood supply to the kidney. Immediate veterinary support, including intravenous fluid therapy, is needed to decrease the chance of permanent damage or death.

Chronic disease may be caused by any number of factors. It may follow an acute problem or result from a slow, smoldering health imbalance. Often, diseases of the kidney are progressive. Addressing the organs' health *before* failure has occurred, as in the senior dog with a mild loss of kidney function, can improve your dog's quality of life and should be your primary concern. However, even when disease is advanced, or when the kidneys are assessed as "in failure," your efforts to treat your dog holistically, with emphasis on improving his overall well-being, can be of enormous benefit.

NUTRITION

- The excessive urination associated with chronic kidney disease results in a loss of water-soluble vitamins and micronutrients. Be sure that your dog gets plenty of **B and C vitamins**.

- **Encourage water consumption** to prevent dehydration and further stress to the kidneys. Provide access to fresh water in a variety of locations throughout the house and yard. Avoid chlorinated water (tap water often contains chlorine and other chemicals), as the chemical taste may discourage your dog from drinking as much as she should. Bottled spring water is a good alternative.

- **Omega-3 fatty acids** benefit the kidneys on many levels, and can be supplied with fish oil, menhaden fish meal, or flaxseed supplements. You can also fortify your dog's diet with small portions of salmon, halibut, mackerel, or tuna each day. To give your dog the maximum level of omega-3s, choose wild rather than farmed fish. (Ask your butcher or grocer about the source.)

- **Antioxidants** can help limit kidney cell damage. Increase the amount of fresh fruits and vegetables in the diet to provide plenty of carotenoids and vitamin C. Try cooked tomatoes for their lycopene content, and cranberry for its quercetin. Supplements such as vitamin E, grapeseed extract and other bioflavanoids also support the health of kidney cells.

- **Avoid excessive amounts of calcium, phosphorous, and salt.** The high salt and phosphorus levels that result from feeding a high protein diet may cause further damage to the kidneys. An excess of calcium can also be troublesome. Your veterinarian can help you determine the correct amount of protein and calcium for your dog. Because commercial pet treats and processed foods tend to be high in phosphorus, calcium, and salt, they should be avoided altogether if your dog is suffering from kidney disease.

- While it's helpful to feed your dog a diet that is lower in protein, take care to see that the quality of the protein is high and that it contains a full complement of amino acids. (See pages 39-40 for information about different kinds and quality of protein.)

- If your dog's appetite is poor, encourage him to eat by:
  - Feeding smaller meals more often.
  - Warming the food to his body temperature (so that it feels warm to the touch).
  - Adding ingredients that he'll find particularly tasty to spark his interest. Many dogs enjoy garlic, clam juice, a light sprinkle of cheese, tomato sauce, olive oil, or even a small amount of butter.

- If your dog is suffering from advanced kidney disease, it's a good idea to enlist the help of your veterinarian or a veterinary nutritionist (available online at www.petdiets.com) to formulate a diet specifically for your dog's needs. Veterinary prescription diets are also an option, although these offer the same limitations in freshness and variety as other prepackaged dog foods.

HOMEOPATHY

- **Arsenicum** – Lethargy, loss of appetite. Scanty urine flow. Elevated protein levels in the urine. A valuable remedy in acute and chronic cases of kidney failure.

- **Colchicum** – Scanty flow, dark in color, foul odor.

- **Lycopodium** – Scanty flow. Loss of weight, exhaustion, chilliness.

- **Nat. mur.** – Large amounts of urine; excessive thirst. Exhaustion; loss of weight; mouth sores or ulcers.

- **Sulphur** – Large amounts of colorless, odorless urine; frequent urination; urgent need to urinate.

HERBS

- **Alfalfa** – An important source of antioxidants, vitamins, and minerals. Helps to balance pH and eliminate toxins.

- **Astragalus** – May protect kidney cells from damage.

- **Cranberry** or blueberry – Inhibits bacteria from adhering to urinary membranes; good source of antioxidants.

- **Gingko** – Useful as a general tonic. Also helps improve circulation. Particularly good for senior dogs who also show signs of mental deterioration.

- **Parsley** – Tonic herb to replenish nutrients lost in the urine; gentle diuretic action helpful for early onset kidney troubles; helps when hypertension present.

- **Golden Book Tea** – A classic Chinese herbal formula; especially good for older dogs with kidney troubles along with poor circulation, a weak or uncomfortable back, poor digestion, and a tendency to be chilly. Give 1 to 6 pills twice daily, depending on the size of your dog.

- **Six Flavor Tea** – A classic Chinese herbal formula; good for older dogs with a weak or painful back, who are restless at night, and who act insecure or agitated. Give 1 to 6 pills twice daily, depending on the size of your dog.

ACUPRESSURE

- **Kidney's Hollow BL23**

- **Great Stream KI3**

- **Foot Three Mile ST36**

- **Repeated Current KI7**

- **Vital Gate GV4**

HOLISTIC VETERINARY TREATMENTS

Many dogs with kidney troubles respond well to acupuncture. For older dogs, early treatment, before kidney failure occurs, can be beneficial and enjoyable. Dogs with kidney failure can benefit from the increase in appetite and energy that acupuncture provides, particularly when they are anemic. Your acupuncturist can provide further guidance on your home acupressure therapy and Chinese herbal formulas.

OTHER

With kidney failure, your dog may not drink enough to flush out all of the toxins in his system. He might need extra support with home fluid and electrolyte injections (given under the skin, to be absorbed over a number of hours). Most guardians master the procedure easily; most dogs tolerate it well, and in fact show an increase in energy with the therapy. Your veterinarian can provide you with more information on home fluid therapy. Information is also available on a variety of websites, including <www.maristavet.com>.

Cancer of the Urinary Tract

See Chapter 10, When Your Dog Is Seriously Ill.

The Female Reproductive System

Your female dog's reproductive anatomy begins with two **ovaries**, one nestled behind each kidney. The ovaries release eggs, a process called ovulation, and produce hormones that regulate the heat cycle and pregnancy. Eggs travel down the small, tubular **oviducts,** that connect the ovaries to the Y-shaped **uterus,** where fertilized eggs are implanted after mating. The cervix joins the uterus to the **vagina,** which opens to the external genital region, or **vulva. Mammary glands** are located beneath the nipples and produce milk in response to hormones released before, during, and after delivery.

When your dog is spayed, her ovaries are surgically removed. The majority of female companion dogs are spayed prior to maturity to prevent potential reproductive problems and cancers, unwanted behaviors, and to help curb canine overpopulation. (See also pages 18-20). Contrary to what you may have heard, there is no proven benefit, physically or emotionally, for allowing your female to have a heat cycle prior to spaying.

Breeding dogs is a complex process that should not be undertaken lightly, as misguided breeding practices have led to many of the health problems that plague our dogs today. It is beyond the scope of this book to cover the vast number of reproductive disorders and breeding difficulties that can arise in unspayed females. If you are considering breeding, talk to your vet as well as respected breeders to become fully informed of the potential risks and consequences to your dog and to the canine population in general. You may change your mind once you realize the commitment needed and the serious complications that could arise.

MAINTAINING HEALTH

Perform regular mammary exams on your dog, for early detection of mammary tumors. (See pages 13-14 for an explanation of the Dog Scan procedure.)

To prevent puppy vaginitis (vaginal infection), minimize exposure to pesticides, chemicals, and environmental toxins. Keep bedding clean, address internal parasites (see pages 21-22), and provide quality nutrition. To prevent vaginitis in your adult dog, maintain optimum body condition (see page 15), keep the hair around the vulva clipped if she is overweight, and guard against foxtails and other plant material that can work their way into the vagina.

SIGNS OF TROUBLE

- Swellings or lumps in or around a nipple, or in the tissue beneath it, may indicate a mammary tumor or infection.

- Any discharge from the vagina or nipples can mean an infection or inflammation in the reproductive tract. If your dog is showing no other symptoms of distress, home therapies may be helpful when started immediately. Seek veterinary advice if a discharge is accompanied by lack of appetite, depression, vomiting, fever, or excessive thirst and urination, or if any abnormal discharge persists more than a few days. When the above mentioned symptoms occur in an unspayed female, it may indicate **pyometra** (pus-filled uterus), even when no vaginal discharge is present. This serious condition can lead to shock and death if surgical removal of the uterus is not done in time. While supportive home care is always beneficial in a crisis, ***prompt veterinary treatment is essential.***

NUTRITIONAL SUPPORT

For breeding dogs, a well balanced, high quality diet is essential for a healthy pregnancy, proper milk formation, and strong healthy pups. **Carbohydrates** are essential; too little carbohydrate during the last few weeks of pregnancy can lead to hypoglycemia and seizures.

During the last month of pregnancy, **calcium** and **phosphorus** requirements increase almost 60% due to rapid growth of fetal skeletons. **The ratio of calcium and phosphorus in the diet should be approx-**

imately **1:1.** Too *much* calcium suppresses parathyroid gland function and can lead to eclampsia (stiffness and seizures caused by low blood calcium, common to miniature breeds). A home-prepared or high quality commercial diet formulated for puppies is also adequate for pregnant and nursing moms. Add a **multivitamin** and an essential **fatty acid** supplement to replace nutrients depleted by lactation.

HOMEOPATHY

- **Aconite** – Anxiousness or fearfulness around delivery.

- **Arnica** – Helps ease pain and exhaustion when labor stops prematurely or after delivery. Oozing blood after delivery.

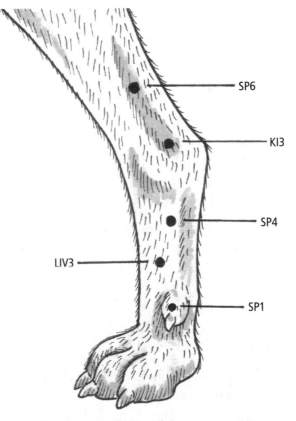

Inside of hind paw and leg with important acupressure points for female reproductive problems

- **Belladonna** – Mammary glands are swollen, hot, painful to the touch. Mammary tumors. Mastitis.

- **Bellis** – Mammary glands are engorged and seem painful.

- **Bryonia** – Mammary glands are hot; tender to the touch; abscessed. Mastitis.

- **Hepar** – Abscesses on the vulva. Vaginal discharge; contains mucus and pus; terrible odor. Mammary glands are tender or abscessed.

- **Hydrastis** – Vaginal discharge; thick, yellow. Mammary tumors.

- **Mercurius** – Vaginal discharge; green; bloody. Exhaustion.

- **Phosphorus** – Mammary abscesses; discharge from nipples. Vaginal discharge that causes discomfort. Bleeding after delivery; blood is bright red. Mastitis.

- **Phytolacca** – Mammary glands are hard, painful to the touch. Mastitis, mammary tumors; abscesses.

- **Pulsatilla** – Vaginal discharge; creamy consistency; causes discomfort. Severe labor pain; contractions are interrupted (give every 15 minutes for 1hour). Insufficient milk production; also helps milk dry up during weaning.

- **Sepia** – Vaginal discharge; green or yellow; causes discomfort. Uterine or vaginal tissue protrudes. Mother won't accept her puppies, or is confused by them.

- **Silicea** – Abscess on the vulva; obvious discomfort. Nipples are sore to the touch; lumps in mammary tissue.

- **Urtica urens** – Insufficient milk production. Bleeding from the uterus.

HERBS

- **Calendula** – Tea makes an effective and gentle douche for puppy vaginitis.

- **Dandelion root** – Tea given after delivery encourages passing of the placenta. Feed the tea and apply a poultice for mastitis, mammary tumors, or mammary absceses.

- **Long Dan Xie Gan Wan** – For vaginitis or an inflamed vulva, unless dog is old or weak.

- **Red raspberry** – Tea from the dried leaves helps tone the uterus a week prior to and after delivery.

- **Spirulina** – A good uterine tonic with broad range of essential vitamins and trace minerals

- **Yunnan Pai Yao** – For abnormal bleeding after delivery. (Always alert your vet when abnormal bleeding occurs.)

NOTE: Because many herbs have not been determined to be safe for use in pregnant dogs, it's wise to use only herbs prescribed by your holistic veterinarian.

ACUPRESSURE

- **Hidden White SP1** and **Grandparent and Grandchild SP4** for excessive uterine bleeding after delivery.

- **Grandparent and Grandchild SP4** and **Three Yin Junction SP6, Sea of Blood SP10, Great Stream KI3, Great Impact LIV3** for irregular heat cycles.

- **Hinge at the Source CV4** and **Sea of Qi CV6** for abnormal bleeding; irregular heat cycles; vaginal discharges.

OTHER

A poultice of grated potato or warm compresses and massage can help in cases of mastitis. Never let pups suckle when the mammary glands are infected.

HOLISTIC VETERINARY TREATMENTS

Acupuncture has been used successfully for difficult delivery and false pregnancy in dogs. It may assist in the regulation of hormones. It can be tried as an alternative to Casearean section surgery.

The Male Reproductive System

The primary organs of your dog's reproductive system are the prostate gland and the testicles. The **prostate** is located adjacent to the bladder, surrounds the urethra, and produces part of the fluid found in the semen. The **testicles** produce the hormone **testosterone**, which influences the development of both physiological and behavioral changes that are related to mating, dominance, and territorial activities. Testosterone also causes the prostate to gradually enlarge throughout your dog's life.

When your dog is neutered the testicles are removed through an incision just in front of the **scrotum**, the sac that houses the testicles. Because neutering removes the source of testosterone, it will control potentially painful prostate enlargement, and help to curb testosterone-driven behavioral problems (fighting, roaming, marking, and mounting), as well as certain types of hernias and anal tumors. Neutered dogs obviously won't develop testicular cancer, and will tend to be more relaxed, less stressed, and a congenial member of your family.

MAINTAINING HEALTH

If your dog is unneutered, palpate the testicles and visually examine the anal area for growths on a regular basis. Early surgical intervention can cure testicular and testosterone-related cancers before they have a chance to spread.

If your dog is over 5 years of age, an annual prostate exam (performed rectally by your vet) is a wise choice for early detection of problems.

SIGNS OF TROUBLE

An intermittent thick, yellow discharge from the penis is quite normal in dogs, especially unneutered ones. Excessive discharge, a bloody discharge, and continual licking at the penis or genitals are abnormal signs that may indicate trouble in the urinary or reproductive tracts.

Straining to urinate and straining to defecate are both symptoms of prostate enlargement, as the enlarged gland can obstruct the flow of material through the urethra or colon. Most commonly, an enlarged prostate is due to benign prostatic hypertrophy (BPH), a condition treated successfully with neutering. More serious disorders such as infections, cysts, abscesses, or more rarely, cancers, can also occur.

If your friend is showing any of the mentioned symptoms above, alternative therapies are useful for support, especially with BPH. However, surgery will often be necessary to treat other conditions.

Your vet will need the diagnostic support of X-rays, urine tests, and ultrasound to help pinpoint the cause and severity of the problem.

NUTRITIONAL SUPPORT

- **Zinc** at 12.5 to 30 mg per day, depending on size.
- **Vitamin E**
- **Omega-3** and **omega-6 fatty acid** supplements.
- **Antioxidants**

HOMEOPATHY

(See pages 222-224 for remedies associated with straining to urinate; see pages 208-209 for remedies associated with straining to defecate.)

- **Conium** – Difficult or interrupted urine flow in older dog. Testicles are hard, swollen. Enlarged prostate.

- **Pulsatilla** – Discharge from the penis; thick, yellow. Urination is difficult and seems painful.

- **Staphysagria** – Frequent urination. Enlarged prostate.

- **Thuja** – Frequent and urgent desire to urinate. Enlarged prostate.

HERBS

- **Astragalus** – For immune support for prostatitis.

- **Goldenseal, Oregon grape** – For prostate infections.

- **Saw palmetto** – For BPH.

- **Turmeric** – As a complementary therapy when treating prostate cancer.

- **Long Dan Xie Gan Wan** – For enlarged prostate with indicators including rapid pulse, dark red tongue, tense behavior, or heat intolerance.

the glandular system

Your dog's body, much like yours, relies on a complex system of glands known as the **endocrine system** to help maintain harmony and homeostasis. The glands release hormones into the bloodstream, where they are then carried to target cells throughout the body. These hormones influence a wide range of metabolic processes, and play a key role in maintaining internal equilibrium. There is new research that centers around the fascinating interconnection between the endocrine and nervous systems, leading many to consider **neuroendocrine system** the most appropriate terminology.

Of the many glands that regulate your dog's body chemistry, the pancreas, thyroid, and adrenal glands are perhaps most commonly involved in disruptions to the health of dogs. The **pancreas** gland rests near the stomach, and helps regulate blood sugar. When your dog eats a meal her blood sugar level rises and, in response, the pancreas releases the hormone **insulin**. The insulin drives the sugar into the body's cells.

The **thyroid** gland, located in the front of the neck, produces hormones that regulate a wide range of bodily processes. In fact, because of the thyroid's overall effect on cellular metabolism, an imbalance in this gland can affect the skin, muscles, nerves, intestines, heart, as well as other organs and glands. You can imagine how varied the symptoms of a thyroid imbalance might be.

The **adrenal** glands, situated in front of each kidney, play an important role in balancing the level of salt in the body, and in regulating the immune and nervous systems. The adrenals help the body respond to stress, and produce a steroid hormone called **cortisol**, which helps control inflammation.

MAINTAINING HEALTH

- Take steps to **minimize physical and emotional stress**. Severe stress of any kind will interfere with the ability of your dog's endocrine system to function smoothly. Chronic stress, whether emotional or physical, causes the continuous release of stress hormones from the adrenals. Obesity taxes your dog's pancreas.

- **Feed a healthy, whole foods diet** to support the health of glandular tissues. Recently it's been theorized that the highly digestible carbohydrates found in dry and semi-moist dog foods lead to insulin resistance and hasten diabetes development in some animals, because these carbohydrates cause broad fluctuations in blood sugar levels. The complex carbohydrates found in fresh vegetables and whole grains (especially barley), on the other hand, are digested more slowly. A diet that consists of natural, whole foods will therefore help stabilize blood sugar levels and protect against the onset of diabetes.

- **Feed a low-fat diet that contains high-quality protein** if your dog is prone to pancreatitis, which can lead to diabetes. A lower carbohydrate diet sometimes helps obese diabetics lose weight.

- **Minimize your dog's exposure to environmental toxins**, many of which are harmful to the glandular system. Lead, mercury, and PCBs have been shown to suppress thyroid and adrenal function. Many other environmental toxins, including the older flea repellent formulas that contain organophosphates, are also suspected of taxing the glandular system. (See pages 26-28 for a list of common household toxins.)

- Your dog's genetic background may also increase his risk of developing common glandular disorders. Consider **periodic monitoring** with lab tests to pick up early dysfunction.

- **Avoid over-stimulating the immune system with repeated vaccinations**, especially if your dog is genetically predisposed to immune system disorders. According to some estimates, an immune system malfunction called **autoimmune thyroiditis** is the cause of more than 80% of the cases of thyroid disease in dogs. A similar mechanism that occurs in the pancreas can cause diabetes.

- Avoid unnecessary use of cortisone, including products that are applied topically. Commonly available cortisone creams, when used excessively, can shut down the normal feedback mechanisms between the brain and adrenal glands. This can lead to Cushing's disease. (See page 242.)

SIGNS OF TROUBLE

A dysfunctional thyroid gland is by far the most common endocrine problem in dogs. When the gland produces *less than* the normal amount of **thyroid** hormone, the disease is called **hypothyroidism.** It's estimated that 1 in every 200 to 300 dogs are affected.

SOME BREEDS AT RISK FOR GLANDULAR PROBLEMS

Diabetes Mellitus

Beagle	Cairn Terrier
Dachshund	Keeshond
Miniature Pinscher	Miniature Schnauzer
Poodle (all sizes)	Puli

Cushing's Disease

Beagle	Boston Terrier
Boxer	Dachshund
Poodle (all sizes)	

Hypothyroidism

Akita	American Cocker Spaniel
Borzoi	Boxer
Dachshund	Doberman Pinscher
English Setter	German Shepherd
Golden Retriever	Great Dane
Irish Setter	Laborador Retriever
Miniature Schnauzer	Old English Sheepdog
Pomeranian	Poodle (all sizes)
Shetland Sheepdog	Weimaraner

Diabetes mellitus occurs when the endocrine portion of the **pancreas gland** is unable to secrete the proper amount of insulin.

Dysfunction in the **adrenal glands** occurs when either too much or too little cortisol is produced. Most commonly, dogs suffer from an *overproduction* of the hormone, causing a disease known as **Cushing's disease**. When a dog has this problem, it's as if he is receiving cortisone drugs on a daily basis. The high levels of cortisol circulating throughout the body have harmful effects on multiple organ systems. **Addison's disease** refers to a condition caused by the *underproduction* of the adrenal hormone.

The symptoms of glandular disease are as varied as the actions of the glands themselves. Early signs are usually subtle. Your dog may have a few minor symptoms or a slowly developing list of problems, or you may simply have an intuitive feeling that she just isn't right. Perhaps you've even tried some home treatment, but she still isn't herself. A thorough veterinary exam at this stage may pinpoint a glandular problem before the imbalance becomes more severe.

The table on page 238 at right lists a wide variety of symptoms that can occur with glandular imbalances. Blood tests are needed to confirm these disorders, and since veterinary medicines are both effective and necessary to control thyroid, adrenal, and pancreas disease, don't put off proper testing. It's important that your dog's condition be rebalanced as soon as possible. Holistic home therapies will be used *in addition* to conventional treatments.

With chronic problems, it's imperative that you have clear communication with your vet. Jot down questions or concerns between veterinary visits, and take your list with you to your appointments. Take time to ask all your questions, and be sure you understand the answers. Always keep your vet informed about your home therapies. Dosages may need to be adjusted as your dog's health improves.

Diabetes

The needs of a diabetic dog can be demanding for a guardian with a busy lifestyle, but once a routine is established and you've mastered the technique of giving insulin injections, you'll find it's easier than you thought. Ask your veterinarian to review all aspects of your dog's care, including her feeding and exercise schedule, how to handle hypoglycemia, and how often her lab tests should be rechecked. Alternative therapies will support her overall health, and particularly that of the liver, which may become overtaxed due to the diabetes.

NUTRITIONAL SUPPORT

- If your dog is overweight, try to **get the extra pounds off slowly,** over a period of 2 to 4 months, to help with insulin regulation. **Avoid strenuous activity** as much as possible, and be aware that physical exertion might *lower* your dog's insulin requirement for the day. **Consistent daily activity** is best.

- Include barley or other whole grains and vegetables in the diet for fiber. **Foods that are high in fiber and complex carbohydrates** slow the digestive process and absorption, which helps prevent wide fluctuations in blood sugar levels. If your dog is thin, however, don't add too much fiber, as it may interfere with her ability to consume and assimilate as many calories and nutrients as she needs. For the latest in nutritional information, consult the nearest veterinary school, or the veterinary nutritionists at www.petdiets.com. They can create a home-cooked recipe tailored to your dog's needs.

- **Glandular supplements** (see page 243, About Glandular Therapy) may be helpful in supporting your dog's pancreas, especially in the early stages of imbalance.

- Current research seems to be divided on the benefits of nutritional supplements to help control blood sugar fluctuations in diabetic dogs. Insulin therapy is always required for diabetic control, but if your dog experiences a dramatic swing in blood sugar despite the recommended insulin regimen, supplementing with the minerals **chromium** or **vanadium** may be beneficial. However, *never use these supplements without veterinary supervision.* No concrete studies have been done to determine the proper dosage for dogs and, regardless of the dose, their use may require an adjustment in the amount of insulin your dog receives.

SYMPTOMS OF COMMON GLANDULAR DISEASES

Condition	Symptoms	Diagnostic Test
Diabetes mellitus	Increased thirst Increased appetite Increased urination Recurrent urinary tract infections Mild to severe weight loss Weakness or fatigue	Fasting blood sugar
Hypothyroidism	Thinning coat Dry, flaky skin Chronic skin infections Mental dullness, lethargy Gets chilled easily, seeks warm places Muscle weakness, particularly in the hind limbs Inability or reluctance to exercise Behavioral changes Signs of aggression in a previously non-aggressive dog Mild neurologic symptoms Seizures Infertility	Thyroid panel blood test Note: Have your vet run a full thyroid panel rather than a single T4 test, which may not be as accurate.
Cushing's disease	Poor coat and skin condition Darkening of the skin Unusual skin bumps Recurrent skin infections Increased thirst and urination Increased appetite Urinary tract infection Weight gain Muscle weakness and difficulty exercising Excessive panting Swollen liver with a distended abdomen; a pot-bellied appearance	ACTH response test, low dose dexamethasone suppression test (LDDST), ultrasound of the adrenals

- Safe supplements for any diabetic dog include antioxidants such as **vitamin E** (to reduce the oxidative stress caused by diabetes) and **vitamin C** (to reduce free radical build-up), marine **fish oils** (to increase insulin sensitivity), and **alpha-lipoic acid** (which may slow cataract development or neurologic symptoms).

- Some dogs develop diabetes after bouts of chronic or recurrent pancreatitis, in which case the pancreas has trouble making insulin *and* the enzymes needed for digestion. If your dog suffers from pancreatitis, and especially if she is underweight, try adding **enzymes** to the diet at each meal.

HOMEOPATHY

Although homeopathy does not replace insulin for the diabetic dog, a remedy based on her complete symptom picture can provide valuable support.

- **Arsenicum** – Excessive thirst; drinks a large volume of water, but little at one time. Urinary tract infections. Weakness, fatigue.

- **Bryonia** – Excessive thirst; increased appetite.

- **Causticum** – Cataract. Loss of weight. Weakness; numbness.

- **Euphrasia** – Cataract.

- **Naphthaline** – Cataract.

- **Nat. mur.** – Excessive thirst; increased appetite; loss of weight. Increased urination. Weakness. Early stage of cataract.

- **Phosphorus** – Increased thirst; increased appetite; loss of weight. Cataract.

- **Sulphur** – Excessive thirst; excessive appetite. Increased urination. Cataract.

HERBS

- Gymnema, an Ayurvedic herb, as well as bitter melon, fenugreek, and ginseng have been used to help slow absorption of sugar or increase insulin secretion in people, however there is a lack of research into their effectiveness in dogs. In small doses these herbs are safe, but because they are intended to lower blood sugar, veterinary supervision is a must.

- Diabetic dogs eventually develop cataracts. Try **bilberry extract** and an antioxidant blend with bioflavanoids to support vision as long as possible.

- If your dog's blood sugar level gets too high, sugar will spill over into the urine, creating a favorable environment for bacteria to multiply. If you see signs of urinary tract infection, refer to page 224 for herbs that can help.

ACUPRESSURE

Points that tonify qi and yin are a good place to start when using acupressure to support a diabetic dog. **Foot Three Mile ST36**, **Three Yin Crossing SP6** and **Middle Cavity CV12** all have the additional benefit of aiding digestion, which is often needed with this disease. Try rotating between these points, massaging one each day after your dog's insulin injection.

Hypothyroidism

If your dog is diagnosed with hypothyroidism, it means her thyroid is underactive—that is, it produces less than the normal amount of hormones, and a variety of metabolic processes become sluggish and inefficient as a result. Most often the condition is caused by **autoimmune thyroiditis**, in which a dysfunctional immune system attacks the thyroid tissue.

Hypothyroidism is generally considered irreversible, and the conventional medical approach is daily hormone replacement therapy. Some vets advise "underdosing," or giving less than a full dose of replacement hormone. They believe the full dose may prevent the thyroid from producing even a small amount of hormone, or from recovering function later on.

At any dose, giving a thyroid supplement doesn't address the underlying problem, so a holistic approach to restoring and maintaining your dog's health is important. In mild cases, of hypothyroidism, alternative therapies alone may be of benefit. However, holistic veterinarians find that in most cases only a partial response is achieved, so it's important that you and your veterinarian monitor your dog closely. When hypothyroidism goes untreated, more serious disturbances in the nervous tissue, heart, and other organs may result.

NUTRITIONAL SUPPORT

- Feed a diet that is **free of chemical additives and preservatives** to avoid overstimulating the immune system, which can be triggered by the presence of foreign substances in the body. Some veterinarians have noted that dogs who develop autoimmune thyroiditis may be at a higher risk for other autoimmune disorders, so caring for the immune system now may prevent further trouble down the road.

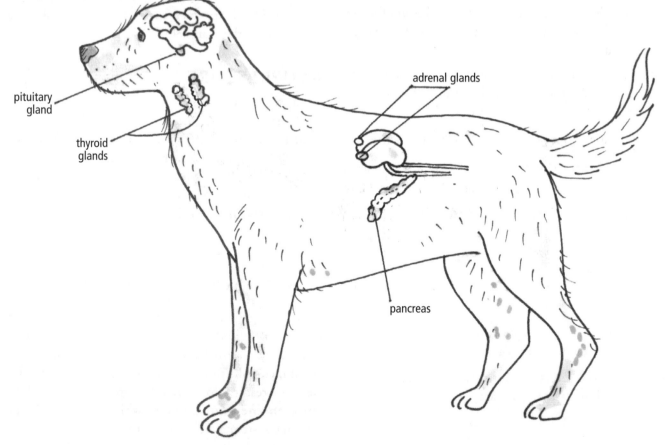

pituitary gland

thyroid glands

adrenal glands

pancreas

The glands most often associated with illness in dogs

- If you're feeding a home-prepared diet, add a daily trace mineral supplement that contains **selenium**. Since much of our food supply is grown on selenium-deficient soil, without supplementation your dog's diet is also likely to be deficient, which may exacerbate thyroid disease. Most commercial dog foods already contain added selenium.

- Because hypothyroidism in humans is often treated with iodine supplementation, it may seem logical to supplement your dog's diet with foods that contain iodine as well. However, since most dogs suffer from an immune destruction of the thyroid gland, this may *not* be the best choice. In fact, some research suggests it might increase the destructive activity of the immune system.

HOMEOPATHY

You may wish to work with a trained homeopath to help you develop an approach to complement conventional thyroid medications. Homeopathic organotherapy may help if your dog's hypothyroidism is *not* due to autoimmune thyroiditis. In any case, a remedy chosen based on the complete symptom picture will benefit her overall health.

- **Conium** – Listless. Muscle weakness, especially in the hind limbs.

- **Gelsemium** – Sluggish, dull, listless; aggressive. Muscle weakness; loss of motor control. Dry, itchy skin.

- **Hepar** – Irritable, depressed, sluggish; aggressive. Muscle weakness. Skin becomes infected easily. Chilly.

- **Kali carb.** – Depressed; irritable. Weakness; legs give out. Overweight; chilly.

- **Phosphoricum acidum** – Dull, indifferent. Muscle weakness; stumbles easily. Thinning haircoat. Better when warm.

- **Phosphorus** – Obesity. Seizures. Bleeding disorders.

- **Veratrum** – Sullen, indifferent; irritable, aggressive. Weakness. Very chilly.

ACUPRESSURE

In TCM terms, hypothyroidism usually involves an underlying sluggishness of the qi in the kidney, spleen, and "triple heater" meridians, which in turn leads to disharmony throughout the body. **Triple Heater's Hollow BL22, Sea of Qi CV6** and **Foot Three Mile ST36 and Repeated Current K7** are all points that can strengthen and balance a hypothyroid dog.

OTHER

- **Natural vs. synthetic hormone replacement** – Some holistic vets recommend trying natural forms of thyroid hormone, derived from cattle or pigs, as a starting place for therapy. Synthetic hormones will be suggested if health is not restored with the natural form. Other vets opt for synthetic from the start, citing more predictable and consistent results.

- **Glandular therapy** – Supplementing with thyroid extract or dessicated thyroid tissue provides gentle organ support in cases of mild disease. (See page 243). Sometimes glandulars can be used in conjunction with homeopathy or TCM therapy in an attempt to support thyroid function while achieving a deeper healing. Monitor your dog closely with regard to her appearance and behavior. Her blood levels should be reevaluated for thyroid function, usually within 6 to 8 weeks of starting support, and every 3 to 12 months thereafter.

- **Minimize vaccination** – Vaccines should be minimized to avoid overstimulation of the immune system. If you do vaccinate your dog, give only one vaccine at a time instead of administering several together, and consider vaccine titers (a simple blood test that measures your dog's antibodies to a given disease) to assess whether your dog truly needs vaccination (See discussion on Vaccination: The New Thinking, beginning on page 29.)

Cushing's Disease

If your dog is diagnosed with Cushing's disease, it means his adrenal glands are producing *too much* hormone. Most often this occurs because of a noncancerous tumor that develops in the pituitary gland in middle-aged dogs. The pituitary gland is located deep inside the brain, and regulates the function of the adrenal glands. Less often, a benign or cancerous tumor in one of the adrenal glands themselves can cause the disorder. The long-term overuse of cortisone medications can also lead to Cushing's disease, but in those cases the problem resolves when the drug is slowly withdrawn.

Conventional therapies include drugs that destroy part of the adrenal glands (hopefully, just the part that is overproducing the hormones!), or surgery if it's found that a tumor is located on one of the adrenals. However, after discussing treatment options with your veterinarian, you both may feel that your dog's symptoms just aren't severe enough to warrant the use of harsh drugs that might create serious side effects, or invasive surgery. This is a great time to explore the option of homeopathy and other alternative healing methods, turning to conventional therapy only *when and if* your dog's symptoms become more severe.

NUTRITIONAL SUPPORT

- As with any glandular condition, a wholesome, natural diet will support overall health.

- A balanced antioxidant supplement along with a multivitamin-mineral complex also lend gentle support.

- Like other endocrine conditions, the use of glandular therapy (see page 243) may help in early or mild cases.

HOMEOPATHY

There are a two homeopathic options for Cushing's disease. Homeopathic organotherapy, a remedy made from the tissue of another animal, may help modify your dog's own production of cortisol. Or, if you prefer using medicine that is not made from animal tissue, apply the standard practice of choosing a remedy that best matches your dog's symptom picture. In either case, you may wish to enlist the help of an experienced veterinary homeopath.

If you choose the latter approach, you might consider the following remedies:

- **Arsenicum** – Increased thirst. Liver enlarged, abdomen swollen and painful. Skin eruptions. Exhaustion.

- **Hepar** – Liver enlarged, abdomen distended and tense. Unhealthy skin; becomes infected easily; bumps on the skin.

- **Mercurius** – Excessive thirst; excessive hunger. Liver enlarged. Skin eruptions. Muscle weakness.

- **Sulphur** – Increased thirst and urination; frequent urination, especially at night; chronic skin eruptions. Depression, weakness.

HERBAL SUPPORT

Herbalists recommend a broad approach, providing tonic support to the whole body and those organ systems, such as the kidney and liver, that may be stressed

about glandular therapy

Glandular therapy, also called organotherapy or tissue therapy, means feeding your dog animal tissues or tissue extracts for specific healing purposes. For example, liver tissue (usually freeze-dried, from cows or hogs) is given to benefit a diseased liver.

Although the practice dates back to Egyptian times, there was little research into the scientific basis or the effectiveness of this practice until the last two decades. Some studies now suggest that active substances found in glandular material—particularly peptide hormones and enzymes—when taken orally, can exert a positive action on the organ from which they are derived. Glandulars can also provide a rich, natural source of fat-soluble compounds that benefit the body. For example, the heart, liver, kidney, and spleen tissues are superior sources of coenzyme Q10. As research continues, it's likely that glandulars will be found to contain additional biochemical compounds that are beneficial as well.

Although glandulars don't contain large quantities of hormones, they may be useful when a small boost in hormone level is needed. A thyroid support supplement that contains glandulars might be all that is needed if your dog's thyroid test shows marginal dysfunction, but if she is severely hypothyroid, you'll want to rely on prescribed hormone replacement therapy.

Controversies do exist around the use of this form of therapy. A common concern is the treatment of animals in advance of slaughter. Veal calves, for instance, may be used as a source, and you may be uncomfortable with the practices associated with veal production. Some people who choose a vegetarian lifestyle for themselves and for their dogs prefer to avoid all products derived from animal sources.

Another issue involves the quality of the animal tissues used to make the medicines. While reputable companies use only USDA-certified sources from animals raised for food in this country, what these animals were fed may be of concern to you. For example, their diet may have included grains or grasses that contained pesticide residue.

Finally, transmission of viruses or other disease agents from one species to another could be cause for concern, particularly if the tissue comes from a country where mad cow or other diseases might be an issue. Fortunately, most glandulars are freeze-dried, a process that eliminates many of the risks of disease transmission.

by Cushing's disease. Some common herbs you may reach for are:

- **Dandelion root**
- **Burdock root**
- **Ginseng**
- **Astragalus**

Recommended Reading

Dogs, Diet, and Disease: An Owner's Guide to Diabetes Mellitus, Pancreatitis, Cushing's Disease, and More. Caroline D. Levin. Oregon City, OR: Lantern Publications, 2001.

my best teacher

No one wants their dog to become diabetic, but my little 14-year-old terrier Silvie has shown me that vibrant health and energy are possible in spite of her disease. A strict feeding and exercise routine keeps her blood sugar well regulated—and that suits her just fine. If I'm even a few minutes late with her after-meal insulin injection, she rousts me from my chair with a single, vigorous yap. I suspect it's the tasty, wafered fatty acid supplement she gets after her shot that keeps her internal clock ticking.

I've come to rely less on blood tests and more on my own intuitive and studied assessment of her demeanor to keep her blood sugar on an even keel. When her pencil-like tail fails to point heavenward, and droops ever so slightly (even if the rest of her seems perky), it's time for a natural fiber biscuit or a little veggie hotdog wrapped in wheat bread for an afternoon "pick-me-up."

I'm preparing myself for the cataract surgery she may need in the future, but she continues to make that flying leap into the back seat of the car without hesitation, and her ophthalmologist is amazed at how slowly her cataracts seem to be advancing. Perhaps it's her diet and the antioxidant, herbal, and acupressure support she receives. But then again, it may just be Silvie's terrier tenacity that keeps her going strong! —*Katy*

the nervous system

When your dog feels your touch, smells the dinner you are preparing for him, or hears your car pulling up in front of your house, he relies on his nervous system to perceive those sensations. In fact, for just about everything he does, from breathing and walking, to conjuring up new ways to engage the cat in a friendly game of tag, he uses his nervous system and its intricate connections to the rest of his body. Twelve pairs of **cranial nerves** leaving the **brain** and 36 pairs of **spinal nerves** branching off from the **spinal cord** all carry electrical impulses to form the communication pathway between the brain and the rest of the body. Chemical substances called **neurotransmitters** are released from the nerve endings, sending information from the brain to muscles, glands, and other nerves.

The nervous system provides clear evidence of the important connection between your dog's emotional and psychological condition and his physical health. Stress, anxiety, and fear cause the release of specific neurotransmitters and hormones such as adrenaline and cortisol. Acute physical problems can occur as a result. Emotional stress has been associated with bloody diarrhea and colitis in dogs, as well as pancreatitis, a severe inflammation of the pancreas gland. Stress hormones can also adversely affect your dog's health by overburdening the immune system, leading to chronic disease.

MAINTAINING HEALTH

- **A nutritious diet** is essential for healthy nervous tissue. Be sure your dog is getting plenty of **B vitamins** and a complement of **trace minerals** by offering fresh foods or adding a daily supplement.

- Create a **supportive home environment** that nurtures your dog's emotional health. If he shows signs of emotional distress, evaluate his lifestyle for possible causes, and remove or minimize them if possible.

- **Mental stimulation**, through training and games, can help maintain good brain function, especially in elderly dogs.

- **Limit exposure to chemicals, toxins, and food additives** as much as possible. Chemical exposure in the diet or through contact with the skin can affect the nervous system, and even precipitate seizures in some dogs.

- **Avoid overvaccinating**. Some reports cite incidents in which dogs began having seizures or other signs of neurologic disturbance shortly after receiving multiple vaccinations.

- **Keep chocolate out of reach**. The theobromine it contains can cause twitching, hyperactivity, and even seizures and coma. Baker's chocolate and the darker chocolates are more toxic than milk chocolate.

SIGNS OF TROUBLE

Because the nervous system involves both a central (brain and cranial nerves) and a peripheral component (nerves that lead to muscles and organs), disorders of the nervous system are numerous and varied. Seizures are the most common central nervous system malady in dogs. Certain infections, such as distemper virus, primarily affect the central nervous system and cause symptoms such as convulsions and twitches. Spinal cord damage from trauma or disc problems in the back can cause weakness, pain, or paralysis in the back or limbs. Damage to the nerves of a limb as a result of an injury may cause lameness, pain, or paralysis in that leg.

Diagnosis of a neurologic disorder is made by first determining which area of the nervous system is affected. A thorough physical exam may be all that is needed, but X-rays, a CAT scan, or an MRI (magnetic resonance imaging) will confirm the diagnosis. Treatments for neurologic problems vary according to the cause. Alternative therapies are often very helpful.

What To Look For:

Seizures, loss of mental function, and paralysis are obvious symptoms, but more subtle signs will also alert you to a potential neurologic disorder.

- **Weakness** can be related to metabolic or muscle disorders as well as a problem in the nervous system.

- **Dragging the limbs.** If you think your dog is not picking up his feet properly, check his toenails for signs of wear. Dogs who drag their feet due to neurologic problems in the hind limbs often have excessively worn nails.

- **Pain or lameness.** A pinched nerve, due to a misalignment or boney inflammation in the skeletal system, can cause severe shooting pains in the back or in a limb. Your dog may lick the area where he feels nerve pain, sometimes to the point of causing a hot spot, or dermatitis. Lameness is another sign of nerve pain. If your dog has a pinched nerve in the neck he may limp on a front leg, and cry out when his neck is rotated one way or another. If the problem is in the lower back, lameness may appear in a hind limb.

- **Balance disturbances** are caused by problems in the middle or inner ear, but also by difficulties in the nerves that supply the ear.

- **Subtle behavioral changes.** Disruption of nerve impulses in certain areas of the brain as a result of tumor growth can produce unusual or even bizarre behavior.

Seizures and Epilepsy

To some people, seizures and epilepsy mean the same thing. In reality, the term **epilepsy** is used when the cause of the seizures is unknown, or when a genetic basis for the seizure is suspected. Either way, these conditions can be extremely frightening.

Seizures come in many forms. Most of us are familiar with those characterized by violent convulsive movements of the body. But seizures may also be so mild that they go unrecognized. These might take the form of trembling or panting, or both simultaneously. Or your dog may become very still, almost as though he's dropping into a trance. In other cases the seizure may affect only one part of the body.

With a holistic approach, you'll *treat the patient rather than the seizure*. Finding the underlying problem and removing the cause of the seizures is the goal. There are many known causes, including but not limited to those listed at left. Your holistic veterinarian will work with you to explore the broad range of health imbalances that may be involved.

CAUSES OF SEIZURES IN DOGS

Genetically based epilepsy

Infections (such as bacteria or distemper virus)

Tick-transmitted diseases (such as Erlichiosis)

Ingestion of lead, snail bait, or other toxins

Metabolic diseases (such as low blood sugar)

Trauma to the brain, or congenital malformations

Brain tumors (benign or malignant)

Low thyroid hormone levels

Excessive parasite load

Chemical or food hypersensitity

Immune-mediated brain diseases

Conventional medicine calls for a thorough work-up with blood tests, spinal fluid analysis, and even CAT scans in cascs where a tumor is suspected. If the cause is not found and treated, then medication to control the seizures is often needed. Drug treatment comes with a price, however. Some side effects are minor annoyances, while others greatly the reduce quality of life; some can even be life threatening.

Complementary therapies are used to reduce the side effects of medication, or to decrease the amount of medication that's needed. Some very fortunate dogs have gradually been weaned off their drugs with alternative care. Luckily, with the right support and monitoring, most dogs who must take antiseizure medications enjoy a good quality life.

The nervous system: note how your dog's sensation and movement of the limbs depends on the connections between the peripheral and spinal nerves and the spinal cord and brain.

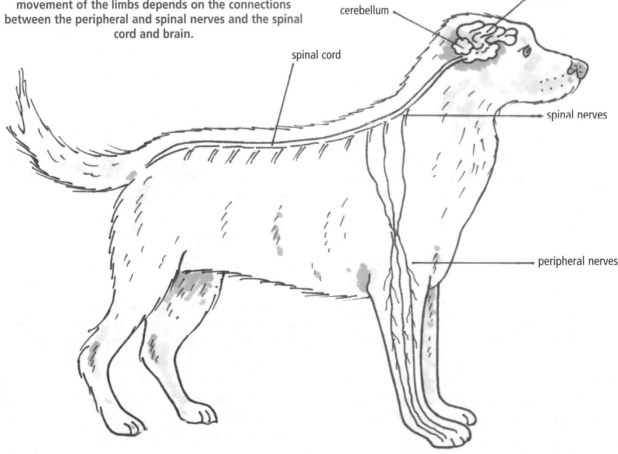

cerebellum

cerebrum

spinal cord

spinal nerves

peripheral nerves

NUTRITIONAL SUPPORT

- Food hypersensitivity, especially in some purebreds, can lead to seizures. Since the list of possible offending substances is endless, try a **home-prepared diet with a very limited number of ingredients**, preferably items your dog's system hasn't been exposed to before. You might choose from lamb, tofu, venison, or even kidney beans as a protein source. For carbohydrates, you might try millet or oatmeal. (See the **8-Week Food Allergy Trial** on page 210) Canned and dry diets made from a limited number of ingredients are also available through your veterinarian. Feed the homemade or prepackaged diet for at least 3 months before you decide whether or not it helps reduce or eliminate your dog's seizures.

- In some dogs, seizures are reportedly the result of chemical flavorings or other additives. **Avoid prepackaged foods or treats** that are laden with additives. Stay away from colored or basted rawhides, and if you are using a heartworm preventive, use the pill form as opposed to flavored chewables.

- Some dogs experience a reduction in the incidence of seizures when **animal products including dairy and eggs are removed from the diet**. Talk to your veterinarian before making this modification, and get her recommendation about additional supplements that may be necessary.

- If your dog is taking potassium bromide for seizure control, avoid diets that are low in salt. The level of potassium bromide in the blood can become toxic without adequate salt. A diet high in salt, on the other hand, may decrease the effectiveness of the drug.

- **Magnesium**, found in most multivitamin-mineral supplements, may play a role in seizure control. Megatherapy (doses that are much larger than what's needed to avoid deficiency) might be beneficial in certain cases, but check with your veterinarian first. Dogs with a history of calcium oxylate stones, kidney disease, or heart disease should definitely not take high doses of magnesium.

- **DMG**, or dimethylglycine, is a very safe supplement that reportedly decreases the frequency of seizures in some dogs.

- The amino acid **taurine**, at a dose of 125 to 500 mg 2 to 3 times daily (depending on your dog's size), reduces seizure activity in some cases. Taurine is present in meat and fish but not vegetables, so this supplement makes especially good sense if your dog is eating a vegetarian diet.

- Although **choline** (a component of lecithin that's a precursor of healthy nerve cell metabolism) is rarely deficient in dogs, adding it as a supplement seems to help in some cases. A veterinary supplement containing choline is available.

- When nighttime seizures are a problem, a nightly dose of **melatonin** (1 to 3 mg), in addition to seizure control medications, reportedly helps reduce the seizure activity in some dogs.

- If you are feeding a home-prepared diet, supplement with **vitamin B complex** to support neurologic function.

HOMEOPATHY

Given the serious and complex nature of this disorder, it's best to enlist the help of an experienced homeopath if you know your dog is prone to seizures. There are many homeopathic remedies that include seizures among their symptoms; the following is a partial list. Of course, the selection of a remedy should be based on your dog's overall symptom picture, *not* just the seizures themselves. In addition, **Aconite** or **Belladonna** may be helpful in reducing the intensity of a seizure if given before or during an event.

- **Aconite** – Fearful or anxious before or during a seizure; seizures that are triggered by stress. (Use on an acute basis only, not as a curative remedy.)

- **Belladonna** – Aggressive or agitated before or during seizure; tries to escape; nausea or vomiting afterward. Mucous membranes or ear flap appear bright red. Pupils dilated; gaze fixed. Grinds teeth.

- **Absinthium** – Tremors before an attack.

- **Artemisia vulgaris** – Cluster seizures (several episodes within a short period of time). Seizures occur after fear or other stress.

- **Cicuta** – Head, neck, and spine bend backward during seizure.

- **Hyoscyamus** – Aggression. Muscular twitching and trembling; every muscle twitches; spasms, convulsions. Deep sleep after seizure.

- **Stramonium** – Trembling; convulsions that affect only 1 part of the body. Tries to escape. Pupils dilated.

- **Strychninum** – Muscle spasms; muscles relax between spasms; violent jerking, twitching, trembling.

- **Nux vomica** – Irritable, aggressive. Conscious during seizure.

- **Silicea** – Chilly before a seizure. Ailments that are caused by vaccination.

HERBS

- **Valerian root:** This common herbal sedative can help when seizures are induced by stressful events.

- **Milk thistle:** May help protect the liver from toxic damage resulting from phenobarbital therapy for seizure control. (See additional ways to support your dog's liver on page 218.)

ACUPRESSURE

If you sense a seizure is coming on, try massaging your dog at **Wind Pond GB20**, and all around the ears and forehead. If your dog tends to seize after an upsetting event, try massaging him right after a stressful occurrence. Put on some soothing music and, in addition to a full body rubdown, take a minute or two to massage **Spirit's Gate HT7** and **Inner Gate PC6**. If your dog has a tendency to have cluster seizures, massage the **External 4 Gates**, which are **Adjoining Valleys LI4** (on both front feet) and **Great Thoroughfare LIV3** (on both hind feet) after the first episode.

During a seizure, 10 to 15 seconds of direct pressure over the enclosed eyelids (enough to *gently* compress the eyeball inward) can help shorten the seizure. Repeat every 2 to 3 minutes.

OTHER

- Find out as much as you can about your dog's underlying disorder and what might trigger his seizures. Keep a log: Is the timing of seizures associated with any event, food, or environmental stimulus? Consider all possibilities—some dogs have been known to have more seizures when the moon is full! Any clues you discover may enable you to reduce or eliminate triggers, or at least know when to prepare for the next occurrence.

- Seizures have been reported following multiple vaccinations given all at one time. Don't vaccinate unless you are positive your dog is at risk for the disease you're trying to prevent. If he is at risk, but has previously been vaccinated, consider getting a vaccine titer to see if he's still protected.

- Seizures have been reported after the application of a topical flea or tick product. Use nonchemical flea and tick control methods whenever possible.

- Have your veterinarian run a thyroid blood panel on your dog, particularly if she is purebred or shows any signs of hypothyroidism (see pages

239-240). Seizures in some hypothyroid dogs are eliminated simply by giving thyroid hormone replacement.

• Because female hormonal changes can precipitate seizures, be sure to spay your dog if she has a seizure disorder.

• Many dogs being treated for epilepsy will have a "breakthrough" seizure when they are under stress. Minimize stress in your dog's routine, and carry Rescue Remedy to use when a stressful situation can't be avoided.

• Some dogs (and their guardians) are able to pick up on signs that a seizure is about to occur. If you're fortunate enough to have advance notice, try some soft music and a dose of Rescue Remedy or valerian for each of you, and sit quietly focusing on your breath or on the gentle rhythm of the music. If you both remain very calm, it may just be possible to ward off a serious episode.

Controlling Difficult Seizures

If your dog is having only the occasional seizure, your veterinarian may recommend a "wait and see" approach rather than prescribe anticonvulsant medication. This makes sense, because once conventional medications are started they can't be stopped abruptly without risk of inducing more severe seizures. It also gives you a good opportunity to work with the diet and natural treatments.

However, if your dog has **cluster seizures** (several seizures within a short period of time), or if his seizures are violent or occurring with increasing frequency, a more proactive approach is warranted. Seizures can cause brain damage that can lead to *more* seizures, so your vet will recommend one or more anticonvulsant drugs. Unfortunately, it's unlikely that these medications will eliminate the episodes completely, and if your friend suffers from a brain tumor the drugs will provide little help in the long run. The following suggestions will help you work with your veterinarian.

• When using anticonvulsant drugs, the goal should be to use the lowest effective dose of the safest drug available in order to decrease the frequency and severity of the seizures, with the fewest possible side effects. Ask your veterinarian to discuss *all* side effects with you, and ways to minimize them.

• Ask your vet about using potassium bromide as an alternative to the more commonly prescribed phenobarbital, which has the possibility of inducing liver damage. If your dog *must* take phenobarbital, request periodic serum drug monitoring for blood levels of the drug, and bile acid testing for liver function. (See pages 216-218, for ways to support the liver.)

• Ask your vet to supply you with valium (to be used in your dog's nostrils or rectally) if his seizures continue despite conventional drug therapy. Many guardians find they can help their dog through a rough episode with this home emergency measure.

• *Do not discontinue medications or reduce the dosage of a drug without consulting your veterinarian.* If your dog is seizure-free for more than a few months, however, ask if the dosage can be gradually reduced.

• Don't isolate yourself. Get support from others who have dogs with seizure disorders. Seizures are a serious health problem, but that doesn't mean you and your dog can't enjoy a great life together. Check out personal experiences from other guardians at www.canine-epilepsy-guardian-angels .com.

HOLISTIC VETERINARY TREATMENTS

Acupuncture is the most widely used and successful alternative therapy for seizures. Tongue and pulse diagnosis, along with a detailed history, help the practitioner choose acupuncture points and herbal preparations suited to the individual. While not all dogs respond, a good number of them do, and *the chance of decreasing or even eliminating lifetime medications makes this therapy well worth investigating.* Long-term control requires long-term therapy, but the surgical implantation of **gold beads** at selected acupuncture sites is an alternative to repeated treatments.

Your holistic veterinarian can also help you support your dog's system, especially her liver, when long-term drug therapy is needed for seizure control.

Intervertebral Disc Disease

This is a common problem that involves the degeneration of the shock-absorbing discs in the spinal column. In some breeds, such as the Dachshund, degeneration of the disc material can begin at a very young age. The problem occurs in the neck or the back, and can leave your dog weak, in pain, or even paralyzed. Your dog may or may not exhibit symptoms, depending on how severe the condition is.

A neurologic examination, X-rays, myelograms (X-rays taken with dye injected into the spinal column), or in some cases MRIs, are needed to confirm the diagnosis. Conventional treatment options include surgery (to remove the disc material pressing on the spinal cord), cortisone and muscle relaxants, pain management, and strict confinement. Alternative therapies that are less invasive and free of side effects are helpful when symptoms are not too severe. When acute paral-

ysis occurs with disc disease, it's a true emergency, because surgery and other therapies are most successful if performed within the first 12 to 24 hours.

NUTRITIONAL SUPPORT

- Keep your dog at an **optimal weight** (see Body Conditioning Score, page 15) to allow the spinal column to move and function without undue stress. This is especially important if your dog is one of the breeds commonly affected by disc problems. An estimated 30% to 40% of dogs with disc disease who are treated with nonsurgical methods (including alternative therapies) have a recurrence of disc problems in their lifetime. Keeping your dog's weight down will help prevent relapses.

- Because excess oxidation (a chemical process that occurs in the cells) can occur at the site of diseased discs, daily **antioxidant** supplements will help by removing the toxic by-products of the oxidation process that can affect other healthy cells in the area. Although not proven, **chondoprotective agents** (see Nutritional Materia Medica) may help maintain the health of disc material.

BREEDS COMMONLY AFFECTED BY INTERVERTEBRAL DISC DISEASE

Basset Hound	Cocker Spaniel
Dachshund	Doberman Pinscher
Great Dane	Lhasa Apso
Pekinese	Shih Tzu

Dogs of mixed heritage with these breeds in their ancestry.

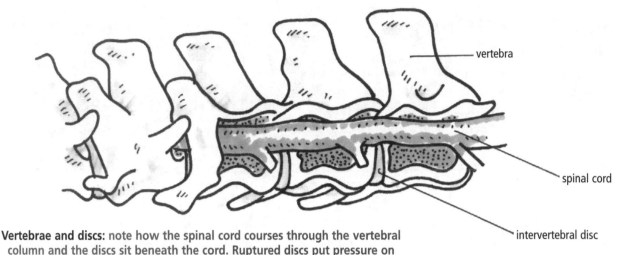

Vertebrae and discs: note how the spinal cord courses through the vertebral column and the discs sit beneath the cord. Ruptured discs put pressure on the spinal cord and nerves, causing pain and paralysis.

HOMEOPATHY

- **Augustura vera** – May help limit nerve damage that is the result of protrusion of a disk.

- **Hekla lava** – If a disk has become calcified (visible on X-ray).

- **Hypericum** – Any problem in which the nerve is traumatized; especially for nerve problems that involve the lower back; can be used in conjunction with **Ruta**.

- **Ruta** – If there is bone involvement, or pain that extends down the hind limbs.

ACUPRESSURE AND MASSAGE

- Gentle acupressure can be used whenever you find an area of mild sensitivity along the neck or spinal column. A daily or weekly light, full-body massage will help you detect areas of tenderness or stiffness, or cold areas that indicate decreased circulation. Attention to minor trouble spots will pay off later. Often, if a dog is having pain in the region of a disc, there will be muscle tightness or spasms nearby. Be gentle and BE VERY CAREFUL! Acupressure or massage that is too vigorous may worsen his condition.

- For general acupressure support of your dog's back, at the end of a massage use a few minutes of light pressure at **Kidney's Hollow BL23** and **Vital Gate GV4**. For strength and energy, add **Three Mile Run ST36**. See Back Pain, beginning on page 182.

- **Moxibustion**, or **moxa**, is a technique used by acupuncturists that involves burning the herb Artemesia vulgaris, or mugwort, over acupuncture points to stimulate the area and increase circulation. If your dog is undergoing acupuncture therapy, ask if home treatment with moxa is appropriate.

OTHER

- A sensible routine of **daily exercise** is the best way to keep your friend fit and help prevent recurrences. Don't let him be a couch potato, but don't force exercise when he's not in shape for it or he's in pain.

- Dogs with pain or difficulty walking associated with disc trouble need strict confinement and **lots of rest**. This means as much as 2 to 4 weeks after an acute episode, depending on the severity.

- **Harnesses** rather than collars are best for leash walking if your dog has a history of neck problems, or as a precaution in Dobermans and Great Danes (susceptible breeds).

- **Feeding on an elevated surface**, on a secure stand or special feeder (available through pet stores and catalogs), is more comfortable for dogs with chronic neck pain.

HOLISTIC VETERINARY TREATMENTS

Be sure to consider **acupuncture** for your dog. Its effectiveness is well-documented as an *alternative* to conventional therapies, and as *additional support* after surgery or other allopathic treatment. In many cases it can provide immediate pain relief. For best results, seek help from a certified veterinary acupuncturist.

Spinal manipulation using **chiropractic** techniques is effective for many neurologic conditions. It is often used in conjunction with acupuncture for disc disease. *It is extremely important that adjustments be done correctly to avoid harm.* Use only certified veterinary chiropractors, or a human chiropractor working under direct veterinary supervision.

SURGERY

There are many ways to approach intervertebral disc disease, depending on the severity of symptoms, your veterinarian's expertise, and the availabilty of referrals to a neurologist or a qualified veterinary acupuncturist. There are times when surgery is the best option. If surgery is affordable for you, consider it when:

1. Your dog has repeated episodes of severe neck or back pain.

2. Your dog has an acute episode of paralysis.

3. Alternative therapies or conventional medical therapies do not provide relief.

If you pinch the toes hard and your dog doesn't feel it, surgery is needed within 24 hours. Even then, he may not recover. A dog who can't walk but can feel deep pain when his toes are pinched is a better candidate for full recovery with surgery.

If you're considering surgery, be sure to ask your veterinarian about possible outcomes of the procedure, the risks involved, and the aftercare you will need to provide during the recovery period. Ask about combining holistic therapies with surgery. Surgery and hospitalization are frightening, so remember to support your friend emotionally throughout the process. Your loving attention will minimize stress, and help speed recovery. (See information about surgical support beginning on page 259.)

TOUGH DECISIONS

Sadly, permanent paralysis from intervertebral disc disease is a reality in some cases. Some dogs, especially miniature breeds, do well with a cart or a sling as a "wheelchair" to help them get around. Providing care for your paralyzed friend requires an enormous commitment. If you are unable to provide this level of care, your local humane society may be able to help you find someone to help in your home, or a foster family who is willing to care for your dog. If adequate care simply is not available, euthanasia is sometimes the kindest option.

Recommended Resources

K-9 Carts, Oak Harbor, Washington, for nursing tips for dogs with paralysis and information on the use of carts and other supplies. 1-800-578-6960, www.k9carts.com.

Baylea (upper right), Border Collie.
1989–2001. Adopted at 3 months
old in Syracuse, New York.

Barney (lower right), Border Collie/
Australian Shepherd cross. Adopted
in 2001 at 5 years old from a family
who could no longer care for him.

3 part three

Dante (left) Labrador/Pit Bull Terrier cross. Adopted in 2003 at 1½ years old from Reunion Rescue, San Francisco, California.

Buddy (right), Labrador/Golden Retriever cross. Adopted in 2003 at 5 years old from the San Francisco Humane Society in San Francisco, California.

part three

when your dog is seriously ill

WHERE TO TURN? WHAT PATH TO TAKE?

alternative modalities can do much to support your dog's system, and play an important role in the elimination of disease. At the same time, conventional medicine offers powerful therapies that can be of tremendous benefit. In the unfortunate event your beloved dog faces a serious illness or traumatic injury, it makes sense to utilize all the best resources that holistic *and* conventional approaches have to offer.

With a broad range of options available to you, choosing the right treatment may be difficult. While most medications or surgeries involve some level of risk, these are usually small when weighed against the outcome of foregoing invasive or aggressive treatment—*usually*, but not always. Ask your veterinarian to discuss the risks and benefits of conventional and alternative options. With all the information in hand, you may decide that a gentle approach with alternative medicines is still the right choice for your dog. When conventional treatments like antibiotics, chemotherapy, or surgery are called for, alternative therapies can help minimize unpleasant and debilitating side effects. Holistic options that complement the conventional approach may offer your dog a way to live with her disease in a fuller and perhaps even more cheerful and comfortable way.

carmel and nicker

Carmel and Nicker are inseparable. A snapshot of these gentle Golden Retrievers romping in their swimming pool is tacked on the wall in my waiting room. When Carmel began experiencing trouble getting up, with pain in her shoulder and hips, her guardians Carrie and Bill listened to all the options and chose an alternative approach. They brought their friend in for acupuncture and trigger-point therapy, and supported her with herbs. Carmel responded beautifully.

A year later, Nick was diagnosed with a highly malignant tumor, called fibrosarcoma, on his muzzle. Again, Carmel and Nick's family listened to all the options. The picture was bleak, to be sure. This time they chose an aggressive approach to fight the cancer, which meant many long trips to an oncology center three hours away so that Nick could receive radiation and chemotherapy. Fortunately, he experienced very few side effects. Through it all, his family supported him with supplements, lots of positive energy, and love. The cancer was treated successfully, extending his life and allowing him to to thrive during remission. Nick gained many new friends in the process.

Carmel and Nicker have different stories to tell. Carrie and Bill's choices represent a thoughtful approach that allows for consideration of more than one alternative, based on a thorough understanding of the options. —*Katy*

A Second Opinion

As veterinary medicine advances, it is impossible for each practitioner to be an expert in all aspects of animal care. There are times when seeking help from a specialist is your best option. A veterinary specialist has additional training and experience in his chosen field. At other times, a second opinion from another general practitioner may be all you need to decide on the right course of therapy for your friend.

The best time to seek a second opinion, whether from a specialist or a generalist, is early on in the crisis. A good primary care veterinarian should support and encourage your interest in doing so. If your vet resists your desire for a second opinion, find one who is more flexible. Similarly, your specialist should be willing to honor your holistic approach by working in conjunction with other practitioners. Conventional and complementary therapies can and should be combined to achieve the ultimate goal of helping your dog.

Finally, keep in mind that getting a second opinion does not mean you must follow the specialist's advice, or that of any other individual. Ultimately, decisions about your dog's course of treatment are *always* up to you.

Surgery
Holistic Support for a Conventional Procedure

PREPARATION

Just the thought of anesthesia and invasive surgery on your beloved companion is stressful, and you can be sure your dog will pick up on the anxiety you're feeling. Preparing for the event, and understanding that there are many ways you can support your dog physically and emotionally, will make the situation easier for both of you.

Begin by providing your dog with excellent nutrition to make sure her healing capacity and immune system are in peak condition. Feed a wholesome diet that includes fresh ingredients and lots of variety. If you are not already giving a multivitamin-mineral supplement and a balanced antioxidant, begin doing so at least a few weeks before surgery. If your dog is older, consider giving **coenzyme Q10**, as this powerful antioxidant may assist the heart muscle during times of stress. Some people feel immune enhancers such as **astragalus** or **echinacea** are helpful. Remember, a healthy animal receiving optimum nutrition is less likely to pick up nosocomial diseases, or "hospital bugs," during her stay.

Have a clear understanding of the procedure ahead of time, including the expected outcome, how long your dog will stay in the hospital, and how long she will take to heal. Surprisingly, some dogs heal best if they spend the night in the hospital after major surgery, including a spay procedure. Excessive movement during the first 12 to 24 hours can increase pain and swelling, which in turn releases unwanted stress hormones. Many dogs, especially those receiving adequate pain management, will sleep soundly at the clinic and

benefit from the needed rest. On the other hand, many dogs are fearful or anxious while in the hospital. These individuals do best if they are treated on an outpatient basis and allowed to go home shortly after surgery, to rest quietly in a small, confined, but familiar space. Discuss these options with your veterinarian. If your dog has outpatient surgery, try to schedule an early morning procedure so she will be fully awake when it's time leave the hospital, and be sure to arrange for pain management at home.

Is your dog prone to anxiety when she visits the clinic? If so, a few drops of **Rescue Remedy** before

VETERINARY SPECIALISTS
Acupuncturist
Behaviorist
Cardiologist
Chiropractor
Dentist
Dermatologist
Emergency/Critical Care
General Surgeon
Homeopath
Internist
Neurologist/Neurosurgeon
Nutritionist
Oncologist
Ophthalmologist
Orthopedic Surgeon
Radiologist
Ultrasonographer

you leave home, another dose when you arrive, and again after the procedure may help. Flower essences do not interfere with medications, and reducing stress always enhances recovery. Some anxious guardians choose to dose themselves, as well, when their dogs are hospitalized!

THE HOSPITAL STAY

Most vets will support your desire to visit your dog while she's hospitalized, or even allow you to hold or cuddle your friend in the recovery room. You may want to bring a favorite blanket or stuffed toy, home-cooked meals, or special comfort food for her. If you can't be around at mealtime, you can instruct the nursing staff about final preparation of your dog's food or supplements.

If your dog needs to stay in the hospital longer than just a day, and your schedule allows, ask when it might be a good time to take her out for some fresh air. Sometimes just a short walk around the hospital, if her condition permits, will lift her spirits—and yours.

Before your dog is discharged, be sure you fully understand any post-operative instructions, such as care of the surgical site or when and how to give prescribed medications, as well as symptoms or side effects to watch for during recovery. Ask how to recognize discomfort or pain, and how to manage it should it occur. Most important, be sure you know how to contact after-hours veterinary support in the event your dog needs it.

RECOVERY: SPEEDING THE HEALING PROCESS

In addition to following your vet's post-surgical recommendations, there are a number of complementary therapies that can help support your dog as she heals.

HOMEOPATHY

- **Arnica** helps minimize bruising, speed healing, and relieve minor pain.

- **Hypericum** will help prevent infection, relieve pain, and promote healing. Alternate doses of these two remedies—a dose of Arnica followed by a dose of Hypericum. Give a total of 4 doses 1 to 2 hours apart immediately after surgery, followed by a total of 4 to 6 doses the next day if your dog shows signs of discomfort. Repeat the remedies only as needed thereafter. Be sure to back off on the frequency of doses as your dog's condition improves. If you bring your homeopathic remedies to the hospital, your vet may be willing to begin giving the remedies immediately after surgery. Since surgery is a severe disruption of the tissues, if your dog's vitality is otherwise strong, this is a time to use a high potency. However, if your dog was very weak before the surgery she might do better with a lower potency, such as 12X or 6C. Check the guidelines in Chapter 5.

- If your dog does not recover from the effects of anesthesia as fast as you'd expect, or if there is blood seepage from the incision or dental extraction site, **Phosphorus** might be of benefit.

- While **Arnica** and **Hypericum** are generally the first remedies to use after any injury, including surgery, there are others that may be helpful after the first 1 to 3 days, as healing progresses. If your dog's surgery involved tendons or ligaments, **Ledum** will help speed healing in those tissues. Use **Symphytum**, or "bone knit," if the surgery repaired a broken bone. If pain is severe or does not subside as you would expect, try **Bellis**, especially after abdominal surgery.

TRADITIONAL CHINESE MEDICINE

- The herbal medicine **Yunnan Pai Yao** is also excellent to enhance healing and limit bleeding and bruising after surgery, especially when there has been extensive tissue damage due to injury or from the surgery itself. Give 1 to 5 pills, depending on your dog's size, twice daily for a week after surgery.

- **Four Ginsengs**, a Chinese herbal patent formula, suppports qi, yin, and yang, and is a good general tonic that can be taken throughout a lengthy recovery.

- **Acupuncture** helps control post-operative muscle spasms, reduces pain, relieves nausea, enhances circulation, and improves mobility.

- At home, **acupressure** can be helpful. **Kunlun Mountain BL60** for low-back or head pain, **Adjoining Valleys LI 4** for face pain, and **Entrusting Middle BL40** for back pain.

- For weakness after surgery, use **Foot Three Mile ST36**. Ask your holistic vet for acupressure points that will benefit your dog's condition.

PHYSICAL THERAPY

Although commonly used to rehabilitate humans after surgery, it's rapidly gaining acceptance in the veterinary community. Luckily, *you* can be your dog's physical therapist. With your intimate knowledge of the kind of touch she likes best and what her tolerances are, you are uniquely qualified to provide this healing therapy.

When your dog leaves the hospital, ask what kind of physical therapy might be appropriate, and when to begin. Although many veterinarians are not yet accustomed to thinking about established physical therapy protocols, they have a good understanding of the healing process and are aware of how positively dogs respond to hands-on attention. Chances are your vet will be more than willing to guide you or give you a referal.

- **Cold and hot applications** are two of the oldest forms of physical therapy. Use cold therapy as soon as your dog arrives home and for the first few days after surgery to help decrease pain and swelling. It is particularly beneficial after limb surgery or following the removal of a tumor. Wrap a plastic bag of crushed ice or a reusable cold pack in a clean towel and gently apply it to the surgical site for 5 or 10 minutes, 5 or 6 times a day. Applications of heat should begin *no sooner than* 10 to 14 days after surgery. Heat treatments will help increase blood flow and promote drainage of lymphatic fluids in the area. For heat therapy, wrap a thick towel or blanket around a hot water bottle or a heating pad on its lowest setting, and apply it to the surgical site.

- **Massage** helps improve circulation, and also soothes your uncomfortable or anxious companion. Daily massage helps prevent compensatory muscle spasms in other parts of the body. Begin on the day of the surgery. Make gentle and light circular strokes, avoiding the swollen and sensitive area around the incision. For deeper massage, consult a veterinary-trained massage therapist. Tellington Touch, which manipulates the skin but not the deeper tissues, may also be used after surgery

- **Passive range-of-motion exercise** is a form of therapy in which *you* move your dog's limbs while she lies still and relaxed. It can usually be initiated the day of surgery and continued throughout the first few weeks of healing, *but check with your vet before you begin.* The simple technique helps minimize tissue adhesions, shortening of the muscles, and stiffening in the joints after surgery or injury.

It also encourages lymph drainage, the production of healthy joint fluid, and the repair of cartilage.

With your dog lying comfortably on her uninjured side with the affected limb on top, gently flex and extend the healing joint in a motion that mimics the normal range of motion that your dog uses when she walks. Perform the therapy for just 1 or 2 minute at each session, and repeat 2 to 4 times each day. If you are unsure what the normal range of motion should be, try exercising the unaffected leg first to get an idea how far it reaches forward and back. Depending on the injury, it may take a few weeks of gentle manipulation before your dog begins to regain her full range of movement. Be gentle, and don't force her to move beyond what is comfortable for her.

- A **planned exercise program** is key to a full recovery after limb or back surgery. If your dog loves to swim, 3 to 5 minutes a day of supervised swimming will boost her spirits while it helps her body heal. In most cases, it's best to wait until after the sutures are removed. On dry ground, work with your dog on a leash to encourage a variety of movements. Walk in circles or figure-eights to improve coordination and range of motion, or climb stairs to strengthen muscles and ligaments. Putting her through a few basic exercises like "sit," "stay," and "come" (for a healthy treat, of course!) will also help loosen up the leg joints.

SUMMARY OF HOLISTIC SUPPORT FOR SURGERY

Optimum nutrition (diet and supplements) for immune enhancement before and after surgery.

Rescue Remedy or other flower remedies before surgery to calm anxiety.

Homeopathic remedies after surgery:

- Alternating doses of Arnica and Hypericum to ease pain and promote healing.
- Phosphorus for bleeding.
- Bellis for prolonged pain.
- Ledum to heal tendons and ligaments.
- Symphytum to mend bones.

Herbal remedies:

- Echinacea or astragalus before surgery to build up immune system.
- Yunnan Pai Yao after surgery.
- Four Ginsengs for long-term support.

Acupuncture and acupressure

Appropriate pain management

Physical therapy:

- Cold and hot applications
- Massage and Tellington Touch
- Passive range-of-motion exercises
- Swimming and walking

Cancer

Cancer. The word itself carries such an emotional charge. Most everyone has watched a loved one suffer at the hands of this devastating disease. The sad fact is, cancer is on the rise among dogs. If your dog lives to be 10 years of age, there is about a 50:50 chance she will die of cancer. Twice as many senior dogs die from this disease as from all other age-related problems combined. Some breeds, such as Golden Retrievers, German Shepherds, and Boxers, face an even greater risk.

The more heartening news is that every year medical research is developing new treatments that are less

the importance of pain management

Holistic-minded individuals are sometimes reluctant to give pain medications for fear of side effects associated with drugs or allopathic treatment. While it's true that side effects are a concern, it's also true that appropriate pain management embodies the very essence of holistic care, and is an important part of your dog's healing process after surgery.

Let's take a look at how pain can be detrimental to the body. When your dog feels pain, her body responds much like yours would, by releasing stress hormones. These hormones have a negative effect on the immune system. This can mean a longer healing time and increased risk of infection. Pain often causes muscle spasms, which create even more problems. Your dog may react to her pain by licking or chewing at the incision, causing still more tissue damage, more pain, and slower healing.

Pain is a subjective experience. In general our nervous systems are all very much the same, but some individuals, whether human or canine, feel more discomfort after a painful procedure than others. When the integrity of body tissue is disrupted by surgery or other injury, nerve fibers transmit signals to the brain that are interpreted as pain. Once it is alerted to the presence of an injury, the nervous system becomes sensitized and the pain threshold is lowered. That is, it takes much less stimulus to elicit a response—just touching the incision can evoke pain. It's a bit like a baseball pitcher who has done his wind-up before a pitch. Once the process is set in motion, it's hard to stop the ball from being thrown. Similarly, if pain management is to be successful, it's best to control the pain before the wind-up occurs.

You may be unaware that your friend is in pain, as signs are often subtle. She may simply be very quiet, sleep or pant more, or get a little cranky with another animal friend. While homeopathic remedies like Arnica and Hypericum can do much to alleviate pain, their action may not be sufficient to minimize your dog's pain when tissue damage is severe. Despite your efforts to control pain with alternative therapies, a more potent pain control measure such as short-term drug therapy may be required to see a dramatic improvement in her condition.

toxic and more effective. On the holistic front, we have new understanding of nutritional, homeopathic, and herbal support for cancer patients, as well as new revelations about the power of positive thought and prayer to promote healing. By utilizing the best that each approach has to offer, we can help prevent cancer. When it does arise we can support, strengthen, and provide comfort for our beloved friends.

WHAT DOES "CANCER" MEAN?

First of all, not every tumor or swelling is cancerous. Many tumors are **benign** growths, which mean they will not **metastasize**, or spread to other areas of the body. However, when we identify a tumor as cancer, we mean it is malignant—that is, it can aggressively invade surrounding tissues. Also, a malignant tumor often sheds its cells into the bloodstream or lymph system, creating new tumors in other areas of the body.

How does this dangerous process get started? Cancer cells arise from *normal* cells that have undergone a malignant transformation, changing into *abnormal* cells that multiply and divide wildly out of control. A complicated series of events leads to this transformation, beginning with damage to the DNA, or reproductive material, within an individual cell. This initial damage can occur spontaneously, with no apparent cause. However, a lifetime of exposure to pesticides, radiation, viruses, parasites, and a variety of biological and chemical agents can promote abnormal cell changes and cause the damaged cell to convert to a malignant one. In fact, when cancer becomes evident, usually in older dogs, the initial DNA damage that triggered the cancer probably happened many years earlier.

Genetic factors play a role, both in protecting against and increasing susceptibility to the DNA damage that ultimately results in cancer. As your dog's immune system ages, her body's surveillance mechanisms that perform search-and-destroy missions weaken, allowing the unregulated growth of cells we identify as cancer to go unchecked.

PREVENTING CANCER

There are many factors that promote the development of cancer. While you cannot change your dog's genetic predisposition to develop a tumor or disease, you can limit the factors that directly promote the development of cancer, which causes DNA cell damage that sets your dog up for a greater likelihood of problems in the future.

The following suggestions may help increase your dog's chances of remaining cancer free:

- As much as possible, limit your dog's repeated or continuous exposure to environmental agents that are known to be capable of inducing cell mutations that lead to cancer. These include herbicides (including lawn care products), pesticides and second-hand cigarette smoke. (See pages 26-28.)

- Avoid overvaccination, which may stress the immune system unnecessarily.

- Spay your female dog before her first heat cycle to eliminate the risk of mammary cancer. In one study, the incidence of mammary cancer in unspayed dogs was 3 times higher than the incidence of breast cancer in women. Unspayed females over 2 years of age should receive monthly "breast exams." You can do this at home by feeling each mammary gland for lumps and checking each nipple for discharge.

- Neuter (castrate) your male dog to prevent testicular cancer, as 1 in 10 unneutered males is likely to develop this malignancy. Neutering is routinely performed at 6 months of age. Unneutered dogs should have their testicles palpated on a regular basis—at least yearly in middle-aged dogs, monthly in seniors—to check for suspicious lumps. You can do this at home by checking for small, firm lumps, or any change in the size of one testicle compared to the other. Prostate palpation by a vet should be done annually on middle-aged dogs to detect prostate and anal gland cancers.

- Avoid chlorinated or fluoridated water.

- Feed the most nutritionally wholesome diet possible, with the least amount of chemical additives, and fortified with supplements that have been shown to provide protection against cancer.

  Buy organically grown foods when possible, or grow your own vegetables—without chemical fertilizers or pesticides.

  Thoroughly wash commercially grown fruits and vegetables to remove pesticide residue. Young pups and senior dogs are probably more susceptible to the damaging effects of pesticides. A 1999 consumer report identified peaches, winter squash, apples, green beans, and pears as the fruits and vegetables with the highest pesticide residues; broccoli, bananas, peas, corn, and sweet potatoes had the least.

- Include brassicas and other vegetables from the cruciferous family (such as cabbage, broccoli, Brussels sprouts, turnips, and cauliflower, as well as many dark green, leafy vegetables like kale, chard, and mustard greens) and cooked tomatoes for their natural, anticancer effect. Experiment with adding shitake mushrooms or maitake and reishi mushroom extracts for their immune enhancing properties.

- Avoid food that might contain rancid fats (such as improperly stored commercial food or fatty acid supplements), which can cause DNA damage due to the production of free radicals.

- Try spicing up your dog's meal with a little turmeric or garlic for their anticancer effects. See the Nutritional Materia Medica for dosage.

- Many cancers can be seen or felt early on in their development. Do a Dog Scan (see page 15) regularly, especially during her middle and senior years. Learn the common signs of cancer (see the table at right), and have your vet evaluate new lumps or suspicious symptoms.

- If your dog is a purebred, find out about cancers that affect her breed, and ask your vet about cancer screening tests for early detection.

DETECTING CANCER

Your veterinarian will evaluate whether a new growth or swelling is benign and nothing to worry about or, in fact, malignant. The good news is, in dogs, only about 30% of tumors are cancerous. Often a simple *needle aspiration* will identify the nature of tumor. A small, hollow needle is inserted into the center of the swelling to withdraw cells for evaluation under the microscope. Sometimes a biopsy is needed to ascertain

---

COMMON SIGNS OF CANCER*

- Abnormal swellings that persist or continue to grow

- Sores that do not heal

- Weight loss

- Loss of appetite

- Bleeding or discharge from any body opening

- Offensive odor

- Difficulty eating or swallowing

- Reluctance to exercise or loss of stamina

- Persistent lameness or stiffness

- Difficulty breathing, urinating, or defecating

(Veterinary Cancer Society)

*NOTE: Before you become overly concerned, keep in mind that most of these symptoms can also be attributed to other less devastating causes. For example, difficulty eating or swallowing may be due to a tooth abscess; persistent lameness may indicate arthritis or an injury. If your dog shows any of these symptoms don't ignore it—but don't panic, either. Have her checked by your veterinarian, and get the information you need to give your friend the care she deserves.

malignancy and, if so, to identify the type of cancer. If the diagnosis is cancer, the sooner you and your vet address the situation the better, so it's wise to have new lumps or bumps evaluated as soon as possible.

WHEN THE DIAGNOSIS IS CANCER

Each of us hopes never to hear the diagnosis of cancer, for ourselves or for our loved ones. If you do hear those words, chances are your fear, anger, sadness, love, and empathy will make it difficult to think clearly about the next step. Your first response might be, "I don't want my dog to suffer," which may lead to thoughts of euthanizing your friend, before you've had a chance to get a clear picture of what lies ahead. More than anything you'll want to preserve your dog's quality of life. This is often more important than *quantity* of life.

Many holistic-minded individuals tend to shy away from major interventions such as surgery, chemotherapy, or radiation because they assume these therapies will affect quality of life dramatically, in a negative way. However, this is not always the case. For instance, surgical removal of an eye or amputation of a leg doesn't have the same social implications for your dog as it might for you, and it may greatly improve the quality of your dog's life by removing a constant source of pain. Guardians often comment on how much better their dogs seem to feel after cancer therapies have begun to work, compared to how they appeared before treatment. When judiciously used, cancer treatments may not *always* extend life, but they frequently make the months or years ahead much more comfortable for the patients and their compassionate caregivers.

Veterinary oncologists, or cancer specialists, realize that, since dogs can't speak for themselves, doctors need to provide the best support possible while minimizing side effects. This may lead to shorter remissions than are typically achieved in human medicine, but the quality of life is better throughout the therapy.

Chemotherapy, surgery, radiation, or a combination of these may eliminate your dog's cancer or dramatically slow its progression. But even the most advanced treatments are not always effective, nor are aggressive treatments appropriate for all dogs. If your friend is very old, she may not be able to handle the stress of these procedures either physically or emotionally. Or, if your dog has a preexisting heart or kidney problem, cancer treatment could make things worse.

Whether you opt for surgery, radiation, or simply plan for loving hospice care until the end is near, compassionate cancer care for your dog means obtaining a clear understanding of what options exist for treatment, support, and comfort, and the benefits and risks of each.

WORKING WITH YOUR VET

While the decisions about your dog's care are ultimately up to you, your veterinarian is an essential resource for the information you'll need to make the right choices. Take your time, ask questions, educate your mind, and follow your heart. The following suggestions will help you through the process.

1. If you need to, take some time to allow the diagnosis to sink in. Let your vet know that you'll have many questions that aren't clear to you now, but that will need answers later. Perhaps you'll want your family to help make decisions. Perhaps you just need time to sit with your friend.

2. Get a basic understanding of your dog's cancer. What kind is it? Where is it? And how advanced is it? Will additional tests or a second opinion be needed?

3. Sit down with other family members, or quietly with your dog at your side, and make a list of all your questions. It may be helpful to make a separate appointment with your vet for the express purpose of getting your questions answered. Have your list with you when you go, and take notes as

needed. Here are some of the things you may want to ask:

- With this type of cancer, what are the goals of treatment for my dog?

- What is her life expectancy, with therapy and without?

- What conventional and alternative treatment options are available? Where will I need to take my dog for treatment? What are the financial implications of each option?

- How will each option improve the quality of my dog's life? How will this differ from her quality of life if the cancer is not treated?

- What are the side effects of each option, and how common are these side effects? What pre-existing conditions does my dog have that might make these options more risky?

- Would a second opinion be advisable for this particular type of cancer, or a referral to an oncologist or cancer clinic?

- What alternative and complementary therapies will help my dog feel better, or help minimize the impact of the disease on her life?

- What else can I do at home to make my dog comfortable? How can I recognize if she is in pain, and what can be done to manage it?

Be sure to seek out and explore the full range of alternative treatment options available to you and your dog. While a serious disease like cancer may well warrant the powerful treatments offered by conventional medicine, there may be less invasive alternative treatments that will help her body fight the disease, without the complication of serious side effects. As a complement to conventional treatment, they may help alleviate side effects, enhance her chances for recovery, and improve her quality of life.

cancer: looking to the future

I can envision the day when chemotherapy and radiation therapy will seem like barbaric and antiquated treatments of the past. Newer therapies will be targeted more specifically to the cancer, like the plant sterols and antiangiogenesis compounds (substances that inhibit tumor growth) currently being researched, so that our own natural defense mechanisms remain active to help keep disease at bay.

I see the future providing an integrative approach to the cancer patient, who will routinely be given supportive care through modalities like acupuncture, homeopathy, nutritional guidance, and massage, and when the guardian and veterinarian will work together to restore health imbalances before cancer occurs.

I hope that more awareness of the environmental stresses and toxins that bombard our immune systems, as well as those of other animals, will lead to a more enlightened way of conducting business on a world-wide scale, so that our holistic efforts to heal the planet will strengthen the health of all beings. —*Katy*

HOLISTIC SUPPORT FOR THE CANCER PATIENT

There are hundreds of types of cancer, and each behaves differently in different individuals. There is no single best way to treat every cancer, just as no two dogs respond to the disease or to its treatment in the same way. With these issues in mind, remember:

- Obtain a thorough understanding of your dog's options.

- Beware of treatments that have as many risks as benefits.

- Financial constraints may affect your choices, but this doesn't mean your dog can't be lovingly supported and kept comfortable during the time she has left.

- Support your dog with excellent nutrition along with gentle alternative and complementary holistic therapies.

- Avoid vaccinations unless recommended by your holistic veterinarian.

- Be mindful of your dog's emotional well-being. Your dog doesn't worry about her cancer, but she does pick up on *your* sadness and anxiety.

- Live each day with love and optimism, and remember the power of positive intention and prayer.

- When your dog can no longer be kept comfortable despite your best efforts, kindly and lovingly let her go.

Nutrition and Cancer

Because cancer cells rob your dog's body of nutrients and energy, altering her metabolism, you will want to modify her diet accordingly.

Benefits of nutritional and herbal support for cancer patients

- improves energy level and quality of life

- decreases metastasis in some cancers

- maintains body weight

- eases nausea and vomiting

- supports immune system; may help extend remission periods

Benefits of homeopathic support for cancer patients

- stimulates the healing response to help the body fight the cancer

- helps the body heal by finding greater emotional balance and ease

- relieves side effects

- enhances vitality, appetite, and quality of life

Benefits of acupuncture and acupressure for cancer patients:

- alleviates pain and discomfort

- improves energy and elevates mood

- reduces nausea and vomiting associated with chemotherapy

- improves appetite

- supports immune system

Reduce carbohydrates, increase fats: Tumor cells prefer carbohydrate sources for energy but have a difficult time using fats. By feeding a diet that's lower in carbohydrates and higher in fats, you can help starve the tumor cells and, in some cases, reduce the spread of cancer or slow the growth of existing tumors. As cancer progresses, the added fat in the diet will help stem the weight loss that often occurs. Maintaining weight means maintaining a healthier immune system and more energy. Increase fats by adding fish oils (or flax oil if you prefer a vegetarian choice), since they contain high levels of omega-3 fatty acids, which have been shown to inhibit tumors and strengthen the immune system.

More protein: Tumor cells rob the body of certain amino acids, the building blocks of protein, resulting in loss of muscle mass, weight loss, and an ailing immune system. Fortifying the diet with a larger proportion of protein can counteract these effects.

Vitamins and minerals: Antioxidants such as vitamin C, vitamin E, and vitamin A or beta carotene may help your dog's immune system and, in some cases, have a direct anticancer effect. Recent studies suggest antioxidants may reduce the effectiveness of radiation and certain chemotherapies, so it's best not to give them within a few days of these treatments. The minerals selenium, iron, and zinc are also recommended. B vitamins help maintain the appetite.

Putting it into Practice:

- **Increase protein to about 60% of the meal;** use poultry, meat, eggs, tofu, liver, salmon.

- **Decrease carbohydrates to 10% of the total meal,** or less (feed only small portions of grains).

- **Increase fresh vegetables to 30% to 35% of the diet;** use a variety of raw, puréed, or lightly cooked vegetables for their phytonutrient and vitamin content.

a sample diet for cancer

(Feeds 1 medium-sized dog for 1 day)

5 ounces chicken, turkey, beef, or lamb, cooked with the fat (For variety, use eggs, cottage or other cheeses, peanut butter, or tofu; beans are not a good choice, as their fat content is too low and their carbohydrate content is too high.)

3 ounces mixed steamed and raw vegetables. (Avoid high-starch and sweet vegetables.)

1/2 ounce cooked grains (such as barley, pasta, oatmeal, or rice)

1 teaspoon 100% pure calcium carbonate powder, or 2 calcium carbonate tablets

1 human daily multivitamin-mineral tablet (Choose a brand with antioxidants and/or bioflavonoids added.)

1 to 2 cloves fresh garlic, minced

200 to 400 IU vitamin E

1/2 teaspoon turmeric powder

2 teaspoons or 2 capsules fish oil. (Work up to this amount of fish oil slowly, over a period of 2 to 3 weeks, to prevent intestinal or pancreatic upset.)

1. Change to this type of diet slowly over several weeks, so your dog's digestive system has time to adjust.

2. Depending on your dog's weight and bowel tolerance, you may double or triple the amount of fish oil for added benefit.

3. Monitor your dog's body condition. You may need to increase portions of grains and protein to maintain optimal body weight. You may also add small portions of olive oil.

4. It is strongly recommended that you discuss any new diet plan with your vet. If your dog has kidney, liver, or pancreatic disease, this diet will need modification.

- **Increase fat (slowly, to avoid diarrhea) to about 1 teaspoon per 20 pounds of body weight twice daily;** use fish oils or flaxseed oil for omega-3 fatty acid content, or olive oil.

- **Give a vitamin-mineral tablet daily, and a digestive enzyme supplement** with each meal.

- **Provide a calcium source,** unless your dog has been diagnosed with high blood levels of calcium, as can occur with certain cancers.

FEEDING PREPACKAGED OR COMMERCIAL FOODS TO THE CANCER PATIENT

There is no commercial food available that meets our recommendations for cancer support, although high quality puppy diets do contain more fat and protein. If you must feed a commercial dog food, add fish oil, fresh foods, and extra vitamins. A canned "cancer diet" formula is available through your veterinarian; it contains added omega-3 fatty acids, added arginine and other amino acids, as well as other nutrients. Studies have indicated that this diet improves the quality of life for cancer patients, and may prolong remission rates in some cases.

SUPPLEMENTS FOR CANCER PATIENTS

Every time you pick up a magazine on natural or holistic medicine, it seems there is a new "cancer cure," or claims about a new supplement that "every cancer patient should be taking." Not only might it be economically devastating to feed your dog all of these supplements, but she probably wouldn't be happy taking all those pills, nor would her kidneys and liver be happy about processing the overload!

Some supplements and natural remedies have more research behind their claims than others; some seem to support certain cancer patients or treat certain types of cancer effectively, but have little effect on others. Ask your holistic vet to help you sort out which supplements will help your dog. In general, use no more than 4 or 5 supplements at one time. (For a more complete explanation of effects and dosages, see the National Materia Medica beginning on page 297.)

Antioxidants – Generally thought to be helpful for cancer patients, recent studies indicate antioxidants may reduce the anticancer effects of omega-3 fatty acids. Before giving those listed below, consult your holistic vet or oncologist, especially if your dog is undergoing radiation or chemotherapy.

- Vitamin C: 200 to 2000 mg per day, depending on your dog's weight; start with lower dosage and work up to as much as your dog can tolerate. Decrease the dose if diarrhea or loss of appetite occurs. Formulas known as Ester-C compounds are usually easier on digestion. Consult your veterinarian for a higher dose or long-term use.

- Vitamin E: (Use the natural form, called d-alpha tocopherol.) 200 to 600 IU per day, depending on your dog's weight. Discontinue 3 days prior to any planned surgery, since vitamin E affects blood clotting.

- Vitamin A: 5,000 to 10,000 units 2 to 3 times weekly, depending on your dog's weight. Always give in conjunction with vitamin E to avoid toxicity. Consult your veterinarian for long-term (more than 1 month) use. Avoid use with lung tumors.

- Coenzyme Q10: 10 to 60 mg twice daily, depending on your dog's weight. Occasionally causes diarrhea at higher doses.

- Bioflavanoids and other plant extracts (green tea extract, Oregon grape seed extract, lycopene, quercetin, fermented Noni-juice). See human dosage on package and dose proportionately to your dog's weight.

Omega-3 fatty acids – Fish oil or flaxeed oil: 1 teaspoon or 1 capsule per 10 to 20 pounds of body weight twice daily. (Studies suggest fish oil may be superior to flax for cancer protection.)

HOMEOPATHY

Although homeopathy has not been evaluated in controlled studies for use as a cancer therapy, many homeopathic practitioners believe it to be effective. There are many, many remedies that are used in the treatment of various types of cancer, and the following are just a few examples of the kinds of treatments available to you. It is recommended, however, that you seek professional assistance before choosing a homeopathic remedy for this kind of treatment.

As a complementary therapy, homeopathy can provide overall support for the cancer patient. In many cases, the symptoms alone will provide an excellent guide to the proper remedy.

- **Arsenicum** – Cancer in the stomach or on the tongue; to relieve pain associated with cancer.

- **Conium** – Tumors associated with weakness in the hindquarters.

- **Hepar** – Liver cancer.

- **Hekla lava** – Cancer in jaw or facial bones.

- **Hydrastis** – Mammary tumors; cancer of the stomach or liver; cancers that are very painful.

- **Phytolacca** – Mammary tumors.

- **Ruta** – Cancer in the lower bowel.

- **Silicea** – Tumors that discharge pus, or where there is a hard swelling.

- **Symphytum** – Cancer of the bone.

- **Thuja** – Warty tumors; cancer of the tongue, eyelid, skin, or connective tissue.

- **Scirrhinum** and **Carcinosin** – These are nosodes made from cancerous tissue; used in the treatment of mammary, uterine and other cancers. Nosodes are available by prescription through a homeopathic practitioner.

CHINESE HERBS

- **Astragalus**

- **Medicinal mushrooms** or mushroom extracts (reishi, cordyceps, tremella, maitake, Coriolus versicolor).

- **Green tea**

- **Licorice** – (Short-term use only.)

- **Ginseng** – Especially with radiation or chemotherapy, for its tonic properties.

- **Yunnan Pai Yao** – For bleeding tumors.

NOTE: Appropriate Chinese herbal therapy, based on your dog's particular health imbalances, should be formulated by a TCM practitioner.

AYURVEDIC HERBS

- **Turmeric** (contains curcumin)

- **Ashwaganda**

WESTERN HERBS

- **Burdock root**

- **Garlic** (fresh, minced cloves) – 1/4 to 2 cloves per day, depending on your dog's weight. Some dogs in poor health may have difficulty digesting garlic.

- **Licorice** – (Short-term use only.)

- **Red clover**

- **Turmeric**

- **Violet leaves** – To make a poultice for external cancers.

OTHER

- **IP-6** (inositol hexaphosphate), modified citrus pectin, and plant sterols as immune enhancers.

- **Hoxsey formula** is a combination of herbs and nutritional supplements; noted particularly for oral melanomas; further studies are needed to confirm its effectiveness.

- **Genestein** and other substances that inhibit the growth of blood vessels that supply tumors; studies are needed to determine the appropriate therapy for dogs.

- **Acemannan** is an extract of the aloe vera plant; can be injected directly into the tumor to shrink certain cancerous growths, particularly fibrosarcomas.

- **Melatonin** is a powerful antioxidant; enhances function of the immune system; may inhibit melanomas, and some other types of cancer cells.

NOTE: Shark cartilage, while anecdotally reported to be beneficial for cancer and arthritis, is unconfirmed as therapeutic. That, combined with the devastating impact that harvesting has on our marine ecosystem, leads us to advise against its use.

PAIN MANAGEMENT IN CANCER

Most dogs suffering from cancer will experience pain at some point in their disease process. Pain may be short-lived, as when your dog undergoes surgery for tumor removal, or when it is due to tissue irritation from radiation. At other times pain may become chronic, as when a growing tumor presses on nerve endings or obstructs the passage of material through the intestines. Chronic pain may be more difficult to recognize, but it is just as important to address. Uncontrolled pain can depress the immune system, further compromising your dog's condition. There is no need for your dog to live with pain—ask your veterinarian for assistance

Recommended Reading

Pets Living With Cancer: A Pet Owner's Resource. Robin Downing. Lakewood, CO: AAHA Press, 2000.

the senior years

h e has grown old by your side. His muzzle is graying and his gait is a little stiff, but he is still a loving and dignified companion with wisdom to share. You are committed to keeping your trusted friend healthy and happy for as long as possible.

Providing for an aging dog *is* a commitment. But with the understanding that growing old is not a disease, and that as a friend and caregiver you can do much to help him age gracefully, you can rest assured that some of the best years are yet to come.

The Aging Process:
What to Expect

"When is my dog considered a senior citizen?

"What should I expect when he grows old?"

Dogs age differently, just like people. Generally speaking, large and giant breeds reach seniorhood at an earlier age than smaller dogs, and have a shorter life expectancy. Age-related problems can begin to appear as early as 7 years of age, or 5 years in giant breeds. The chart on page 274 will help you compare your dog's age to your own. Happily, our dogs are living longer today than ever before. One Australian Cattle Dog named Bluey was reported to have achieved the ripe old age of 29 years!

There is a predictable pattern of aging that holds true for most dogs. Diminished sight and hearing are somewhat inevitable. Other symptoms indicate health problems that can be treated or, in some cases, even reversed. Early detection may avoid a serious disease that can shorten your dog's life span.

The more you know about the aging process, the better prepared you'll be to help your dog remain healthy for a long time.

AGE CONVERSION CHART				
Dog Years	**Approximate Age in Human Years – according to size variations**			
Age	Small	Medium	Large	Giant
5	35	36	39	50
7	44	48	50	62
9	53	58	62	74
11	63	66	72	86
13	70	74	82	101
15	76	83	93	
17	84	92	104	
19	92	101	115	
21	99	109		

- **Your dog will become more sensitive to drugs**. Older dogs have about a 30% reduction in the functioning of most body systems, including the kidneys and liver (the organs that metabolize drugs and many herbs). For this reason, do not give seniors over-the-counter medications without checking with your veterinarian.

- **She might experience muscle atrophy and some related weakness.** Provide regular exercise to strengthen the muscles (which support the back and joints, protecting them from injury), improve circulation and digestion, and slow the progression of arthritis. Supplement with vitamin B complex, MSM, and coenzyme Q10.

- It is normal for aging dogs to be a little stiff when they first get up in the morning, but **limping or persistent difficulty rising are definite indicators of chronic pain**. Surveys have shown most guardians fail to recognize the subtle behavioral changes associated with chronic pain. (For more information, see page 280, The Hidden Disorder: Chronic Pain and Arthritis.)

- **Your dog may not think, listen, or understand what's going on around her as well as she once did**, due to changes that occur within the brain. Free radicals (molecules produced during normal metabolism) tend to build up more rapidly as your dog ages, shrinking brain tissue and wreaking havoc on the rest of the body. Mitigate these effects by providing him with supplements that scavenge free radicals, like vitamin E and other antioxidants. Supplementing in advance of seniorhood is even better.

If your dog shows signs of **senility**, gingko biloba may also help, although it may take several months to see results. Don't use gingko if your dog has a bleeding problem or if you are giving him aspirin, as gingko can slow blood clotting. The herbs for neurologic support listed on page 278 may also help with senility.

facing the fear

The fear that an older dog's condition could be terminal causes many loving guardians to delay a visit to the vet. Family members may feel medical costs will be too high, or they simply may not be ready to hear the words they suspect and dread: "Nothing can be done." I've known guardians to put off scheduling an appointment for a few days, weeks, or even a month after their dogs show symptoms of distress, only to find that the news is far better than they had feared. I often see their relief as we work together to develop a treatment plan for their companion, and I find myself explaining how old age is not necessarily a death sentence! The response, usually accompanied by a hug, is invariably, "Thanks, Doctor. We just knew you were going to say we had to put him to sleep!" Instead, they leave the clinic with lighter, happier hearts, a new sense of purpose, and the knowledge and tools to help their friend age gracefully. —*Katy*

- **Separation anxiety** (your dog feels insecure or anxious when left alone or when separated from you) is more common in senior dogs. Valerian is particularly effective, as well as herbal preparations that contain oyster shell or gotu kola. Kava kava can be used short-term for anxiety, but consult your holistic veterinarian first, due to recent concerns about liver problems associated with this herb.

- **Skin tends to be drier, thinner, and more prone to infection if torn or scratched.** Reach for your Holistic Medicine Chest whenever the skin is damaged. Calendula-hypericum lotion or ointment is very soothing and helps heal any abrasion. Daily (or at least weekly) grooming with a soft brush or cloth mitt not only brings out the natural oils in the skin and coat, but also gives you a chance to perform your Dog Scan (see page 14) more regularly. Fatty acid supplements, such as fish or flax oils, improve the coat and also benefit the kidney, brain, and heart.

- **Aging dogs are subject to a number of diseases that are similar to those that affect aging humans.** Obesity, cancer, kidney and liver failure, dental disease, arthritis, and senility are common. While older dogs do experience heart failure, they do not suffer from arteriosclerosis or heart attacks. Osteoporosis is also uncommon in older dogs, unless their diet has not included the proper balance of calcium and phosphorus.

NUTRITIONAL SUPPORT

By paying close attention to your dog's diet, you have an opportunity to improve his quality of life and maximize his lifespan by preventing or minimizing the progression of disease. No two dogs of any age have the same nutritional requirements, but there are a few basic considerations that are important for most seniors.

Aging decreases your dog's ability to handle poor quality food, dietary excesses or deficiencies, and abrupt changes in menu. Adding enzymes and probiotics, feeding top-quality home-prepared meals or commercial foods made from premium ingredients, and making dietary changes slowly over several weeks will benefit all older dogs. Be aware that senior dogs may have trouble digesting raw foods and handling bones.

Physical activity and metabolic rate tend to decrease as dogs age, leading to lower calorie requirements in most. As many as 40% to 50% of seniors suffer from obesity. Obesity in animals has been associated with other diseases such as cardiovascular problems, diabetes, arthritis, cancer, and shorter lifespan. Use the Body Conditioning Score on page 15 to evaluate your dog's fitness, and decrease (or increase) calories and food portions accordingly until optimal weight is achieved.

It was once thought that all older dogs should receive less protein for maximum health, but newer studies indicate that many senior dogs actually need *more* protein than younger dogs. Protein is especially important to support an aging immune system and to promote cell replacement and enzyme activity. These functions decline with age so, if protein is restricted, wounds may not heal as well and the immune system may function poorly. Very lean dogs also benefit from increased protein in the diet.

However, if your senior dog has been diagnosed with kidney failure, restricting his intake of protein is advised. Because excess protein and phosphorus contributes to the progression of kidney disease, consult your veterinarian for dietary guidelines. Likewise, sodium restriction is not necessary in all older dogs, but only in those with kidney or heart disease.

Some geriatric dogs need a little coaxing to get them to eat. Feed by hand, heat the meals, or add favorites like chicken breast to spark interest. Vitamin B complex also stimulates the appetite.

HOMEOPATHY

Homeopathic remedies are wonderful allies when your dog faces the multiple symptoms that sometimes accompany aging. Their gentle support, and your ability to tailor the potency of remedies to the vitality of your dog, mean they're ideally suited to the sensitivity and the varied complaints so common in the senior years.

The diversity of symptoms may actually make it easier for you to find a remedy that will improve your dog's quality of life. Chances are that changes in his mental function or mood, preferences for food and water intake, stool or urinary habits, and even chronic pain or stiffness will all point to just one remedy that will address all of his needs. If symptoms are mild, choose a low potency and administer it with minimal frequency (just once a day, or even every second or third day), monitor his response, then follow the guidelines on pages 83-84 for modifying potency, and pages 84-86 for dosing.

To find the remedy that's best suited to your dog:

- Make a list of the most pronounced symptoms.

- Refer to the various sections in Chapter 9, Treatment of Illness and Injury, for remedies associated with each symptom.

- Plot the symptoms, along with other traits like preferences and modalities, and the remedies on a chart like the one on pages 312-313.

- Use the Homeopathic Materia Medica to determine which remedy matches the most symptoms and traits on your list.

ACUPRESSURE AND MASSAGE

Regular massage and acupressure sessions can stimulate your aging friend's circulation, tone his muscles, help maintain his fitness and flexibility, and provide comfort when he's just plain tired.

a warning from shamrock

Jeff was devastated when his best buddy Shamrock, a friendly and gentle Irish Setter, began to growl at visitors and even snapped at a neighbor girl. Shamrock had just celebrated his thirteenth birthday, and Jeff's family blamed senility, suggesting it was time to have Shamrock "put to sleep" before serious injuries occurred. But Jeff was committed to his friend, and he noticed that *most* of the time Shamrock was loving and good-natured around children and adults. Jeff brought his companion to me for advice.

Together we discovered a painful area in Shamrock's hip. As is common with large dogs, he had given little indication he was hurting. But his short temper was his way of protecting himself from being touched. In fact, just having people in close proximity made him irritable; he never knew when someone might reach out or bump him accidentally.

Dealing with Shamrock's pain through acupuncture, herbs, and massage alleviated the aggressive behavior. Jeff also gave Shamrock a quiet and private area to which he could retreat when visitors, especially children, were around. Finally, Jeff made it a daily habit to gently check him over with a brief massage that clearly delighted his elderly friend. —*Katy*

A good place to start is to gently stroke along the Bladder meridian, the longest energy channel in your dog's body—which courses down the back on either side of the spine. Start behind the skull, and massage along the top of the neck, between the shoulder blades, and continue with long strokes along each side of the spine, all the way to the base of the tail. From there, continue with gentle massage down the back of the legs to the feet. If you find areas of tension, spasm, or soreness along the way, you can give them extra attention with light acupressure. Remember that if he moves away from you, the pressure is too firm and you'll need to lighten your touch.

Special attention to key acupressure points seems to help increase the energy of some geriatric dogs, improving their spirit and attitude. Refer to the chart on pages 98-102 and the illustrations on pages 103 and 183 to locate the acupressure and trigger points.

- **Great Stream KI3** – For hearing imbalances; strengthens the kidney energy.
- **Foot Three Mile ST36** – Classic qi-building and strengthening point; helps with digestion and many other body functions.
- **Hundred Meetings GV20** – Clears the mind, calms the spirit.

Aggression and the Senior Dog

Why would a good-natured dog show signs of aggression? Physical pain is a common reason for an elderly animal to become bad-tempered. At the first sign of grumpiness or irritability, be sure to address any physical ailments; seek veterinary advice if you suspect your dog is hurting somewhere. You may need to protect him from certain triggers, such as a younger or bigger dog who plays too rough. When there is a lot of activity around the home, make sure he has a safe and quiet place to retreat. Remind friends and family always to approach your aging friend with respect, and to play more gently with him—after all, he's earned it.

Mental deterioration that sometimes comes with age can also make your dog more irritable. Holistic veterinarians have seen aggression resolve simply by changing to a home-prepared, nutritious diet. Improve your dog's brainpower with antioxidants, vitamin supplements, and plenty of fresh food. Keep his mind active by spending quality time interacting with him. Let him practice his old tricks, or even learn a few new ones.

As physical limitations increase, an older dog may become sullen, depressed, or cranky. Loss of hearing or sight can impact his ability to recognize a friend—dog or human—and he may startle and snap out of fear or surprise. Keep him involved with familiar people and friendly dogs to maintain his social skills, and to help him feel safe and ward off aggressive feelings even when his senses are diminished.

Your dog's spirits need to be nurtured more than ever as he ages. Reassure him that he's still an important member of the family, and make an effort to keep his spirits high by engaging him every day in activities he loves, whether it's a special walk, performing for a treat, a ride in the car, or quality time with you.

NUTRITIONAL SUPPLEMENTS AND HERBS FOR SENIORS

Nutritional Supplements

Antioxidants

Coenzyme Q10

Digestive enzymes

Multivitamin-mineral with vitamin B-complex

Omega-3 fatty acids

Probiotics

Psyllium husks

Spirulina or blue-green algae

Tonic herbs

Ashwaganda

Astragalus

Dandelion

Garlic

Ginger

Ginseng (American, Red, or Korean)

Herbs for neurologic support
(including senility and anxiety)

Gingko biloba

Gotu kola

Oats or oatstraw

St. John's wort

Valerian

Herbs for pain and stiffness

(see page 187)

Five Special Treats for Senior Dogs

Your older dog may no longer chase you around with that Frisbee in his mouth, but that doesn't mean he's not interested in interacting with you. Even so, he may not seek you out as often simply because of the discomfort he feels just getting up to walk across the room to greet you. Some dogs interact less, as a result of confusion related to oncoming senility. Your aged friend may need special attention, and that doesn't just mean extra food treats. Here's a list of nonfood "treats" your older dog will enjoy:

- **Give your dog a massage.** You'll be amazed at how relaxing this is for both of you.

- **Take a walk, but don't go anywhere.** Even if your dog is unable to go for long walks, he'll still love to get out and smell the roses. To him, this might be the enticing scent of another dog, or the bouquet of something your human nose will never perceive. Don't rush your geriatric dog when he's sniffing the bushes on his walk. His sense of smell may be the keenest sense he has left. It gives him plenty of joy, and will keep him alert and interested in his surroundings.

- **Spruce up the bed.** Older dogs need more cushioning for painful joints and aching backs, and protection from drafts, so consider upgrading his bed. (The senior years are a time when it's more difficult than ever for a dog to live outside your home. If your dog has been living outdoors, allow him to join your family in the house, or at least move into an enclosed garage for the winter. In fact, it may be time to move him in permanently.)

- **Offer more bathroom breaks.** Older dogs often have diminished bladder and bowel control. More frequent opportunities to eliminate are essential. This prevents overdistension of the

---

SENIOR HEALTH CARE HOME CHECK LIST

Eyes – Cloudiness is a normal change associated with aging and may not impact sight, but vision problems should be checked by your veterinarian.

Ears – Wax tends to build up more quickly and may need to be removed. Check for odors indicating infection, which are more common in seniors.

Nose – The tip of the nose can become dry and cracked. Try topical applications of olive oil, vitamin E oil, or lanolin.

Mouth – Odors may indicate infected teeth or tumors.

Breathing – Some increase in noisy respiration (snoring) is normal in older dogs as they sleep, especially if they are overweight. Labored breathing or coughing, however, is abnormal.

Lumps and bumps – Many are benign, but older dogs have a higher risk of malignancy. Fine needle aspiration can detect which lumps are serious and which are not.

Coat and skin – A little dryness can be minimized with grooming to stimulate oil glands. Add extra vegetable or fish oils to the diet.

Stool health – Seniors tend to become constipated. To soften stools, add cooked pumpkin (canned is fine) to the diet (1 to 3 Tablespoons, depending on weight) or bran. For bowel incontinence, try a low fiber, highly digestible diet (based on eggs and white rice, for example).

Urinary health – Increased urination or a gradual or sudden increase in water consumption may indicate diabetes, kidney or adrenal disease, urinary tract infection, or other disorders.

the hidden disorder: chronic pain

Denise was baffled when her beautiful older shepherd Maya began pacing, rearranging her bed, and making several trips to the kitchen for water each night. During the day, she panted more than usual but her appetite was fine; her movement had become a little stiff but she enjoyed her daily walks as much as ever. When the strange behavior persisted for a few weeks, Denise became worried.

Maya seemed in very good health on physical exam, except for stiffness in the lower spine and pain in the lumbar muscles when I pressed with my thumb. Geriatric lab tests were normal. My diagnosis: I believed all of Maya's symptoms were the result of chronic pain in her back. Maya was hurting at night, didn't know how to show it, and couldn't find a way to get comfortable.

Denise was shocked—and bewildered to realize she'd been unaware her companion had been suffering from chronic pain.

Dogs are remarkably stoic in the face of chronic pain. They rarely whimper, and unless the pain is excruciating they still want to walk with you (though they may pay for it later!), eat their meals, and carry on with life. Symptoms are often more severe at night, for the simple reason that other distractions are absent, and lying in one position for several hours can aggravate the condition that's causing the pain. The signs can be as subtle as a change in the expression on your dog's face, or an unprecedented tendency to be grumpy.

The first step towards addressing chronic pain is to recognize it. As guardians, we owe our dogs the right to live without pain, and there are many options for treatment. My approach to chronic pain disorders usually begins with a combination of acupuncture, herbs, bodywork, and supplements, tailored to the needs of the individual dog. This is often all it takes, but I will use oral drug therapy, "pain patches" glued to the skin to slowly release pain medication, or even surgery when necessary. In response to clients who are concerned about side effects of drug therapies, my position is this: Although there are risks and side effects associated with these medications, you must ask whether the benefits outweigh the risk. If you have not achieved the degree of pain control you had hoped for with gentler therapies, wise and carefully monitored use of drug therapy may truly help with healing by removing the chronic pain that was taxing the immune system and eroding your dog's spirits. —Katy

bladder, which causes further weakening of the bladder sphincter. Some geriatrics become less aware of the fullness of their bowels. Help him avoid the embarrassment of an indoor accident with more frequent trips outside.

- **Never stop communicating!** If your dog's hearing is failing, you may have to speak louder, or start teaching him sign language. If her sight is poor, use guide sticks when he is out on a walk with you. Even if your dog is completely deaf, keep up the conversation. Your body language and facial expressions speak volumes. Also, your words will help focus your thoughts, which may make it easier for him to pick them up telepathically. And if both his hearing and vision are fading, you can still communicate with your loving touch.

OTHER

Veterinary visits twice a year are a good idea at this stage of your dog's life. If that sounds like a lot, remember that, because dogs age differently, this is similar to a human senior citizen visiting her doctor every four years. Geriatric lab tests will screen for health problems typical in older dogs. Acupuncture is particularly helpful for seniors, and your holistic veterinarian can prescribe other gentle therapies to improve the quality of your dog's life.

Perhaps most importantly, savor each day. Celebrate the very special moments, as well as the more mundane ones you spend together. Caring for an elderly dog is sometimes frustrating, and will even try your patience. But when you remember the unconditional and boundless love your friend has given you, and take the time to appreciate the very *special* attributes that age and wisdom bestow on him, you will find that you treasure each day of his golden years as much as or more than you did his youthful ones.

Recommended Reading

Old Dogs, Old Friends: Enjoying Your Older Dog. Bonnie Wilcox, DVM and Chris Walkowicz. New York: Howell Book House, 1991.

Cleo, Alaskan Malamute. 1988–1999.
Adopted at 2 years old in Hayward,
California, when her first family could
no longer care for her.

letting go

Perhaps the most challenging aspect of caring for our dogs comes when we must begin to let them go. Nothing demands more of us as caretakers than when the end of our beloved friend's time as a physical presence in our lives draws near, and we realize we must move beyond our own wish to have her close to us forever, and honor her need to make the transition toward death.

As you approach the end of your dog's life, there are many decisions to be made regarding how best to support her as you honor your own needs, with consideration for physical, emotional, as well as spiritual concerns. Healing foods, homeopathic remedies, herbs, and other therapies can provide medicine to ease her through her last days. You'll draw on the strength of your emotional relationship to find love and beauty even in the most trying times. You might explore the possibility of entering this transition as a spiritual process that the two of you share, even allowing your dog to lead you through it and bring you to a new understanding of death—and of life.

Is It Time to Let Go?

The revelation that your dog is near death may come abruptly and undeniably, in the form of a critical injury or an acute, untreatable illness. Often, however, the signs are less clear. Perhaps the years have gradually taken their toll, and one day you realize her quality of life has declined significantly. Or maybe you've been treating your friend for a slow-growing cancer or a chronic heart problem, and suddenly it appears she is no longer responding to treatment.

As her guardian you will be faced with many decisions, among them whether to continue to administer treatments—perhaps invasive ones, at that—or allow your dog to die. What seems like an impossible choice can be made a little easier if you begin by gathering all the facts available to you, and then employ your personal resources—most of all, your knowledge of your dog's physical and emotional strengths, and your commitment to her best interest—trusting your own wisdom and compassion to guide you.

283

GET THE FACTS

To make an informed decision you'll need a thorough understanding of your dog's condition, as well as the treatment options available and the effects—good and bad—of those treatments. As always, alternative therapies will be enormously valuable as supportive treatment with a minimum of side effects. However, if your dog is struggling with a life-threatening illness you will also want to explore every conventional medical option that is available to her.

This is a time when the relationship you've established with your vet will prove invaluable. Schedule time to sit down with him and ask questions:

- What is the exact nature of your dog's condition? What organ systems are involved? Is your dog in pain?

- If no treatment is given, how quickly is the illness likely to progress? As it progresses, what additional symptoms should you expect to see? How quickly are they likely to develop?

- What treatment options are available? What is the likelihood that the treatment will improve or cure her condition? If improvement is unlikely, will the treatment at least slow her decline?

- What are the side effects of treatment? Will your dog recover from the side effects? If so, how long will that recovery take?

- What will be the financial cost of treatment? Are payment options available?

Once you have the facts in front of you, you can evaluate whether or not continuing treatment makes sense. Will the benefits of treatment outweigh the physical and emotional cost to your dog and to you? Your vet may be able to perform surgery to remove a tumor from your dog's throat, but if her liver is also riddled with cancer, she may not survive long enough to recover from the throat surgery. If her cancer is localized, radiation therapy may slow its progression, but if advanced arthritis prevents her from getting out of bed, it may be kinder to let her rest comfortably at home rather than haul her to the clinic every other day for treatment.

It's important to evaluate the impact treatment will have on you, as well. If intensive home therapy is required, will you have the time and the physical stamina to administer it? What about the emotional toll it will take on you and other members of your household?

Don't feel guilty about considering your own needs as you make these difficult decisions. If changing dressings on a daily basis or injecting fluids to keep your dog hydrated is beyond your capabilities, be honest with yourself. You are not helping your dog if you sign up for a task that you are unable to cope with. Nor is it necessary to bury yourself and the rest of your family under extreme financial hardship to pay for treatment that may only buy your dog a few more weeks or months. Weigh the benefits against the costs for *all* members of the family, including yourself.

TUNE IN TO YOUR DOG

No one knows your dog as well as you do. Your ability to read the signs she gives you puts you in a unique position to evaluate how she is likely to respond to treatment.

- How is her energy level? Does she still greet you at the door with a wagging tail and a bounce in her step? Is she still happy to trot after a tossed ball now and then? Or does getting through the day seem to take more energy than she can muster?

- How is her appetite? Is dinner still her favorite time of the day, or does she eat a few handfed morsels, seemingly just to please you?

- How resilient is she? Does she bounce back when treatments are administered, or does she seem more tired and listless these days, in spite of your best efforts?

- Look into her eyes. Do they still sparkle now and then? Or does the light seem to be fading?

- Listen to your heart. As difficult as it is, trust that you know deep down what is best for your dog. The bond you share with her will help you to know what she needs. Be open to the possibility that your intuition may in fact be *her* voice, sending you a very personal message.

Whatever you decide, allow yourself the comfort of knowing that healing takes many forms. Sometimes it means the removal of every remaining cancer cell. At other times, it means a quiet acceptance of the natural phases of life. If you decide to let her go, remember to honor your courage and your compassion, and your willingness to put her needs before your own wish to keep her at your side for as long as possible.

Supportive Care

Once you've made the decision to allow your dog to move peacefully through her final months, weeks, or days, your care will take on a different form. Rather than focusing on the removal of illness, your efforts will be directed toward keeping your friend comfortable, and making the most of this very special time.

MANAGEMENT OF PAIN AND OTHER PHYSICAL DISTRESS

- Your veterinarian can help you monitor your friend's level of pain, and provide medication to help alleviate it should the need arise. A variety of medications are available that are easily administered at home. (See page 265, The Importance of Pain Management.)

- Homeopathic remedies may help alleviate pain in some cases. Depending on the cause of your dog's discomfort, **Arnica**, **Hypericum**, **Bryonia,** or **Rhus tox.** may provide some palliative relief. Check the Materia Medica to see which remedy best matches your dog's symptoms.

- The calming effect of herbs, such as **valerian** or **kava kava**, may help your dog relax, and therefore be less distressed by pain.

- **Acupressure** or **acupuncture** are useful in alleviating pain, and will help your dog rest more comfortably.

NUTRITIONAL SUPPORT

You may find that your dog's appetite declines along with her health, or that it becomes difficult for her to keep her food down. A few simple modifications to her diet will help her get the most out of her food when she does eat.

- Avoid rich or spicy foods in favor of a diet that is easy to digest, but still tasty. Sometimes a little extra protein or fat will provide energy for a dog whose appetite is weak. Try cooked chicken or turkey, scrambled eggs, cottage cheese, and rice along with vitamin supplements.

- Feed smaller, more frequent meals to help minimize stomach upset.

- Perk up her appetite with a sprinkle of cheese, nutritional yeast, or broth. Try breaking her favorite cookies into small bits and mixing them into the meal. Warm the food.

- Make mealtime a quiet time for the two of you. Minimize noise and distractions, and give her time to pick through a meal a few morsels at a time.

- Feeding your dog by hand, bit by bit, may encourage her to eat when nothing else does.

MAXIMIZE HER COMFORT

- Create a quiet space for your dog to rest, where she won't be bothered by a pesky puppy or boisterous children.

- Make it easy for her to be close to you. Arrange her bed in a place where she can monitor your activities even though it may be difficult for her to get up and follow you from room to room.

- Since she may be spending more time sleeping, she'll appreciate an extra layer of bedding to cushion her body while she rests. Now might be a nice time to indulge her with an orthopedic cushion or foam bed.

- Though she may have difficulty controlling her bowels or her bladder, she'll find it distressing to soil in her bed or on the carpet. Help her get out of doors at frequent intervals throughout the day so she can relieve herself with dignity. If she does eliminate indoors, reassure her with your understanding. If her control is severely diminished, with a little creativity you may be able to modify a human disposable diaper to fit her comfortably.

- Change her bedding promptly if it does become soiled. An absorbable bed liner, available at your pharmacy, will make it easier for you to keep her bed clean and dry.

- She may become chilled more easily, or have difficulty dealing with warm weather. Watch her body language for signs. If her ears feel cold or if she's curled into a tight little ball, she may be struggling to retain body heat. Be prepared to put on her winter sweater, cover her with a light blanket, or tuck a hot water bottle in beside her (be sure it's not hot enough to cause a burn). Be extra vigilant to avoid overheating. A sunny porch might be an ideal spot for a morning nap, but much too warm when the afternoon sun intensifies. Check her often and remember that she may need your help to move to a more comfortable resting place.

SAVOR THE JOY

Now is the time for both of you to relish the simple pleasures of life. While the quantity of your time together may be limited, the quality need not be.

- Take time now to spend special moments together. Perhaps your busy schedule makes it difficult for you to spend as many hours with your friend as you'd like on a daily basis. But whenever you can, try spending just two or three minutes sitting quietly at her side, stroking her fur, being fully present with her. These will be moments you'll treasure in the years to come.

- Indulge her a little—or a lot. A favorite cookie or a dish of ice cream may bring a moment of earthly bliss. Both you and your dog will delight in a few of the decadent treats you've always saved for special occasions. As long as those treats don't compromise her health (sorry—a big chunk of chocolate is still a bad idea!), go ahead and make her gastronomical dreams come true.

- Although your walks together may be much slower and shorter, they're still a great boon to her well-being. The stimulation of a variety of sights and smells will bring pleasure to her days, and may help her get the rest she needs when you're back at home.

- There's nothing more healing for body and soul than the loving energy of someone you hold dear. That's true for your dog, just as it is for you. Chances are she has human and canine friends whose company she enjoys. Encourage them to stop by for a visit. A friendly voice or a wagging tail will provide a welcome boost to her spirits. They'll also be a source of valuable support for you.

When the End Is Near

As your dog's health continues to fail, there may come a time when you question whether it's in her best interest to facilitate her death. **Euthanasia** is an option that, in many cases, is embraced as a welcome opportunity to alleviate the suffering of a terminally ill animal. Some caretakers choose to allow their dogs to die a natural death, rather than speed the process with an injection. Many report that their dogs appear to experience a very personal process of release when allowed to approach death in their own time, in their own way. Under the right conditions, allowing your dog to die a natural death in your own home may be a richly meaningful time for both of you. How will you know which choice is right for you and, most important, for your friend?

EUTHANASIA OR NATURAL DEATH?

This may be the most intimate decision you ever make for your dog. Much as you may feel overwhelmed by the task, be comforted in the knowledge that no one is better equipped to make it than her closest life companion. Your veterinarian will be a valuable resource at this time; input from other family members or friends who are also close to her will help as well. Above all, trust *yourself* to make the right choice.

Consider the following questions:

- Is your dog in pain? How severe is it? Are there medications that can alleviate her discomfort? Keep in mind that every individual has a different tolerance for pain. Have you seen indications that your dog is suffering? Does she frequently cry out or whine? Does she tremble or pant, when temperature is not an issue? Does she seem to prefer to be alone, or stare blankly off into space? Does her face have an expression of distress, or does it have a look of serenity when she's at rest? A dog who is in pain that does not respond to medication may be most kindly served by releasing her from that pain through euthanasia. If pain is not a factor, you may be able to allow death to come naturally.

- What practical considerations are involved in caring for your dog at this stage of her life? Is she able to move around? Is she able to control her bowels and her bladder? These issues are significantly affected by your ability to tend to her needs. If she's lost her mobility and needs to be carried from place to place, you may be able to manage if she's a 12-pound terrier. But if she's a 150-pound Great Dane it's fair to recognize that your back may not be as strong as your heart. Carefully consider what her needs are, and what you can realistically provide for her. No one benefits if you put unreasonable demands on yourself.

- What is your dog's quality of life? Does she still wag her tail when you walk into the room? Does her expression brighten when you sit down to spend a quiet moment with her? If your friend is resting peacefully, you may be able to make the journey toward a natural death together.

- Talk to your veterinarian about what form your dog's death is likely to take. Based on knowledge of her condition, he may be able to provide valuable insight into what you can expect in the final days. Will she become very weak and slip into a deep and final sleep? Is pain likely to become unreasonable? The information will make your decision much clearer. Whatever choice you make, it will help you to be prepared.

- Do you have an adequate network of support to help you through the process? Whether you choose euthanasia or natural death, accept the aid of family and friends. If your dog needs extra care

providing for your dog after your death

Most of us put a high priority on giving our dogs the best care we can. We even plan for a compassionate and meaningful way to care for her remains after she dies. But what if you should be the first to die? Who will love and look after your friend when you're gone?

The death of a guardian can throw the life of a well-loved animal into a nightmare of uncertainty. Too often a dog who was once the center of someone's life shows up at an animal shelter, or on the doorstep of a distant and disinterested family member, all because the passing of the dog's human suddenly left her homeless. While it's something we rarely think of, and hardly ever plan for, it's a good idea to look ahead. Select a loving friend or relative to take your dog into his home should such a need arise, to become an "alternate guardian." It will give you peace of mind, and could prove to be one of the most important things you do to ensure your dog's continued well-being.

🐕 While no one will love your dog quite like you do, choose a friend or family member who cares about her, and who is sensitive enough to understand that she will be suffering a loss when you're gone. Be sure the individual has a home that will be safe and comfortable for your dog, and the financial resources to provide adequate physical care.

as the end draws near, having other loving people to assist you will ease the process, as well as offer an opportunity for all of you to draw together in love and mutual support.

Keep in mind that the choice you make now is not etched in stone. You may decide that a natural passing at home is what you want for your dog, only to find that circumstances change and euthanasia becomes the kinder option. Be open, be flexible, and in your compassion for your dog find compassion for yourself as well. Most of all honor your choice, and know that if it's made from your heart it is undoubtedly the right one.

HOSPICE

The last days of your dog's life are sacred days. They will be filled with the practical matters of caring for your friend, and also with preparations for releasing a loved one into death. The journey will be unique, just as your dog is unique. The following are a few thoughts to help you create a meaningful passage.

• Ask your vet what hospice services, if any, are available in your community for you and your dog, through the veterinary hospital, humane society, or other resource. Organizations that provide hospice for humans in your area may be able

🐕 Ask your alternate guardian if he is willing to make a commitment to adopt your dog under those circumstances. Let him know that your request reflects your trust in him, and your knowledge of him as a gentle and compassionate person. Be straightforward and practical. While the issue is an emotional one, it requires careful consideration of the responsibilities associated with adoption. Give your friend time to think about your request and make a thoughtful decision. Make it comfortable for him to decline your request if he does not feel able to assume the responsibility.

🐕 If possible, make arrangements to leave funds to help cover the costs of caring for your dog. Even a small amount could make it easier for your dog's alternate guardian to make necessary modifications to his home, such as fencing or a gate, or cover any veterinary expenses that may arise.

🐕 If it's not already part of your routine, try to make time for your dog to spend time with her alternate guardian on a regular basis. Visit his home together, and consider letting your dog spend short visits there on her own. The more familiar she is with the person and the place, the easier it will be for her to adjust to her new home should she ever need to.

to offer emotional support, or direct you to other local resources geared specifically to animal care.

- Become familiar with any medical procedures you may need to perform for your dog, including pain management. If your veterinarian is not comfortable supporting you in providing hospice for your dog, consider working with another vet who is.

- If rituals are meaningful to you, allow them to bring meaning to this important event in your life. You might create a very private ceremony for just you and your friend, or invite others to share in or even help create a ritual.

- Talk to your dog about what is happening. Share your feelings. Verbalize (or visualize, if that is more comfortable for you) all the things you hope she knows—how much she added to your life, the qualities you admire in her, that she'll always hold a special place in your heart. Tell her it's okay for her to leave. Let her know that while you'll miss her a great deal, the love you shared will sustain you and bring you happiness forever. Consciously releasing her into death may make it easier for her to slip away, and may also help you to let go.

- Chances are that other animals in your family are aware of what is happening. Include them in special moments with your dying friend. Be aware that they feel your sadness. Talk to them about your feelings, and acknowledge the importance of their relationship to the one who is soon to leave. Observe their responses, how they interact with her, and be open to what they may have to teach you about death and dying. Allow yourself to receive the loving support they offer you.

- Consider the use of homeopathic remedies to help ease your dog into death. While they will not *cause* death, when given in high potencies (10M or higher), some remedies may help bring about a more peaceful passage. **Arsenicum album** is most commonly used for this purpose, but depending on your dog's condition **Antimonium tartaricum**, **Carbo veg.**, **Lachesis** or **Phosphorus** may be appropriate choices. Consult the Materia Medica and choose the remedy that best matches your dog's symptoms.

Euthanasia:
When and How?

As the health of your beloved dog continues to decline, you may begin to wonder, "Is it time?" Even if you've made the decision that euthanasia will be the kindest, most sensible way to ease your dog into death, while she is still having good days and bad days, rough nights and brighter mornings, you may wrestle with the decision to call in the vet for the last time. "When?" may seem like a question with no clear answer.

But more often than not, once the decision has been made, a loving caretaker reports, "I just knew." Somehow there comes a day when it's no longer a question. It might be a look in your dog's eyes—a vacancy, a sense that she's already gone, the light has dimmed. In other cases there might be signs that pain has escalated;

she may cry through the night, or come to your bed in the morning with her ruff standing on end. Or perhaps it's simply an intuitive sense that the time has come... "She just looked at me and I knew."

Factual information about your dog's condition and options for her support will guide your mind to a sound, intellectual judgment. But the heart connection that you share with her, and the keen awareness you've developed as you've seen her through years of health and, especially, her transition toward death, will enable you to know at your deepest level when it's time to help her leave.

Euthanasia is an intimate, tender event in the life you share with your dog. If you are able to carry that awareness through the process, and allow it to inform the arrangements you make for how it takes place, it will be a sacred testimony to the love you share, and help ease the grieving process for you after she's gone. If time allows, making some arrangements in advance may prove to be a blessing when the time comes.

- If possible, arrange to have the euthanasia performed by a veterinarian your dog knows. Both you and your friend will appreciate the comforting presence of a gentle and familiar healer.

- Talk to your vet about making a house call to perform the euthanasia. Many veterinarians are willing to provide this service. It's a comfort to all if you can avoid transporting your dog, and say good-bye to one another in the comfort and privacy of your home.

- If you have young children, discuss the appropriateness of their presence during the euthanasia procedure with your family and your vet. He can also provide resources for helping your child through this time.

- Whether the euthanasia takes place at home or at your vet's clinic, remain at your dog's side in her final moments if at all possible. If you can manage it emotionally, allow her to die in the arms of the one she loves, rather than in the hands of strangers.

- Remain calm. Remember that releasing your dog into death may be the greatest act of love you can offer her. Focus on the joy you've shared, rather than on the pain of your loss. In whatever manner is appropriate to your belief system, be mindful of the form her spirit may take after it is freed from her aging or ailing body.

- Talk to her. Tell her all that's in your heart. Thank her for sharing her life with you. Let her know how much her loving presence enriched yours.

- Tell her it's okay to go.

Final Arrangements

Whether your dog is euthanized or dies naturally at home, you'll need to make some final decisions about the handling of her body. Your choice will depend on your spiritual beliefs, your personal wishes, and your physical and financial resources.

- You may simply allow your veterinarian to dispose of the body for you. In most cases it will be cremated along with the remains of other companion animals. In rare cases, it may be turned over for rendering. If this is a concern for you, get details ahead of time from your vet.

- If you would like your dog's body to undergo a postmortem examination (termed autopsy in humans), for your own information or for the benefit such an examination might bring to other dogs, discuss this option with your veterinarian.

- Most veterinarians can arrange to have your friend's body cremated individually and the ashes returned to you. Your vet may even be able to offer you a choice of urns to hold the ashes. These options can be expensive, so if finances are a concern inquire about cost before you proceed. Once the ashes are returned (this may take a couple of weeks) you may wish to scatter them in your dog's favorite spot, bury them in the urn, or keep them.

- If you choose not to have your dog cremated, and need a day or two to arrange for burial or to plan a ceremony to honor the event, your veterinarian may be able to hold and preserve your dog's body, usually under refrigeration, until you are ready.

- If you have property available, you might simply bury your dog in your backyard, or on your land. To avoid predation by wild animals, be sure to bury her body deep enough, or cover the area with heavy rocks, so that scavengers will not unearth it.

- Consider burying your dog in a pet cemetery. Ask your veterinarian for contact information for facilities in your area. The services offered vary, and may include transportation of your dog's body from your home or from the hospital, use of a viewing area where you can have a wake for your dog prior to burial, and perhaps perpetual care of the gravesite. Some grieving guardians even find it to be a place where they can meet others who are dealing with a similar loss. At the very least, if your friend's remains are in a cemetery you will always have a site that you can visit where you may feel a special connection to her after her death.

Time to Grieve

Now that your friend has passed on, you'll need some time to grieve. It's important that you honor this process, and recognize the significance of this event in your life. If someone tells you, "Oh—she was only a dog!" take some distance from that friend for a while, and choose instead the company of those who understand. You've just lost the company of your beloved companion, the one who greeted you every day with a smile, who wanted nothing more than to be at your side. She made your life richer, put a smile on your face when you were glum, and licked your tears away when it was time to cry. Most people have few relationships in their lives that are more unequivocally loving and supportive than the relationships they have with their dogs. There's no question that you'll need time to adjust to the empty space on the couch, or the silence when you come through the door at the end of the day.

Remember, too, that the other animals in your family have also lost a companion. Take the opportunity to spend some extra, quality time with them. Watch for signs of grieving among them, and pay special attention to those who seem to be suffering. Accept their offers of kisses when they decide you need them. Let them lavish you with love, and show you that there's still a reason to laugh and play.

Above all, don't underestimate the significance of your loss. Understand that grieving takes as much time as it takes—for you that may be a few weeks, or it may be a year or more. Give yourself whatever time you need. Consider it one of the ways you honor the wonderful creature who graced your life.

COPING WITH YOUR LOSS

There are as many ways of coping with grief as there are people who love. Here are a few ideas from others who have loved as you have—and healed.

- Take care of yourself. Remember to eat and rest. Be sure that other animal family members who may be grieving also get the nourishment they need.

- The homeopathic remedy **Ignatia** is a wonderful aid in dealing with grief and loss. It will not suppress your pain, but it will soften its sharp edge and help you get through the most difficult days and nights. If other family members, including animals, are showing signs of grief, Ignatia may also help them get back on course. The flower

remedy **Star of Bethlehem** is another option that can offer gentle, healing emotional support.

- If you can, take some time away from your normal routine to simply be present with your emotions. Try not to avoid feeling all of the feelings, painful as they may be. Allow them to flow through you. If you feel the need, cry long and loud.

- Gather up all of the photographs you have of your friend into a beautiful photo album. You'll relive happy memories you'd forgotten, release those pent-up emotions, and have a wonderful tribute and keepsake when it's finished.

- Write, sing, or paint her story. It might describe her whole life, from puppyhood to the final days, or just your favorite afternoon with her. Whether it's a poem, a sculpture, or a sonata you play on your piano, create something in the world that expresses who your friend was.

- Notify her friends. Send a brief announcement to others who knew and loved her. You might use your poem or drawing to create a note card in her honor, and thank recipients for the happiness they brought into her life. Include a favorite photo of your friend in her more vibrant days.

- Create a shrine in your home or backyard. Include a few photos, her collar, a favorite toy, and any other mementos or symbols that are meaningful for you. You might add her ashes when they arrive. Her shrine will create a special place where you can reflect on her presence in your life, and celebrate the wonderful creature that she was.

- Be open to the possibility of her continued presence in your life. Depending on your spiritual beliefs, this may or may not seem like a reality to you. But many guardians find a great sense of comfort in an ongoing awareness of the energy of the dogs who once shared their lives in physical form.

- If you buried her body or her ashes on your land, consider adding a commemorative headstone, or planting a tree, bush, or perennial flower to mark the site.

- Consider joining a support group for people grieving the loss of companion animals. Ask your veterinarian if one exists in your area, or check online resources. If no group exists in your area, you may wish to start one. You can be sure that there are others in your community who are dealing with a loss similar to yours.

- Browse through your local bookstore, library, or websites for books that will support you at this time.

- Enjoy the healing friendship of other dogs. Take a neighbor's dog for a walk, or volunteer at your local animal shelter. Offering a gentle touch to a homeless animal will be nurturing for you and for him.

- When the time is right—not a day sooner or later—bring a new dog into your life. Adopting a dog in need of a home will bring a new source of love and joy into your life, and fill your heart with the contentment that comes from bringing happiness to another being. Ultimately, that may be the greatest tribute that you can make to your departed friend.

Most important of all, remember the loving. As painful as this time is, keep in mind that it is only painful because you loved—and were loved—greatly. There is no greater beauty in this world, and no more sacred gift we can give one another. You and your beloved friend shared that joyous bond. Allow the experience of that love to transform your pain and heal your aching heart.

Recommended Reading and Resources

Blessing the Bridge: What Animals Teach Us About Death, Dying, and Beyond. Rita Reynolds. Troutdale, OR: NewSage Press, 2001.

Conversations with My Old Dog: For Anyone Who Has Ever Loved and Lost a Pet. Robert Pasick. Hazelden Transitions, 2000.

Saying Goodbye to the Pet You Love: A Complete Resource to Help You Heal. L.A. Greene and J. Lanis. New York: New Harbinger Press, 2002.

Delta Society, Renton Washington, an excellent resource for books, information, and web links about bereavement. 1-425-226-7357, www.deltasociety.org.

Washington State Veterinary Medical Association Pet Loss Support Group. www.wsvma.org/pet_loss.htm.

FOR CHILDREN:

I'll Always Love You. Hans Wilhelm. New York: Crown, 1985.

The Tenth Good Thing About Barney. Judith Viorst. New York: Macmillan. 1971.

Jamie (right), Australian Shepherd/
Siberian Husky cross. Jamie was
adopted in 2003 at 5 months old
through the Milo Foundation in Willits,
California.

Henry (left), Australian Shepherd/
Border Collie. Adopted at 2 years old
from the ASPCA in Oakland, California.

4 part four

Bunny (above), Australian Shepherd.
Adopted in 1994 at 6 months old when
his first family could no longer care
for him.

Minky (below), Australian Shepherd.
Adopted in 1996 at 1 year old
from Australian Shepherd Rescue
of Northern California.

part four

nutritional materia medica

U NLESS OTHERWISE NOTED, give a dose that is proportional to a human dose (as recommended on product label), based on your dog's body weight. If your dog is under medical care, let your veterinarian know about any supplements you are giving. To be sure you are able to identify any side effects, always add new supplements one at a time.

Alpha-lipoic acid (Lipoic acid)

- Powerful, natural antioxidant found in all cells; enhances the function of other antioxidants and supports the liver's ability to remove toxins.

- When combined with other antioxidants, omega-3 fatty acids, and L-carnitine, can help reduce symptoms associated with senility.

- A good supplement for diabetic dogs, to help slow development of diabetic cataracts and, in some cases, stabilize blood sugar.

- Dose at 25 to 150 mg daily, depending on dog's size.

Antioxidants

- See listings for individual antioxidants. See also Chapter 3.

Berberine

- The active ingredient in many antibacterial herbs, including goldenseal, goldthread, coptis, and Oregon grape.

- Used for support in cases of bacterial infection, particularly of the respiratory or intestinal tract; has been shown to be effective for clearing Giardia, a protozoal intestinal parasite.

Bioflavonoids (Flavanoids, proanthocyanidins)

- Plant pigments that are responsible for the many medicinal actions of foods; found in abundance in many varied sources (citrus fruits, berries, legumes, green tea, and many herbs).

- Powerful antioxidants and potent free-radical scavengers; they can inhibit the enzymes that break down cartilage in arthritic joints; they also help slow the progression of other degenerative disease processes, such as cataracts.

- Supplemental sources include quercetin (especially good for allergies and bee stings), mixed citrus bioflavonoids, pine bark, grapeseed extract and rutin.

Bromelain

- A plant enzyme derived from pineapple that can reduce swelling and pain associated with tissue trauma, when given in large doses.

- Aids digestion and relieves pain and inflammation due to arthritis in some dogs.

- Give 50 to 300 mg 2 to 3 times daily 30 minutes before meals (use short term for tissue trauma such as sprains or strains, longer term for pancreas insufficiency).

- *Susceptible animals can develop allergic reactions with long-term use.*

Calcium

- An important mineral that is present in sufficient quantities in commercial dog foods; supplementation is needed in home-prepared diets.

- Sources include raw bones (as recommended in raw food diet plans), bonemeal, calcium carbonate, and eggshells. See Chapter 3 for sources and recommended dosage.

- Seek veterinary advice before supplementing when kidney disease, cancer, parathyroid disorder, or urinary stones are present.

Carnitine (L-carnitine)

- An amino acid needed by the body to convert fat into energy.

- Supplementation can reduce the production of damaging free radicals.

- Some cases of the heart disease called Canine Dilated Cardiomyopathy are associated with carnitine deficiency, so supplementation may be helpful; may also lead to improvement in other forms of heart disease.

- When combined with antioxidants (such as vitamins C and E), alpha-lipoic acid, and omega-3 fatty acids, may help reduce behavior changes caused by senility.

- Diarrhea and gas have been reported in rare cases, usually only when high doses were given.

Choline

- Found in the diet as a component of lecithin; supplementation has been shown to benefit some cases of seizures and cognitive dysfunction (senility); may be of benefit in some cases of liver disease.

- Commonly found in veterinary supplements for senior dogs

Chondoprotective agents (glucosamines, chondroitin sulfate, glycosomminoglycans, injectable Adequan-R)

- Agents which reduce joint inflammation associated with arthritis, joint injury, or surgery.

- Help heal injured cartilage by assisting in the production of the joint's lubricating fluids and controlling enzymes that break down cartilage in joints.

- Natural sources include sea cucumber, green-lipped mussel (*Perna canniculus*), shellfish, and bovine trachea and cartilage.

- Use twice daily for 4 weeks, then decrease to once daily. Expect results in 4 to 8 weeks.

- Sensitive dogs can experience nausea, poor appetite, or diarrhea. Side effects are usually related to the size of the dose.

- *Theoretically, could raise blood sugar in diabetics and promote bleeding when used with any blood-thinning herbs or medications.*

Coenzyme Q10 (CoQ10)

- Important natural antioxidant and free radical scavenger, used in cases of periodontal disease, heart disease, and for geriatric support. Natural stores in the body are depleted at times of stress, with age, and in some diabetics.

- May help reduce toxicity of chemotherapy.

- For early stage periodontal disease give 10 to 60 mg with a meal for best effect.

- To improve function of heart muscle, or in conjunction with medications for congestive heart failure, give 30 to 90 mg twice daily, depending on size.

- Use oil-based capsules for best absorption.

Digestive enzymes

- Enzymes derived from plant and animal (pancreas) sources can help dogs with poor digestion (excessive gas, large stool volume, chronic intermittent vomiting).

- May benefit some dogs with allergies and arthritis.

- Pancreatic enzymes are a mainstay for treating pancreatic insufficiency.

DLPA (dl-phenylalanine)

- A mild natural analgesic; may stimulate the body's production of endorphins (morphine-like compounds); used for arthritis, back pain, or other forms of mild pain.

- Give 100 to 500 mg twice daily, depending on size.

- *Not for use during pregnancy.*

DMG (Dimethyglyceine)

- Enhances oxygen use and increases cellular energy; boosts immune function.

- Considered an anti-stress nutrient for the heart and muscles; has been known to inhibit seizures in some dogs when dosed at 50 to 125 mg 3 times daily.

- May help treat arthritis at doses of up to 500 mg per day, depending on size.

Essential fatty acids

- See omega-3 fatty acids, omega-6 fatty acids, alpha-lipoic acid.

Flaxseed

- See omega-3 fatty acids.

Glutamine (L-glutamine)

- Amino acid found in high concentration in muscles and gastrointestinal tract; helps promote a healthy digestive tract and support muscle tissue during chronic disease.

- Preferred fuel for small intestinal cells, making it a good supplement for acute intestinal injury as well as chronic problems.

- Best given on an empty stomach. If your dog has liver problems, consult your vet.

Glucosamines

- See **Chondoprotective agents**

Grapeseed extract

- A potent antioxidant (in various studies, shown to be 4 to 20 times more powerful than vitamins C and E) and vascular strengthener.

- Contains procyanidolic compounds that scavenge free radicals, leading to its recommended use in cancer prevention.

- Give 50 to 100 mg twice daily.

IP-6 (Inositol hyxaphosphate)

- A naturally occurring carbohydrate that can help inhibit cancer by stimulating "suppressor genes," inhibiting blood vessel formation (angiogenesis), and increasing the formation of "natural killer" cells.

- Used as support for blood, organ, or skin cancers.

- Exact therapeutic dosage is unknown, but it appears to be a very safe nutrient. Studies suggest 100 to 1000 mg per 20 pounds body weight

- *Seek veterinary support for long-term use.*

Lactoferrin

- An immune modulating supplement derived from colostrum.

- When applied to gums, it binds iron, which bacteria need to thrive.

- For periodontal (gum) disease, mix the contents of 1 capsule with a small amount of milk or water and apply to gums twice daily.

- Allergies can develop with long-term use.

Lecithin

- Derived from soy or eggs, its primary benefit comes from a phospholipid that provides increased choline for the body, which may be deficient in certain neurologic disorders, especially those associated with aging.

- An excellent supplement for senior dogs, or dogs who exercise heavily.

- *Safety in pregnancy has not been established.*

Melatonin

- A natural hormone (produced by the pineal gland) that helps control sleep cycle. Also a powerful antioxidant. Vegetarian sources are available.

- Can help control some cases of nighttime seizures, certain seasonal hair loss conditions, and nighttime restlessness.

- Reported to be of benefit in treating noise phobias and other anxiety related issues. May be of increased benefit when combined with valerian root. (See Herbal Materia Medica.)

- Suggested dose: 1 mg for dogs up to 25 lbs; 3 mgs for medium-sized dogs; 3 to 6 mg for giant breeds.

- Best to give at night. May cause sedation. More frequent doses (2 to 3 times a day, which is safe for short-term use) may be needed for thunderstorm or other noise phobias. (Consult a veterinarian or behaviorist.)

- Possible anticancer effect with high doses for certain cancers that are affected by hormones (such as mammary or prostate cancers) reported in human clinical trials.

- May effect fertility and diabetic regulation.

MSM (Methylsulfonylmethane)

- A natural compound that contains sulfur, which declines in the body with aging.

- As a dietary supplement, provides needed sulfur for cartilage synthesis and healing when joint disease is present; has a mild antiinflammatory effect and is considered a natural mild painkiller.

- Used for arthritis at dosages of 100 to 300 mg twice daily, depending on size; a common ingredient in multi-nutrient arthritis formulas.

N-acetylcysteine

- A modified form of cysteine, an amino acid that is

needed for the production of glutathione, an important antioxidant and liver-protective enzyme.

- Strengthens the mucous layer in the respiratory and intestinal tract.

- Used for respiratory disease and liver support. Reported to be useful in treatment of degenerative myelopathy, a nerve disease.

- Dosing information in dogs is not well established at this time.

Nutritional yeast

- Flavorful supplement that most dogs enjoy; rich in B vitamins.

- To be sure the supplement does not create a gummy residue that adheres to the teeth, mix it into food rather than adding as a top-dressing.

- *Allergic reactions occur in very rare cases.*

Omega-3 fatty acids

- An essential component of every dog's diet; a valuable antiinflammatory supplement; also reported to have antitumor effects.

- Used for a variety of problems including allergies, skin disease, arthritis, intestinal problems, cancer, diabetes, kidney and heart disease, hyperlipidemia in Schnauzers.

- Studies in dogs have been done with fish oils, reportedly the best source of usable omega-3s. Studies on congestive heart failure and cancer reported improved survival, and inhibition of tumor metastasis.

- Give 1 fish oil capsule (assuming the standard dose of 180 mg EPA, or eicosapentaenoic acid) per 10 to 15 pounds body weight daily. Consult a vet for higher dosages.

- Flaxseed oil, a vegetarian alternative, may not be as effective as fish oil, due to dogs' inability to fully convert adequate amounts of alpha-linoleic acid (ALA) to the beneficial eicosapentanenoic acid (EPA). If using flaxseed oil, feed at higher doses than fish oils, or 1 to 2 teaspoons daily per 20 lbs. Works well to improve skin and coat (contains some omega-6).

- Give omega-3 supplements with antioxidants daily, particularly vitamin E. Check with your vet if your dog has cancer, as antioxidants may reduce anti-cancer effects of omega-3s.

- Store in a tight container, protected from light, preferably in refrigerator.

- *Occasionally causes loose stools in some dogs. Avoid using long-term with aspirin or other anticlotting substances. May cause weight gain.*

Omega-6 fatty acids

- An essential component (in the form of linoleic acid) of every dog's diet; important for healthy skin and coat. Add as a supplement when there is a history of poor nutrition.

- Evening primrose oil is an excellent source; also borage, black currant, and vegetable oils.

- Store as with omega-3 supplements.

Prebiotics (Fructose oligosaccharides, FOS)

- Short-chain sugars that nutritionally support the beneficial bacteria (such as *Lactobacillus acidophilus*) that live in a healthy gastrointestinal tract.

- May inhibit the ability of certain harmful bacteria to adhere to the intestinal lining.

- Used for inflammatory bowel disorders, food allergies, chronic colitis.

Probiotics

- A supplement that contains live microorganisms, such as *Lactobacillus acidophilus, Lactobacillus bifidus*, and *Bifidobacterium bifidum*, the beneficial bacteria that reside in the intestinal tract and promote normal digestive health.

- Can be used for the prevention and treatment of disease, and to repopulate the intestinal tract after disruption occurs due to infection, poor diet, stress, or the use of antibiotics, steroids, and other medications.

- Recent reports suggest organisms frequently "die on the shelf" and may not be viable by the time of purchase. Larger doses (as for humans) often get a better response. With most products, refrigeration is necessary to maintain viability of the bacteria. Ongoing studies at the University of Guelph may help determine which microorganisms are most beneficial in dogs, as compared to those marketed for human consumption.

Psyllium

- Seed husks from the plantain plant, used to treat constipation and to support gastrointestinal health.

- ½ to 2 teaspoons 1 to 2 times daily, depending on the size of the dog and the desired stool effect.

- Do not give if your dog is dehydrated.

Quercetin

- See bioflavanoids.

SAM-E (S-adenosylmethionine)

- For arthritis – studies in humans showed increased cartilage production and decreased pain and inflammation; may be as effective as NSAIDs.

- For liver support – helps make glutathione, an important detoxifying antioxidant.

- For senility and depression – may help relieve symptoms, although it occasionally leads to increased restlessness in some dogs.

- Dose is roughly 10 mg per pound daily on an empty stomach, or follow recommended dose on Denosyl (veterinary brand) package. If stomach upset occurs, reduce the dose for a few days then try to increase it gradually up to the desired dose.

- *Product potency varies widely. Purchase only enteric-coated varieties (not capsules) to ensure freshness and stability. Store according to package directions.*

Selenium

- A powerful antioxidant that can enhance immune function; works synergistically with vitamin E; concentrations in some commercial foods may be inadequate.

- Plays a vital role in normal thyroid function.

- May help decrease the risk of cancer and reduce side effects associated with chemotherapy. Check with your vet if your dog has cancer.

Spirulina

- A fresh-water blue-green algae that contains B-vitamins, minerals, and numerous antioxidant phytonutrients.

- May support healthy intestinal bacterial populations, improve skin and coat conditions, and possibly provide an anti-tumor effect.

SOD (Super oxide dismutase)

- Antioxidant (extracted from bovine liver cells) with good antiinflammatory properties; helpful for arthritis.

- 100 to 200 mg per day. Reduce the dose if loose stools occur.

Taurine

- Important amino acid for the heart, eyes, muscles, and many tissues.

- Vegetarian diets tend to be deficient; deficiency can lead to heart failure.

- May be helpful in treating dilated cardiomyopathy, especially in American Cocker Spaniels and Golden Retrievers.

- May be of benefit in some cases of epilepsy or hepatitis.

- A very safe supplement. Give 250 to 1000 mg 2 to 3 times daily.

Vitamin A

- Supports immune response for use with skin disease, intestinal disease, eye disorders, and cancer.

- 500 to 5000 IU per day. Higher doses are sometimes beneficial, especially in Cocker Spaniels with seborrhea or in cancer cases. Check with your veterinarian first. Overdose can lead to bone pain.

- *Do not use with "dry eye" condition or liver disease without checking with your veterinarian. High doses are not recommended during pregnancy.*

Vitamin B

- A complex of several different vitamins (commonly called B_1, B_2, B_6, B_{12}, biotin, choline, folic acid, inositol, PABA, and pantothenic acid) needed to maintain healthy nervous tissue, skin, eyes, liver, and muscle. Because dog foods are fortified, and most foods contain B vitamins, deficiencies are rare. Dogs on vegan diets need added B_{12}. May be helpful in some cases of senility, epililepsy, and liver disease; may help stimulate a poor appetite.

- A good supplement for acute diarrhea; works synergistically with probiotics and can help transport potassium (an electrolyte often lost during bouts of diarrhea) into the cells.

Vitamin C

- Natural antioxidant; added to some dog foods to help preserve freshness; may be helpful in cases of arthritis, or any other disorder where antioxidants are beneficial.

- Dogs synthesize their own vitamin C, however at times of stress or illness supplementation may be of benefit.

- Diarrhea may occur at higher doses (over 200 mg) in some dogs. The non-acidic form (ester-C) helps prevent intestinal upset.

Vitamin E

- A natural antioxidant vitamin that normalizes immune function.

- Used in skin disease, inflammatory disease, epilepsy, and to promote the healing of wounds; strengthens the immune system.

- Also a good supplement for diabetics, cataracts, dogs with intervertebral disc disease, or nerve problems.

- A good supplement for senior dogs, especially those with cancer; may help with senility.

- Daily dose: For small dogs, 200 IU; medium dogs, 400 IU; large dogs, 800 IU, unless higher doses are recommended by your veterinarian for a specific condition.

- The preferred form is natural, whole-food-based, and labeled "mixed tocopherols" or the d-alpha form.

- *May cause thinning of the blood. Consult your vet before giving long-term with aspirin, gingko, or any other anticlotting substance, especially prior to scheduled surgery.*

Zinc

- An important component of many types of enzyme activity; assists in several immune mechanisms.

- May help promote the healing of wounds and assist in the regulation of blood sugar in diabetics.

- Useful in treating certain skin disorders and chronic degenerative disease.

- Available as zinc sulfate. Usually dosed at 5 to 15 mg per day, depending on size, unless a different dosage is prescribed by your veterinarian. Can interfere with absorption of copper and iron.

- *May cause vomiting, diarrhea, or loss of appetite (less likely when using time-released form). Discontinue if side effects occur.*

homeopathic materia medica

WHEN SELECTING A REMEDY for an injury or acute illness, the most prominent symptoms and any changes in his behavior or emotional state will generally guide you to the right remedy. However, if your dog is dealing with chronic illness, it's important to consider all of the symptoms, characteristics, moods, and even history that you know about him. The following guidelines will help you get started, however it is not intended to be a complete course of instruction. The use of homeopathy to treat chronic illness is a skill and an art that requires training and experience to master. If possible, work with an experienced homeopath who can teach you. If none is available, the approach described here will allow you to begin your exploration of homeopathy as a valuable healing tool.

Selecting a Remedy for Chronic Illness

Begin by gathering a list of symptoms and traits that describe your dog as a *whole* individual. Include the following kinds of information:

- Your dog's normal body type and personality traits

- His preferences, habits, and tendencies

- Any physical, emotional, and behavioral symptoms of his illness

- "Modalities," or the conditions under which your dog feels better or worse

The symptoms listed in your material medica are broken down as follows:

- Mind, emotions and behavior
- Head
- Eyes
- Ears
- Nose
- Mouth (includes teeth, tongue and gums)
- Throat
- Stomach and abdomen (includes preferences regarding food and water)
- Stool
- Respiratory and circulatory systems
- Urinary tract
- Reproductive system
- Back, limbs, and paws
- Neurologic system
- Generalities (symptoms that affect the entire body, such as fever, sleep habits or energy level)
- Modalities (conditions under which symptoms are better or worse)

Many of the symptoms and traits that guide you to the correct remedy will seem completely irrelevant in the context of conventional medicine. Because you're treating the whole individual, you'll consider things that may seem to have no relationship to the problem you're worried about. For example, your dog has developed some stiffness in his hind legs, but gathering information beyond the condition of his knees, hips and spine will be important. For instance, knowing that his left eye is a little runny, that he likes to drink large amounts of water all at one time, and that he sometimes has tiny red bumps on his belly may complete the symptom picture that leads you to the remedy that will best help balance his system and stimulate his healing energy. It takes a little practice, but learning to "think homeopathically" will allow you to develop your eye for the *seemingly* unrelated symptoms that are part of the overall picture of his energy system, and that may be key to finding a cure.

The survey on pages 312 and 313 will help jog your memory and stimulate your powers of observation. At this stage be generous—write down everything that comes to mind. You can tease out the most meaningful information later. Begin by describing your dog's normal characteristics and habits, both physical and emotional, including his body type, his medical history and his diet. List any previous health problems and the treatments he received. Make a note of any routine vaccinations or medications you give him, such as heartworm preventive or flea and tick deterrents.

Next, list the symptoms of his current illness. Go through all of his body parts and systems to be sure you've noted all the clues that may lead you to the correct remedy. Finally, think carefully about what modalities you've observed, or what circumstances seem to make your dog feel better or worse.

Once you've completed the survey, **review your notes and eliminate any items that might be considered normal behavior** for a dog, such as "gets excited when strangers come to the door," or "loves raw meat." On the other hand, if your dog has a distinct dislike of raw meat, that's a bit unusual for a dog, so be sure to include it on your list.

Once you've completed the survey, **fill in a chart like the one on pages 312-313.** In the left hand column list symptoms and traits you noted in your survey. Turn to Chapters 9 and 10, and read the sections that describe the problem you'd like to treat. Make a list of the remedies associated with the symptoms you've observed in your dog. Enter those across the top of your chart.

using a homeopathic materia medica designed for humans

The Materia Medica that follows will help you get started using homeopathic remedies to care for your dog. As you become more experienced, you'll want to expand your reference library to include other materials. Unfortunately, while there are many excellent resources designed for use with human patients, there are very few good materia medicas that are written specifically for animals.

With a little practice, however, you can learn to interpret the information in reference books written for humans and apply it very effectively to help you treat your dog. The biggest difference to keep in mind is that you will generally have much less information about your dog, or any animal, than is available when dealing with a human patient. For example, a typical material medica will rely on information that a patient provides regarding his *subjective* experience of pain or other symptoms, such as whether the pain feels like pressure, tearing, burning, or cutting. Of course, while it may be obvious that your dog is in pain, it is difficult to know what *kind* of pain he is feeling. Your dog may be rubbing his eyes, but are they burning or itching? It's hard to say. Also, most material medicas rely heavily on mental, or emotional, symptoms. Much as we may have a good understanding of the emotions our animals feel, it is often difficult to be certain whether she is feeling angry or frustrated, whether she is sad or simply feels like being alone. Did she bite that boisterous stranger out of aggression or because she was frightened?

Regardless of the type of materia medica you're using, It is very important to use only the information you can be relatively sure of when listing your dog's symptoms and looking for a remedy that matches those symptoms. Using inaccurate symptoms may lead you to the wrong remedy, so you'll be better off to omit a symptom rather than guess. —*Jan*

Next, go to the List of Remedies beginning on page 314 and read through the description of each remedy you've listed across the top of your chart. As you do, mark an "X" on your chart next to any symptom listed for that remedy that you also noted as present in your dog.

Don't expect your dog to exhibit all the symptoms related to any one homeopathic remedy. Many remedies list dozens of symptoms. In some cases they may be even associated with symptoms that seem to contradict one another. For example, the remedy Lycopodium is associated with a huge appetite and also with an ability to eat only small amounts of food. Obviously, both of those tendencies would not be present in your dog at the same time. Stick with your list of the symptoms and traits you've observed in your friend, and choose the remedy associated with as many of those as possible. In most cases you can simply ignore symptoms listed in the Material Medica that do not apply to your dog.

Finally, review your chart to see if one of the remedies has more Xs in its column than the others. If so, that's the remedy to choose for your dog. If two or more remedies have the same, or nearly the same, number of Xs, choose the one that is the best match in the areas of emotional/behavioral symptoms and modalities. Check to see if there are any notes with regard to dosage listed for that remedy in the material medica. If not, follow the general guidelines for potency and dosing frequency in Chapter 5.

Survey

Describe your dog:

How old is your dog? This is particularly important if your dog is very young or very old.

What is his body type? Is your dog lean, muscular or does he tend to be overweight? Is he very thin, even though he has a good appetite?

What color is his coat?

Describe his personality. Is he a happy, playful guy? Does he tend to be very sensitive? Does he whine when he doesn't get his way, or is he fairly adaptable? Does he love to be touched or does he keep his distance from strangers? Is he very active or more of a "couch potato"?

What is his medical history? Make a list of any illnesses or injuries your dog has had through the course of his life, along with the treatments he received for each. Be on the lookout for any recurring problems, such as infections or lameness.

What is his vaccination record? Does he receive annual vaccines?

Describe his diet. Does he eat fresh food, or does his diet consist of commercial dog foods that may contain chemical additives?

Are there any chemicals in his environment that he may eat, sniff or absorb through his skin? Identify any environmental toxins he may be exposed to.

In the following section, write down only those abnormalities that you can identify with a reasonable degree of certainty. For example, if you're not sure if your dog's skin eruptions are itchy or painful, leave that question blank. It's better to have fewer symptoms to work with than inaccurate ones, since an *inaccurate* symptom will be more likely to lead you to the wrong remedy than will a *lack* of symptoms. Skip any section in which your dog shows no sign of trouble.

Mind:

Describe any unusual emotions or behaviors you've observed. Does he want to be held all the time? Is he irritable or aggressive? Is he anxious, fearful, or depressed? Remember that emotions can be difficult to identify precisely. If you're not sure, it's best not to list an emotion at all.

Head:

List any symptoms that pertain to the head. In most cases this will apply to skin problems or unusual growths that are concentrated on and around the head.

Eyes:

Is there a discharge? Is it more apparent in the left eye or the right? Note the color and consistency of the discharge.

Does your dog rub or try to scratch his eyes? Again, be sure to note whether one eye or the other seems to bother him the most.

Are there any visible changes to the eyelids or to the eyeball itself? Are the lids red or swollen? Does the eyeball look cloudy? Do his eyes look dull or glassy?

Does she seem uncomfortable in bright light?

Is her vision impaired? Get a veterinary diagnosis of the cause, if possible. Note any information you have regarding the parts of the eye that are affected.

Ears:

Is there a discharge? Describe the color and odor.

Are there signs of discomfort? Is he shaking his head or trying to rub his ears? Does he cry out when you handle them?

Does he seem to be bothered more than usual by loud noises?

Is there a loss of hearing? Get a veterinary diagnosis to determine the cause, if possible. Make a note of any parts of the ear that are affected.

Nose:

Is there any discharge? Is it clear and watery, or thick? Is it ropey or creamy? What color is it? Is it constant or does it occur only under certain circumstances?

Is your dog sneezing? Note the frequency and intensity, and whether there is any discharge when he sneezes.

Note any unusual conditions on the surface of his nose. Are there any unusual growths? Is his nose dry and crusty? Is it warm or cool?

Mouth:

How does his breath smell? Try to describe any odor. Does it smell like old cheese, or like dead tissue?

What is the condition of his teeth? Are they covered with plaque? Has he lost teeth due to gum disease?

Are his gums healthy? Do they seem to bleed easily? Note any signs of gum infection or deterioration.

Describe the surface of her tongue. Does it have a white or yellowish coating? Is there a line down the center? Does the saliva appear foamy around the edges?

Is there any excessive salivation? Does the saliva have an unusual odor?

Are there any unusual growths? Describe the location and appearance. List your veterinarian's diagnosis of the type of growth.

Throat:

Does your dog have a cough that sounds like it originates in the throat? Describe the sound. Does it sound like a try, tickling cough? Does it sound as though something is caught in his throat? Does he cough when you apply gentle pressure to the area?

Is he coughing up a discharge? If so, describe its color, consistency, and odor.

Is there any alteration in the sound of his voice? Is he unable to bark, cry, or "talk"?

Is there breathing difficulty that seems to originate in the throat area? Is it more noticeable when your dog inhales or when he exhales? Is it worse during or after physical activity? Is it worse in warm weather? Note any veterinary diagnosis of the problem and its cause. Be sure to note any parts of the throat that are affected, and the nature of the trouble.

Stomach and Abdomen:

Describe your dog's drinking habits. Does he drink a lot of water or very little? If he drinks a lot, is it all at one time or a few laps frequently throughout the day?

Does your dog have an unusual relationship to food? Is he a ravenous eater or a picky one? Has he lost his appetite entirely, or nearly so? Does he stay very thin even though he eats well? Does he have any unusual food preferences?

Is there any vomiting? How often? Does it occur immediately after a meal or at some other time of the day? What does the vomitus look like?

Does your dog get hiccups?

Is there pain when you apply gentle pressure to the stomach or abdominal region?

Has your veterinarian diagnosed a problem? If so, list the diagnosis and the particular body parts that are affected.

Stool:

Describe any unusual bowel habits. Does your dog have diarrhea or is he constipated? Does he strain when trying to move his bowel? Does he pass one piece of stool at a time?

Describe any unusual color or consistency. Is there blood or mucus in the stool? Does it look small and dark, dry or greasy?

Is there any sign of pain during or after a bowel movement?

Does your dog show signs of pain or itching in the anal area?

Has your veterinarian diagnosed a problem? If so, list the diagnosis and the particular body parts that are affected.

Urinary System:

Is your dog incontinent? Describe the nature of the incontinence. Does he dribble when he walks? Does he wet his bed when he sleeps?

Does your dog show signs of difficult urination? Does he strain when he tries to pass urine? Does he cry out during or after urinating?

Does he seem to urinate more frequently, or with a greater sense of urgency, than usual? Does he pass small amounts of urine frequently, or a large amount at one time? Does he suddenly need to go outside in a hurry?

Is there pain when you apply gentle pressure in the region of his kidneys?

Does your dog show signs of burning or itching after urinating? A male dog might lick his penis after urinating. A female might lick her vulva or perhaps try to "scoot" on the grass. Either gender might run away, looking distressed, after passing urine that burns.

Does his urine have an unusual color or odor?

Has your veterinarian diagnosed a problem? List the diagnosis and the particular body parts that are affected.

Reproductive System:

Is there a discharge from the penis or vulva? Describe the color, consistency, and odor. Ask your veterinarian to help you determine whether it is in fact originating from the reproductive system or the urinary tract.

Are there any growths in the area of the nipples, vulva or penis? Describe the location and appearance. List your veterinarian's diagnosis of the type of growth.

Respiratory and Circulatory Systems:

Are there any breathing abnormalities? Describe any unusual sounds or rhythms associated with the breath. Note any activities or other circumstances that seem to make the problem better or worse.

Does your dog cough? Describe the sound of the cough. Describe the color, consistency, and odor of any sputum that your dog produces. Note any activities or other circumstances that seem to trigger the cough.

Has your veterinarian diagnosed a problem? Note any irregularities in the functioning of the heart or lungs.

Back, Limbs and Paws:

Does your dog show any signs of lameness or uneven movement? If he seems to favor one leg consistently, note which one.

Did the lameness develop gradually or did it appear suddenly?

Note the circumstances that seem to make him better or worse. Does he get better with rest or is he stiff after a nap? Is he more lame after exercise, or in cold, rainy weather?

Is there any heat or swelling in any of his limbs or paws? Note the location.

Does your dog indicate pain when you apply pressure to a particular joint or other area? Note which limb and the location of the painful area.

Does your dog show signs of weakness or loss of coordination? Describe his movement as you see it.

Is there any sign of pain when you run your fingers along your dog's spine? Describe the location, and your dog's response to your touch.

Neurologic System:

Does your dog show signs of weakness or paralysis? Describe the symptoms as you see them. Note which limbs or which parts of the body are affected.

Is there lameness that seems to be the result of a spinal injury or irregularity? Note your veterinarian's diagnosis, as well as her description of the body parts affected.

Has your dog had seizures? Note the frequency, and the time of day or any other pattern in their occurrence.

Describe the nature of his seizures. Does he have convulsions, or does he simply tremble or become very drowsy?

What events are associated with the seizures? Describe your dog's behavior immediately before and after the seizures, and any circumstances that seem to trigger them.

Note your veterinarian's diagnosis and the body parts affected.

Skin and Coat:

What is the condition of your dog's coat? Is it thick and shiny, or dull, dry, or brittle? Is the hair thin, or even balding in places? Note the location of trouble spots.

Describe any skin eruptions. If there are bumps or sores, describe their appearance.

Is there any discharge? Describe its color, consistency, and odor, if any.

Does your dog scratch or lick a particular part of his body? Does he appear to be itching or in pain? Note the exact location, and any circumstances that seem to make him more or less comfortable.

Generalities:

Note any abnormalities that affect the entire body, such as fever, restless sleep, or lack of energy.

Modalities:

Note any circumstances or events that make your dog feel better or worse. Under what conditions is your dog particularly happy or irritable, or are his symptoms notably better or worse? Is there a time of day, season of the year, or type of weather that seems to make a difference? Is he better before or after meals, or when he first wakes up in the morning? Is he better when you comfort him, or does he prefer to be left alone?

Does your dog seek heat or cooling? Does he like to lie in a sunny spot, or on the cool bare floor?

When he sleeps, does he lie on his left or right side most of the time?

MATCHING THE ILLNESS AND THE REMEDY

Dog's Name _____   Date _____

Symptom/trait	Remedy 1	Remedy 2	Remedy 3	Remedy 4	Remedy 5
Age (puppy/senior)					
Body type					
Coat color					
Personality					
Medical history					
Vaccines?					
Chemicals ingested?					
Mind/emotions/behavior					
Head/eyes/ears/mouth					
Throat					
Stomach/abdomen					

Symptom/trait	Remedy 1	Remedy 2	Remedy 3	Remedy 4	Remedy 5
Stool					
Urinary system					
Reproductive system					
Respiration/circulation					
Back/limbs/paws					
Neurologic system					
Skin/coat					
Generalities					
Modalities					

The Remedies

Absinthium (Wormwood)

May be useful in treatment of epilepsy, distemper, early stages of tetanus. Symptoms resemble those associated with epileptic seizures, although symptoms may also be due to other causes.

Mind: Wants to be left alone.

Mouth: Jaws are rigid. Bites tongue; tongue protrudes.

Stomach/Abdomen: Vomiting, retching; loss of appetite. Abdomen is enlarged.

Urinary Tract: Frequent urination. Dark yellow urine, with strong odor.

Respiration/Circulation: Irregular heartbeat.

Back/Limbs/Paws: Paralysis.

Generalities: Seizures. Tremors, alone or prior to an attack; movements are jerky; rapid, irregular, involuntary spasmodic movements. Loss of consciousness; sleeplessness.

Aconite (*Aconitum napellus*, Monkshood)

Aconite is noted as a remedy for fear or anxiety, for symptoms of shock, and for symptoms that arise suddenly or that are brought on by trauma or a sudden chill.

Mind: Fear, anxiety, restlessness. Does not want to be touched.

Eyes: Red, swollen eyelids; bothered by bright light; clear, watery discharge.

Ears: Acute sensitivity to noise; ear canal is red, swollen and painful when touched.

Mouth: Gums red and swollen. Tongue appears to be coated with a white film. Moves lower jaw as if chewing.

Nose: Sneezing with a watery discharge.

Stomach/Abdomen: Very thirsty; vomiting; vomitus contains mucus or is green or bloody. Abdomen is tender when touched.

Stool: Straining at stool; frequent bowel movements; small stool or watery diarrhea that is green in color, like chopped herbs. Pain or itching in anus.

Urinary Tract: Excessive urination; small amounts of urine; painful urination; blood in urine. Pain in back over kidneys.

Respiration/Circulation: Unproductive cough; breathing is noisy and difficult; gets winded easily; cough is worse at night and after midnight. Bleeding from the lungs. Pneumonia. Hard, pounding pulse.

Back/Limbs/Paws: Pain in back, particularly at nape of neck and between shoulders. Coldness and loss of feeling in paws; fore paws are hot while hind paws are cold; lameness or unsteadiness in hind limbs, worse after rest; joints crack.

Generalities: Sudden loss of strength; fever. Restless sleep, fearful dreams. Chilly, trembling fever.

Modalities: Worse from exposure to dry, cold weather or winds; very hot weather; emotional distress; at night; after midnight. Better when out of doors.

NOTE: Aconite is best used in the early stages of any illness, before any physical or structural change in the tissues has occurred.

Alumina (Aluminum oxide)

The Alumina patient is often an older dog, one that is prematurely old, or a weak young dog. Feebleness, loss of weight and dryness of skin and mucous membranes are characteristic.

Mind: Depressed, easily confused.

Eyes: Chronic conjunctivitis. Each eye seems to gaze in a different direction.

Nose: Tip of nose is dry and cracked. Discharge that is watery or thick and yellow.

Mouth: Foul odor, unhealthy gums, teeth covered with plaque. Dryness, minimal saliva.

Stomach/Abdomen: Unusual cravings, such as dirt.

Stool: Dry, hard. Bleeding from the rectum; anus itches or burns. Much difficulty passing stool.

Urinary Tract: Frequent urination. Strains to begin urinating.

Respiration/Circulation: Cough, especially in the morning; wheezing.

Back/Limbs/Paws: Weakness, paralysis; spinal degeneration. Staggers when walking. Lameness in forelimbs. Brittle nails.

Skin: Dry, flaky; itching.

Generalities: Restless sleep. Low body weight, weakness.

Modalities: Worse after waking in the morning; afternoon. Better out of doors; from bathing; in the evening. Symptoms cycle better and worse, sometimes on alternate days.

Angustura vera (Bark of *Galipea cusparia*)
A remedy for musculoskeletal problems, including paralysis and stiffness.

Head: Facial muscles appear tense.

Mouth: Dry; thick mucus.

Stomach/Abdomen: Pain in abdomen. Belching; excessive thirst. Diarrhea; diarrhea associated with weakness and loss of weight; stool is very soft. Straining at stool. Burning in the anal region.

Back/Limbs/Paws: Pain anywhere along the spine, from the neck to the lower back; painful to the touch. Itching or twitching along the back. Joints and muscles of the legs are stiff and tense. Lameness; weakness; joints crack when moving. Pain in the extremities, particularly the knees. Paralysis; paralysis in a single limb.

Generalities: Tetanus. Hypersensitivity.

Antimonium tart (Tartrate of antimony and potash)
Most often associated with respiratory problems.

Mind: Depressed. Does not want to be left alone. Whines when touched.

Mouth: Mucus. White coating on tongue, with redness at edges; dry, red tongue. Lower jaw quivers.

Stomach/Abdomen: Vomiting, retching, especially after eating. Drinks small amounts of water frequently. Passes gas.

Stool: Diarrhea; mucus.

Urinary Tract: Painful urination. Mucus.

Respiration/Circulation: Rattling mucus in lungs, but little expelled. Breathing is difficult; rapid, short. Pneumonia. Rapid, weak pulse.

Back/Limbs/Paws: Pain in lower lumbo-sacral region. Muscles twitch; limbs tremble.

Skin: Eruptions with pus. Warts.

Generalities: Chilly, shivering; very hot; fever comes and goes. Very sleepy.

Modalities: Worse in evening; lying down; from warmth, damp, cold weather.

Apis (*Apis mellifica*, Honey bee)
Apis is commonly used where symptoms resemble those of a bee sting: swelling with redness and pain.

Mind: Listless, unconscious; fearful, restless, whining.

Eyes: Interior of eyelids red and swollen; eyelids everted; clear, watery discharge; sensitive to light; squints and rubs eyes as if they are painful; cornea inflamed; styes.

Ears: External ear canal red, swollen, painful.

Face: Swollen.

Mouth: Gums, tongue and lips swollen and red; blisters on tongue. Cancer of the tongue.

Throat: Red and swollen interior; lesions; edema in exterior.

Stomach/Abdomen: Complete lack of thirst; vomiting; "afternoon chill, with thirst." Abdomen extremely tender when touched; swollen. Peritonitis.

Stool: Passes stool involuntarily; bloody stool or watery, yellow diarrhea; constipated.

Urinary Tract: Urination painful; frequent, involuntary; passes small amounts of brightly colored urine; casts in urine.

Reproductive System: Inflammation or other abnormalities of the ovaries.

Respiration/Circulation: Difficult, labored breathing; dry cough. Swelling in the larynx.

Back/Limbs/Paws: Swollen legs, feet and joints; joints painful to the touch; stiffness; hives on limbs; numbness in toes.

Skin: Swelling and pain after bites or stings; painful cysts.

Generalities: Sensitive to touch; symptoms affect the skin and the outer surfaces of internal organs. Acute swelling of the entire body. Body feels hot to the touch. Excessively sleepy; fearful, worrisome dreams. Chilly fever.

Modalities: Worse from external heat or warmth; touch; after sleep; in the afternoon; right side of the body. Better out of doors; from a cool compress or a cool bath.

NOTE: Use lower potencies where swelling is prominent.

Argentum (*Argentum metallicum*, Silver)
Effective in treating symptoms associated with joints and associated bones, cartilages, ligaments; stiffness in older dogs.

Mind: Depressed.

Head: Painful to the touch.

Eyes: Eyelids are thick and red.

Respiration/Circulation: Cough; difficult breathing. Altered sound of the bark or whine.

Back/Limbs/Paws: Severe pain in the back. Pain in joints, particularly the elbow and knee; pains may come on gradually. Weakness and trembling in legs, particularly when going down stairs. Swelling in the lower limbs.

Urinary Tract: Increased production of urine; frequent urination; urine is cloudy, with a sweet odor.

Generalities: Loss of weight.

Modalities: Worse when touched; around noon. Better when out of doors.

Arnica (*Arnica montana*, Leopard's bane)
Arnica is the primary remedy for any injury, bump, bruise, sprain, strain or overexertion, to help promote healing and prevent or reduce pain and swelling. It is a valuable aid to healing after surgery.

Mind: Does not want to be touched; fearful when approached. Depressed.

Eyes: Trauma to the eyes. Retinal hemorrhage.

Mouth: Offensive odor; pain and tissue trauma after extraction of a tooth.

Stomach/Abdomen: Thirsty; ravenous hunger; little interest in milk or meat. Vomiting; vomitus is bloody, with terrible odor. Abdomen distended; passes gas with offensive odor.

Stool: Diarrhea with straining or involuntary. Stool is bloody, with terrible odor. Passes stool during sleep.

Urinary Tract: Urination is difficult and painful.

Respiration/Circulation: Difficult breathing; coughs up bloody mucus. Pulse is irregular and weak. Fluid around the heart. Enlarged heart.

Back/Limbs/Paws: Swelling, lameness, painful to the touch.

Skin: Hematoma. Clusters of small cysts.

Generalities: Use after any physical trauma, strain or injury, including surgery. Tissue degeneration. Restless or excessively sleepy; fearful dreams. Fever with hot head and cool body, or hot body and cool feet.

Modalities: Worse with touch, activity, after rest, cold environment. Better while at rest.

Arsenicum (*Arsenicum album*, Arsenic trioxide)

Arsenicum is a valuable remedy for a variety of illnesses, often indicated by a marked weakness or lack of energy, with degeneration of tissues or body systems, and symptoms that get worse at night. It is frequently helpful in treating toxic conditions caused by ingestion or injection of a poison or drug, or by an internal disease process. It is also noted for use in high potency (10M) to help ease the passage into death.

Mind: Fearful, anxious, restless, irritable. Does not want to be left alone. Aggressive.

Eyes: Clear, watery discharge. Margin of eyelids irritated. Painful swelling around eyes. Squints and rubs eyes as though in pain. Severe aversion to light.

Ears: Ear canal is raw and painful. Discharge has offensive odor.

Nose: Watery discharge; sneezes; worse when out of doors. Rubs nose as if in pain.

Mouth: Gums are unhealthy, bleed easily; pain when eating or chewing; bloody saliva. Gums or tongue appear blue. Ulcers in the mouth. Benign growths or tumors on the lips.

Throat: Swollen, constricted. Difficulty swallowing.

Stomach/Abdomen: Extremely thirsty; drinks large amounts of water, but in small portions. Aversion to food. Vomiting, particularly after eating or drinking. Belches. Abdomen is enlarged and painful to the touch. Enlarged liver or spleen. Abdomen is distended.

Stool: Straining at stool. Stool is small, hard and dark, or bloody diarrhea, with terrible odor. Rectum protrudes; anal tissue is raw. Licks or "scoots," as if in pain in anal area.

Urinary Tract: Incontinent; passes small amounts of urine; painful urination. Urine contains protein, epithelial cells, blood clots, blood or pus.

Reproductive System: Vaginal discharge that burns, with terrible odor.

Respiration/Circulation: Difficult breathing; breathing made difficult by inflammation and mucus in the respiratory tract; cough is dry, or with a small amount of frothy sputum. Cough is worse after drinking water.

Back/Limbs/Paws: Weakness and pain in back and limbs; trembling or twitching of limbs; walks as if limbs are heavy; swollen feet; paralysis and atrophy in hind legs.

Skin: Skin is dry, scaly, itchy; edema, hives, eruptions, hot spots, ulcers; infected wounds. Benign skin growths. Patchy hair loss. Gangrene.

Generalities: Great lack of energy and strength; exhausted after minimal activity; restless; fearful, anxious dreams. Slow but steady loss of weight. Anemia. Diabetes. General decline in vitality and functionality. Illness as a result of ingestion of poison or decayed material, from stings or bites, from severe infections. Supports the body while it is dealing with malignancy. Discharges are green, have a terrible odor. Generalized retention of fluids. High fever; temperature rises and falls; fever rises around 3 a.m.; body feels cold to the touch.

Modalities: Worse at night, from cold; during rain or damp weather; on the right side. Better from warmth.

Artemisia vulgaris (Mugwort)

Known for its use as a treatment for seizures, particularly those that occur without warning or after emotional stress; also for cluster seizures.

Head: Drawn toward the back during seizure.

Belladonna (Deadly nightshade)

Belladonna symptoms generally come on very quickly and are very intense. They often include severe pain, heat, redness and agitation.

Mind: Agitated, excited; symptoms cause much distress. Wants to escape. May become aggressive. Hypersensitivity. Loss of consciousness.

Face: Muscles twitch.

Eyes: Pupils are dilated; conjunctiva are red; eyelids swollen. Bothered by bright light.

Ears: Pain in interior; pain may be so severe that the dog presses head into bedding or wall; inflammation. Ears feel hot. Hypersensitive to noises.

Mouth: Dry. Abscessed teeth or gums. Tongue is red; swollen. Gums are bright red; hot.

Stomach/Abdomen: Loss of appetite. Vomiting, retching. Excessive thirst; complete lack of thirst. Abdomen swollen and hot; painful to the touch.

Stool: Diarrhea; thin, green; lumpy. Discomfort in rectum.

Urinary Tract: Strains to urinate. Frequent urination. Urine is dark and cloudy; bloody; scanty; contains high level of phosphates. Incontinence.

Reproductive System: Mammary tumors. Mammary glands swollen; hot; painful to the touch. Mastitis.

Respiration/Circulation: Dry cough; cough with bloody sputum; breathing is difficult, uneven. Pulse is hard, pounding; rapid but weak.

Back/Limbs/Paws: Stiffness or pain in the neck; glands in the neck are swollen. Pain in back, hips, thighs. Joints are swollen. Lameness. Legs and feet are cold.

Skin: Dry, hot; hypersensitive. Abscesses; infected wounds.

Generalities: High fever. Heat stroke. Distemper. Restless sleep; cries out in sleep. Unsteadiness with a tendency to fall sideways or backward.

Modalities: Worse at night; after noon; from being touched; when lying down.

Bellis (*Bellis perennis*, Daisy)

An excellent remedy for injury to deep tissues due to surgery, or for sprains and bruises that are very painful. Follows Arnica favorably after a trauma.

Reproductive System: Mammary glands or uterus are engorged and painful.

Stomach/Abdomen: Pain after surgery. Injury to the pelvic organs. Abdomen is enlarged; rumbling in intestines. Diarrhea with yellow, foul-smelling stool; worse at night.

Skin: Abscesses; painful bruises.

Back/Limbs/Paws: Painful sprains; pain in joints and muscles. Itching over the hamstrings.

Generalities: Injury to tissues due to surgery. Injuries to the nerves. Swelling.

Modalities: Worse on the left side; before a storm; in cold wind; cold bath.

Berberis (*Berberis vulgaris*, Barberry)

Conditions that affect the liver, urinary tract, with pain in the lumbar area.

Mind: Depressed, listless. Reluctant to move, as from pain.

Mouth: Dry; saliva is foamy. Blisters on the tongue.

Stomach/Abdomen: Disturbances in liver function;

promotes the flow of bile. Enteritis. Diarrhea. Pelvic organs engorged.

Stool: The color of clay.

Urinary Tract: Kidney disease. Blood or mucus in the urine. Painful or frequent urination; increased flow of urine may alternate with decreased flow. Cystitis due to diminished output of urine.

Reproductive System: Vaginal irritation; discharge.

Back/Limbs/Paws: Pain in the lumbar region, particularly after surgery; muscles in back are tense. Lameness in the forelimbs, shoulders, front and hind paws. Legs become tired easily; weakness. Arthritis associated with urinary disturbances.

Skin: Itching and irritation, made worse by scratching, better with cold compress. Small pustular eruptions.

Generalities: Symptoms change or alternate rapidly, e.g., excessive thirst and lack of thirst, excessive hunger and no desire for food. Jaundice. Fleshy body type.

Modalities: Worse from activity.

Bryonia (Wild hops)
Noted as a remedy for painful musculoskeletal conditions that get worse with movement. Also useful for other painful conditions that get worse with movement.

Mind: Very irritable.

Eyes: Glaucoma.

Mouth: Dry.

Stomach/Abdomen: Excessive thirst; drinks a large amount of water at one time. Vomits bile and water after eating. Abdomen is painful to the touch, particularly over liver; swollen.

Stool: Large, dry, hard, dark; brown, thick and bloody. Constipation.

Urinary Tract: Urine is red or brown; scanty flow.

Reproductive System: Mastitis; mammary glands hot; tender to the touch; abscessed.

Respiration/Circulation: Dry cough; productive cough with sputum the color of rust, the consistency of jelly. Takes deep breaths; breathing is difficult, rapid. Pulse is strong and rapid. Pericarditis.

Back/Limbs/Paws: Stiffness in the nape of the neck; lower back; knees. Feet or joints are hot and swollen. Pain in limbs gets better from pressure.

Skin: Hair is greasy. Itching. Hair loss; dermatitis.

Generalities: Weakness. Complaints develop slowly. Body feels cold to the touch.

Modalities: Worse from motion; hot weather; entering a warm room; after eating. Better from rest; lying on painful side; cool, open air.

NOTE: Do not give before, after, or with Calc. carb.

Calc. carb. (*Calcarea carbonica*, Calcium carbonate)
One of the most valued constitutional remedies, where poor nutrition and skeletal conditions are present, and the dog is overweight and sluggish. Symptoms may be due to poor diet or an inability to assimilate nutrients, particularly calcium.

Mind: Fearful, particularly of unfamiliar things or change in the routine. Prefers inactivity to exertion.

Eyes: Sensitive to bright light. Watery discharge in open air. Corneal ulcers. Pupils remain dilated. Cataract. Eyelids swollen, itching.

Ears: Discharge of pus and mucus.

Mouth: Bleeding gums. Delayed teething in puppies. Breath is offensive.

Stomach/Abdomen: Thirst. Excessive appetite. Unusual cravings; eats dirt, charcoal. Dislikes milk; difficulty digesting milk. Abdomen painful to pressure; swollen; hard.

Stool: Large, hard. Sour odor. Diarrhea; looks like undigested food.

Urinary Tract: Large amounts of urine; dark in color; bloody; white sediment. Incontinent while sleeping.

Reproductive System: Milky vaginal discharge.

Respiration/Circulation: Foul-smelling, yellow discharge from nose. Difficulty breathing.

Back/Limbs/Paws: Difficulty rising due to pain in back; pain between shoulders. Fractures are slow to heal. Weakness in lower back, limbs. Bone tumors. Calcium deposits around joints. Muscular weakness and spasms. Feet are cold.

Skin: Unhealthy; minor wounds are slow to heal. Abscesses. Flat warts.

Generalities: Slow to heal. Poor development of bones and other structures. Sour body odor. Wakes frequently during the night.

Modalities: Worse from activity; cold weather, water or food; bathing; during a full moon. Better in dry weather; lying on painful side.

NOTE: Do not give before, after or with Bryonia or Sulphur. Should not be given in very frequent doses to older dogs.

Calc. fluor. (*Calcarea fluorica*, Calcium fluoride)
In its natural form, this substance is found in the bones, tooth enamel and skin. The potentized form is useful for conditions affecting those tissues, particularly where an excess or deficiency of calcium is a factor.

Mind: Extremely depressed.

Eyes: Cataract. Conjunctivitis. Blocked tear ducts.

Ears: Chronic infections. Hardening of the tissues in the middle or inner ear; calcium deposits.

Mouth: Hard, painful swelling on the jaw bone or cheek. Abscess on the gums. Teeth are weak and brit-

tle, decay easily; loose; dog is reluctant to eat due to painful teeth.

Stomach/Abdomen: Vomiting; undigested food. Hiccups. Passes gas. Appetite is reduced. Itching in the anal area. Painful crack in the anus.

Stool: Diarrhea.

Respiration/Circulation: Large amounts of thick, lumpy, foul-smelling, green or yellow nasal discharge. Tumors of the blood vessels; enlarged veins.

Reproductive System: Hardened mammary glands.

Back/Limbs/Paws: Bones are weak and brittle. Bone tumors. Muscular pain in the lower back. Inflammation of the joint capsule in the knee.

Skin: Unhealthy coat, pale skin. Hard growths. Ulcers or infections that have hard edges; ulcers that secrete yellow pus.

Generalities: Underweight, undernourished, generally unhealthy. Asymmetrical body shape due to poor bone structure. Adhesions after surgery. Hardening of tissues. Slow to heal. Active dreams.

Calc. phos. (*Calcarea phosphorica*, Calcium phosphate)
Another important constitutional remedy, similar to Calc carb. However, dogs who respond well to Calc phos tend to be thin, weak and malnourished, as opposed to the overweight, sluggish and malnourished Calc carb dog.

Mind: Fretful; difficult to satisfy. Ailments that arise after grief or stress.

Eyes: Cloudiness on the cornea; cataract.

Mouth: Delayed teething in puppies. Teeth decay rapidly.

Stomach/Abdomen: Excessive hunger and thirst. Poor digestion; vomiting; stomach pains after eating. Passes gas, with foul odor.

Stool: Hard, followed by bleeding. Diarrhea; green, "sputtering"; undigested food.

Reproductive System: Vaginal discharge looks like raw egg white.

Back/Limbs/Paws: Stiffness, pain, coldness in limbs. Tires easily when going uphill or climbing stairs. Diseases of the bone; problems related to bone growth in young dogs; fractures that do not heal.

Generalities: Underweight, undernourished. Chronic wasting disease. Anemia that follows acute illness. Symptoms that appear in puppyhood.

Modalities: Worse, damp, cold weather; any change in the weather. Better in warm, dry weather.

Calc. sulph. (*Calcarea sulphurica*, Calcium sulphate; Plaster of Paris; Gypsum)
Characterized by a thick, yellow discharge from some part of the body.

Eyes: Infection with thick, yellow discharge. Cornea is cloudy.

Ears: Discharge of pus, may be mixed with blood.

Stool: Diarrhea mixed with pus, blood, mucus. Abscesses of the anal glands.

Respiration/Circulation: Thick, lumpy, yellow discharge from the nose or from cough, often mixed with blood.

Skin: Wounds become infected, discharge pus, are slow to heal. Skin eruptions that discharge pus.

Generalities: Persistent infections. Cystic tumors. Swollen glands. Infections, after pus has begun to discharge. Abscesses.

Calendula (*Calendula officinalis*, Marigold)
Calendula is well known as an aid to healing when applied topically, in the form of a lotion, cream, ointment or gel. In the potentized form it works internally to speed the healing of wounds.

Eyes: Infected injuries to the eyes. Aids healing after surgery.

Mouth: Aids healing of gums after tooth extraction.

Skin: Speeds healing of wounds; reduces pain; minimizes scarring. In infected wounds, help clear infection and promote healthy drainage.

Back/Limbs/Paws: Torn muscles.

NOTE: In very deep wounds, Calendula alone may cause the skin to close before the deeper tissue has healed. In these cases, use in alternate doses with Hypericum; in puncture wounds use Hypericum in alternate doses with Ledum.

Candida albicans (Yeast)
A potentized form of the organism that causes a common yeast infection. It may be helpful in treating those infections.

Cantharis (Spanish fly)
Intense irritation and inflammation of the urinary tract, mucous membranes and skin.

Mind: Anxious, restless; whining; agitated due to irritation of sensitive tissues. Heightened interest in sexual behavior. May become aggressive.

Mouth: Blisters on tongue and mucous membranes. Throat inflamed.

Stomach/Abdomen: Loss of appetite. Excessive thirst. Vomiting; retching; vomitus is streaked with blood. Abdomen is swollen and tender. Enteritis; peritonitis.

Stool: Diarrhea; mucus or blood in stool; looks like scrapings of intestines. Straining at stool; burning.

Urinary Tract: Intense urge to pass urine; constant urging; straining; burning; passes only a few drops at a time. Passing urine is very painful. Urine is bloody; the consistency of jelly. Inflammation of the bladder or kidneys. Cystitis.

Reproductive System: Swelling and irritation of the vulva; blisters.

Respiration/Circulation: Pulse is weak and irregular. Pericarditis. Bleeding from the nose.

Back/Limbs/Paws: Pain in lumbar region or in limbs. Paws are cold.

Skin: Eruptions that itch or burn; heat, redness. Eruptions on or near the genitals. Painful, inflamed burns that are better with cold compress. Painful insect bites.

Generalities: Symptoms arise suddenly.

Modalities: Worse from touch; passing urine. Better from rubbing.

Carbo veg. (*Carbo vegetabilis*, Vegetable charcoal)
The dog who benefits from Carbo veg is usually very lethargic and often overweight, with poor circulation, cold body temperature and a tendency to chronic ailments.

Mind: Inactive; very low vital energy; becomes tired easily. Desires fresh air.

Mouth: Small white or grey blisters on the tongue. Gums are blue; recede and bleed easily. Mouth and tongue feel cold.

Stomach/Abdomen: Abdomen is bloated, tense; painful; causes discomfort when lying down. Belches; passes gas, offensive odor. Pain after eating. Food passes through digestive tract very slowly; difficulty digesting even bland food. Thirsty.

Stool: Painful diarrhea, particularly in older dogs. Discharge of jelly-like substance or blood from the rectum; burning. Pain after stool. Stool smells like rotting flesh; passes involuntarily.

Respiration/Circulation: Bleeding from the nose; nasal discharge. Cough. Breath is cold. Pneumonia. Pulse is weak and thready.

Back/Limbs/Paws: Legs appear heavy, stiff, lacking in muscular strength.

Skin: Feels cold to the touch. Loss of hair. Ulcers, with foul-smelling, watery discharge; abscesses.

Generalities: Shock due to trauma; collapse. Body feels cold while head is warm. Succumbs easily to infection. Lingering effects of a previous illness.

Modalities: Worse, evening; out of doors; warm, damp weather. Better in drafts of air or breeze.

Carduus mar. (*Carduus marianus*, St. Mary's thistle)
A valuable remedy for liver ailments. Can be used to cleanse the liver and stimulate function when herbs are not tolerated well.

Mind: Depressed.

Stomach/Abdomen: Reduced appetite. Vomiting; retching; vomits green liquid. Liver region is painful to pressure. Liver is enlarged.

Stool: Constipated; constipation alternates with diarrhea. Stools are hard, difficult to pass; bright yellow. Burning in the rectum.

Urinary Tract: Urine is cloudy; a deep gold color.

Back/Limbs/Paws: Hip joint is painful; has difficulty getting up.

Generalities: Edema. Jaundice.

Causticum (Potassium hydrate)
Dog is weak and run down, from illness or old age, often with progressive loss of muscular function.

Mind: Does not want to be left alone.

Face: Paralysis of the facial muscles. Has difficulty opening mouth.

Eyes: Eyelids are inflamed; corneal ulcers. Cataract.

Ears: Chronic ear infection. Excessive ear wax.

Mouth: Tongue is paralyzed. Bleeding gums.

Stool: Soft, small or hard and covered with mucus; shiny. Strains at stool. Burning in the rectum. Paralysis of the rectum.

Urinary Tract: Urine passes very slowly or not at all. Incontinence while asleep, while coughing, or from excitement. Chronic cystitis.

Back/Limbs/Paws: Pain in joints and bones. Weakness; progressive paralysis; single-limb paralysis. Lameness; sciatica with lameness in the left hind limb. Limbs appear heavy. Contracted tendons.

Skin: Burns. Flat warts; warts that bleed easily. Old scars open up.

Generalities: Very sleepy; restless at night. Entire body seems stiff. Localized paralysis of particular body parts, e.g., vocal cords, tongue, bladder, limbs. Loss of weight, due to disease or stress. Symptoms that are rooted in emotions. Lead poisoning.

Modalities: Worse from dry, cold wind. Better in damp weather; from warmth.

NOTE: Do not give before or after Phosphorus. Causticum is a powerful constitutional remedy; it should be used in low potency for acute symptoms only, or under the guidance of an experienced homeopath.

Chelidonium (*Chelidonium majus*, Celandine)
This remedy is primarily used as a treatment for liver ailments.

Mind: Lethargic. Very sleepy.

Eyes: Whites of the eyes appear yellow. Profuse watery discharge. Conjunctivitis.

Mouth: Foul odor. Gums appear yellow.

Stomach/Abdomen: Vomiting. Abdomen is enlarged. Liver is enlarged; obstructed.

Urinary Tract: Large amounts of urine. Urine is yellow and foamy, or dark and cloudy. Hepatitis.

Stool: Hard, round balls; bright yellow; the color of clay. Constipation; constipation alternating with diarrhea. Irritation in the anal area.

Respiration/Circulation: Difficulty breathing; short, rapid breaths. Cough.

Back/Limbs/Paws: Neck is stiff; head is drawn to the left. Lameness. Limbs are painful to the touch. Hind limbs are paralyzed, muscles are rigid.

Skin: Dry; itching. Yellowish color, most visible in the ears.

Generalities: Jaundice. Body feels cold to the touch.

Modalities: Worse from a change in the weather; movement; early in the morning; touch.

Cicuta (*Cicuta virosa*, Water hemlock)
Cicuta has a particular affinity for the nervous system, and may be considered in the event of trauma to the brain or spinal cord. Symptoms are often extreme in nature, as in violent convulsions or spasms.

Head: Brain injury; concussion.

Eyes: Persistent stare. Pupils dilated. Each eye appears to look in a different direction.

Ears: Bleeding from the ears.

Mouth: Foaming.

Stomach/Abdomen: Abdomen is enlarged.

Stool: Diarrhea. Itching in the rectum.

Back/Limbs/Paws: Head, neck and spine are bent backwards in spasm or convulsion; head is twisted to one side. Odd distortions in body position; limbs are rigid, joints cannot be moved. Tends to fall to one side when walking or standing. Injuries to the spinal cord.

Neurologic System: Brain damage or malfunction. Injuries to the spinal cord.

Generalities: Spasms, convulsions; twitching. Tetanus. Epilepsy. Meningitis.

Modalities: Worse from touch; sudden movement.

Colchicum (Meadow saffron)

A remedy for very painful symptoms that involve the joints.

Mind: Exhausted; weak. Restless; irritable; sensitive. Cries out when touched, as from pain.

Eyes: Pupils are unequal in size. Watery discharge, particularly when out of doors.

Stomach/Abdomen: Loss of appetite. May salivate or lick lips as though nauseated, at the sight or smell of food, or simply when called to dinner. Vomits mucus, green fluid or undigested food. Very thirsty. Abdomen is enlarged; bloat.

Stool: Scanty; painful or very difficult to pass. Stool contains mucus; large amounts of white shredded material.

Urinary Tract: Urine is dark in color; bloody. Passes small amounts or none at all.

Respiration/Circulation: Heart palpitations.

Back/Limbs/Paws: Symptoms that affect the muscles and bone surfaces near the joints, and the joints themselves. Severe pain. Joints feel hot.

Generalities: Pains are very intense; has trouble resting comfortably. Great weakness; collapse.

Modalities: Worse with motion; evening; nighttime; warm weather. Better from rest.

Conium (*Conium maculatum*, Poison hemlock)

In its undiluted state, Poison Hemlock causes paralysis that begins in the lower or hind extremities, and progresses upward or forward through the body, culminating in death due to paralysis of the lungs and heart. Homeopathic Conium is used to treat symptoms that resemble that pattern.

Mind: Depressed; lack of interest in surroundings; confused. Does not want to be left alone.

Eyes: Bothered by light. Watery discharge. Corneal ulcers. Muscles of the eyes become paralyzed.

Stomach/Abdomen: Nausea; better immediately after eating, worse a few hours later. Abdomen enlarged, tense.

Stool: Hard, difficult to pass.

Urinary Tract: Has difficulty passing urine; inability to control the muscles of the bladder; flow starts and stops..

Reproductive System: Hard mammary tumors.

Respiration/Circulation: Dry cough, worse at night.

Back/Limbs/Paws: Symptoms first appear in the hind limbs. Weakness; trembling; numbness; paralysis in the hind limbs; progressive. Limbs appear very heavy. Difficulty walking; stumbling; stiffness; sudden loss of strength. Paralysis due to tumors; Coonhound paralysis.

Generalities: Progressive weakness due to debility in older dogs or to illness. Paralysis that progresses from the hind limbs forward. Hard swellings of the lymph nodes and glands.

Modalities: Worse from exertion; cold; lying down. Better from movement.

Crataegus (Hawthorn berries)

Crataegus has specific action on the muscle of the heart, and may help to regulate the heartbeat.

Mind: Irritable; nervous; fearful.

Stomach/Abdomen: Bleeding from the lower bowels.

Respiration/Circulation: Irregular heartbeat; rapid; feeble. Heart murmur. Irregular or difficult breathing. Chronic heart disease.

Back/Limbs/Paws: Legs and feet are cold.

Generalities: Edema. Chilliness. Extremely weak. Older dogs with heart ailments.

Modalities: Better with rest.

Crotalus (*Crotalus horridus*, Rattlesnake)

This remedy is made from the venom of the rattlesnake. It is useful in treating snakebite or symptoms that resemble snakebite.

Mind: Depressed; sad. Agitated.

Eyes: Hemorrhages. Sensitive to light. Pain. Whites of eyes appear yellow.

Mouth: Tongue is bright red; swollen. Excessive salivation.

Throat: Dry; swollen; dark red.

Stomach/Abdomen: Severe vomiting; unable to keep food or water down. Vomitus contains blood; green liquid; dark green material; mucus; is black, like coffee grounds. Stomach ulcer. Cancer of the stomach. Abdomen is enlarged, tender to the touch.

Stool: Black; the consistency of coffee grounds; foul odor. Bleeding from the intestines; dark blood that does not clot; seeps out of rectum.

Urinary Tract: Urine is dark in color, contains blood; passes small amounts. Kidney is inflamed.

Respiration/Circulation: Bleeding from the nose; blood does not clot. Cough; sputum contains blood. Pulse is weak; palpitations.

Back/Limbs/Paws: Paralysis on the right side of the body.

Skin: Snakebite. Very painful swelling, with discoloration of the tissue. Blood oozes into the skin. Skin is very sensitive. Insect bites and stings. Blisters; abscesses; eruptions are surrounded by discolored skin and edema. Vaccine reactions. Gangrene.

Generalities: Hemorrhages; blood is dark in color; oozes from the tissues. Abscesses. Jaundice. Infections. Symptoms return annually.

Modalities: Worse after sleeping; right side of the body; evening and morning; damp and wet weather; weather becomes warm.

NOTE: Low potencies, such as 3C or 6C are often effective. Ask your pharmacy about remedies made from other species of rattlesnake that may be present in your area, such as Crotalus atrox, or Crotalus cascavella.

Digitalis (Foxglove)

Stimulates heart function.

Mind: Depressed; lethargic. Fearful; anxious.

Eyes: Whites of the eyes appear yellow. Crusty deposits around eyelids after sleep.

Mouth: Gums appear blue. Excessive salivation.

Stomach/Abdomen: Vomiting; nausea; worse from motion. Stomach is tender to the touch. Liver is enlarged and sore.

Stool: White, like chalk or paste. Diarrhea.

Urinary Tract: Constant desire to urinate. Urine passes a drop at a time, or not at all; burns; sediment the color of rust. Inflammation of the urethra.

Reproductive System: Prostate is enlarged.

Respiration/Circulation: Breathing is irregular; difficult; takes deep breaths. Cough; sputum contains blood.

Pulse is weak, irregular, very slow; palpitation. Weak pulse becomes rapid with movement. Mitral valve disease. Pericarditis. Enlarged heart. Heart failure after a fever.

Back/Limbs/Paws: Paws feel cold. Joints are painful, swollen. Muscles are weak.

Generalities: Internal and external edema. Very weak; easily exhausted. Body feels cold to the touch. Jaundice, particularly when associated with heart disease. Heart ailments in older dogs.

Modalities: Worse after eating.

NOTE: Use in low potencies to help regulate heartbeat.

Equisetum (Scouring rush)
This remedy has a particular affinity for the bladder.

Urinary Tract: Frequent desire to urinate. Painful urination; flows one drop at a time or not at all; contains mucus or high levels of protein. Incontinence, particularly in very young or old dogs. Urination accompanied by the passage of stool. Cystitis.

Modalities: Worse from movement, touch or pressure. Better from lying down.

Euphrasia (Eyebright)
Like the herbal form of this medicine, the potentized form is an excellent remedy for injuries or illness that affect the eyes.

Eyes: Conjunctivitis; abundant, thick discharge; mucus sticks to cornea. Profuse, continuous watery, burning discharge. Eyelids swollen; upper eyelid droops. Corneal ulcers; cloudiness.

Stool: Constipation. Diarrhea, with blood and mucus in stool.

Urinary Tract: Dribbling incontinence in males.

Respiration/Circulation: Discharge of mucus from the nose. Cough, with much sputum.

Modalities: Worse in the evening; from bright light; in a warm room; respiratory symptoms worse in the morning. Better when in the dark; out of doors.

Generalities: Chilly; body feels cold to the touch.

Gelsemium (Yellow jasmine)
Gelsemium patients typically are very sluggish, with a heaviness to their movements. May help curb aggression in some dogs.

Mind: Depressed; listless; not interested in surroundings. Wants to be left alone. Fearful. Uneasy in unfamiliar situations. Aggressive.

Head: Wants to lie with head elevated.

Eyes: Upper eyelids droop. One pupil is contracted while the other is dilated.

Mouth: Terrible breath. Tongue trembles, or is paralyzed.

Stomach/Abdomen: Drinks very little. Hiccups.

Stool: The color of green tea or cream. Diarrhea, particularly after excitement or fear. Incontinence; paralysis of the sphincter.

Urinary Tract: Passes large amounts of urine; clear, like water. Difficult or painful urination.

Respiration/Circulation: Sneezing. Watery nasal discharge. Very slow respiration. Dry cough. Pulse is slow and weak; or full and strong. Poor circulation.

Back/Limbs/Paws: Muscular weakness; trembling; paralysis. Muscles are completely relaxed. Pain deep in muscles of back, hips and legs. Poor muscular coordination.

Skin: Brings out emerging eruptions.

Generalities: Ailments that follow emotional excitement, anxiety, or fear. Becomes exhausted very easily;

body is limp. Paralysis of various muscle groups, e.g., those around the eyes, throat, sphincter. Never falls deeply asleep; yawns. Chilly. Continuing lethargy after an acute illness.

Modalities: Worse from hot sun; before a storm; cold, damp weather; excitement; at 10 a.m. Better after passing large amounts of urine; out of doors.

Hekla lava (Volcanic ash from Mount Hekla, in Iceland)
This remedy has a particular affinity for the jaws, and ailments in surrounding areas.

Mouth: Tooth decay, with swelling in the jaw; pain after extraction. Abscessed gums. Puppies have difficulty teething. Bony growths in the mouth and jaw.

Back/Limbs/Paws: Lymph glands in the neck are enlarged and hardened.

Generalities: Bone cancer. Inflammation of the bone or membrane covering the bone. Tumors. Swellings are painful.

Hepar (*Hepar sulphuris calcareum*, Calcium sulphide)
Hepar is best known as a remedy for abscesses and other infections that produce a large amount of pus. The lowest potencies are particularly effective in helping to promote drainage of infections.

Mind: Irritable. May become aggressive, particularly when touched. Sad; distressed. Extremely sensitive.

Eyes: Conjunctivitis, with abundant discharge. Eyes and eyelids are red and swollen. Ulcers on the cornea. Pus in the anterior chamber of the eye. Whites of the eyes may appear yellow.

Ears: Infected, with foul-smelling pus; painful to the touch.

Mouth: Abscessed teeth or gums. Excessive salivation. Gums bleed easily; dog is reluctant to eat or chew due to pain.

Stomach/Abdomen: Belches. Abdomen is enlarged and tight. Liver region is painful to the touch. Hepatitis; liver abscesses.

Stool: Soft, the color of clay; white; looks like undigested food; foul odor. Has difficulty passing stool, even though it is soft.

Urinary Tract: Urine passes very slowly, as though bladder lacks strength to expel it.

Reproductive System: Vaginal discharge of mucus and pus, with terrible odor.

Respiration/Circulation: Heavy discharge from any of the mucous membranes, particularly of the respiratory tract. Nasal discharges smell like old cheese. Sneezing, coughing, particularly when body becomes cold, in cold, dry wind, or after eating cold food. Difficult breathing. Heart palpitations.

Skin: Abscesses; infected ulcers, bleed easily. Skin is unhealthy; even minor injuries become infected. Recurring eruptions.

Generalities: Swollen lymph glands. Very chilly, seeks warm places. Abscesses and lesions are extremely painful, sensitive to the slightest touch.

Modalities: Worse from dry cool air or drafts. Better from warmth; damp weather; after eating.

NOTE: Very low potencies, such as 1X to 6X, will hasten the release of pus in infections, or drainage in respiratory illness.

Hydrangea (*Hydrangea arborescens*, Seven barks)
A remedy for stones in the urinary tract.

Stomach/Abdomen: Very thirsty.

Urinary Tract: Frequent urination; burning; has difficulty passing urine. Urine contains mucus; white sediment. Urinary stones.

Reproductive System: Prostate gland is enlarged.

Generalities: Older dogs. Diabetes insipidus.

NOTE: Use the lowest potency available, such as 1X or 3X.

Hydrastis (*Hydrastis cadensis*, Goldenseal)
An excellent remedy for infections, particularly those that produce thick, yellowish, ropy discharges.

Mind: Depressed. Becomes tired easily. Irritable; worse after eating.

Ears: Infected, with discharge of mucus and pus. Deafness.

Mouth: Tongue is white, swollen, slimy. Ulcers on the tonge.

Stomach/Abdomen: Difficult digestion. Gastritis. Ulcers. Cancer. Liver is enlarged, painful to pressure.

Stool: Dry. Constipation. Pain when passing stool, or afterward.

Urinary Tract: Discharge of mucus from the urethra; thick, yellow discharge.

Reproductive System: Vaginal discharge. Mammary tumors.

Respiration/Circulation: Thick, ropy, yellowish discharge from nose and bronchial tubes. Watery nasal discharge. Dry cough, followed by a productive cough; sputum looks like yellow mucus.

Back/Limbs/Paws: Back appears stiff; has difficulty rising.

Skin: Severe infections. Ulcers. Cancer, where ulcers are present or imminent.

Generalities: The characteristic thick, yellow discharge may appear anywhere in the body, e.g., mucous membranes, urethra, reproductive tract, digestive tract. Loss of weight. Particularly helpful in older, feeble dogs. Jaundice.

Hyoscyamus (*Hyoscyamus niger*, Henbane)
Behavioral changes are key indications for this remedy. The dog is extremely agitated or excited, and may show signs of aggression, nervous sexual behavior, extreme playfulness, or a combination of manic behaviors. Many of the symptoms are similar to those of rabies, and may be brought on by administration of the rabies vaccine.

Mind: Aggression, may be fear-based. Uncharacteristic sexual behavior, such as mounting or rubbing the genitals. Deliriously happy. Alternates between various moods. Jealous. Does not want to be left alone.

Eyes: Pupils dilated, fixed. Each eye appears to be looking in a different direction.

Mouth: Tongue is red and dry. Foams at the mouth. Lower jaw droops.

Stomach/Abdomen: Nausea, vomiting. Abdomen is swollen and tense. Hiccups. Gastritis.

Stool: Diarrhea. Incontinence.

Respiration/Circulation: Dry cough, worse at night, or while lying down.

Back/Limbs/Paws: Weakness; twitching. Shakes head back and forth.

Generalities: Convulsions; spasms. Restless sleep. Loss of consciousness. Symptoms may be brought on by rabies vaccination.

Modalities: Worse at night; after eating; while lying down.

Hypericum (*Hypericum perforatum*, St. John's wort)
An excellent remedy for injuries that involve the nerves, or tissue that contains an abundance of nerve endings. It eases pain in many kinds of injuries, and helps prevent infection in lacerations.

Mind: Depressed; sad.

Head: Brain injury.

Eyes: Painful cuts or scratches.

Mouth: Pain after tooth extraction. Injuries to the teeth, gums or tongue.

Back/Limbs/Paws: Pain in the lower back; base of the neck; tail. Impaired coordination; paralysis; twitching; spasms. Quiets irritated nerves in spinal misalignment, or where disks are pressing on the nerves. Injury to the spinal cord.

Skin: Cuts, scrapes, puncture wounds.

Neurologic System: Spasms; twitching.

Generalities: Eases pain after surgery. Tetanus.

NOTE: Follows Arnica in cuts or abrasions. For puncture wounds, give alternately with Ledum. For back pain or for pinched nerves, give alternately with Arnica.

Ignatia (St. Ignatius bean)
Ignatia is known for it's ability to help resolve grief, and physical symptoms associated with grief.

Mind: Dull; depressed. Sighs heavily. Mood changes frequently. Lack of interest in activities or surroundings; withdrawn.

Mouth: Excessive salivation.

Stomach/Abdomen: Vomits due to emotional stress. Loss of appetite; lack of interest in customary diet; eats indigestible materials. Belches; passes gas. Rumbling sound in belly. Hiccups.

Stool: Difficult to pass. Diarrhea due to emotional stress. Itching.

Urinary Tract: Passes large amounts of urine; clear, watery.

Respiration/Circulation: Dry cough, worse in the evening. Frequent, deep sighing.

Skin: Itching. Eruptions.

Generalities: Symptoms that arise after, or can be traced to, an emotional loss, such as loss of a companion or a move from familiar surroundings; also, symptoms associated with a frightening event. Sleep is excessive or restless; much dreaming.

Modalities: Worse in the morning; out of doors; after eating; in a warm room or warm weather. Better during meals.

NOTE: Ignatia is often used for recent or acute grief, or for illnesses associated with a recent loss. For more long term affects of grief, consider Nat mur.

Iodum (Iodine)
For dogs who are extremely thin, in spite of an excellent appetite.

Mind: Anxious. Depressed. Sudden bouts of aggression.

Eyes: Excessive tearing.

Mouth: Gums bleed easily. Excessive salivation. Foul breath. Thick coating on the tongue.

Throat: Thyroid gland is enlarged. Swollen lymph glands.

Stomach/Abdomen: Extremely hungry, eats well; very thirsty. Enlarged liver or spleen. Diseases of the pancreas.

Stool: Bloody. Pale, foamy diarrhea. Constipation. Alternating constipation and diarrhea.

Urinary Tract: Frequent urination; large amount of urine; urine is dark yellowish-green.

Reproductive System: Swelling in the testicles. Vaginal discharge.

Respiration/Circulation: Acute respiratory illness; excessive flow of mucus; cough, productive or dry; sneezing; pneumonia. Breathing is difficult, particularly on inhalation. Shortness of breath. Cough is worse indoors or when weather is warm or wet.

Back/Limbs/Paws: Joints are swollen and sore to the touch; lameness. Paws feel cold.

Generalities: Easily exhausted; weakness. Swollen lymph nodes. Elevated temperature. Lead poisoning. Tremors. Jaundice. Seeks a cool place to rest.

Modalities: Worse from warmth. Better after eating; with movement; out of doors.

Ipecac (*Cephaelus ipecacuanha*)
A favorite remedy for nausea and vomiting.

Mind: Irritable.

Eyes: Excessive tearing. Sensitive to light.

Mouth: Excessive salivation.

Stomach/Abdomen: Vomiting. Vomitus contains undigested food, blood, or mucus. Drinks little.

Stool: Bright green; foamy; contains or is coated with mucus. Diarrhea with straining.

Respiration/Circulation: Runny nose: bloody nose. Labored breathing; shortness of breath that recurs annually. Cough; produces bloody mucus.

Generalities: Body is held rigid, stretched out. Hiccups. Fever comes and goes. Symptoms recur periodically.

Kali bich. (*Kali bichromicum*, Potassium bichromate)
A valuable remedy for illnesses that affect the mucous membranes throughout the body, particularly those of the respiratory tract. Thick, ropy mucus is a key symptom.

Mind: Irritable; better after eating.

Eyes: Yellow, stringy discharge. Conjunctivitis. Eyelids are swollen. Corneal ulcer.

Ears: Infection; discharge is thick, stringy, yellow; foul odor; pain in ear.

Stomach/Abdomen: Cirrhosis of the liver.

Mouth: Dry; saliva is thick. Tongue is red and shiny, or has a thick coating.

Throat: Swollen glands.

Stomach/Abdomen: Drinks little. Vomiting; vomitus is bright yellow, thin and watery.

Stool: Diarrhea; contains mucus; the consistency of jelly; foamy; worse in the morning. Straining.

Urinary Tract: Burning in urethra. Urine contains mucus, blood, pus, protein, epithelial cells. Kidney disease.

Reproductive System: Vaginal discharge; mucus; thick, yellow; burning. Itching or burning in the penis.

Respiration/Circulation: Discharge of mucus from nose and respiratory tract; mucus is thick, stringy; greenish-yellow; forms crusts; foul-smelling; may be clear, watery. Sneezes; coughs.

Back/Limbs/Paws: Pain in lower back and at base of tail; sciatica, particularly on the left side. Joints are painful, stiff, swollen; joints crack when moving. Difficulty walking; weakness. Lameness moves from one leg to another.

Skin: Eruptions; lesions. Itching.

Generalities: Dog is extremely weak. Anemia. Most symptoms are generally mild or moderate rather than severe. Dogs who respond to this remedy often tend to be overweight.

Modalities: Worse in the morning; in hot weather. Better from hot applications.

NOTE: Do not give this remedy if fever is present.

Kali carb. (*Kali carbonicum*, Potassium carbonate)
A remedy for hypothyroidism, or for other illnesses with a similar symptom picture.

Mind: Depressed; very irritable. Moods change frequently. Overly sensitive to noise or touch. Does not want to be alone.

Mouth: Infected gums. Excessive salivation. Tongue appears white.

Stomach/Abdomen: Nausea; vomiting; carsickness. Poor appetite; chokes when eating. Passes gas. Bloated. Liver region is painful to the touch.

Stool: Large; bloody; difficult to pass. Anus burns or itches.

Urinary Tract: Must urinate several times during the night; incontinence when coughing or sneezing.

Respiration/Circulation: Nasal discharge; thick, yellow; bloody; forms crust. Cough. Pulse is weak and rapid.

Back/Limbs/Paws: Weakness; numbness; paralysis; hind legs give out. Muscles twitch. Pain in kidney region; behind right shoulder; hip joint; lower back and into the back of the leg. Pain, stiffness, or lameness in the hip joint.

Skin: Coat is dry; hair falls out.

Generalities: Weak; lethargic; exhausted; chilly; numbness. Sensitive to touch. Dogs who respond to this remedy often tend to be overweight. Jaundice. Edema. Hypothyroidism.

Modalities: Worse early in the morning; cold weather; any change in the weather; around 3 a.m; lying on left side. Better in warm, damp weather; with movement.

NOTE: Do not give this remedy if fever is present.

Lachesis (Venom of the Bushmaster snake)
Commonly used as an alternative to Crotalus for rattlesnake bite, or for poisoning from other causes.

Mind: Depressed, especially in the morning. Restless; anxious; timid, especially with strangers. Jealous. Prefers to be alone.

Head: Head is swollen. Bones of head, jaw, and face are painful to pressure.

Ears: Pain. Earwax is hard and dry.

Mouth: Gums are swollen; bleed easily. Tongue is swollen and red.

Throat: Glands are swollen. Painful to external touch or pressure. Interior membranes are bright red or purple.

Stomach/Abdomen: Stomach and liver regions are painful to the touch. Very hungry.

Stool: Bloody. Offensive odor. Constipated.

Respiration/Circulation: Bloody nose. Sneezing. Cough.

Back/Limbs/Paws: Pain in the back of the neck; sciatica. Paws are cold.

Skin: Abscesses; ulcers; blisters; bruising, hemorrhage. Appears blue from blood seepage. Wounds are slow to heal.

Generalities: Exhaustion; debility. Trembling. Hemorrhage. Poisoning from chemical or bacterial agents.

Modalities: Worse after sleep; in the springtime; on left side of the body. Better with warm applications.

NOTE: Give one dose at a time, then wait for a response.

Ledum (*Ledum palustre*, Marsh tea)
An excellent remedy for injury to the tendons or ligaments, and also for bites, stings and puncture wounds.

Mind: Irritable; indifferent. Prefers to be alone.

Eyes: Injury; bruising.

Stomach/Abdomen: Retching.

Respiration/Circulation: Cough; bloody sputum.

Back/Limbs/Paws: Lameness; joints crack when moving. Swelling may be hot or cool. Sprains; injuries to tendons or ligaments; bone bruises.

Skin: Stings. Puncture wounds; bites. Eruptions; red, itchy bumps.

Generalities: Lack of body heat; swellings and wounds are cold.

Modalities: Worse when warm; at night. Better from cold applications.

NOTE: For puncture wounds, alternate with Hypericum. For tendon or ligament injuries that are very painful, alternate with Arnica.

Lycopodium (*Lycopodium clavatum*, Club moss)
Mind: Premature senility. Wants company, but prefers not to be touched. Anxious.

Head: Shakes head.

Mouth: Foul odor.

Stomach/Abdomen: Extremely hungry; eats very quickly; eats very little. Drinks little. Abdomen becomes bloated after eating even a small amount. Hepatitis.

Stool: Diarrhea. Stool very hard; straining.

Urinary Tract: Straining. Produces large amounts of urine, particularly at night.

Reproductive System: Vaginal discharge; burning.

Respiration/Circulation: Nasal discharge. Cough; bloody discharge; grey, thick. Shortness of breath. Pneumonia.

Back/Limbs/Paws: Pain between shoulder blades; in lower back. Lameness; numbness in legs and feet. Legs twitch. Sciatica, particularly on the right side.

Skin: Hair falls out; turns grey, even in a young dog. Itching. Abscesses; hives; worse with warm applications.

Generalities: Hiccups. Body feels cold.

Modalities: Worse on the right side of the body; from warm room, bed, or applications. Better from being cold; eating warm food; with motion.

NOTE: Do not repeat dosage too frequently.

Lyssin (*Hydrophobinum*, Saliva of a rabid dog)
Believed by some to help reduce the effects of rabies vaccine when vaccination cannot be avoided. As with rabies, the symptoms have a marked effect on the neurologic system.

Mouth: Excessive salivation; saliva is thick, foamy.

Stool: Diarrhea; watery; large amounts of stool; worse in the evening.

Respiration/Circulation: Spasmodic breathing.

Neurologic System: Seizures.

Generalities: Hypersensitivity.

Mercurius (*Mercurius vivus*, Mercury)
As with mercury poisoning, the symptoms associated with this remedy may affect many different bodily systems, with inflammation, offensive discharges, exhaustion, and great sensitivity to heat and cold.

Mind: Dullness. Easily frightened or confused. Very irritable. Depressed.

Eyes: Discharge. Change in the color of the iris.

Ears: Infection. Discharge is thick, yellow, bloody; foul odor. Painful.

Mouth: Excessive salivation; thick; bloody. Foul odor. Gums bleed easily. Mucous membranes inflamed. Ulcers.

Throat: Ulcers; inflammation. Mucous membranes bright red or blue.

Stomach/Abdomen: Very thirsty. Always hungry. Stomach region is sensitive to the touch. Liver is enlarged; painful to the touch. Passes gas.

Stool: Green or pale grey; contains blood or mucus. Straining.

Urinary Tract: Frequent urination; passes small amounts of urine; blood or protein in urine. Straining. Itching or burning in urethra; discharge.

Reproductive System: Vaginal discharge; green; bloody.

Respiration/Circulation: Sneezing. Nasal discharge; mucus; pus; yellowish-green; foul odor. Cough; sputum is yellow; contains pus or mucus.

Back/Limbs/Paws: Lameness; joints are painful to the touch. Weakness; legs tremble. Legs and paws are swollen.

Skin: Lesions; ulcers; abscesses; eruptions become infected. Itching. Foul odor. Unhealthy coat.

Generalities: Very sensitive to heat and cold. Tremors; weakness; exhaustion. Alternately hot and panting, then cold and shivering. Discharges are foul smelling. Loss of weight and muscle mass. Anemia. Jaundice. Hiccups. Mercury poisoning.

Modalities: Worse at night; in a warm bed or warm room; from cold, damp weather.

NOTE: Do not give before or after Silicea. Female dogs are generally more responsive to Mercurius than males; male dogs may respond better to Mercurius corrosivus.

Merc. cor. (*Mercurious corrosivus*, Mercuric chloride)
Considered one of the best remedies for straining at stool or urine.

Eyes: Sensitivity to light. Excessive tearing; burning. Lids are swollen. Change in the color of the iris.

Ears: Infection; foul smelling discharge.

Mouth: Gums and tongue are swollen and red. Excessive salivation. Foul odor.

Throat: Mucous membranes red, swollen. Difficulty swallowing. Swollen glands.

Stomach/Abdomen: Vomiting; vomitus is green. Stomach and abdomen are painful to the touch. Bloated.

Stool: Diarrhea; stool contains blood, mucus, or bits of white tissue; very foul odor. Continuous straining, even after passing stool.

Urinary Tract: Much straining. Small amount of urine; contains blood or protein. Pain in urethra; thick, green discharge.

Reproductive System: Penis and testicles swollen.

Respiration/Circulation: Nasal discharge; mucous membranes are bright red.

Generalities: Easily chilled; body feels cold.

Modalities: Worse in the evening or at night. Better when resting.

NOTE: Male dogs are generally more responsive to Mercurius corrosivus than females; female dogs may respond better to Mercurius.

Naja (*Naja tripudians*, Virus of the Cobra)
A remedy for heart disease.

Mind: Depressed. Does not want to be alone.

Mouth: Excessive salivation; drooling.

Throat: Difficulty swallowing.

Urinary Tract: Incontinence due to loss of control of the sphincters.

Stool: Incontinence due to loss of control of the sphincters.

Respiration/Circulation: Shortness of breath. Pulse is slow, weak; irregular. Disease of the heart valve or lining. Enlarged heart. Heart disease caused by infection.

Back/Limbs/Paws: Poor coordination; weakness.

Generalities: Very deep sleep.

Naphthalene (Tar camphor)

This remedy is particularly useful for symptoms that affect the eyes.

Eyes: Cataract. Cloudiness. Detached retina. Degenerative eye disease. Irritation of the eyes due to allergy.

Urinary Tract: Bladder or kidney infection; pain in the urethra. Urgent need to urinate. Urine is very dark in color; offensive odor.

Respiration/Circulation: Sneezing. Cough. Shortness of breath.

Skin: Itchy eruptions.

Nat. mur. (*Natrum muriaticum*, Sodium chloride, Table salt)

Symptoms that respond well to Nat. mur. can often be traced to old grief, loss, or other emotional trauma. Since the remedy is made from common table salt, many of the symptoms are similar to those that would occur as a result of excessive salt intake.

Mind: Unresolved grief, fear, or other emotional distress. Depressed. Irritable. Prefers to be alone.

Eyes: Excessive tearing. Blocked tear duct. Early stages of cataract.

Mouth: Eruptions on tongue and mucous membranes. Mucous membranes are dry.

Stomach/Abdomen: Excessive thirst. Excessive hunger. Nausea; vomiting. Abdomen is bloated.

Stool: Dry; crumbles. Constipation or diarrhea. Pain after passing stool. Anus bleeds.

Urinary Tract: Passes large amounts of urine; urine passes involuntarily when walking or coughing. Pain after urinating.

Respiration/Circulation: Nasal discharge; clear, watery; mucus. Sneezing. Cough. Shortness of breath.

Back/Limbs/Paws: Weakness; numbness. Tightness and soreness at the back of the thighs. Joints crack when moving. Nails are dry, brittle.

Skin: Skin and coat are greasy. Eruptions, particularly where the limbs bend; hives; itching or burning. Hair loss.

Generalities: Disease that has its roots in emotional trauma. Exhaustion; weakness; lack of body heat. Severe weight loss. Restless sleep. Hypersensitivity. Edema. Systemic infection. Anemia. Addison's disease. Diabetes.

Modalities: Worse when warm; when consoled. Better out of doors.

NOTE: When the emotional cause of disease occurred some time ago, Nat. mur. is often the remedy; for more recent emotional trauma, consider Ignatia.

Nat. sulph. (*Natrum sulphuricum*, Sodium sulphate)

An important remedy for liver ailments, particularly for dogs who feel worse in damp weather.

Mind: Depressed. Prefers to be left alone. Emotional or behavioral disorders that are associated with a head injury.

Head: Injuries to the head.

Eyes: Sensitive to light.

Ears: Painful when touched.

Mouth: Thick mucus. Brown coating on the tongue.

Stomach/Abdomen: Vomiting; vomitus is green. Abdominal region is painful to the touch. Passes gas. Hepatitis.

Stomach/Abdomen: Vomiting; vomitus is yellow or green. Passes gas. Hepatitis.

Stool: Very large stools. Diarrhea, with yellow stool. Burning at the anus.

Urinary Tract: Passes large amount of urine.

Respiration/Circulation: Nasal discharge; thick, yellow. Nosebleed. Shortness of breath, particularly during damp weather. Cough; sputum is thick and stringy; green.

Back/Limbs/Paws: Pain between shoulder blades; at the back of the neck; in hips. Lameness or stiffness in the hips or knees. Joints crack when moving. Paws are swollen. Licks between the toes, as though itching. Swelling and redness at the base of the nails.

Nervous System: Injuries to the brain or spinal cord.

Skin: Growths, warts; blisters; red bumps. Itching.

Generalities: Changes position frequently. Jaundice. Diabetes. Tetanus. Strychnine poisoning.

Modalities: Worse in damp weather, or when exposed to water in any form; in springtime; lying on the left side. Better in warm, dry room or weather.

Nit. ac. (*Nitricum adicum*, Nitric acid)
This remedy is associated with very painful skin eruptions or ulcers, particularly those that appear where skin and mucous membranes meet, such as the edges of the mouth, the anus, or the genitals.

Mind: Very irritable or aggressive, particularly when touched, or after passing stool. Very sensitive to noise or touch. Depressed.

Eyes: Dullness. Sensitive to light. Excessive tearing. Corneal ulcer.

Mouth: Pale mucous membranes. Foul odor. Excessive salivation; saliva streaked with blood. Gums are soft, bleed easily. Tongue appears to have a groove down the center.

Throat: Ulcers on mucus membranes.

Stomach/Abdomen: Very hungry; excessive desire for fats. Unusual cravings, as for non-food matter; eats dirt.

Stool: Offensive odor. Straining. Diarrhea; contains mucus. Constipation. Pain when passing stool. Ulcer at the edge of the anus or in rectum. Passes bright red blood.

Urinary Tract: Passes small amounts of urine. Burning in urethra when urinating. Urine is dark in color, with foul odor; contains blood or protein.

Reproductive System: Discharge has offensive odor.

Respiration/Circulation: Nasal discharge; yellow or clear and watery; foul odor. Nosebleed. Hoarse. Dry cough.

Back/Limbs/Paws: Arthritis.

Skin: Blisters; ulcers; abscesses; warts. Eruptions are very painful; cannot tolerate being touched; discharges have foul odor. Bleeds easily.

Generalities: Dogs who respond well to this remedy often have dark skin and coat, or are in their senior years. Abscesses, ulcers, and inflammations may spread throughout body, on skin, organs, bones. Loss of weight. Jaundice. Anemia. Mercury poisoning.

Modalities: Worse in evening or at night; in cold weather; in very hot weather.

NOTE: Skin eruptions may initially appear worse as healing begins.

Nux vomica (Poison nut)
A valuable remedy for many common acute illnesses, particularly of the digestive system, and for dogs who have a history of conventional drug treatments or exposure to environmental toxins, such as chemical food additives, which suppress the vital force and compromise the immune system.

Mind: Hypersensitive; nervous; irritable. Aggressive. Does not want to be touched. Disturbed by noise.

Eyes: Sensitive to light, particularly in the morning. Excessive tearing. Paralysis of the muscles of the eyes. Inflammation of the optic nerve.

Ears: Itching deep in the ear. Very sensitive to noise.

Mouth: Saliva is streaked with blood. Gums are swollen; pale; bleed easily.

Stomach/Abdomen: Very hungry. Nausea; vomiting; worse after eating. Belches up stomach contents. Repeated retching; tries to vomit, but produces no vomitus. Stomach region sensitive to pressure. Abdomen distended; tight; painful. Liver is swollen. Bloat.

Stool: Constipated; straining. Alternates between constipation and diarrhea. Passes small amounts of stool. Itching or pain in the anal region.

Urinary Tract: Sudden desire to urinate; frequent urination. Passes small amounts of urine frequently. Straining; pain or itching during urination. Blood in the urine.

Respiration/Circulation: Nasal discharge; thick, watery. Nosebleed, particularly in the morning. Hoarse. Cough; sputum contains blood. Breathing is shallow; difficult.

Back/Limbs/Paws: Pain in lumbar area; at the back of the neck; behind shoulder blades. Paralysis; numbness; weakness; drags toes when walking. Joints crack when moving.

Neurologic System: Seizures; remains conscious during seizure.

Generalities: Dogs who respond well to this remedy are often thin, overly sensitive to physical stimulation and change (such as a change in the diet), with a history of conventional drug treatments. Very chilly. Wakes very early in the morning. Jaundice.

Modalities: Worse in the morning; when out of doors, particularly in dry, cold weather; in a warm room; after eating; from being touched. Better while resting; after a short sleep; in the evening; in wet weather.

Phos. ac. (*Phosphoricum acidum*, Phosphoric acid)
Low energy, exhaustion, debility are key symptoms associated with this remedy.

Mind: Dull; listless; indifferent; depressed. Grief. Emotional exhaustion after stress. Sensitive to noise. Emotional distress or debility precedes physical symptoms.

Eyes: Pupils dilated. Sensitivity to light.

Mouth: Gums bleed easily. Thick mucus on tongue.

Stomach/Abdomen: Nausea. Abdomen is bloated. Passes gas.

Stool: Watery diarrhea; passes involuntarily.

Urinary Tract: Frequent urination, particularly at night. Pain or burning after urination. Passes large amounts of urine.

Respiration/Circulation: Nosebleed. Hoarse. Dry cough. Labored breathing.

Back/Limbs/Paws: Weakness. Lameness. Stumbles frequently. Licks skin between the toes, as though itching. Pain or sensitivity in stump after amputation.

Skin: Eruptions filled with blood. Ulcers that become infected; foul odor. Thinning haircoat.

Generalities: Exhaustion; sleeps long and deep. Very chilly. Young dogs who grow rapidly. Hair turns grey prematurely. Diabetes. Hypothyroidism.

Modalities: Worse from activity. Better when warm.

Phosphorus

This is an important remedy for bleeding. It is also valuable for a broad range of illnesses including those that affect the mucous membranes, nervous system, bones, liver, and blood.

Mind: Easily startled or frightened; anxious. Hypersensitivity. May become anxious in response to one or more of a variety of triggers, particularly sound or electrical stimuli, such as light, lightning, or thunder. Very depressed; indifferent. Irritable. Restless.

Eyes: Skin around the eyes appears swollen. Conjunctiva are very pale. Degenerative changes; atrophy of the retina, optic nerve. Cataract. Glaucoma.

Mouth: Mucous membranes inflamed; bleed easily. Bleeding after tooth extraction. Swelling or degeneration of the bone in the lower jaw.

Stomach/Abdomen: Hungry, even after eating. Very thirsty. Vomiting; vomitus contains water or undigested food. Vomiting after surgery. Stomach region is painful to the touch; walks stiffly, as though due to pain in the stomach region. Passes gas; very foul odor Diseases of the pancreas. Acute hepatitis.

Stool: Long, thin, and hard; white. Straining. Diarrhea, with large amounts of stool. Contains green mucus; blood. Incontinence. Foul odor. Bleeding from the anus.

Urinary Tract: Blood in the urine.

Reproductive System: Mastitis.

Respiration/Circulation: Nasal discharge of mucus, blood, or both. Hoarse, particularly in the evening or in cold air. Breathing is rapid; difficult. Cough due to irritation in throat or congestion in lungs; dry or productive; sputum contains blood or pus. Pulse is rapid and weak. Pneumonia.

Back/Limbs/Paws: Paralysis; begins in paws and progresses upward. Weakness; trembling; numbness; loss of coordination. Legs give out. Bones break easily. Bone infection.

Neurologic System: Irritation or inflammation of the spinal cord or nerves.

Skin: Bleeds easily and profusely, even from a minor injury. Bruising. Dry, flaky skin and coat.

Generalities: Dogs who respond well to this remedy are often long and lean, with a brown or red coat. Symptoms arise suddenly. Exhaustion; very sleepy, particularly after eating. Hemorrhage. Jaundice.

Modalities: Worse when lying on the left side; lying on the painful side; in a cold room; from touch; from stress; from activity; after a change in the weather or during a thunder storm; when strangers are present. Better when lying on the right side; out of doors; from sleep.

NOTE: Do not give Phosphorus immediately before or after Causticum.

Phytolacca (Poke root)

This remedy is particularly for disease that affects the glands. It is a key remedy for mastitis or for tumors of the mammary glands.

Mind: Restless. Indifferent.

Mouth: Teeth are tightly clenched. Tongue is red at the tip. Excessive salivation; contains blood.

Eyes: Excessive tearing.

Throat: Mucous membranes are dark red or blue; excessive mucus. Swollen glands.

Stomach/Abdomen: Loss of appetite. Constipation, particularly in older dogs.

Stool: Bleeding from the anal area.

Reproductive System: Mammary glands are hard; painful to the touch; dark red or blue. Mastitis. Mammary abscesses. Benign or cancerous tumors of the mammary glands.

Respiration/Circulation: Nasal discharge; clear and watery. Hoarse. Breathing is labored. Dry cough.

Back/Limbs/Paws: Weakness. Stiffness in the back, particularly after sleep. Lameness or stiffness, particularly in the right foreleg. Swelling in the paws.

Skin: Dry; itching. Eruptions; ulcers; abscesses; discharge pus. Warts.

Generalities: Exhaustion. Swollen glands. Tetanus.

Modalities: Worse with exposure to dampness or cold weather; at night; on the right side of the body; when moving. Better when warm; at rest; in dry weather.

Pulsatilla (Wind flower)

This remedy is most often used to treat females, particularly those who are sweet and gentle, but emotional or needy.

Mind: Gentle; accommodating. Becomes distressed easily; sensitive; emotional. Moods change readily. Needs a great deal of attention; clinging; loves sympathy, being fussed over. Does not want to be alone. Timid.

Eyes: Excessive tearing. Discharge is thick and yellow; clear and watery; mucus. Itching or burning. Eyelids are swollen, stuck together due to discharge. Conjunctivitis.

Ears: Infection. Discharge is thick; yellow; foul odor. Inner ear is painful to the touch. Earflap is inflamed.

Mouth: Dry. Excessive salivation; thick mucus. Foul odor.

Stomach/Abdomen: Lack of thirst, even though mouth is dry. Dislikes warm or fatty foods. Vomiting; vomitus contains undigested food, long after it was eaten. Abdomen is distended; painful to pressure; gurgling noise. Passes gas.

Stool: Watery diarrhea; contains mucus or blood. Every bowel movement is of different consistency. Pain in rectum.

Urinary Tract: Frequent desire to urinate. Burning during and after urination. Incontinence at night; when coughing; when passing gas.

Reproductive System: Vaginal discharge; the consistency of cream; burning. Discharge from penis; urination is difficult and painful. Inflammation of the prostate gland or testicles.

Respiration/Circulation: Nasal discharge; thin and watery; yellow mucus; worse in the morning. Cough; dry at night; productive in the morning; sputum contains mucus; is thick and green. Shortness of breath.

Back/Limbs/Paws: Lameness that moves from one leg to another. Pain between shoulder blades; in lower back; in hips. Moves as though legs are heavy. Arthritis.

Skin: Hives.

Generalities: Gets chilled easily; hot and panting at night. Symptoms change frequently. Wide awake in the evening, deep sleep in the afternoon.

Modalities: Worse in a warm room; from fatty foods; after eating; lying on the left side; lying on the pain-free side. Better out of doors; with cold applications. Likes to sleep with head resting on a pillow.

NOTE: The emotional traits are key guiding symptoms for this remedy.

Pyrogenium (Rotten meat or pus)

Since this remedy is made from rotting meat or septic pus, it is valuable for treating illness that involves putrefying infections or septic conditions. It is also useful for chronic illness that has its roots in a septic condition.

Mind: Restless; anxious.

Mouth: Terrible odor.

Stomach/Abdomen: Nausea; vomiting. Vomitus has terrible odor; looks like coffee grounds; water. Abdomen is distended and painful.

Stool: Very offensive odor. Diarrhea; dark in color. Straining. Incontinence. Constipation; impaction. Stools are large and black; like small black balls.

Respiration/Circulation: Pulse is rapid, weak.

Urinary Tract: Straining.

Reproductive System: Infection after giving birth.

Skin: Minor injury becomes infected quickly; discolored.

Generalities: All discharges are extremely foul smelling; infections are very painful. Chilly. Fever; temperature increases quickly. Abscesses. Food poisoning. Gangrene.

Modalities: Better when moving.

Rhus tox. (*Rhus toxicodendron*, Poison ivy)

Known as the "rusty gate" remedy, Rhus. tox. is suited to lameness or stiffness that gets better with movement. It's also valuable for skin eruptions that resemble poison ivy or poison oak.

Mind: Listless; dull; depressed. Restless. Anxious, particularly at night.

Eyes: Discharge; yellow pus. Excessive tearing. Eyelids and tissue around the eyes is swollen. Sensitive to light. Corneal ulcers. Change in the color of the iris.

Ears: Painful infection. Discharge contains blood; pus.

Face: Swollen. Facial bones are painful to the touch.

Throat: Swollen glands.

Stomach/Abdomen: Loss of appetite, very thirsty. Nausea. Abdomen is distended after eating. Gurgling noise, better with motion.

Stool: Diarrhea; stool contains blood, mucus. Terrible odor, like a dead animal.

Urinary Tract: Passes a very small amount of urine. Urine is dark in color.

Reproductive System: Intense itching of the vulva or penis.

Respiration/Circulation: Sneezing. Nosebleed. Cough is dry or productive; sputum contains blood; small chunks of mucus. Pulse is rapid, weak.

Back/Limbs/Paws: Pain between shoulder blades; in sacral area; in the knee. Injuries to the tendons or joints. Strains; overuse. Joints are hot, swollen, painful. Pain and stiffness gets better from movement. Paralysis; trembling. Arthritis. Sciatica.

Skin: Very itchy. Red; inflamed. Eruptions; blisters; hives. Infected blisters.

Generalities: Problems that arise after surgery. Chilly fever.

Modalities: Worse during sleep; from rest; cold, damp weather. Better from moving around; changing position; from stretching legs; in warm, dry weather; from warm applications.

Ruta (*Ruta graveolens*, Rue, Bitterwort)

An excellent remedy for injuries to the tendons, periosteum (surface of the bone) and cartilage.

Mind: Listless; depressed. Irritable. Restless.

Eyes: Red. Excessive tearing. Sensitivity to light.

Stool: Straining. Frequent urge to pass stool. Constipation. Stools contain mucus; foam; blood. Cancer in the lower bowel.

Urinary Tract: Continuous desire to urinate.

Respiration/Circulation: Nosebleed. Cough; large amounts of thick, yellow sputum. Shallow breathing.

Back/Limbs/Paws: Pain in the back of the neck; lumbar area; sacral area. Injuries to the tendons, particularly those that cause the joints to bend; ligaments, periosteum, joints. Overuse; strains; sprains. Lameness; weakness. Legs give out. Sciatica.

Generalities: Jaundice.

Modalities: Worse when lying down; from cold; dampness. Better from movement.

Sepia (Ink of the cuttlefish)

Thick, green, ropy discharges are the hallmark of this remedy. Dogs who respond well are often females with dark haircoat.

Mind: Depressed; indifferent. Irritable; anxious, particularly in the evening. Does not want to be alone.

Stomach/Abdomen: Poor appetite. Nausea. Vomits after eating. Dislikes fatty foods. Liver region is painful to the touch. Passes gas.

Stool: Constipation; stools are large and hard; difficult to pass; dark in color; contain mucus. Bleeds from the rectum when passing stool.

Urinary Tract: Incontinence while sleeping. Bladder infection.

Reproductive System: Vaginal discharge; green or yellow, thick; intense itching.

Respiration/Circulation: Nasal discharge; thick, green; crusty. Deep cough, dry or productive. Shortness of breath. Pulse is prominent in all arteries.

Back/Limbs/Paws: Jerks head forward and back. Weakness and pain in lower back. Lameness; stiffness. Twitching. Legs and paws feel cold.

Skin: Itching, especially where elbows and knees bend. Skin is dry and scaly, coat is dull. Hives. Ringworm.

Generalities: Very chilly, even in a warm room; seeks a warm place to rest; lack of body heat. Weakness; exhaustion.

Modalities: Worse after sleeping; when out of doors; mornings and evenings; dampness. Better in a warm room; from hot applications; after sleeping.

Silicea (Silica, Flint)

This is a valuable remedy for helping the body expel foreign matter, whether it be in the form of a splinter or foxtail, carrying agents of drugs or vaccines, or toxins. It helps abscesses to soften, open, and drain, and is also well known as a remedy for illness that has its roots in vaccination.

Mind: Easily intimidated; anxious; overly sensitive.

Eyes: Aversion to light. Corneal ulcer; abscess after an injury. Cataract.

Ears: Infection; discharge has a foul odor. Bothered by noise.

Mouth: Abscessed gums; at root of teeth.

Throat: Infected glands.

Stomach/Abdomen: Poor appetite. Very thirsty. Dislikes meat; warm food. Vomits after drinking water. Stomach region is painful to pressure; abdomen is bloated. Gurgling noise. Liver abscess.

Stool: Constipation. Stool is difficult to pass; is partly expelled, then drawn back in. Diarrhea; smells like a dead animal.

Urinary Tract: Incontinence. Urine contains blood.

Reproductive System: Burning or itching of the vulva or penis. Abscess on the vulva. Nipples sore to the touch; lumps in mammary tissue.

Respiration/Circulation: Discharge from the nose or respiratory tract; contains mucus and pus. Cough; sputum consists of hard pellets with foul odor; yellow lumps; blood or pus.

Back/Limbs/Paws: Back is weak; pain at base of tail. Legs are weak; tremble. Joint abscesses. Paws are cold. Diseases of the bones and nails. Sciatica.

Neurologic System: Seizures.

Skin: Abscesses; infections; ulcers; foul-smelling pus. Even minor injuries become infected. Irritation on the inner thigh. Overgrowth of scar tissue.

Generalities: Illness that is the result of vaccination. Always chilly; lack of body heat. Delicate, weak constitution. Exhaustion. Interrupted sleep; dreams; sleepwalking. Abscesses.

Modalities: Worse during the new moon; in the morning; when lying down; when lying on the left side; in dampness or cold. Better when warm, or in warm weather.

NOTE: Because of its ability to expel foreign matter or dissolve scar tissue, Silicea should not be used if your dog has implants, such as an artificial joint, or plates or pins inserted to help mend a broken bone. Silicea should not be used before or after Mercurius.

Spongia (*Spongia tosta*, Roasted sponge)
A valuable remedy for respiratory illness.

Mind: Anxious; fearful.

Eyes: Discharge; clear, watery, sticky; mucus.

Throat: Swollen glands. Sore to the touch.

Respiration/Circulation: Watery nasal discharge. Labored breathing; shortness of breath. Dry cough that originates in throat or lungs; better after food or water. Cough that is associated with heart disease. Enlarged heart.

Skin: Itching.

Stomach/Abdomen: Very thirsty; extremely hungry.

Back/Limbs/Paws: Moves as though the body is heavy.

Generalities: Dogs who respond well often have a pale skin and light-colored coat. Easily exhausted. Wakes abruptly from sleep. Hiccups.

Modalities: Worse after sleep; from activity; in cold wind. Better from warmth.

Staphysagria (Stavesacre)
A remedy for dogs who are extremely sensitive emotionally or physically.

Mind: Extremely sensitive to disapproval, anger, or scolding. Inappropriate behavior due to emotional stress. Likes to be alone. Cranky; difficult to comfort or satisfy.

Eyes: Eruptions at the margin of the eyelid; itching. Laceration of the cornea.

Mouth: Excessive salivation. Gums are soft, bleed easily. Pain after tooth extraction.

Throat: Pain when swallowing. Swollen glands.

Stomach/Abdomen: Excessive hunger. Digestive upset that follows emotional stress. Distended abdomen. Passes gas.

Stool: Diarrhea or constipation. Straining.

Urinary Tract: Frequent urination. Burning when urinating, or when not urinating. Bladder infection.

Reproductive System: Enlarged prostate.

Skin: Cuts that are clean and straight but very painful. Helps heal incisions after surgery, particularly when site is extremely painful. Dry, scaly patches; intense itching.

Modalities: Worse after emotional distress. Better with warmth; at rest.

Strychninum (Strychnine, Alkaloid of Nux vomica)
An important remedy for symptoms that involve the central nervous system and motor function.

Mind: Restless. Hypersensitive; irritable.

Face: Facial muscles are rigid, tense. Lower jaw is rigid.

Eyes: Pupils dilated. Eyelids twitch.

Throat: Difficulty swallowing.

Stomach/Abdomen: Nausea. Severe vomiting; retching.

Stool: Constipation. Passes stool during seizure or spasm.

Respiration/Circulation: Rapid breathing; shortness of breath. Cough.

Back/Limbs/Paws: Muscles of the neck, back, and legs are rigid. Head and neck are drawn toward the back. Muscle spasms; twitching; trembling; cramps.

Neurologic System: Diseases that affect the spinal cord.

Skin: Itching, particularly on the nose.

Generalities: Hypersensitivity of all the senses. Muscle spasms or stiffness. Symptoms are recurring; they arise suddenly then subside. Seizures. Tetanus.

Modalities: Worse from touch; in the morning; from noise or motion; after eating.

Sulphur (Sulphur)

This is an important remedy with many symptoms and a broad range of action. It is most often used to treat chronic rather than acute illness, so careful matching of the symptoms is key.

Mind: Irritable; cranky. Depressed; indifferent.

Eyes: Eyes burn or itch. Conjunctiva are bright red. Corneal ulcer.

Ears: Old infections that have been treated with antibiotics, but return.

Mouth: Bright red edges and mucous membranes. Foul odor. Gums are swollen. Tongue is white in the center, red around the edges.

Throat: Mucous membranes are red and dry.

Stomach/Abdomen: Very thirsty or lack of thirst. Extremely hungry or loss of appetite. Very thirsty *and* disinterested in food. Belches, with foul odor. Abdominal region is sensitive to pressure.

Stool: Stools are hard, small, difficult to pass. Frequent urging; straining. Diarrhea in the morning. Anus is bright red. Itching or burning in the anal area.

Urinary Tract: Frequent urination; urgent need to urinate. Incontinence at night. Burning in the urethra during and after urination. Passes large amount of urine; clear like water; contains mucus, pus.

Respiration/Circulation: Labored breathing. Hoarse. Cough; sputum is green; contains pus.

Back/Limbs/Paws: Stiff neck. Pain between the shoulder blades. Legs or paws tremble. Moves as if legs are heavy; gait is stiff.

Skin: The skin and coat appear dirty or greasy; dry, dull; flaky. Skin is unhealthy, becomes infected easily; has a foul odor. Hot spots. Itching. Eruptions like small bumps or pimples. Loss of hair. Made worse by washing.

Generalities: Dogs who respond well to this remedy are generally dirty or greasy with a foul odor, also depressed and underweight, even when eating well. Weakness; exhaustion. All body openings (mouth, anus, ears, etc.) are red. Dislikes being bathed. Recurring symptoms. Active dreams; jerking, twitching; wakes up frequently.

Modalities: Worse when standing or resting; in a warm bed; from being bathed. Better with fresh air; warm, dry weather; when lying on the right side.

NOTE: This remedy should be used only when the dog has many symptoms that clearly point to it; begin with a low potency. Do not give before, after, or with Calc. carb.

Symphytum (Comfrey, Bone knit)

This remedy has a very narrow range of symptoms, but is extremely effective when called for. It is a primary remedy for the healing of broken bones, and for injuries to the eye.

Eyes: Injury to the eye. Pain in the eye after trauma.

Stomach/Abdomen: Stomach ulcer.

Back/Limbs/Paws: Broken bones; broken bones that fail to rejoin. Injuries to the tendons, ligaments, periosteum, joints. Sensitivity in the stump after amputation. Bone bruise.

Skin: Ulcers. Abrasions.

Thuja (*Thuja occidentalis*, Arbor vitae)

As a veterinary remedy, Thuja is best known for treating illness that has its roots in vaccination, most commonly with symptoms that affect the skin and urinary tract.

Mind: Sensitive; emotional.

Eyes: The white of the eye is inflamed; appears bluish-red. Tumors.

Mouth: Tooth decay. Unhealthy gums.

Stomach/Abdomen: Increased thirst. Loss of appetite. Dislikes meat. Abdomen is distended. Gurgling noise. Passes gas.

Stool: Diarrhea. Constipation. Painful straining. Growths in the anal region.

Urinary Tract: Frequent urination; sudden and urgent need to urinate; difficulty retaining urine. Severe pain after urinating. Paralysis of the sphincter.

Reproductive System: Growths on the vulva. Vaginal discharge; thick, green. Enlarged prostate.

Respiration/Circulation: Nasal discharge; thick, green; contains blood; pus. Hoarse. Dry cough.

Back/Limbs/Paws: Lameness; weakness. Twitching; trembling. Joints crack when moving. Nails are dry; soft; break easily.

Skin: Eruptions that will not heal. Dry skin; loss of hair. Growths; ulcers.

Dark spots. Skin has a sweet odor. Sensitive to the touch. Tumors.

Generalities: Illness that is the result of vaccination; vaccinosis. Exhaustion; weakness. Loss of weight. Difficulty sleeping. Easily chilled. Tumors. Fungal infections; bacterial infections.

Modalities: Worse from vaccination; at night; when resting; from cold; in damp weather. Better in dry weather.

Urtica urens (Stinging nettle)

An effective remedy for skin eruptions and urinary problems.

Respiration/Circulation: Discharge of mucus from nose and respiratory tract.

Urinary Tract: Incontinence, particularly at night. Suppressed urination. Urinary stones.

Neurologic System: Irritation and inflammation of a nerve.

Stool: Diarrhea; contains mucus.

Back/Limbs/Paws: Joint pain; uric acid deposits.

Reproductive System: Insufficient milk production. Bleeding from the uterus.

Skin: Hives. Skin is red; itching; burning. Hot spots. Traumatic burns.

Generalities: Symptoms recur with a particular season.

Modalities: Worse from dampness; cool air; touch.

Uva ursi (Bearberry)

A primary remedy for conditions that affect the urinary tract.

Stomach/Abdomen: Nausea. Vomiting.

Urinary Tract: Frequent desire to urinate; urgent desire; difficult to retain urine. Straining. Burning after urination. Passes a very small amount of urine. Urine is green; contains mucus; pus; blood; blood clots. Incontinence. Bladder or kidney infection. Kidney stones.

Reproductive System: Bleeding from the uterus.

Respiration/Circulation: Shortness of breath. Pulse is weak.

Sasha (left), Labrador/
Shepherd/Pit Bull Terrier
cross. Adopted at 8 weeks
old in 1999.

Sierra (right), Labrador/
Golden Retriever/Doberman
cross. Adopted at 8 weeks
old in 1996.

herbal materia medica

When no dose is listed for an herb, use the dosage recommendations on page 94, or use a dose that is proportional to the human dose (as recommended on the product label), based on your dog's size. Keep in mind that extracts, tinctures, and concentrates can be 3 to 10 times more potent than the dried herb. Mild stomach upset or diarrhea may occur in sensitive individuals; discontinue use if a side effect or allergy is suspected.

If your dog is under medical care, let your veterinarian know about any herbs you are giving, especially if you are also giving prescribed drug therapy. Veterinary monitoring is suggested when using any herb long term.

Single Herbs

Alfalfa (*Medicago sativa*)
- Nutritive herb that provides antioxidants, vitamins, and minerals.

- Considered a heart tonic, with mild diuretic effect; contains estrogen-like bioflavanoids such as genistein, a potential anti-cancer nutrient.
- Good for dogs with poor digestion or who've been on poor nutrition.

Aloe vera (*Aloe barbadensis*)
- Soothing to skin, topical antibacterial and antifungal properties, antiinflammatory.
- Used for burns, skin irritations, superficial wounds; check with your holistic vet for internal use.
- Fresh gel straight from the plant is best, or purchase 99% gel, in alcohol-free form.
- Acemannan, an injectable aloe extract (administered by your veterinarian), can shrink fibrosarcomas and some other tumors when used prior to surgery; may help prevent recurrences after surgery.
- This herb has side effects if given orally. Consult an herbalist.

Ashwaganda *(Withania somnifera)*

- Aryuvedic tonic herb for increasing energy and a state of well-being.

- Shown in lab studies to be antiinflammatory, anti-tumor; human studies support use for arthritis (antiinflammatory and antioxidant).

- Use for relief from stress, or the effects of arthritis, aging and cancer.

- Rare side effects are diarrhea or dermatitis.

Astragalus *(Astragalus membranaceus)*

- Immune enhancing, mild antiinflammatory, Traditional Chinese tonic, considered the counterpart to Echinacea.

- Use short term for infections, when immune system is acutely stressed, and for chronic immune problems or cancer support; may protect kidney cells from damage.

- 1 to 2 drops of tincture per pound, 3 times daily.

Bilberry *(Vaccinium myrtilus*, Huckleberry*)*

- Good source of antioxidants (vitamin C, quercetin, and other flavanoids).

- Anthocyanosides present reported to help with degenerative eye diseases (cataracts, retinal diseases); European herbalists use it for diarrhea, urinary tract infections, and diabetes (contains chromium).

- Dose at 20 to 100 mg 3 times daily, depending on size (using common 25% bilberry extract).

Black walnut *(Juglans nigra)*

- Anecdotal reports suggest the use of black walnut hulls in treatment of intestinal worms or heartworms. However, proof of effectiveness is lacking at this time; use of this herb should not replace heartworm preventive medication.

- *Side effects, including vomiting and diarrhea, may occur; use only under supervision of a holistic veterinarian experienced with its use.*

- *Severe, life-threatening gastrointestinal toxicity due to fungal contamination of walnut hulls has been reported. Use only packaged products.*

Boswellia *(Boswellia serrata)*

- Strong antiinflammatory, similar to NSAIDs (nonsteroidal antiinflammatory drugs) for arthritis, and in some cases of IBD or bronchitis; administer twice daily for best results.

- *Consult your veterinarian if currently administering NSAIDs; may cause stomach upset; avoid during pregnancy.*

Burdock root *(Arctium lappa, Arctium minor)*

- Known by herbalists as a "cleansing" herb for the blood, liver, and kidneys, with diuretic and antioxidant properties.

- Used as one ingredient in the popular herbal cancer remedies known as Essiac Tea and Hoxsey's formula. (Scientific evidence of the effectiveness of these remedies has not yet been demonstrated.)

- Can lower blood sugar, so an adjustment in diabetics' insulation dosage may be required.

Calendula *(Calendula. officinalis, Calendula marigola)*

- Reported antibacterial, antifungal, and antiinflammatory properties in the flower.

- Use topically for skin irritation, superficial wounds, and minor ear and eye infections.

- Use the tincture to make a lotion or ointment according to directions on page 123. Apply to cuts, puncture wounds, abrasions, burns, hot spots.

Cat's claw *(Una de gato, Uncaria tomentosa)*

- Peruvian rainforest vine, traditional Amazon remedy for cancer and gastrointestinal problems.

- Possible immune-enhancing properties, antioxidant and antiinflammatory properties.

- Avoid with other blood-thinners.

Chamomile *(Matricaria chamomilla)*

- Soothing flower useful for compress on inflamed skin, mucous membranes of the eyes and mouth; can promote wound healing; make infusion as described in Chapter 6.

- Use internally for calming effect; may help with digestive disturbances, particularly if related to anxiety or nervousness; for tincture, use ¼ to ½ milliliter (cc) per 20 pounds twice daily.

- *Not for use in pregnancy or with anticlotting herbs; rarely, dogs can be allergic. If symptoms get worse, discontinue immediately.*

Coleus *(Coleus forskohlii)*

- From the mint family; lowers blood pressure.

- Consult a vet before use, as it can affect dosage of heart medication.

Comfrey *(Symphytum officinale)*

- Use as infusion, ointment, or poultice (from pureed leaves) for sprains, strains, and bruises.

- *Caution: Do not give orally (pyrrolizidine alkaloids may damage the liver) without guidance by a qualified veterinary herbalist.*

Cornsilk *(Zea mays)*

- Soothes mucous membranes; a gentle antiinflammatory; good for bladder discomfort.

- 1 cup finely chopped fresh silk per 40 pounds body weight as a tea twice a day.

Cranberry *(Vaccinium macrocarpon)*

- Prevents bacteria from adhering to bladder lining; makes the urine acidic so that bacteria such as E.coli will not thrive.

- For prevention of recurrent urinary tract infections, dose at 50 to 500 mg, based on size, dried cranberry extract 1 to 2 times daily, or 2 drops tincture per pound of body weight; in dogs with history of calcium oxalate or other urinary stones, consult vet before use.

- Can cause diarrhea in some dogs.

Dandelion *(Taraxacum officinale)*

- A cleansing, nutritive antioxidant herb used in kidney and liver disorders; bladder infection or small stones; indigestion, poor appetite, constipation; mild heart disease.

- Leaves are used for their diuretic action, are high in vitamins, minerals (potassium). Root stimulates bile production and liver circulation. Flowers provide mild pain relief.

- As a therapy for liver disease, increases bile secretion and rids the body of excess fluid build up.

- Should not be used in severe liver disease with bile obstruction, or in cases of low blood pressure.

Echinacea *(Echinacea purpurea, angustifolia, and pallida)*

- Popular for use with viral and bacterial infections of urinary or respiratory tract, mouth or skin sores or wounds, and as a topical and oral folk remedy for insect and snakebites.

- Believed to enhance the immune system by increasing and activating white blood cells and macrophages, and stimulating interferon; suspected antibacterial effect may result from inhibition of certain bacterial enzymes.

- Best not to use with autoimmune (immune mediated) diseases, parvovirus, or in highly allergic individuals without veterinary supervision.

- Best for short-term support (5 days), sometimes in conjunction with Oregon grape, goldenseal, goldthread, or other herbs that contain berberine. Not recommended for daily use for more than 8 weeks, or with immunosuppressive drugs.

- May be endangered. Use cultivated (not wild-crafted) or certified organic echinacea.

Eyebright (*Euphrasia officinalis*)

- Available as a bulk herb, tincture, or eye drops for eye problems.

Garlic (*Allium sativum*)

- Known for antibacterial, antifungal, antioxidant, anticancer, and immune enhancing effects.

- Has suppressed the growth of cancer cells in the lab; reduced the risk of certain cancers in human studies where consumption of garlic was high.

- Cardiovascular tonic; can help lower high blood pressure, inhibit clot formation, and improve circulation; may help lower high triglyceride levels (common in some Schnauzers).

- Some caregivers report benefit with control of fleas and certain parasites (giardia and tapeworms) although scientific proof is lacking.

- May benefit diabetics by improving circulation and increasing insulin half-life

- *Gastrointestinal upset and flatulence can occur in some sensitive dogs; do not use large amounts (more than ¼ clove daily in small dogs or 1 to 2 cloves in large dogs) without veterinary supervision due to the possibility of developing anemia (may be more common in Akitas and Shibu Inus).*

Ginger root (*Zingiber officinale*)

- Mild pain relief; antiinflammatory.

- Soothes indigestion, combats nausea; use for motion sickness, indigestion, and intestinal gas.

- Considered a heart tonic; may inhibit blood clotting; use with caution in conjunction with anticlotting drugs or other substances that effect clot formation (garlic, high dose vitamin E, gingko), especially prior to surgery.

- Not for use in dogs with stomach ulcers. Large doses on an empty stomach can cause nausea.

- For motion sickness, make a tea with 2 slices of fresh ginger root per cup of hot water, steeped 10 minutes. Give ⅛ to ½ cup, ½ hour before travel. For a more potent tea, make a decoction or use ½ to 1 capsule twice daily during the journey.

Gingko leaf (*Gingko biloba*)

- A general tonic herb that contains antioxidants, anticoagulants, and constituents that can improve circulation, memory, and mental functions.

- Used with senior dogs to increase energy and for cognitive dysfunction.

- *Avoid when bleeding or coagulation problems exist, or with aspirin or other blood thinners.*

Ginseng root (*Panax ginseng, Panax quinquefolius, Eleutherococcus senticosus*)

- There are two types (American and Asian). Both are considered tonic herbs, with Asian being the strongest.

- Used to invigorate, combat fatigue and declining mental ability, and to strengthen when convalescing from a prolonged illness. Limit use to 2 to 3 weeks at a time.

- May increase blood pressure, protect against cancer when taken regularly, and decrease blood sugar in diabetics.

- *Consult vet before use if your dog has heart disease, kidney disease, diabetes, or is pregnant; may increase nervousness or insomnia in some dogs.*

Goldenseal *(Hydrastis canadensis)*

- Contains berberine; considered antibacterial; used topically for mouth sores, conjunctivitis, and skin infections.

- May cause gastrointestinal upset when taken orally. Not for long-term use. Can affect dosages of heart medications.

- Goldenseal is an endangered plant. Use only cultivated (certified organic) and not wild-crafted varieties. See berberine in Nutritional Materia Medica for alternative therapies.

Green tea *(Camellia sinensis)*

- Excellent antioxidant; is reported to have anticancer properties, good astringent for minor skin wounds when applied topically.

- Mouth rinses (2 to 3 times daily) with tea provide comfort for dogs with mouth sores.

- Used for immune support during chemo and radiation therapy; reported to provide support for cancer prevention.

Hawthorn *(Crataegus oxyacantha)*

- Improves the heart muscle's pumping action, dilates blood vessels, and improves coronary blood flow; may help protect against rhythm disturbances.

- Used for early stages of congestive heart failure, and as a heart tonic with antioxidant effects; look for hawthorn in "combination heart formulas" with CoQ10, taurine, carnitine, and other nutrients.

- May affect dosage of heart medications; veterinary monitoring is recommended.

- *Not for use during pregnancy.*

Hypericum *(Hypericum perforatum*, St. John's wort)

- See St. John's wort.

Kava kava *(Piper methysticum)*

- Sedative and muscle relaxant, used for anxiety, night restlessness, muscle spasms associated with intervertebral disc problems or overuse of muscles.

- *Recent reports indicate liver toxicity in humans, possibly related to extract constituents. Not for use in cases of liver disease, or in dogs who are being medicated with drugs that are potentially toxic to the liver. Consult your holistic veterinarian before using.*

Licorice *(Glycyrrhiza spp.)*

- Antiinflammatory, expectorant, cough suppressant; soothes gastric mucous membranes; may enhance liver repair.

- Used for arthritis, skin inflammation, stomach ulcers, some liver and intestinal conditions, constipation.

- Due to its cortisone-like effect, has been suggested for use with allergies as a way to lower drug doses in some animals on cortisone therapy.

- Dilute the tincture (10 drops per ounce of spring water) and use one to three dropperfuls daily, based on size. Higher doses may be used with veterinary supervision.

- For stomach ulcers, mouth sores, and inflammatory bowel disease, use the tableted deglycyrrhizinated form (DGL) at dose of 100 to 400 mg, 2 to 3 times daily, depending on size.

- Limit use to 2 to 4 weeks. Can suppress adrenal gland function when used long term.

- If your dog is on drug therapy, has kidney, liver, or heart failure, diabetes, or high blood pressure, or is pregnant or nursing, consult your vet first. The less potent DGL form doesn't have the same cautions or side effects, and works well for digestive problems.

Marshmallow *(Althaea officinalis)*

- Used to soothe and heal irritated membranes of the bronchial and urinary tract.

- An expectorant and cough suppressant for kennel cough.

- Use glycerine tincture orally, or make an infusion from the leaves, or a decoction from the roots.

- *May delay absorption of drugs taken at the same time.*

Medicinal mushrooms (Includes *Cordyceps sinensis* (Caterpillar mushroom), *Ganoderma lucidum* (Reishi), *Lentinula edodes* (Shiitake), *Coriolus versicolor* (Turkey Tail) *Tremmella fuciformis* (White wood ear) and *Polyporus umbellatus* (Maitake); available as a dried concentrate, or add mushrooms to the diet.

- Used widely in Japan and China to strengthen the immune system during stress, as a support during chemotherapy, or when long-term immune support is needed.

- Safe and gentle support for cancer patients; may increase natural tumor necrosis factor, stimulate "natural killer cells," and improve antibody and cell mediated immunity.

Milk thistle *(Silybum marianum)*

- Bioflavanoid components act as antioxidants; silymarin content supports liver cell regeneration.

- Good for liver stress, damage, or disease; can help prevent liver damage from certain medications; antidote for some poisonous mushrooms.

- Give 100 to 250 mg milk thistle extract (80 % silymarin) 1 to 3 times daily or 1 to 2 drops per pound of alcohol tincture; diarrhea or nausea have occasionally been reported at higher doses; may increase insulin requirements in some diabetic dogs.

- Use the tea to aid digestion and as a gentle liver support.

- Avoid long-term use, or use during pregnancy.

Mullein *(Verbascum spp.)*

- Soothes mucous membranes and breaks up mucus; possible antibacterial, antiviral, and mild antiinflammatory properties.

- Prepare a strong infusion of the leaves, and give 1 teaspoon to 1 tablespoon (depending on size) twice daily to relieve bladder or respiratory irritation.

- Occasional allergic reaction or nausea.

Oregon grape *(Berberis* or *Mahonia aquifolium)*

- Contains the same antibacterial berberine alkaloid as goldenseal. Can be used as a replacement for over-harvested goldenseal or echinacea for immune support with infections. Use 1 to 2 drops per pound of tincture.

- Most commonly used to treat skin, ear, digestive, and urinary tract infections. Should not be used to replace antibiotics prescribed by your veterinarian.

- Not for use during pregnancy; veterinary supervision is advised when liver disease or diabetes present; not for long-term use; may deplete B vitamins.

- Occasional gastrointestinal upset or allergic reaction.

Parsley *(Petroselinum crispum)*

- Excellent nutritive herb, especially for animals on home-prepared diets; gentle diuretic, can help with mild hypertension.

- Leaves contain vitamins A, C, B, and K, as well as potassium and other minerals, fiber, and protein.

- Root is used in arthritic conditions (along with other herbs); dose tincture at ¼ teaspoon per 25 pounds daily.

Plantain *(Plantago spp)*

- Leaves soothe irritated mucous membranes and reduce phlegm in the respiratory tract; also used for urinary tract irritations.

- Press fresh leaves to make a juice; give ¼ to 1 teaspoon 3 times daily.

- *Some dogs are allergic. Discontinue if itching, hives, or other sign of allergy appears.*

Red clover *(Trifolium pratense)*

- Nutritive, tonic, diuretic, and blood-cleansing; contains bioflavanoids that may help with allergies and skin diseases.

- *Do not give with blood-thinning medications or herbs.*

Red raspberry *(Rubus idaeus)*

- High in vitamin C; use as a tea for mild diarrhea; tones the uterus after delivery.

Saw palmetto *(Serenoa repens)*

- Known to shrink prostate and relieve symptoms of benign prostatic hypertrophy in men after 4 to 6 weeks of treatment. To date, only anecdotal reports of effectiveness in dogs.

Slippery elm bark *(Ulmus fulva)*

- Soothes and heals inflamed intestines. Soothes sore throat; helps diarrhea and constipation.

- Dose at 1 to 3 capsules, depending on size, mixed in a little broth twice a day; or try a tea for diarrhea or intestinal upsets.

St. John's wort *(Hypericum perforatum)*

- Used internally for depression or anxiety (may act as a serotonin reuptake inhibitor); can take 6 to 8 weeks to see results. Give with food to avoid stomach upset.

- Used topically to relieve pain, promote healing, and prevent infection in injuries to the skin.

- Make a lotion or ointment according to directions on page 123. Apply to cuts, puncture wounds, abrasions, burns, hot spots.

- *Topical or internal use may cause photosensitivity in some dogs, especially those with short hair or light skin. Try on a small area of skin first.*

- *Consult your veterinarian before using with any other drug therapy; may increase the effects of sedatives and anesthetics, or decrease the effectiveness of other drugs.*

Thyme *(Thymus spp.)*

- Used as a tea or tincture for loosening congestion and suppressing cough in respiratory infections; also as a warming digestive remedy or hot compress to promote circulation.

- Use 1 to 2 drops per pound of a glycerin tincture or 1 teaspoon of a tea per 30 pounds body weight twice daily.

- To make a tea, bring to a near boil to remove the volatile oils, then steep for 15 to 20 minutes. *Do not use the essential thyme oil, orally or topically— it's too toxic when taken internally, and will burn the skin if applied topically.*

Turmeric *(Curcuma longa)*

- A common spice that contains curcumin, a powerful antioxidant and safe antiinflammatory; may protect liver cells from damage; enhances the body's natural antioxidant system, and has demonstrated anti-tumor effects.

- Reported to be useful for arthritis, liver disease, supportive therapy for cancer, infection, and some gastrointestinal disturbances.

- Curcumin extract, in a fish oil base to enhance absorption, is more potent than tumeric spice.

Valerian root (Valariana officinalis)

- Used for anxiety, stress-related problems, and sleeping difficulty; may help calm a dog in pain, treats digestive upsets caused by stress or nervousness, and aids in seizure control in some dogs. May take 2 to 4 weeks to see maximum effect.

- For phobias that have a specific trigger (firecrackers, thunderstorms, etc.) give 3 to 5 drops of the tincture, 4 times daily. If possible, begin dosing 1 day before the stressful event. Can increase to 1 drop per pound if needed, twice daily.

- For help when a seizure is anticipated, or in high-stress situations for a seizure-prone dog, give ¼ teaspoon of the tincture per 30 pounds of body weight, 3 to 4 times daily.

- *In rare cases, dog may become more agitated than sedated. Do not use during pregnancy. Large doses can cause vomiting in some dogs. ALWAYS consult your veterinarian if you are giving other prescribed medications.*

Wild cherry bark (Prunus virginiana)

- Sedates cough reflex; expectornat; commonly found in cough suppressants for humans.

Witch hazel (Hamamelis virginiana)

- Astringent, soothing formulation used for minor skin irritations and hot spots

- Your own preparation is likely to be more effective than commercial distillations. To prepare, dilute 30 to 40 drops of tincture into 1 pint of water. Use a mister to spray affected areas.

Yarrow (Achillea millefolium)

- As a poultice, can help control bleeding, inhibit growth of bacteria, and speed healing of bruises.

- A topical application of the tea can help relieve pain and itching; also a good antiseptic rinse.

- Tinctures are sometimes given orally to treat inflammatory conditions.

- *May cause allergic reactions if used topically or internally. Not for use during pregnancy or lactation.*

Yucca root (Yucca schidigera)

- Antiinflammatory for short-term use with arthritis flare-ups. Recent studies question effectiveness.

- A good source of vitamin C, B, beta-carotene, and a number of minerals.

- Dose with the glycerin tincture at ⅛ teaspoon per 20 to 25 pounds daily or ¼ to ½ teaspoon daily of dried herb.

- May cause digestive upset in sensitive individuals, or with longer term use.

Chinese Herbal Combination Formulas

Chinese herbalists create specific formulas by combining herbs based on symptoms (much like homeopathy) as well as physical signs, such as the appearance of the tongue and the quality of the pulse. There's a host of Chinese Herbal Combination Formulas available at health food stores or Asian markets that may help for a general set of symptoms you notice in your dog. The traditional patent or "tea" pills are round and easy to administer. Many American manufacturers are making variations of these classic formulas, in tablet or capsule form, and have a good reputation for quality and purity. See page 94 for general dosing information. The lower end of the dose is all that's usually needed for a well-chosen formula. Always reduce or discontinue an herb if symptoms worsen or if signs of gastrointestinal distress develop. Use only short term (two weeks or less) unless you're working with a qualified veterinary herbalist, and never give them with other drugs or if your dog is pregnant, unless properly guided by your vet.

Chin Koo Tieh Shang Wan (Traumatic Injury Pill)

- Excellent for sprains, strains, and bruises. 1 to 5 pills, depending on dog's size, twice daily
- Use for up to 2 weeks.
- *Not for use in pregnant dogs.*

Four Ginsengs (Dragon Eggs formula)

- Combines four types of ginseng (yang) herbs with other (yin) herbs; revitalizes after illness and a good long-term tonic formula.

Golden Book Tea (Jin Gui Shen Qi Wan)

- Good for senior dogs with kidney troubles and poor circulation, weak or uncomfortable back, poor digestion, urinary incontinence, and a tendency to be chilly.
- Give 1 to 6 pills twice daily, depending on size.

Lien Chiao Pai Tu Pien (Lien Chiao Pai Tu Lien)

- For itchy, red rashes and hives; drives infection to the surface.

Long Dan Xie Gan Wan (Gentiana Combo, Gentiana Purge Liver Pills)

- Classic formula to reduce Damp Liver Heat.
- Liver Heat symptoms may include red, itchy eyes, ringing in the ears, and sometimes constipation.
- Also used with urinary tract infections or damp skin eruptions in the groin area, and hepatitis.

- Give 1 to 3 pills 2 to 3 times daily for no more than 2 weeks. Cut the dose in half if loose stools or poor appetite develop.
- Do not use if your dog is weak or has a pale tongue.

Pill Curing (Curing Pill, Kang Ning Wan)

- Used for acute onset overeating, indigestion, vomiting, and diarrhea.
- Also used long term for sluggish digestion.
- Give ¼ to 1 vial for an acute problem. Can be used up to 3 times daily at a dose of 1 vial per 20 pounds, divided in 3 equal portions and given throughout the day.

Six Flavor Tea (Liu Wei Di Huang Wan)

- Good for senior dogs with a weak or painful back and nighttime restlessness, who are insecure or agitated, and may be thirsty or constipated, or have urinary incontinence.
- 1 to 6 pills twice daily, depending on size.

Yunnan Pai Yao (Yunnan Bai Yao, Unnan Pai Yao)

- Used as an aid to control bleeding, enhance tissue healing, and provide pain control in an injury or recovery from surgery.
- Helps platelets (a type of blood cell) clump together to form a strong clot; can be used topically on a bleeding area, such as a torn or cut toenail, or a wound in the mouth. (Open a capsule and put herb directly on the bleeding area.)
- Can be given orally for support with bleeding mouth tumors or spleen tumors, under advice of veterinarian. (Usual dose is 1 to 3 capsules twice daily orally, or opened and sprinkled onto food.)
- For emergency bleeding situation, give 1 capsule or tablet per 10 pounds body weight as a 1-time dose, then seek veterinary support immediately.

Bibliography

Ackerman, L. Nutritionally responsive dermatoses. *The Five Minute Veterinary Consult*, L. Tilley, W.K. Smith, ed. Williams and Wilkins, 1997.

Ackerman, L. 1995. Symposium on fatty acid supplements. *Veterinary Medicine* 90(12): 1136-1159.

Agar, S. *Small Animal Nutrition*. Butterworth Heinemann, 2001.

American Veterinary Chiropractic Association. www.animalchiropractic.org

Aronson, L. 1999. Animal behavior case of the month. *Journal of the American Veterinary Medical Association* 215(1):1045.

Balch, J., P. Balch. *Prescription for Nutritional Healing*. Garden City Park, New York: Avery Publishing Group, 1997.

Basko, Ihor, D.V.M., flea and tick control, personal communication, 1999.

Bear, J. *Practical Uses and Applications of the Bach Flower Emotional Remedies*. Balancing Essentials Press, 1993.

Beaver, B.V. *Behavior Companion: A Clinical Reference Guide for Veterinarians*. Friskies Pet Care Company, 2000.

Beaver, B.V. *Canine Behavior: A Guide for Veterinarians*. Philadelphia: W.B. Saunders, 1999.

Blake, S.R. Bach flower therapy: a practitioner's approach. *Complementary and Alternative Veterinary Medicine: Principles and Practice*, A.M. Schoen, S.G. Wynn, ed. Mosby, Inc,1998.

Boericke, W. *Pocket Manual of Homeopathic Materia Medica, Comprising the Characteristic and Guiding Symptoms of All Remedies [Clinical and Pathogenetic]*, 9th ed.

Repertory by O. Boericke. Philadelphia: Boericke & Runyon, n.d.

Boik, John. *Natural Compounds in Cancer Therapy*. Princeton, Minn: Oregon Medical Press, 2001

Boothe, D. M. 2001. Nutraceuticals: indications, contraindications and practial use. *Second Annual Tufts Animal Expo Educational Conference*.

Bratman, S., and D. Kroll. *Natural Health Bible*. Prima Publishing, 2000.

Budiansky, S. *The Truth About Dogs*. New York: Penguin Books, 2000.

Bui, L.M., T.L. Bierer. 2001. Influence of green lipped mussels (perna canaliculus) in alleviating signs of arthritis in dogs. *Veterinary Therapeutics* 2(2):12-16.

Byrd, R.C. 1988. Positive therapeutic effects of intercessory prayer in a coronary care unit population. *Southern Medical Journal* 81(7):826-29.

Carmichael, L. 1999. Canine viral vaccination at a turning point – a personal perspective. *Advances in Veterinary Medicine* 41:289-307.

Carson, K. 2002. Herb-drug interaction awareness. *Veterinary Practice News* (14)6:36.

Chadwicke, C.E., S.C. Zicker, S.R.Lowry, D.E. Jewell, D. Fritsch, P.W.Toll. 2002. Effects of an investigational food on age-related behavioral changes in dogs. *Symposium on Brain Aging and Related Behavioral Changes in Dogs*. Veterinary Healthcare Communications.

Chambreau, C. 1999. Integrating homeopathy and holistic medicine into your veterinary practice. Southeast Holistic Veterinary Conference.

Corson, B. 1999. The role of S-Adenosylmethionine in hepatic structure and function. *Pathways*, Nutramax Laboratories Inc, Veterinary Science Division.

Coyne M., J. Burr, T. Yule, M. Harding, D. Tresnan, D. McGavin. 2001. Duration of immunity in dogs after vaccination or natural acquired infection. *Vet Record* 149(17):509-15.

De Guzman, E. Western herbal medicine: clinical applications". *Complementary and Alternative Veterinary Medicine*, A. M. Schoen, S.G. Wynn, ed. Mosby,1998.

DeNapoli, J.S., N.H. Dodman, L. Shuster, W.M, Rand, K.L. Gross. 2000. Effect of dietary protein content and tryptophan supplementation on dominance aggression, territorial aggression, and hyperactivity in dogs. *Journal of the American Veterinary Medical Association* 217(4):504-508.

Dodds, Jean, D.V.M., Hypothyroidism, vaccination reactions, personal communication, 2001.

Donaldson, Jean. Canine behavior, personal communication, 2002.

Dossey, L. *Healing Words: The Power of Prayer and the Practice of Medicine*. San Francisco: HarperSanFrancisco, 1993.

Dove, R. 2001. Nutritional therapy in the treatment of heart disease in dogs. *Alternative Medicine Review* 6(Supplement):38-45.

Ettinger, Stephen J. *Textbook of Veterinary Internal Medicine*. W.B. Saunders Company, 2001.

Fleming, T., ed. *PDR for Herbal Medicines*. Medical Economics Co.,1998.

Fratkin, J. *Chinese Herbal Patent Formulas: A Practical Guide*. Shya Publications, 1986.

Freeman, L. 2000. Nutritional modulation of cardiac disease. *Waltham Focus* 10(2):19-24.

Gaeddert, A. 2002. What is the safety and benefit of kava? *Professional Health Concerns* 11(3):1-8.

Glinski, M. Point Selection. *Complementary and Alternative Veterinary Medicine: Principles and Practice, A.M. Schoen*, S.G. Wynn, ed. Mosby, Inc, 1998.

Goodwin, J.K., D.R.Strickland. 1998. The role of dietary modification and nondrug therapy in dogs and cats with congestive heart failure. *Veterinary Medicine* 93(10): 919-926.

Grossi, Sophia. Puppy socialization, personal communication, 2002.

Hamilton, D. *Homeopathic Care for Cats and Dogs: Small Doses for Small Animals*. Berkeley: North Atlantic Books, 1999.

Hand, M. S, C. D. Thatcher, R. L. Remillard, and P. Roudebush. *Small Animal Clinical Nutrition*, 4th Edition, Mark Morris Institute, 2000.

Head, K.A. 2003. Astragalus membranaceus - monograph. *Alternative Medicine Review* 8(1):72-77.

Hepatic toxicity possibly associated with kava-containing products-United States, Germany, and Switzerland, 1999-2002. 2002. *Morbidity and Mortality Weekly* 51:1065-1067.

Hoffmann, D. *The New Holistic Herbal: A Herbal Celebrating the wholeness of life*. Barnes and Noble, Inc., 1995.

Hofve, J. 2002. A holistic look at commercial pet food. Annual Conference of the American Holistic Veterinary Medical Association.

Impellizeri, J.A., M.A.Tetrick, P. Muir. 2000. Effect of weight reduction on clinical signs of lameness in dogs with hip osteoarthritis. *Journal of the American Veterinary Medical Association* 216(7):1089-1091.

Integrative Medicine Communications. *Professional Guide to Conditions, Herbs, and Supplements*. Integrative Medicine Communications, 2000.

Janssens, L.A. 1997. Treatment of trigger points. *Veterinary Acupuncture Course Notes, 6th edition*. International Veterinary Acupuncture Society.

Jensen, C.L. 2001. Flower essence therapy for animals: bach flower remedies. Second Annual Tufts Animal Expo Conference.

Kaptchuk, T. J. *The Web That Has No Weaver: Understanding Chinese Medicine.* Congdon & Weed, Inc. 1983.

Karch, S. B. *The Consumer's Guide to Herbal Medicine.* Advanced Research Press, Inc., 1999.

Kendall, R.Therapeutic nutrition for the cat, dog, and horse. *Complementary and Alternative Veterinary Medicine: Principles and Practice*, A.M. Schoen, S.G. Wynn, ed. Mosby, Inc, 1998.

Kodama, N., K. Komuta, H. Nanba. 2002.Can maitake md-fraction aid cancer patients?" *Alternative Medicine Review* 7(3):236-239.

Lade, A. *Acupuncture Points: Images and Functions.* Seattle: Eastland Press, Inc., 1989.

Lanci-Altomare, M. *Good-Bye My Friend: Pet Cemeteries, Memorials, and Other Ways to Remember; a Collection of Thoughts, Feelings, and Resources.* Irvine, CA: BowTie Press, 2000.

Levin, C. *Dogs, Diet, and Disease: An Owner's Guide to Diabetes Mellitus, Pancreatitis, Cushing's Disease, and More.* Lantern Publications @petcarebooks.com, 2001.

Lewis, A.E, A.M. Schoen. Glandular therapy, cell therapy, and oral tolerance. *Complementary and Alternative Veterinary Medicine: Principles and Practice*, A.M. Schoen, S.G. Wynn, ed. Mosby, Inc, 1998.

Longwood *Herbal Task Force on Milk Thistle*, www.mcp.edu.herbal/milkthistle

Macleod, G. *A Veterinary Materia Medica and Clinical Repertory With a Materia Medica of the Nosodes.* Essex: C.W. Daniel, 1995.

Macrae, J. *Therapeutic Touch: A Practical Guide.* New York: Alfred A. Knopf, 1998.

McCluggage, D. 2000. Applied clinical nutrition: clinically effective protocols. Annual Conference of the American Holistic Veterinary Medical Association.

McCluggage, D. 1999. Introduction to nutraceutical, food, and herbal therapies. Annual Conference of the American Holistic Veterinary Medical Association.

McKenna, D., K. Hughes, K. Jones. 2000. Green tea monograph. *Alternative Medicine Review* 5(4):234.

Marks, S.L., Q.R. Rogers, D.R. Strombeck. 1994. Nutritional supplementation in hepatic disease. *Compendium on Continuing Education for Practicing Veterinarians* 16(8):971-978.

Mathews, K.A., A.G.Binnington. 2002. Wound management using honey. *Compendium on Continuing Education for Practicing Veterinarians.* 24 (1):53-60.

Messonnier, S. *Natural Health Bible for Dogs and Cats.* Prima Publishing, 2001.

Miller, L.G., ed, W.J. Murray, ed. *Herbal Medicinals: A Clinician's Guide.* Pharmaceutical Products Press, 1998.

Mishra, L., B. Sigh, B., S. Dagenais. 2000. Scientific basis for the therapeutic use of witharia somnifia (ashwaganda): a review. *Alternative Medicine Review* 5(4).

Moore, M. *Medicinal Plants of the Pacific West.* Red Crane Books, 1993.

Moore, A. 1999. Healing with the bach flower remedies. Annual American Holistic Veterinary Medical Association Conference.

Ody, P. *The Complete Medicinal Herbal.* Dorling Kindersley, 1993.

Ogilvie G.K., S.L.Marks. Cancer. *Hills Monograph 2001*, adapted from Small Animal Clinical Nutrition, 4th editions, Mark Morris Institute, 1998.

Ogilvie, G.K. Nutritional approaches to cancer therapy. *Complementary and Alternative Veterinary Medicine: Principles and Practices*, A.M. Schoen, S.G. Wynn, ed. Mosby, Inc, 1998

O'Brien, M.G. 1999. Mammary neoplasia in the dog and cat. *Proceedings of the North American Veterinary Conference* 13:408-409.

Packer, L. 2002. The antioxidant response to oxidative stress: from free radicals to genes. *Symposium on Brain Aging and Related Behavioral Changes in Dogs.* Veterinary Healthcare Communications.

Phillips, T., R. Schultz. Canine and feline vaccines. *Current Veterinary Therapy XI.* Saunders, 1995

Pitcairn, R.H., S.H. Pitcairn. *Dr. Pitcairn's Complete Guide to Natural Health for Dogs and Cats.* Rodale Press, Inc, 1995.

Pizzorno, J.E, M.T. Murray. *Textbook of Natural Medicine*, 2nd edition. Churchill Livingstone, 1999.

Pollen, S. M. 2001. Renal disease in small animals: a review of conditions and potential nutrient and botanical interventions. *Alternative Medicine Review* 6 (Supplement):46-61.

Porter, M. Physical therapy. *Complementary and Alternative Veterinary Medicine: Principles and Practices*, A.M. Schoen, S.G. Wynn, ed. Mosby, Inc, 1998.

Rush, J.1996. Alternative therapies for heart failure patients. 14th Annual American College of Internal Medicine Forum.

Santillo, H. *Natural Healing With Herbs.* Prescott, Arizona: Hohm Press, 1989.

Scanlon, N. 1999. The use of antioxidants and coenzyme Q-10 in the prevention and treatment of cancer. *Annual Conference of the American Holistic Veterinary Medical Association.*

Scanlon, N., 2002. Oriental Massage Therapy. Annual Conference of the American Holistic Veterinary Medical Association.

Schoen, A. *Veterinary Acupuncture: Ancient Art to Modern Medicine*, Mosby, 2001.

Schultz, R. 1999. Current and future canine and feline vaccination programs. Southeast Holistic Veterinary Conference.

Schwartz, C. *Four Paws, Five Directions: A Guide to Chinese medicine for Cats and Dogs*, Berkeley, CA: Celestial Arts, 1996.

Strombeck, D. *Home-prepared Dog and Cat Diets: The Healthful Alternative.* Iowa State University Press, 1999.

Tams, T. 2001. Management of chronic liver disease in dogs. Atlantic Coast Veterinary Conference.

Tapp, L. 2000. Introduction to homeopathy. Annual Conference of the American Holistic Veterinary Medical Association.

Tteam Training USA. www.lindatellingtonjones.com

Twark, L., J. Dodds. 2001. Clinical use of serum parvovirus and distemper virus antibody titers on determining revaccination strategies in healthy dogs. *Journal of the American Veterinary Medical Association* 217(7):1021-1024.

Veterinary Information Network, Inc. How Does Your Garden Kill? On line course, 2002. www.vin.com

Veterinary Information Network, Inc. Nutritional Tune-ups: Bringing Your Practice Up to Speed. On line course, 2001. www.vin.com

Weed, S. S. *Wise Woman Herbal: Healing Wise.* Woodstock, New York: Ash Tree Publishing, 1989.

Willoughby, S. Chiropractic care. *Complementary and Alternative Veterinary Medicine: Principles and Practices*, A.M. Schoen, S.G. Wynn, ed. Mosby, Inc, 1998.

Wulff-Tilford, M., G.L. Tilford. *All You Ever Wanted to Know About Herbs for Pets*, BowTie Press, 1999.

Wynn S. *Emerging therapies: Using Herbs and Nutraceutical Supplements for Small Animals.* AAHA Press, 1999.

Wynn, S., Marsden, S. *Manual of Natural Veterinary Medicine: Science and Tradition.* Mosby, 2003.

Wynn, S. 2001. Nutrients and botanicals in the treatmen+t of diabetes in veterinary practice. *Alternative Medicine Review* 6(Supplement):17-23.

Index